THE CAMBRIDGE ILLUSTRATED HISTORY OF
France

THE CAMBRIDGE ILLUSTRATED HISTORY OF
France

COLIN JONES

CAMBRIDGE
UNIVERSITY PRESS

For Kelsey and Blanche, affectionately.

Published by the Press Syndicate of the University of Cambridge
The Pitt Building, Trumpington Street, Cambridge CB2 1RP
40 West 20th Street, New York, NY 10011–4211, USA
10 Stamford Road, Oakleigh, Melbourne 3166, Australia

First published in 1994

Typeset by Wyvern Typesetting Ltd., Bristol

Printed in Hong Kong
A catalogue record for this book is available from the British Library

Library of Congress Cataloging-in-Publication Data

Jones, Colin. 1947–
    The Cambridge illustrated history of France / Colin Jones. —
1. ed.
        p.   cm. — (Cambridge illustrated histories)
    Includes bibliographical references and index.
    ISBN 0-521-43294-4
        1. France—Civilization.   I. Title.   II. Series.
DC33. J66   1994
944—dc20   94-19310
                                                                        CIP

ISBN 0 521 432944 hardback

This book was laid out and produced by
CALMANN & KING LTD
71 Great Russell Street,
London WC1B 3BN

Picture research: Susan Bolsom-Morris
Layout: Andrew Shoolbred

Contents

Preface

With the explosion of historical knowledge in this century, professional historians have rarely been rash enough to try to cover the whole of the history of France in a single volume, and have largely abandoned the field to amateur historians and professional writers, who have had few of their qualms. As I explain in the Introduction, I have tried to dodge the pitfalls and embrace this Cinderella among historical genres with some warmth. My aim has been to provide an accessible account that is more than a chronicle of the political history of the social and governmental elite; that gives economic, social and cultural history their due; that respects the regional as well as the national framework; and that gives full weight to questions of gender, class and race.

As Richard Cobb – the greatest British historian of France this century – has put it, history contains "a wide element of guesswork. It is like attempting to sound the unsoundable, and to penetrate the secrets of the human heart". The amount of guesswork is all the more extensive for the historian roaming well outside his professional area of scholarly expertise, not to mention approaching the history of France as a foreigner. How well I have come to terms, first, with national preconceptions and misconceptions, second, with my inevitable deficiencies of specialized knowledge over much of the historical record, and, third, with the challenge of writing a new sort of national history will be for readers to judge.

It remains to thank most warmly those colleagues and friends who have helped by reading drafts of various parts of the typescript and saved me from more egregious errors than I care to relate. Fellow historians at Exeter University – notably Jonathan Barry, David Braund, Bryony Coles, Julia Crick, John Critchley, Robert Hudson, Linda Hurcombe, Nicholas Orme, Tim Rees and Peter Wiseman – were especially helpful. My thanks, too, to Roger Chartier and Emmanuel Le Roy Ladurie. Numerous other friends and colleagues – including those at Stanford University, where I spent 1993–94 as Visiting Professor of European History – helped too, in all sorts of ways. All should be absolved from blame for any problems that remain, which are my responsibility. On the production side Rosemary Bradley, Melanie White and Damian Thompson provided advice and support, and Susan Bolsom-Morris was a superb picture researcher. Finally my thanks go to Josephine McDonagh, for being there.

Colin Jones

Foreword
by Emmanuel Le Roy Ladurie

In its way, *The Cambridge Illustrated History of France* is a striking example of the seductive yet thorny topic of Anglo-French or Franco-English relations. It is a topic about which much could be said.

In Carolingian times, while "France" and "Germany" were central to the immense and fragile European state constructed by Charlemagne, England kept itself to itself, with the Continent – to adopt a famous phrase – "cut off". From 1066 and throughout the Middle Ages, William the Conqueror and his successors controlled from Normandy an England that was not always appreciative of contacts, though it would be churlish and anachronistic to see this in terms of occupation, collaboration and resistance . . . The Plantagenets brought British influence down to the Garonne before the Hundred Years War, that stunning and long-lasting catastrophe. Contacts between the two countries subsequently became less explosive. Despite religious differences, most cultivated French people valued contacts with the English. Every period of intellectual and political openness from 1595 down to 1925 was marked by a dose of cultural and diplomatic anglophilia. Henry IV counted on his "good sister Elizabeth"; Mazarin was Cromwell's ally; the ministries of Dubois and Fleury marked a period of cross-Channel friendship, coinciding with the impact of Newton and Shakespeare on the French Enlightenment; and in the nineteenth century, too, numerous economic and political models (parliamentarism, free trade and press freedom) came from England.

The obverse of this relationship, however, was conflict. From the time of Richelieu France was generally on top, but this changed dramatically from the Seven Years War onwards. A period of nearly two centuries had opened up in which France would be constantly defeated, at first by the English (along with the Prussians), subsequently by the Germans (now enemies of the English). The 1914–18 war was in theory a French victory; but the million-and-a-half French deaths made it a disaster all the same – and one followed by an even greater catastrophe, 1940.

One can understand why, following these disasters, the French proceeded to a national stock-taking after 1945–50. They came to seek reconciliation with Germany and threw themselves unconditionally into the European adventure. Post-war Britain, in contrast, retains a certain distance towards, even a suspicion of, the Continent.

Colin Jones' work is of course utterly antithetical to such an approach. His *Cambridge Illustrated History* is a book which should allow his compatriots to become better acquainted with their neighbour. The French past, which Jones explores using the techniques of the New History, reveals unexpected riches and highlights material overlooked by the old school of event-oriented, positivist historians (both French and English). Authoritative, well written and solidly thought through, this book, which has no recent equivalent in writing about French history, should reach out beyond the British Isles to the English-speaking world in its entirety.

Introduction

We can draw a line, roughly from north to south, across the middle of the department of the Hérault, on the Mediterranean coastline in Lower Languedoc, dividing the area into eastern and western sectors. In the east, soccer is played as the first winter game (Montpellier fields, at the time of writing, a first-division team in the national soccer league); in the western half, rugby has the same role (in the 1970s and 1980s Béziers was the premier rugby club of France). This bifurcation of the department – roughly along the line of the Hérault river valley – corresponds, broadly speaking, with a split detectable throughout the long history of the region. Predominantly left-wing voters to the west have traditionally been distinct from right-wing supporters in the east; supporters of the Revolution of 1789 in the east could be distinguished from dissidents in the west; sixteenth-century Protestants in the east, from Catholics in the west; late medieval Cathars in the west, from orthodox Catholics in the east. The division recurs in the diocesan framework created in the early Middle Ages. And it probably dates back to pre-Roman times; archaeologists confirm the presence of a cultural frontier here, with one grouping, the Volcae Arecomici in the west, having a different material culture from the Volcae Tectosages in the east.

Such stories could be told about a great many regions within France. If we are not generally aware of them or have lost them from sight, this is partly because professional historians tend to work in relatively short time-periods, eschewing the broadest angles of vision. It also owes something to the fact that most multi-period histories of France prefer to commemorate national unity rather than exploring division, divergence and variety within French borders. Such histories have tended to be written as if the frontier separating the French from undifferentiated "Others" was the only cultural boundary worth investigating. In this, they remain true to the penchant of national histories for blatant, often flag-waving chauvinism.

Historians in the nineteenth century – when national histories came into their own – conceived of the French nation as comprising a group of men with a common language, common racial features and a common culture that distinguished them from their neighbours. In so far as these characteristics were not shared in the past within the boundaries of the present-day state, then the historian's task was to show, through the prism of the nation state, how men came to possess a common ethnic, cultural and political heritage. The common identity was often viewed as being centred on Paris and its environs: "The real France," Michelet (a Parisian) had announced, "is northern France" – a phrase echoed in the doubtless apocryphal remark of Charles de Gaulle (a Lorrainer), that "Africa begins at Lyon". It was in the Paris region, declared one of the most prestigious of these national histories at the turn of this century, "where national history essentially took place".

Yet, as the example of the Hérault department suggests, if we stick to this increasingly outdated model, then we miss a lot. If we want to understand what motivated

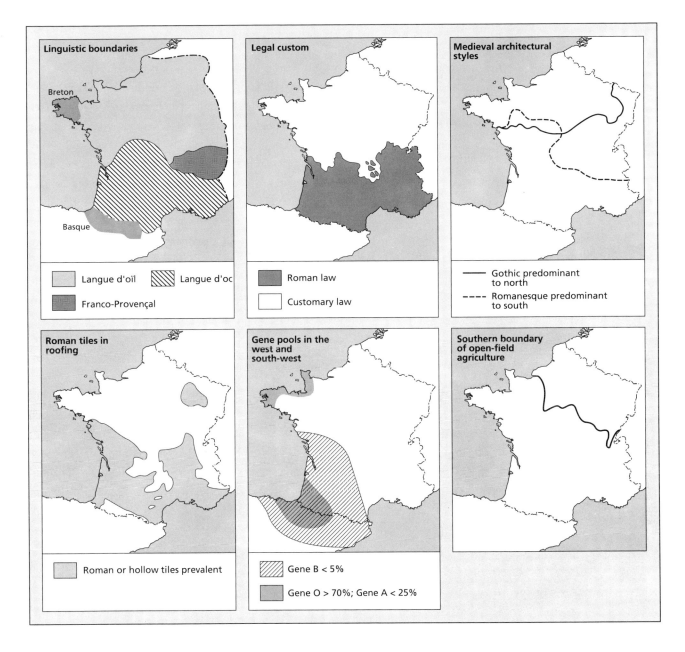

people in the past, it is as rewarding and helpful to examine the major internal, cultural frontiers as the political boundaries defining the limits of national territory. Even at the very end of the twentieth century identity in France is local and regional: in certain respects, many individuals still count themselves as much Auvergnats, Bretons or Basques as French. This testifies to the enduring character of regional divisions.

The long-term persistence of linguistic frontiers within France mocks the assumption that the French nation has ever been linguistically unified in any meaningful sense until very recently. The major division – between the *langue d'oc* in the south and the *langue d'oïl* in the north – is only one of a range of important dividing lines. In the

Cultural boundaries. Deep internal boundaries highlight differences in everything from language to building style. The lines of division cut different ways – the genetic geography, for example, seems quite distinct. Overall, an anthropologist would have little difficulty positing a strong north–south profile.

middle of the nineteenth century a quarter of the French population did not speak French, and another quarter understood it very imperfectly. Many of these were located in the north: fifty kilometres outside Paris, peasants spoke Picard as their first language; and we may also note northern cohorts of Breton speakers in the Armorican peninsula, Germanists in the east and a smattering of Flemish speakers on the Belgian frontier. The bulk of those resistant to the French language, however, were situated in the Midi, the area of the *langue d'oc*.

The line of cultural demarcation between north and south occurs remarkably frequently in France's history. The map distinguishing a north, where customary law obtained, as against a Midi, where Roman law was the basis of local legal codes, is an extraordinarily important one linked to the transmission of property. The line also broadly corresponds with differences in more everyday material culture: as for example, types of roofs and water-mills. It is interesting, too, to compare this with a rather different medieval boundary – that marking the areas where Gothic and Romanesque architecture was prevalent in the Middle Ages.

One could draw other important lines of division besides the north–south one. In genetic terms, for example, there is a strong case for seeing the Basque area and southwest Gascony as very different from the rest of France (and indeed most of western Europe), and this forms a boundary which has had other significant cultural expressions. So too in many respects – such as style of farming and social structure – a line running from the Channel coast to Geneva has constituted a marker of difference.

It should not, however, be imagined that cultural boundaries are solely geographical, and that only localism counts. Although I have placed particular emphasis on geographical factors to illustrate a point, gender and social class are every bit as crucial areas of demarcation, difference and identity as region. Much of the finest work in French history in recent decades – notably that in the tradition of the so-called *Annalistes* – has sought to uncover the worlds of workers, peasants, marginal groups and women, and it has striven to extend the boundaries of the past to include private as well as public life. Drawing on these rich sources, we can now, for example, incorporate women into French history as more than queens or royal mistresses. Peasants may now be viewed as more than brakes on "Progress"; marginal groups as more than threats needing to be repressed; colonial societies as more than "primitives" awaiting the metropolitan civilizing mission. French history now appears more complex – and more interesting – than the chronicle of the achievements of a limited group of, we might say, Dead White Northern Elite Males.

The *Cambridge Illustrated History* format lends itself particularly well to an analysis that gives due attention to questions of locality, class, gender and other principles of difference. Cartography allows many of the regional distinctions to be highlighted and explored. In addition, the illustrations allow us to portray diversity at all levels of French society. Representations of royal coronations stand alongside primitive contraceptive devices. The Gothic cathedral is juxtaposed with the mass-produced Citroën car (post-structuralist Roland Barthes, as we shall see, actually compared the two).

Opposite The ceremony of healing the "King's Evil" (scrofula), as practised by Henry II (r. 1547–59). The belief in the divine power of the "royal touch" dated from the eleventh century, and the Capetians exploited the ritual for propaganda purposes. As the king touched the sick person, he would say, "The king touches you; God cures you." By the eighteenth century, this formula had changed to: "The King touches you; may God heal you" – a shift to the subjunctive which reflected a scepticism on the part of the toucher, if not the touched. This example comes from a sixteenth-century illuminated manuscript, *Les Heures de Henri II*.

The regions of France

Since 1789, France's administrative framework has been provided by the departments (see below, p. 308), which replaced the ancient territorial units amassed over the millennia. Some provincial names date back to a pre-Roman past: Auvergne, for example, was the home of the Arverni, Julius Caesar's most redoubtable foes. Others had a post-Roman ancestry – such as Burgundy, the home of the barbarian Burgundes – or a later, usually medieval, pedigree: Guyenne and Languedoc, for example, dated from the thirteenth century.

Canonical works of art take their place alongside chapbook illustrations; a medieval manuscript illumination, alongside twentieth-century street graffiti; the royal palace at Versailles, alongside a twentieth-century slum; a prehistoric menhir, alongside the Pompidou Centre.

Not that we should assume that the kind of imagery we will sample in this volume is only illustrative. Images tend to have a prescriptive as well as a descriptive face. Something as apparently straightforward as the image of a monarch on a coin had telling political force. As we shall see, too, a painting of the king of France, engaged in "touching" the sick poor to cure them of the "King's Evil" (scrofula), may attest to a long-enduring cultural practice: but, with its assumption that French monarchs had miraculous powers, it also needs to be placed within the context of royal propaganda. So, too, the pictorial images of French history present in the school textbooks of the late nineteenth century may be viewed not simply as out-of-date narratives, but as part of a broader project of instilling metropolitan and nationalistic values into a recalcitrant provincial population and turning, as Eugen Weber has put it, "peasants into Frenchmen". More recently the newspaper photographs and television news bulletins on the Events of May 1968 were important not simply for recording what occurred on the capital's streets as for forming public opinion and conditioning political responses. Repressive regimes have, tellingly, tended to censor images as well as books, for visual representations make history as much as they illustrate it.

From this angle of vision, the history of France begins to look rather different from how it has normally been presented in old-style multi-period histories. What emerges is less the progressive unveiling of essential truths about "France", "Frenchness" and "the nation" than a sense of the malleability, even fragility of such everyday terms. We can make an optimistic wager that there have developed a resilience and durability about French social, political and cultural life which make it unlikely that events similar to those unfolding in the former states of Yugoslavia and the Soviet Union will occur there. Yet these events have sensitized us to the sometimes exhilarating, sometimes frightening notion that they can decay and deconstruct – and also be created, almost invented. As our news bulletins also show, moreover, the process of state formation (and deformation) can have major knock-on effects for seemingly well-embedded notions of class, regionalism, ethnicity, masculinity, femininity and so on. In this context one begins to grasp the extent to which even in the most solidly founded of national states, ideas of identity are continually negotiated and renegotiated, and are subject to endless definition and redefinition. In some senses, the political reaches into the heart of social and cultural experience. Terms like the "nation" and "national identity" – in this context "France" and "Frenchness" – seem to be as much problems as solutions. My aim in this volume has been to try to write a history of France which is alert to that fact.

CHAPTER 1   *France Before the Romans*

The human species tiptoed imperceptibly into French history. Although Europe cannot compete with the archaeological record of Africa, where hominid remains four million years old have been discovered, the ancestors of *Homo sapiens sapiens* were already to be found in France two million years ago. Notable here was *Homo erectus*, whose physical remains have been found dating to approximately half a million years ago. Then came the Neanderthals, who were present from about 100,000 BC, and who were characterized by a short, stocky stature and a large, rugged, deep-featured head. Only from around 40,000 BC did these begin to be replaced – for reasons which remain entirely unclear – by modern humans (*Homo sapiens sapiens*), in whose more conventional bodies we recognize ourselves.

These developments took place in the context of huge environmental changes wrought by the Ice Age. Geologists distinguish four periods of glaciation, or freezing, in the far-distant past: ice-sheets reached down from the north into England, northern Germany and the Low Countries; a smaller icecap centred on the Alps; glaciers spread far out from the Pyrenees and Massif Central; and conditions of permanently frozen soil prevailed as far south as the Loire valley. Phases of ice advance were, however, interspersed with times of thaw – and it was during a warmer, interglacial phase of the Würm period, which lasted between roughly 90,000 and 9,000 years ago, that *Homo sapiens* appeared.

For the little we know about these early humans we are dependent upon the archaeological record. Archaeologists divide this prehistoric past into periods characterized primarily by the type of tools which societies employed. The Stone Age, in which stone-based tools were used, is divided into two distinct eras: the Old Stone Age, or palaeolithic period (from earliest times to *c*. 6,000 BC in France) and the New Stone Age, or neolithic period (*c*. 6,000 to *c*. 1,800 BC), in which polished stone tools were used. The transition from Old to New Stone Ages was one of the most crucial in human history, namely, the shift from hunting and gathering lifestyles to those characterized by more settled communities practising farming. The Age of Metal began in roughly 1,800 BC, when societies began to employ copper, then bronze, in their tool-making. The Bronze Age (1,800 to 700 BC) was followed by the Iron Age (*c*. 700 BC to the time of the Romans), so called because of the widespread use of this tough and resilient metal.

Throughout this early period France was subject to migratory movements, especially from the east, whose rationale and extent remain clouded in mystery. Demographic pressure caused by population levels outstripping food supplies may well have been the major factor in making peoples mobile. Ecological deterioration – changes in animal populations on which peoples depended for their foods, for example – may also have played a part. New peoples brought new cultural patterns and modes of behaviour, which could then be adopted and further spread by indigenous peoples. The Romans, who arrived and settled in France in the first century or so before

Christ, brought with them not only a relatively complex and sophisticated culture, they also introduced writing to France. With the Romans, pre-literate prehistory passes into the realm of history.

THE OLD STONE AGE

Early societies affected their environment less than they were affected by it, especially during the geological and climatic upheaval of the Ice Age. Glacial advance and retreat caused spectacular shifts in the native flora and fauna. While freezing, steppe-like conditions prevailed in ice-age periods, the interglacial periods could be hot, with tundra giving way to jungle-like forest. A surprisingly wide range of animals lived at some time or other over this early period, ranging from Arctic species (musk ox, reindeer) to carnivores more at home in subtropical climes (hyena, lion), temperate-zone herbivores (red deer, aurochs), mountain species (chamois, bear, ibex) and grassland grazers (bison, horse) – to say nothing of now extinct species, such as the mammoth (whose remains are found throughout France down to the Mediterranean coastline), the woolly rhinoceros and various types of hippopotamus. All these animals were at some time important food sources of early hominids.

This is a period frequently characterized as the "Age of Man the Hunter". Yet the label seems doubly inappropriate. Plants rather than game probably provided the bulk of the food of these prehistoric populations. Moreover, it seems likely that the

The Lascaux caves, from 16,000 to 14,000 BC, the most celebrated example of cave art.

The Venus of Lespugue, Haute-Garonne. This ivory figure, around 20,000 years old, is typical of similar portable objects and wall representations, which depict the female figure almost as a caricature (large belly, breasts, bottom). It may have formed part of a fertility cult.

gathering of plants and berries was the preserve of women rather than men, and took more time and effort than hunting. If women left mammoths, woolly rhino, reindeer and their ilk to men, they themselves probably engaged in the hunting of smaller animals such as rabbits and other rodents. A division of labour between the sexes may well have developed, with men specializing in big-game hunting, war-waging and possibly tool-making, and women in gathering staple foodstuffs and – probably – child-care. It is too easy to portray this period as a golden age of communal living, but group survival did depend on co-operation, so that mutual support was given priority over individualism. The earliest inhabitants about whom we have much direct information lived in caves or rock shelters and hunted game in packs, using stone axes, rocks and cunning (notably in the organization of pits and cliff-falls). The fact that these people were quarry themselves as well as hunters was a further reason to foster collective values.

This Stone Age existence was in part nomadic. Hunter-gatherers, who can rarely have exceeded several tens of thousands in France, were parasites as well as predators on the herds that in cold phases wandered the semi-Arctic tundra wastes. Some regions seem to have been little more than big-game hunting parks – makeshift hunting lodges provide the only clear evidence of early human presence in, say, the Paris basin, Brittany, Alsace and Champagne. Areas with more varied forms of cave shelter may have provided a more welcoming setting for *Homo sapiens*. In the Dordogne area, for example, the steep, south-facing cliffs of the Dordogne and Vézère rivers housed settlements for twenty millennia. The remains of the "reindeer culture", present here between *c.* 16,000 and *c.* 14,000 BC, reveal heavy dependence on a quarry which provided the bulk of the society's food, clothes and shelter. They also bear witness to an astonishingly rich expression of skill and imagination: cave art.

Much of the Ice Age fauna that cave art celebrates eventually became extinct. Though some argue that this ecological transformation was due to over-hunting by human predators, it seems more likely to have been a consequence of climatic change. A warming-up period from around 10,000 to 9,000 BC caused glaciers to recede and water levels to rise. The land-bridges which had joined Corsica to Sardinia, and northern France to southern England, narrowed and were eventually submerged; and the low-lying Mediterranean coasts took on roughly their present shape. Tundra and grasslands permanently gave way to forest, stimulating a major change in wildlife. Mammoths disappeared; the great wandering herds of reindeer moved northwards to a Lapland home where they have remained; chamois and ibex took to the Alps; deer, wild boar and other forest fauna appeared in greater numbers. Human groupings adopted more intensive, less mobile hunting strategies. The appearance of the bow around this time and, from around 8,000 BC, the domestication of the dog as a hunting-companion testify to new forms of predation. The rubbish-tips of these peoples show greater exploitation of forest produce – berries, chestnuts, hazelnuts and so on – and a growing dependence on snails and other molluscs, which were seemingly consumed in vast quantities. Changes in ecology and lifestyle were laying the groundwork for the shift from hunting and gathering to settled farming.

FROM PREDATORS TO PEASANTS

From roughly the seventh millennium BC onwards, a major transformation took place in the relationship between early peoples and their milieu. During the New Stone Age or neolithic period, early societies began to produce their own foodstuffs, notably through cultivation of edible plants and herding. This had a feedback effect on the environment: humans began purposely to shape their surroundings rather than being shaped by them, to produce environmental change rather than merely responding passively to it.

The process involved the gradual spread of new lifestyles, but also involved some groups adapting biologically to new challenges. Changes in fauna, as tundra gave way to forest, may have predisposed some groups to abandon predation for pastoral or peasant life, particularly if reduced returns from hunting were making it difficult to maintain existing population levels. Migration of peoples from the east who had already made the shift to farming also played a role. Farming had appeared in western Asia in the eighth millennium BC and spread outwards. In France the change took the form of a crude pincer movement. Around 6,000 BC an area on the coast of Provence became the first to adopt sedentary farming as a way of life. The local variety of wild sheep seems to have been domesticated first, followed by goats and cattle, then came limited cereal cultivation (corn, barley, millet) and pottery manufacture. Hunting and gathering continued to provide extra forms of subsistence, but it is noticeable that the proportion of wild game consumed at the hearth fell drastically: by around 3,500 BC it was down to about 60 per cent of total consumption, while by the first millennium BC it had fallen to only 10 per cent. New industries developed too: novel forms of toolmaking (now in polished stone as well as bone and wood), weaving and milling, as well as pottery.

Around 4,500 BC, a separate current of change from the Danube valley in the east started to permeate northern France. Whereas in the south, the shift towards farming was largely through a process of slow cultural adaptation, in the north conquest had a role. The so-called "Danubian" culture originated among peoples widely scattered through parts of Romania and the Ukraine. Danubian material culture differed from that of the south: herding concentrated on cattle and pigs rather than sheep and goats, and there was a greater emphasis on cereal cultivation. This form of farming spread south and west, reaching Picardy in 4,000 BC, for example, and fizzling out in the foothills of the Massif Central – while the southern form gradually spread northwards, reaching Geneva and Franche-Comté in approximately 3,000 BC, to complete the pincer movement.

The process by which the peoples of France shifted from predatory to sedentary farming lifestyles, based on herd and plant management, was completed under the so called Chasseyan culture. Originating in the south, from 3,800 to 2,700 BC this spread slowly north to cover virtually all of French territory and much land beyond French borders. In some respects the bearers of Chasseyan culture were a warlike group of

The most ancient form of cultural expression to take place within French borders, far predating that of Greek and Roman civilizations, cave art has been recognized only very recently as a part of France's cultural heritage. At first archaeologists, used to thinking of prehistoric peoples as primitive savages, found it difficult to accept the authenticity of decorated prehistoric objects. Professional endorsement was swiftly followed by wider public interest, when some were shown at the Universal Exhibition held in Paris in 1867. Paradoxically, prehistoric art entered the public sphere only shortly before the advent of Impressionism in 1874.

The great Lascaux cave in the Dordogne was found as late as 1940, and discoveries continue to be made. The most striking recent find was in July 1991 by the diver Jean Cosquer, at Cape Morgiou, twelve kilometres south-east of Marseille. The paintings, engravings and daubings found in the Cosquer cave date from the Magdalenian period, between 18,000 and 16,000 years ago. The cave was probably ten kilometres from the coast during the Magdalenian period, but the rise in sea level by over one hundred metres at the end of the Ice Age sealed normal access, thereby reducing environmental damage.

The location of this cave, in Provence, is unusual. Though cave art is found over an area ranging from Paris and Rouen in the north to Gibraltar and Sicily in the south, most of it is located in south-west France (notably in the Dordogne and the Pyrenees) and in north-east Spain – indeed cave art is often called Franco-Cantabrian art. In other respects, however, the pictorial contents of the Cosquer cave are fairly representative of prehistoric parietal (or wall) art. Though cave art dates back to before 30,000 BC, the Magdalenian period saw a veritable artistic explosion.

Prehistoric art: the Cosquer cave

The most brilliant examples – Lascaux in the Dordogne, Altamira, near Santander in Spain and Niaux in the French Pyrenees – date from this period.

A host of different methods is evident at Cosquer as elsewhere: finger marks, stencilled hands, rock engravings and paintings. Charcoal and ochre were the preferred media. As is typical, animals make up the bulk of the subjects represented at Cosquer: of nearly fifty representations so far listed, horses, bison and ibex are the most common, but there are also chamois, felines, a megaceros and some marine species, notably seals and penguin-like great auks. (By contrast Lascaux, whose "Hall of Bulls" is a veritable Sistine Chapel of cave art, contains 600 paintings and nearly 1,500 engravings.) The Cosquer cave has not yet yielded examples of portable art. Elsewhere engraved, painted and sculpted objects are extremely numerous. The fifty prehistoric caves of the Dordogne region alone have produced over 2,000 objects:

carved bone, stone, antler, ivory objects, clay figurines and the like.

Though access to the Cosquer cave is now difficult because of the rise in sea level, there is every reason to believe it has never been easy. Cave art is frequently located in dark, secret places, usually far away from normal habitations and intended to be illuminated only by fat-burning lamps. In some cave sites paintings are over a mile from the cave entrance, through chambers that professional speleologists find challenging. In the caves at Lascaux, moreover, some of the paintings are fifteen feet from the ground, which would have necessitated the use of scaffolding.

The identities and intentions of the cave artists remain a profound mystery. Stylistic similarities between paintings in different caves suggest schools of cave artists, or systems of apprenticeship. It is conceivable that the artists served a magical function for the societies involved, and that the painted caves were sites for initiation ceremonies aimed at bringing good luck in the hunt. Cave art seems replete with meanings; yet we lack the codes for discovering what they were.

Auks, here depicted on the roof of the Cosquer cave (*c.* 16,000 BC), may have formed a part of the diet of the coastal cave-dwellers.

newcomers – they drove existing shepherd communities up into the Alps and the Massif Central, for example. However, the shift to the Chasseyan also operated through peaceful acceptance by existing groups, for it represented a new style of life in France as a whole, as much as a new layer of immigrants.

The shift towards a farming existence is conventionally identified as one of "Man's" greatest achievements. Yet a great deal of archaeological and ethnographic evidence suggests that the initial impetus came from women rather than "Man". Selecting and planting seeds seems a natural extension of the food-gathering activities in which women probably specialized. As long as farming resembled horticulture – that is, while it was close to human dwellings in which women attended to child-care – it probably allowed women to maintain a high status. At all events the impact of the transformation on the scale of human enterprise was dramatic: population increased, it can be surmised, ten-, then a hundredfold, reaching 100,000 by 3,700 BC, one million over the next millennium, and peaking at perhaps four to five million by the beginning of the first millennium BC. The phenomenon was at the same time cause and consequence of social change.

Statue menhirs from Filitosa, Corsica. The island contains more than one third of the total number of such effigies located on French territory. The Corsican standing stones are distinctive not just for having the rudiments of features (nose, eyes, mouth), but also for representing the paraphernalia of Bronze Age warfare (helmets, shields, daggers). They seem to be a commemoration of the heroic.

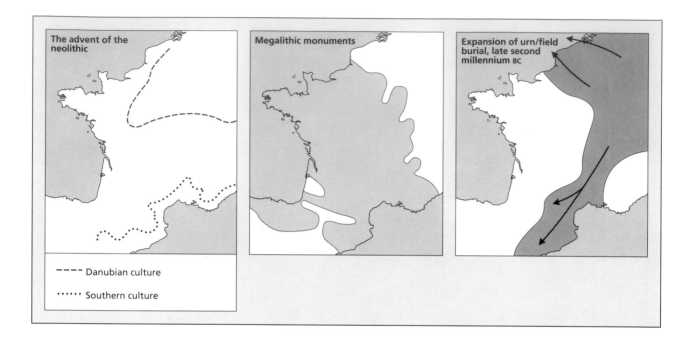

The advent of the neolithic

Megalithic monuments

Expansion of urn/field burial, late second millennium BC

– – – – Danubian culture

· · · · · · Southern culture

The area of France underwent a number of significant transformations in the six millennia before the modern era. The passage from hunting and gathering to pastoral and farming lifestyles (left) was diffused from two main centres – the Mediterranean in the south and so-called "Danubian culture" from the east. Megalithic culture (centre), which appears to have originated on the Atlantic seaboard, in time spread throughout France and beyond. Customs of urn/field burial, in contrast, originated in the east.

The slowness as well as the complexity of the cultural currents by which the shift to farming life was achieved makes archaeologists wary of using the term "neolithic revolution" to describe the process. After all, can any change which lasted three millennia – it was in place throughout France by 3,000 BC – seriously be considered "revolutionary"? In fact the so-called neolithic or Stone Age "revolution" was essentially evolutionary. It made, moreover, a major impact on the landscape: early farmers scooped out areas for cultivation from the primeval forest, using slash-and-burn techniques and often moving on to new areas within a generation or two. Grazing, too, affected the ecosystem, banishing forever forest cover on some highland areas with poor soils. The bare, goat-cropped flanks of Mont Aigoual and Mont Ventoux in the south are testimony in our own day to the impact of early farmers on landscape.

The relative homogeneity of cultural forms under the Chasseyan began to break down in the third millennium BC. In the Armorican peninsula a distinctive grouping developed, flourishing especially between 3,500 and 1,800 BC, whose most characteristic cultural expression was megalithic monuments. The so-called Seine-Oise-Marne (SOM) culture, originating in northern France, extended far and wide during the same period. In the Alps and the Jura a distinctive lakeside-dwelling civilization evolved, and from around 2,200 BC we begin to see traces of "Bell Beaker" culture, characterized by distinctively shaped pottery. The latter may have represented a new style of life, but alternatively it may have been brought by new, incoming groups originating either in Spain or in central and eastern Europe. Bell Beaker culture was especially important in its use of copper – for decorative ware, utensils, arms and armour. The Age of Metal was coming to supersede the Stone Age.

THE AGE OF METAL

The emergence of metallurgy highlighted growing social and economic complexity among early farming communities. Experiments with copper at the beginning of the second millennium BC led to the invention of bronze, a tough and resistant alloy of copper and tin. The new metalworking technology, adopted throughout France from around 1,400 BC, was passed on after 1,250 BC by populations practising "urn/field burial". This entailed cremation of the dead and and the interment of their ashes in urns that were placed in cemeteries outside the village. The practice of urn/field burial swept most of France, except the Atlantic seaboard. It reached the Rouergue, for example, by 950 BC, flourished there until 725 BC, and was still being practised on the Languedoc coast in the third century BC. By then, however – and notably from the eighth century BC – fresh migrant groups were already invading northern climes. Though these groups – the Celts – probably had much in common with the urn/field burial peoples, they were culturally distinct from them. They swept south and westwards and by 700 BC they were present in the Armorican peninsula. All of France north of a line between Carcassonne and Geneva bore marks of their presence by 400 BC.

This migratory phase had its roots in the east. The Scythian peoples of the Steppes, and societies in the Near and Middle East, seem to have been the epicentres of waves of turbulence which travelled outwards across Europe, triggering short- and long-term migratory waves over several centuries. Greek and Roman writers at first used the term "Gauls" to denote these restless and footloose Celts, who spread widely throughout Europe. Some pushed south-east as well as westwards, reaching "Galatia" in the Balkans and Asia Minor (hence the name "Gaul"). Another group, the "Cisalpine Gauls", had marauded into Italy, sacking Rome in 390 BC, before settling down in the Po valley. Others penetrated the Iberian peninsula. Still others had settled in Great Britain and Ireland by the third century BC: the Parisii tribe, based in the Paris basin, established a colony in Yorkshire. These mobile populations appear to have communicated exclusively in Indo-European languages, established from around 2,000 BC, on which the major European tongues would be based. They provided a dense cultural covering over France in which there were relatively few cracks: French placenames bear virtually no traces at all of pre-existent languages.

The Celts constituted a sprawling, untidy but powerful set of groupings whose area of influence far surpassed the frontiers of what would soon be Roman Gaul. Archaeologists classify the material culture of the eighth-century-BC Celts as belonging to the "Hallstatt" stage of Iron Age civilization (named after a site in Austria near Salzburg). The iron cutting-edges on their ploughs, for example, allowed them to extend cultivation on to heavy soils, while their weighty iron swords, stronger than defensive armour made of bronze, plus their mastery of horsemanship, made them formidable warriors. From the fifth century BC a variant form of Iron Age culture – the La Tène stage, named after a village on Lake Geneva, and characterized by distinctive styles of pottery, weapons and jewellery – began to predominate.

This terracotta representation of a Gaulish warrior, dating from *c.* 200 BC, was found in Lombardy, which Gaulish tribes had invaded several centuries earlier. This wild and valiant warrior was typical of a breed of foot soldiers that could be found from Britain to the Black Sea. By the time of Caesar's invasion of Gaul in 58 BC, more sophisticated military techniques were being employed, including chariots and cavalry.

The Celts came bearing ploughshares as well as arms. The Celtic warrior elite formed a landed aristocracy. They made use of a variety of tenancy arrangements and were based in large estates that were characterized by open fields. Their iron ploughs, sickles and reapers boosted agricultural production and stimulated demographic growth. Population, which had slumped dramatically under the impact of the warfare they had initially waged, increased from two to three million in 500 BC to probably between six and eight million at the time of the Roman annexation in 51 BC. This demographic expansion may have been accompanied by a deterioration in the position of women. Celtic warfare was largely man's work, while the heavy, iron-trimmed plough needed a masculine hand too, it would appear. Ploughing the fields became a male preserve, as did large-scale herding for milk, hides and other secondary goods besides meat. The status of Iron Age women was apparently in decline.

Opposite Constructed between 2000 and 1400 BC, the stone alignments around Carnac in Brittany cover several square kilometres, making it the largest and most concentrated site of its kind in the world. Whether they commemorate a cult of the sun and other religious rituals or whether they acted as a kind of astronomical observatory is unknown.

The martial Iron Age culture of the Celts was firmly hierarchical, with the warrior elite dominating subservient tenants, clients and maybe slaves too. Among some southern and central tribes, a powerful aristocracy had replaced the traditional Celtic system of a hereditary monarchy by one of annual elected magistrates – a system which seems better to have enshrined their power. In the new social order tribal units were broken up into a bewildering patchwork of lesser subtribes, each occupying a smallish natural unit. The Romans estimated that Gaul possessed some sixty tribes, which between them controlled some three hundred territorial entities, to which the Romans gave the term *pagus* (whence the later French term, *pays*). Roughly 1,200 to 2,000 square kilometres in size, these units constituted a crucial element of political differentiation and were destined for a long, if unsung, role in French history as the framework within which much local history would take place. As the conquering Julius Caesar was later sardonically to note, the region as a whole was "divided by language, customs and laws".

This bronze mask representing a Celtic god was discovered in 1839 at Montsière in the Hautes-Pyrénées, and dates from the second century BC. The eye-holes may have been filled with glass or ceramics.

The Celtic cult of the severed head, mentioned by a number of ancient writers, lies behind this ceremonial gateway from Roquepertuse, near Marseille, dating from between the third and the second century BC. Recent archaeological research suggests that the lintel between the pillars may have been longer, and that the skulls faced into the household rather than outwards.

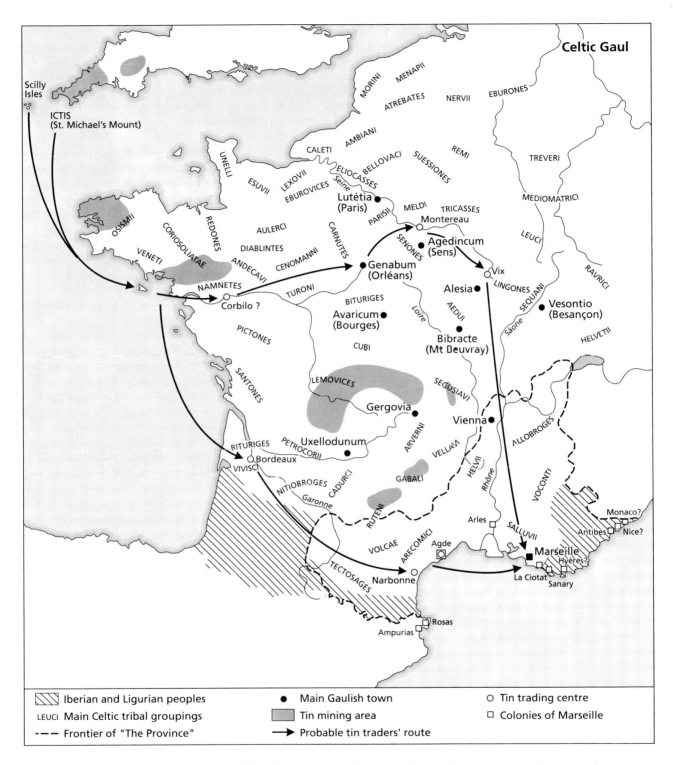

Celtic Gaul

Scilly
Isles

ICTIS
(St. Michael's Mount)

MORINI   MENAPII

ATREBATES   NERVII   EBURONES

CALETI   AMBIANI

ELIOCASSES   BELLOVACI   SUESSIONES   REMI   TREVERI

UNELLI   LEXOVII   Seine   MEDIOMATRICI

ESUVII   EBUROVICES   Lutétia
(Paris)   MELDI   TRICASSES   LEUCI

REDONES   PARISII   Montereau
Agedincum
(Sens)

OSISMII   CORIOSOLIATAE   AULERCI   CARNUTES   SENONES   Vix   RAVRICI

VENETI   DIABLINTES   Genabum
(Orléans)   Alesia   LINGONES   Vesontio
(Besançon)

ANDECAVI   CENOMANNI   SEQUANI

NAMNETES   TURONI   BITURIGES   AEDUI   HELVETII

Corbilo ?   Avaricum
(Bourges)   Bibracte
(Mt Deuvray)

PICTONES   CUBI   Saône

SANTONES   LEMOVICES   SEGUSIAVI

Gergovia   Vienna   ALLOBROGES

BITURIGES   PETROCORII   Uxellodunum   ARVERNI   VELLAVI

Bordeaux   VELLAVI   HELVII   Rhône   VOCONTI

VIVISCI   NITIOBROGES   CADURCI   GABALI

Garonne   RUTENI   Arles   SALLUVII   Monaco?

TECTOSAGES   VOLCAE   ARECOMICI   Agde   Antibes   Nice?

Narbonne   Marseille
Hyères?

La Ciotat   Sanary

Rosas

Ampurias

⬚⬚⬚ Iberian and Ligurian peoples	● Main Gaulish town	○ Tin trading centre
LEUCI Main Celtic tribal groupings	▨ Tin mining area	☐ Colonies of Marseille
– ∙ – Frontier of "The Province"	→ Probable tin traders' route	

Prior to Roman colonization, the Celts had established themselves throughout Gaul, leaving only marginal areas in the south-east and south-west still dominated by indigenous peoples. Celtic Gaul formed a crazy-quilt of tribes and sub-tribes making shifting alliances and frequently resorting to war. Farming techniques were fairly advanced. In addition, the tin trade established currents of movement and exchange from the far west and centre, where the tin deposits lay, through to the Mediterranean coast.

The Vix princess

In 1953 archaeologists discovered at Vix in Burgundy, just north of Châtillon-sur-Seine, the grave of what appears to have been an Iron Age princess or priestess buried in a ceremonial four-wheeled chariot and dating from around 525 BC. Pride of place among the artefacts uncovered, which rank among the richest aristocratic grave goods in prehistoric Europe, is taken by a massive bronze crater (or ceremonial vessel). Five feet high, and weighing over 440 pounds, the vessel is decorated with a bronze frieze showing a cavalcade of warriors, and there are elaborate handles supported by gorgons. The princess had been dressed in ceremonial finery, though all that remained were amber, schist, pearl and

The gold diadem of the Vix princess.

silver jewels, earrings, necklaces and other decorations. Around her head, which had been severed from her body, was an exquisitely elegant gold diadem.

The most exotic goods came from afar: coral from the Mediterranean, amber from the Adriatic, bronze goods with Etrurian designs from central Italy. The constituent parts of the crater appear to have been manufactured either in Corinth or in Greek colonies in southern Italy, transported to the Vix site and reassembled there. The diadem may hail from the Scythian peoples, who lived beyond the Greek world on the banks of the Black Sea. All highlight the strong currents of exchange in which Iron Age Gaul had begun to be involved. Vix was a key trading post in the tin market, linking sources in the south-west of England and the Armorican peninsula with bronze-smiths in the Graeco-Roman world. It was close to the end of the navigable part of the river Seine, and well situated at the head of passages towards the Saône and Rhône rivers – and thus to Marseille.

The Vix crater, bronze, *c.* 550–500 BC.

Bronze calendar from Coligny, near Bourg. Dating from the late first century BC, it constitutes the oldest and most extensive example of Celtic script. The Celts did not have their own alphabet – here they employed the Latin alphabet, but at other times used the Greek. The calendar was possibly consulted by Druids for calculating ceremonial days to honour the gods.

The *pays* formed, as it were, the building blocks from which political coalitions were formed. Certain tribal groupings were able to amass a good deal of power through a loose system of clientage and alliance. In the second century BC the Arverni, based in the Massif Central, imposed their will on smaller groups and forced them to submit hostages and pay tribute, building up an extensive "Arvernian empire" in the process. Loose political arrangements of this sort were fragile, however, and easily fell apart. Gaul as a whole was marked by profound political discord, only partly offset by the rough cultural unity inspired by their polytheistic religion. Tribes accorded importance to a special priesthood, the druids. Each year the druids of the whole of Celtic Gaul held a convention at a ritual location, possibly close to Orléans, in the middle of the forest of the Carnutes tribe. Impressive as a show of cultural unity, the druid convention had no broader political significance, however. Though Celts may sometimes have felt a crude sense of fellow-feeling, there was no "Gaulish nation".

A new element was introduced into the region when, in *c.* 600 BC, the Greek colony of Massalia (present-day Marseille) was established by the (now Turkish) city of Phocea. Massalia helped to create a web of similar Greek-based trading cities on and near the French coast and in the Rhône valley. Hitherto trade had not been extensive and was largely restricted to the coasts. Through greater involvement in the tin trade – tin for making bronze came notably from Devon and Cornwall, Brittany and Bohemia – Massalia developed as the hub of a trading network in which much of France came to be involved. The trade built up more land routes through France, partly to avoid piracy from the Carthaginians of north Africa. The routes developed for the tin trade became available for other commodities too, and trade broadened into a more general north–south trading pattern: northern goods such as tin, copper, iron, glassware, leather goods, cereals, salt, slaves and maybe charcuterie were exchanged against Mediterranean luxury goods – jewels, for example, decorative ware and wine. The birth of French wine-growing, as well as olive cultivation, probably took place under the auspices of the Massalia merchants. The widespread diffusion of Greek coins from this period throughout France testifies to the importance of the role of the Phocean colony in the development of the Gaulish economy.

Gallo-Roman god with a torque. Dating from the first century AD, this bronze statue was found at Bouraye in the Paris region.

The growth of commerce and the development of agriculture boosted urban development. Small bourgs and embryonic towns emerged. Their material structures were unimpressive compared with what was going on south of the Alps; apart from stone-built defensive walls, for example, virtually all urban building was in wood. Yet some centres, such as Ensérune in Lower Languedoc, were impressive. And all contributed to the construction of an urban network which covered virtually all of France, except for the north beyond the Ardennes forest and the far west. The emergence within cities of neighbourhoods of traders and artisans and the appearance of separate areas for the town houses of aristocratic landlords signalled progress too. The archaeological finds in the princely tombs at Vix in Burgundy graphically illustrate the formidable extent of aristocratic wealth.

Economic growth was not, however, matched by greater political co-ordination. All roads might seem to lead to Massalia, but the Phoceans were merchants, not conquerors nor imperialists. They preferred to establish trading counters, not to impose new structures of political domination. Significantly, French words influenced by Greek are found predominantly in the fields of navigation, fishing and meteorology, while only a tiny number of Greek words remain in placenames.

Greek merchants did pave the way, however, for Roman legionaries and administrators. Massalia supported Rome in its struggle with Carthage and proved to be, as the Roman orator Cicero later put it, "the most faithful ally of the Romans". Rome valued such support. Its initial expansion towards the Alps brought the Italian city-state into contact with the Cisalpine Gauls based in the Po valley, while extension beyond the Alps caused potential friction with local Celts. The Romans sought friends and allies amongst the tribes – the Aeduans, based in Franche-Comté, were special favourites. The degree of support which tribes gave the Carthaginian general Hannibal, as he trudged Alpwards with his elephants in 218 BC, impelled the Romans towards closer control. From 125 to 121 BC Rome answered calls by Massalia for protection against hostile neighbours, plus an appeal for help by the Aeduan tribe against the Allobroges and the Arverni. The upshot was direct Roman control over the entire coastal strip. "The Province" (*provincia* – whence "Provence"), soon to be called Gallia Transalpina or Gallia Narbonensis, was to prove the springboard for the Roman annexation of the Celtic tribes to the north, and the establishment of Roman Gaul.

CHAPTER 2

Roman Gaul

The incorporation of the southern part of France into the Roman sphere of influence proved to be only the first act of a long-lasting saga in which France became the core of Roman Gaul – a province, or set of provinces, within one of the great world-historical empires. In acquiring Gaul, Rome increased the size of its empire by one third – an empire which, in time, would stretch from the Scottish borderlands in the north to the shores of the Upper Nile in the south, from Morocco and Portugal in the west to Armenia in the east. Roman authority brought in its train Rome's taxes, conscription, coinage, markets, officials, soldiers, language and writing. All in their different ways would immeasurably enrich the cultural fabric of a massive, sprawling area which included not only the whole of future France, but also all of Belgium and Luxembourg plus much of the Netherlands, western Germany and Switzerland and some Alpine fringes of Italy. Roman Gaul was far more than "France" under the Romans.

CONQUEST AND CONTROL

The Roman Empire was assembled by force of arms. Its rationale in Gaul as elsewhere was conquest, pacification and exploitation; anything else was a bonus. Like any imperial power Rome was sensitive to developments outside the immediate orbit of its control. Roman armies had, for example, beaten back an invasion of southern France by the Germanic Cimbri and Teutones from 109 to 101 BC. Alleged preparations for another such invasion in 58 BC – by the Helvetii, who were preparing to migrate from southern Switzerland into southern France – alerted Rome to the coming danger. This was combined with the threat of destabilization further north, where the Germanic chieftain Ariovistus had joined in a squabble involving the Arverni, the Sequani and Rome's long-standing allies, the Aeduans. To combat this politico-military threat Rome sent Julius Caesar.

"There was a time," Caesar later noted in his *Gallic Wars*, "when the Gauls were more warlike than the Germans." That day, he claimed, had passed, and Gaul required occupation and control if it was not to fall into the hands of the Germans, who would be unruly neighbours for Rome. Ambitious, already prominent in Roman domestic politics and seeking a wider stage for his talents, Caesar took on the task of subjugating Gaul with relish. It probably took longer, and needed more force – and more luck – than he had anticipated. The Gauls overcame their famed divisiveness and, under the Arvernian leader Vercingetorix, fought a relatively united struggle against the Roman armies. Caesar's victory in 52 BC at the siege of Alésia, however, forced Vercingetorix to yield. Mopping-up operations continued into 51/50 BC; but the back of Gaulish resistance had been broken.

Roman Gaul was thus a creature of the Roman army, and the threat of naked coercion was never far away. The legionary presence on the Rhine frontier stood permanently on guard. The fact that colonized settlements were staffed by army veterans also

Vercingetorix

The first move was made by Vercingetorix, a young Arvernian with very great power in his tribe ... He called his dependants together and had no difficulty in rousing their passions. When it was known what he intended to do, there was a rush of armed men to join him ... He (also) raised a band of beggars and outcasts from the countryside. Once he had recruited these, he brought over to his side all the Arvernians he approached, and he soon collected a large force of men, by urging them to take up arms in thecause of Gaulish freedom ...
He quickly won the support of the Senones, the Parisii, the Pictones, the Turoni, the Aulerci, the Lemovices, the Andes and all the other tribes of the Atlantic coast. By general consent he was given the supreme command.

Julius Caesar's *Gallic Wars* is a justification as well as an account of his conquest of Gaul between 58 and 51 BC, and we may reasonably suspect that this portrait of his most redoubtable Gaulish opponent inflates the Arvernian's importance, so as to make Caesar's victory over him all the more impressive.

Yet although there seems little doubt that Vercingetorix was a formidable opponent, it is altogether more questionable whether he was acting in the cause of "Gaulish freedom". An

aristocrat from the powerful Arverni tribe, based in the Massif Central, which had quite recently switched from a monarchy to an oligarchic republic, he may well have been promoting his own cause. Caesar describes him as "a man of enormous

Gold coin, with the head of Vercingetorix.

energy" and "a very strict disciplinarian", using "savage means" – cutting off an ear or putting out an eye for even slight offences, for example – to put together a powerful army.

By this time, however, the wars were going badly for the Gauls. In 58 BC

Caesar had dealt with the main causes of the wars, forcing the migrant Helvetii back into Switzerland and clipping the wings of the German leader, Ariovistus, who returned across the Rhine. The following year, he had brought the Belgi and north-western tribes to heel, then in 56 BC pacified the west and south-west, winning a naval battle over the powerful Venetii near Vannes. Sorties into England and across the Rhine in 55 BC and 54 BC were crowned with less obvious success, however, and though Caesar was establishing his position in 53 BC, the Vercingetorix coalition caught the Roman commander off balance.

The war was fought with great ferocity. The Arvernian leader enjoyed some successes, but in 51 BC was finally hemmed in with his troops at the stronghold of Alésia (near Alise Sainte-Reine in Burgundy). The conflict was effectively over. Vercingetorix was taken to Rome to appear in chains at Caesar's official triumph in 46 BC, and was then strangled.

Caesar's conquest was achieved with the loss of much Gaulish blood. Battlefield losses and civilian massacres amounted to over a million dead, and it seems likely that between half a million and a million Gauls over the next decade were exported to the Italian peninsula, where they flooded the slave-markets.

played a role in exerting authority. The network of Roman roads developed out of politico-military rather than economic motivation: troops could travel fast to any point where order had broken down. The symbolic language of Roman power had a strongly militaristic flavour which seemingly affected even Rome's Gaulish adversaries. Significantly, Julius Sabinus, leader of the most notable rebellion, in AD 69–70, postured not as the heir of Vercingetorix but rather as a descendant of one of Caesar's bastards. Overall Gaul was far less rumbustious and rebellious than the neighbouring

Iberian peninsula. The "Roman peace", or *pax romana*, won support from most Gauls, who perhaps felt that Rome had more to offer than their bellicose, barbarian neighbours in Germany.

The Gaul which stopped at or around the Rhine was only in certain respects a single area. Caesar remarked that it was divided into three parts, Gallia Belgica (in the north), Gallia Iberica (in the south-west) plus the sprawling trunk of Gallia Celtica. The list excludes, however, already Romanized Gallia Narbonensis, the firm springboard for Caesar's conquests – "more like Italy than a province," as the Roman first-century naturalist, the Elder Pliny, put it. In the administrative settlement of the region by Augustus in 13 BC, this four-part organization was retained – albeit with considerably reworked frontiers and different names (Aquitania, Belgica and Lugdunensis to the north of Narbonensis). With some minor retouching this structure stayed in place until the third century.

But although the region's administration was subdivided, the term "Gaul" did come to denote a certain cultural entity, at least as regards the three northern provinces. In 43 BC Lugdunum (Lyon) was designated the capital of the "Three Gauls". Its role as a

The sight of manacled Gaulish prisoners on the triumphal arch in Carpentras was a powerful reminder of Rome's martial superiority. After the fall of the Roman Empire the arch was converted into the porch of the city's first cathedral.

symbol of Gallo-Roman unity was endorsed by the construction in 12 BC of an Altar of Rome and Augustus at the meeting-point of the rivers Rhône and Saône. Representatives from the Three Gauls were permitted to hold an annual conference on the site, to discuss judicial and administrative affairs and formulate grievances to be passed on to Rome – as well as to participate in public worship of the Roman emperor. The high priest in these annual ceremonies of the imperial cult was, moreover, a Gaul.

Such measures formed part of a standard imperialistic strategy aimed at eliciting political consent without the need for coercion. The institution of administrative division within a vaguer cultural union typified a more general policy of divide and rule. The Arverni, for example, the leading edge of Gaulish resistance in the Gallic War, were divided up. Other tribal units competed against each other to gain tax and other privileges. Despite the massacres committed by him and in his name, Julius Caesar showed clemency to many of his erstwhile enemies, and incorporated them into his train of dependants. Caesar and Augustus liberally gave Roman status to magistrates – this long before the Emperor Caracalla (r. AD 211–17) made all free men within the empire Roman citizens in AD 212. In Gaul, moreover, this status could be inherited by children, thus increasing the spread of citizenship. The army too became an important career channel for ambitious Gauls, along with administration and local government. In AD 48 Emperor Claudius (r. AD 41–54) persuaded the Roman senate to admit Gauls among their number. This decision, part of broader moves to widen the Roman governing class, established a ladder of ascent which reached the very highest levels: the grandfather of Emperor Antoninus Pius (r. AD 138–61) had come from Nîmes.

The impact of the Gauls on Rome's central governmental apparatus was never considerable. Virtually all Gauls in the Roman governing class originated in more heavily Romanized southern Gaul, and their number in the senate was far exceeded by Africans, for example. Yet if Gauls made little impact in Rome, Romans were relatively few in administrative and governmental posts within Gaul. To a great extent, in fact, the Roman Empire in Gaul was administered by Gauls – and largely for Gauls too. Immigrants from the Italian peninsula seem to have been few, and one numerous category, military veterans, was clustered in southern Gaul. Generally the Roman authorities followed the inclination of Julius Caesar to graft local government on to pre-existing tribal forms. The Celtic tribe was transmuted – often literally – into the Gallo-Roman city-state, or *civitas*. Pre-conquest tribal groupings formed the basis of the sixty *civitates* of the Three Gauls, while the twenty-two administrative units of Gallia Narbonensis were also closely linked to pre-conquest divisions.

To most intents and purposes the *civitas* was the tribe in a toga. The Gaulish elites were allowed to dominate, if they submitted to Roman orders. Magistrates still often used the Gaulish title of *vergobret*. The *curia*, or city council, introduced in each local capital, owed much to pre-conquest forms. At village level no change was probably detectable. The new taxes may have been Roman in origin, but they were assessed and collected according to existing forms – and were still rather low. Not surprisingly Celtic tribal elites welcomed being refashioned into Gallo-Roman notables.

Was *romanitas* – Roman identity – more than skin-deep, however? Just as Roman political forms overlay older Celtic institutions, so Latin culture influenced, but never erased, the pre-conquest linguistic heritage. Latin replaced the Gaulish tongue as the language of written communication, but Celtic had in any case been an oral rather than a written language – the druids had been wont to educate the Gaulish political elite without the benefit of writing or even their own alphabet. Under Rome, Latin became the language of education for the elite: many towns – Marseille, Autun, Reims, Toulouse, Bordeaux and others – contained schools in which the Gallo-Roman aristocracy, by imbibing Latin, could learn the language of power, social ascent and cultural clout.

The imposition of Roman power was successful in creating a new, Gallo-Roman cultural amalgam. But the blend of Gaulish and Roman elements varied according to time, place and social level. It was in the interests of anyone who had dealings with political and cultural institutions to know Latin. In the towns potters dependent on wealthy clients learnt in time to put *fecit* instead of the Celtic *avot* on the bottom of their pots and vases. Yet even the heavily Romanized social elite never totally lost contact with its Celtic roots, while the further one descended the social ladder, and the further one moved from the towns, the more the balance between Celtic and Roman was weighted towards the former. The heavy concentration of Gaulish words in placenames, outliving Roman and later Germanic accretions, underlines this, as does the fact that many contemporary French words for agricultural implements and techniques have Celtic origins, for example *arpent* (acre) and *soc* (ploughshare).

The longer Roman occupation lasted, however, the more Latin penetrated and won over even backward rural areas. Rome's merchants, officials, labourers and soldiers acted as vectors of everyday Romanization. For some time bilingualism must have been the norm for many: one talked "up" in Latin, "down" in Gaulish. But in the long term a vulgar Latin far removed from the language of the rhetoricians prevailed. By the fifth century AD there is evidence that Gaulish was no longer understood in rural areas. Significantly, the Germanic invaders of the period called the inhabitants of Gaul "Romans". Even as Rome fell Latin was triumphing – and was to prove the basis for the development of the French language.

Evidence suggests that religion also evolved by cultural mixing rather than replacement. Roman government launched a campaign against druidism, whose secrecy, practice of human sacrifice and potential for subversion marked it out as dangerous. Emperors regulated the polytheistic cult that was to be followed in the empire, adding worship of themselves in the form of the so-called imperial cult. So closely was religion tied into the imperial system that it would have been unthinkable for the Gaulish political elite to shun the pagan and imperial cults, which appear to have prospered in Gaul. There were strong efforts to assimilate earlier beliefs within the accepted framework. Thus the annual religious ceremony at the Altar of Rome and Augustus in Lyon attended by representatives of the Three Gauls could be seen as echoing the annual druidic ceremony held in the forest of the Carnutes. It was held on 1 August, the

Opposite This arch at Saintes contains a Gaulish genealogy. The Roman-sounding name of the constructor, Caius Julius Rufus, contrasts with the semi-Romanized name of his grandfather Caius Julius Gedomo and his great-grandfather, the utterly Gaulish Epotsorovidus. In such ways the Gaulish elite assumed a Roman identity.

Statue of the god Mercury, from the Clermont-Ferrand region, dating from the late first to the fourth century AD. Mercury was one of the most popular Roman gods, probably because he corresponded fairly closely to a similar pre-Roman god. The horns represent virility, aggression and fertility.

ceremonial birthday of Emperor Augustus, but also the festival day of the Celtic god Lug, whose cult had given Lugdunum (Lyon) its name. In addition, despite official pressure towards conformity, many Roman gods were "gallicized". Roman temples too were often erected on Celtic shrine sites; while Roman thermal spas were built around the healing springs allegedly inhabited by Celtic deities. Gallo-Roman polytheism was thus a distinctive blend of two strong and resilient cultural forms.

The strength of the Gallo-Roman religious hybrid may also explain Christianity's slowness to penetrate Gaul. It was merely one of a number of usually Greek-speaking, Eastern mystical cults (worship of Isis and Osiris, for example, and Mithraism) that followed the lines of trade and administration into the province from the late second century onwards. Lyon seems to have harboured the first Christian community, and initially the cult was closely linked to the towns of the Rhône corridor. Only from the fourth century were the churches making efforts to organize rural parishes and to spread the cult into country areas – significantly, the Latin term *paganus* came to denote both "peasant" and "pagan". The sect's apparent secrecy triggered rumours of horrible and murderous rituals. Monotheistic, exclusive and intolerant – yet heroically committed to an interior ethic – Christianity seemed the polar opposite of Roman religion's open willingness to assimilate.

Diocletian (r. AD 284–305) stepped up the intensity of the persecution to which Christians had sporadically been subjected. Yet within a couple of decades Christianity had been transformed from a minor cult into the official religion of the Roman Empire. In the Edict of Milan in AD 313 joint-emperors Licinius and Constantine (the latter a Christian himself) restored freedom of worship to Christians. The earlier pattern was now reversed. By the end of the fourth century Christianity was the religion of the state and emperors were persecuting pagans and closing down their temples. The diocesan framework that developed in the fourth century underpinned the *civitates*, and closely integrated civil and religious power. Latin became the language not only of liturgy and theological dispute, but also of conversion. This was a tribute to how deep Roman culture had penetrated, and the Church acted as an important channel for the relaying of Latinate culture into rural areas.

PAX ROMANA AND THE "ETERNAL CITY"

The incorporation of Gaul into the Roman Empire not only created new political, administrative and cultural forms; the *pax romana* also transformed the region's economy. Julius Caesar had found Gaul politically anarchic, and the imposition of Roman authority allowed its economic potential to be realized. The effect of the Roman presence was that much of the wealth of the eastern Mediterranean moved west. The relatively underdeveloped Gaulish economy received a boost from Roman investment, immigration, urban building, road improvement, tax demands and military occupation. The prolonged period of internal security – both against incursions from outside the empire and from banditry within – plus the fact that Roman taxes were generally low and still collected by local agents also facilitated steady economic growth.

Nowhere was economic prosperity more in evidence than in the cities, where life blossomed under the Romans. Cities were constructed in stone rather than wood and wattle-and-daub, and were planned imaginatively. Sometimes laid out geometrically, their model was often "the eternal city", Rome itself, and many buildings were virtual replicas of Roman originals. Private dwellings coexisted alongside an impressive array of commercial and public buildings. Towns housed a colourful artisans' sector: besides the building trade, which employed large numbers, there was a whole range of urban trades and occupations. Lyon, for example, had guilds for shippers, rafters, wine importers, corn and oil merchants, cloak-makers, plasterers, silversmiths, glassmakers, potters, wool-carders, linen-weavers and soap-makers. Among public buildings there were the *forum*, market and meeting-place; the *curia*, or town hall; the *basilica*, or law courts; and sundry temples. These urban institutions, which beggared Gaulish precedents, were complemented by an impressive range of leisure facilities. Baths were a staple feature of the urban landscape. The cities of Gaul boasted no fewer than seventy-nine theatres, thirty-five amphitheatres and a score of other entertainment centres, including circuses and odeons. The logistics and engineering required to construct and maintain these edifices were immense: stone used in the construction of Lyon, for example, was hauled some 200 kilometres, while the city's water supply was brought from a distance of over seventy-five kilometres away.

In towns material life could be good. Full participation in the public life of the city was, however, almost wholly male. Women had no place in decision-making in politics, law or in regard to questions of city defence. Roman law was sternly patriarchal: for example, fathers had the right to order the exposure of unwanted babies, and could make offspring stay minors, sometimes even beyond their marriage. It is difficult to judge how far social practice conformed with legal precept. Despite their saturation with patriarchal power, family relationships could be affectionate. The state, moreover, increasingly acted to bolster women's civic rights. Women could inherit, for example; they could initiate divorce; and, on getting married, their property was kept independent. They also played an important role in the clientage relationships on which Roman political and family life depended. Women of high social status also benefited from the considerable volume of trade in luxury goods – jewellery, gold- and silverware, fine cloth and cosmetics. How far such benefits reached down to women of lower social status outside the cities is, however, debatable.

A host of new towns emerged under Roman rule, and so, consequently, did a new urban network, which has endured astonishingly well: of 55 cities in France with a population of 100,000 in the late twentieth century, 37 had been Gallo-Roman cities, while out of 107 sites which served as capitals of *civitates*, 94 are towns today. Gaul lacked a monster city like Rome (perhaps 700,000 inhabitants); its biggest conurbations – Narbonne, Nîmes, Lyon, Autun, Reims and Trier – did not exceed the 20,000 to 30,000 population band. Most cities were far smaller, though they tended to look larger than they were. Indeed the monumentalism of gates and walls owed more to the desire to impress than to military needs. Leisure facilities were also designed on an

Head of Venus, based on Greek models, found at Nîmes in 1853.

Roman Nîmes

Nîmes provides an excellent illustration of what provincial urban life must have been like under the Roman Empire in southern Gaul. It was one of Gaul's larger cities, with a population of perhaps 20,000. Located on seven hills, which gave it more than the usual claim to replicate the "eternal city", Rome itself, it was founded by Emperor Augustus in 16 BC as a military colony for his veterans. Several monuments are based closely on Roman models, notably the amphitheatre, based on the Colosseum, and the famous temple Maison Carrée. The latter closely resembles the Temple of Apollo in Rome. Constructed by Agrippa, son-in-law of Augustus, to commemorate Augustus' grandchildren, Gaius and Lucius Caesar, it was dedicated to the imperial cult.

Nîmes contained the full paraphernalia of Roman leisure. The 23,000-seater amphitheatre, constructed late in the first century AD, still stands, and is still in use, though a circus, a theatre and extensive baths have been destroyed. Before the arrival of the Romans, the city had been the capital of the powerful Volcae Arecomici tribe, and the focus of important regional trading links. On top of the Mont Cavalier, overlooking the city, sat a look-out tower which the

Coin with crocodile motif minted at Nîmes, or COL(onia) NEM(ausus).

Romans built over and renamed the Tour-Magne (again still in existence).

The city had a cosmopolitan reputation. The military veterans attached to the city by Augustus hailed from Egypt, following Augustus' capture of Alexandria in 30 BC, and early coins minted here depict a crocodile chained to a palm tree, a design which passed into the city's arms. Nîmes was also a key staging post on the Domitian Way, the main economic and administrative artery connecting northern Italy with Spain (which had been a Roman province since 202 BC). Hence the city must have witnessed the passage of large numbers of travellers, merchants, soldiers and administrators, as well as pilgrims.

Nîmes was very much a city of waters. The sacred spring of Nemausus had long given the settlement some repute. Pre-conquest Celtic religion had set great store by springs, wells and caves, which were viewed as housing deities and serving as thresholds to the underworld. By naming the new city "Colonia Augustus Nemausus", thereby associating himself, as a deity within the Roman pantheon, with a pagan god, Augustus showed characteristic Roman pragmatism. Rather than obliterating the Celtic gods, the Romans preferred to assimilate them.

Water was also provided in abundance from outside the city walls. The Romans created a hydraulic system which transported 20,000 cubic metres of water per day from Uzès, a distance of fifty kilometres away. The aqueduct across the river Gardon at the Pont-du-Gard, constructed in 19 BC, is the highest surviving bridge structure from the Roman world, and (as one of the most impressive pieces of civil engineering in France until the reign of Louis XIV) a visible link with the past.

The Maison Carrée at Nîmes, first century BC: a perfect example of classical style.

extravagant scale: Lutetia (Paris) boasted a population of some 8,000, yet its arena contained 15,000 places.

The urban network was created remarkably swiftly. Massive building programmes in Gallia Narbonensis and some other sites (notably Lyon) were instituted by Augustus, using booty acquired from his victories in the east. Emperor Claudius' preparations for the invasion of Britain in AD 43 were important in filling out the urban and communications infrastructure of northern Gaul. But the rage for building also testified to the growth of indigenous urban prosperity and civic pride among local elites. The Gallo-Roman elite drew much of its wealth from the business and administrative networks into which cities were plugged. Roman roads, replacing the winding Celtic pathways with rectilinear masterpieces of civil engineering, may have been built for armies, but they also stimulated and facilitated economic exchange. Similarly the presence of troops could boost trade and wealth – the development of Trier as a major imperial city in the third and fourth centuries owed much to its strategic position close to the Rhine armies. Those cities did best which were able to turn this communications network to their advantage: with security less of a problem in the *pax romana*, fortified hill-towns either were left to rot, or else adapted and slid down the hill towards road and river junctions.

If towns derived wealth from their position on the networks of trade and administration, they also drew heavily on their surrounding countrysides. To be a city, chronicler Gregory of Tours was later to note, one required "walls, an imperial edict, and a rural hinterland". Town and country were locked into a symbiotic relationship, with the towns providing the markets and the commercial skills which rural inhabitants required. Many rural workers actually lived in towns, and would set off for the fields at dawn. Urban growth demanded a degree of efficiency in agricultural production and distribution: it was asking a great deal of any pre-industrial economy to feed the 6 to 7 per cent of the population who lived in towns. The achievement was all the more important because it was made without any major breakthroughs in agrarian productivity. The growth in production came from the extension of cultivable land, greater use of the sturdier wheeled ploughs already widely used before the conquest, crop diversification and vast improvements in distribution and exchange.

The backbone of Gallo-Roman agriculture was the villa economy. Villas were often continuations of pre-conquest Gaulish estates and the standard operation was large-scale farming on open fields. In time they spread to even apparently inhospitable localities such as Brittany. Villas tended to be farmed for their owners by individuals working under various kinds of contract and tenancy arrangements, plus some slaves. Many villas were large, factory-like complexes, with buildings set aside for agricultural and manufacturing functions (weaving, brewing or basket-making). Some may have contained as many as 100 individuals and been potentially self-sufficient.

In general, however, in the period of the *pax romana*, the triumph of large property stimulated not self-sufficiency but rather a willingness to enter into commercial arrangements. Villa owners were excellently placed to commercialize their production,

The third-century stone frieze from the tomb of a merchant at Cabrières-d'Aygues shows a convoy of wine barrels on its progress along the river Durance. The wine barrel was a Gaulish invention – wine was otherwise stored in the kind of amphora depicted on the top of the frieze.

and some independent peasants also profited from those propitious economic conditions. Certain areas, like the Beauce, concentrated on grain production. Other regions began to specialize too: wine in Languedoc, Roussillon, Alsace and the Touraine; hemp in the Auvergne; flax in the Berry; geese in the Artois; sheep in the Ardennes; and so on. Roman tastes spread and brought changes: hazelnuts and apples gave way to the spread of the olive and the vine, and to cherry and peach trees. As time went on landowning came to be seen increasingly as a symbol of honour and gentility as well as potential wealth among the social elite, and the ideal of the "gentleman-farmer" achieved a certain vogue. Increasingly, however, villas and villages seemed prey to a growing wave of insecurity. The *pax romana* was coming to an end, under the pressure of barbarian raiding.

THE FALL OF ROMAN GAUL

Julius Caesar had blamed the aggressive turbulence of the barbarian German tribes for Rome's annexation of Gaul. The erection of a defended frontier – the so-called *limes* – to repel Germanic invaders played a crucial role in establishing the *pax romana*. Yet from the late second century, and even more obviously in the third and fourth, Germanic pressure was threatening to overturn Roman political structures. The *limes* was leaking like a sieve. Yet it would be grossly misleading to assert that the fall of the Roman Empire in the west, conventionally placed at AD 476, was solely due to barbarian pressure from without. Roman authority was also crumbling from within, due to varied social, political and demographic problems. Indeed it is a curious paradox that the barbarians were instrumental in propping up Roman power in these centuries of decline, and giving it an extra lease of life.

Romans and barbarians were not polar opposites: they had been living in close cultural association for centuries. The seismic language of "flood", "waves" and "engulfment" which historians often adopt to describe the Germanic invasions (or migrations?) is quite inappropriate. It obscures the long history of earlier "trickle migration", and the relatively small size of the Germanic contingents in the third and fourth centuries, which should probably be counted in tens rather than hundreds of thousands. As we shall see, moreover, most were only too keen to settle down and adapt to Gallo-Roman ways, and indeed many already bore a strong Roman imprint. The flood metaphors also obscure the fact that a great many areas had only limited experience of barbarian destruction till the fifth century: parts of Franche-Comté, close to the *limes*, were virtually unmolested, and many south-western areas experienced a golden age in the third and fourth centuries.

Too much emphasis on the role of the "barbarians" in the fall of Rome obscures the gravity of the empire's internal difficulties. At the centre political anarchy from the middle of the third century made stable policy-formation impossible, but the problem was about more than political will. The empire was also faced by declining population levels. The legal situation of the Roman family did not favour large families. The fact that women could inherit, and that individuals could choose to adopt an heir towards the end of their life, meant that there was less stimulus to procreate than is usually the case in societies characterized by high infant mortality. While Roman family law may have deterred large families among the urban elite, population decline in rural areas was probably caused more by financial and social pressures.

The Roman Empire had been created at very little expense to the taxpayer: systematic pillaging had allowed the initial costs of establishment to be transferred from the Roman taxpayer to the colonized peoples. In time, however, the plunder was exhausted and payment for the military and bureaucratic costs of empire fell more

The *limes*

The defended frontier marking the Germanic limits of the Roman world – known as the *limes* – was at first merely a rough track interspersed with look-out stations. It was gradually bolstered by a complex system of forts, walls, palisades and support roads, and by the third century featured watchtowers every half a kilometre, and a sophisticated and wide-ranging military-style administration, containing one of the heaviest densities of Roman troops in the empire.

In military terms the wall was only as effective as the strength of the armies behind it and constituted an administrative and symbolic marker more than an impregnable barrier.

Indeed its varied fortunes at the hands of barbarian raiders from the second century onwards highlighted its military limitations. It did not insulate Gallo-Roman civilization from what Romans perceived as the home of barbarism, since it proved impossible to prevent contacts between peoples on either side of the boundary. Trade flourished across the divide: the barbarians provided slaves, animal products and amber, while the Roman side supplied precious metals, silver drinking vessels, arms and armour and other luxury goods; these were aimed primarily at the Germanic tribes' warrior elites. Nor did the *limes* prevent settlement. Indeed the Roman authorities came to depend on Germanic tribes from across the frontier to defend the *limes*.

Primarily, perhaps, the *limes* represented a political attempt to set limits and to bring order and fixity to a fluid world. By marking off the Roman from the Germanic worlds, and by settling for security in the area rather than expansion, Rome constructed a notion of "Germany" as a symbol of barbarism just as surely as it constructed, out of a divided and idiosyncratic region, the fictive unity of Roman Gaul.

This poignant and evocative second-century funerary monument from south-western Gaul depicts a ten-year-old child holding its toys: a cat and a tame cockerel – also a symbol of resurrection – who nibbles the cat's tail.

squarely on Romans. The Roman tax system was regressive, which placed a heavy burden on peasants, many of whom were already living close to the breadline. The problem was aggravated when, from the third century, taxes began to be imposed individually rather than collectively. Severe inflation and outbreaks of epidemic disease only made matters worse. Many peasants were forced to sell up to big property-owners. Others abandoned their small-holdings to migrate to towns, which offered public assistance – everything from bread to circuses – and in which employment possibilities were more varied. There are signs in some areas of a return to mesolithic-style cave occupation. Some peasants chose to take to the woods, to live a shadowy life of banditry and highway robbery. The so-called Bagaudae movement of rebellious peasants grumbled through Gaulish agrarian history from the third quarter of the third century onwards. Shortage of labour led villa owners to tighten up the regulations tying their peasants to the land – a process supported in Rome; yet one effect of this was to create a wave of resentful refugees from the fields, who swelled the ranks of the Bagaudae.

The shift of large numbers of peasants out of productive employment into service-sector work or economic dependency increased the strain on an arguably over-urbanized empire. Given stable levels of agrarian productivity, prosperity had been ensured only by the excellence of Rome's distribution and exchange networks. That these were breaking down was signalled by the appearance of large-scale famines, even from the late second century. The Bagaudae aggravated rural insecurity; so, on a much larger scale, did the migrations of the Germanic peoples, who wreaked damage not only on property and persons but also on the smooth operation of the systems of exchange on which prosperity had been built.

There had been Germanic incursions beyond the Rhine in AD 162 and 174 in the Strasbourg region, but it was from the second third of the third century that the phenomenon began to assume a more consistently threatening form. In 253 the Rhine legions marched to Italy to sustain the claim of Valerian to the imperial title, leaving the frontier undermanned. Two tribes, the Franks (situated on the lower reaches of the Rhine) and the Alamanni (based on the river's upper reaches), punctured the security cordon, the former even reaching Paris and causing the Lutetians to cower on the Île de la Cité. Gaulish coasts also began to be harassed by Frankish and other Germanic pirates. In 260 the Roman general Postumus declared himself emperor and, with the support of the Rhine legions, established a Gallic empire independent of Rome. Significantly, most of northern Gaul, no doubt feeling that he would exhibit more commitment to the Germanic problem than a remote and insecure emperor in Rome, supported him. Postumus did indeed check the barbarian advance, though following his death, the Roman emperor Aurelian (r. 270–5) brought Gaul back under the Roman aegis. Almost at once – in 275 – the continuing nature of the threat was highlighted by a further attack by the Alamanni and the Franks, who sacked between sixty and seventy cities.

Roman emperors finally began to give higher priority to problems on the Rhine, and sought to find more appropriate administrative structures for coping with social, economic and political difficulties. Diocletian (r. 284–305), in particular, completely reorganized the structures of imperial administration. He divided the empire between east and west, each part to be ruled by an emperor ("Augustus"), assisted by a subaltern ruler ("Caesar"). This attempt at "tetrarchy" (rule by four) spawned imperial claims and counter-claims. Although Emperor Constantine (r. 306–37) temporarily united the empire under his authority and shifted its seat to the new city of Constantinople, this was a prelude to the definitive division of the empire into eastern and western halves in the year 395.

Diocletian also undertook root-and-branch reform of local administration in Gaul. His decision to create a more decentralized structure – two super-provinces centred on Trier and Vienne, including between them 17 provinces and 112 *civitates* – provided a more flexible and responsive apparatus. Military defences on the frontiers received particular attention. Diocletian also introduced important financial, currency and military reforms, in order to make the empire more able to resist incursions from outside. He offset the costs of maintaining a huge army by allowing troops to requisition more extensively for their requirements, and he also allowed taxes to be paid in kind. In this

Mosaic of bread-baking. Gaul was exceptionally fertile, and wheat and other grains were the most widely-grown crop. Caesar managed to survive the lengthy Gallic Wars without a serious food-supply problem.

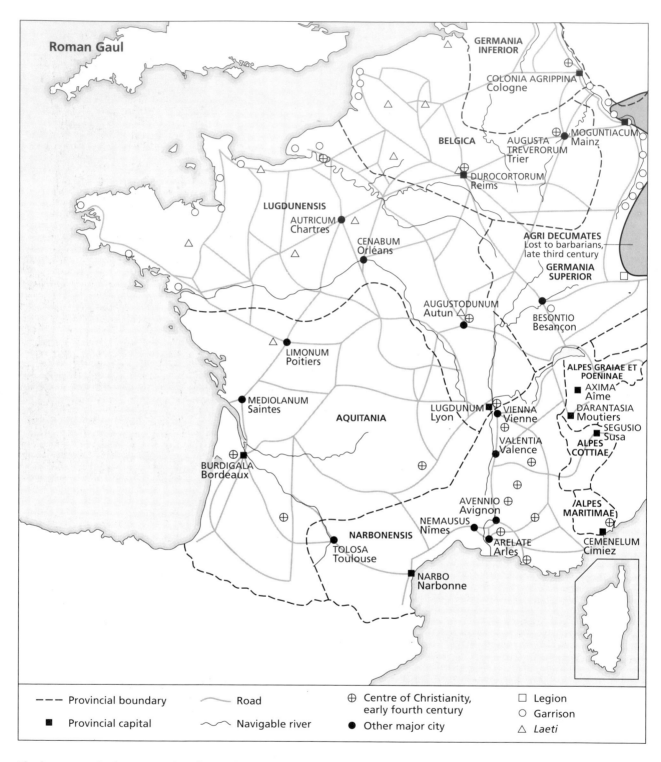

Roman Gaul

GERMANIA INFERIOR

COLONIA AGRIPPINA
Cologne

BELGICA

AUGUSTA TREVERORUM
Trier

MOGUNTIACUM
Mainz

DUROCORTORUM
Reims

LUGDUNENSIS

AUTRICUM
Chartres

CENABUM
Orléans

AGRI DECUMATES
Lost to barbarians,
late third century

GERMANIA SUPERIOR

AUGUSTODUNUM
Autun

BESONTIO
Besançon

LIMONUM
Poitiers

ALPES GRAIAE ET POENINAE

AXIMA
Aîme

DARANTASIA
Moutiers

MEDIOLANUM
Saintes

AQUITANIA

LUGDUNUM
Lyon

VIENNA
Vienne

SEGUSIO
Susa

ALPES COTTIAE

VALENTIA
Valence

BURDIGALA
Bordeaux

AVENNIO
Avignon

ALPES MARITIMAE

NEMAUSUS
Nîmes

NARBONENSIS

TOLOSA
Toulouse

ARELATE
Arles

CEMENELUM
Cimiez

NARBO
Narbonne

- - - Provincial boundary
■ Provincial capital
〜 Road
〜 Navigable river
⊕ Centre of Christianity, early fourth century
● Other major city
□ Legion
○ Garrison
△ *Laeti*

The dense network of Roman roads and navigable waterways combined military with economic functions. In the north and east in particular they serviced the military establishment required to keep the Gaulish provinces safe from Germanic attacks. In the south they highlighted the main commercial currents. It was along such trade routes that Christianity – an eastern import – penetrated the region from the second century AD.

way he had to raise fewer taxes. He struggled to control inflation, albeit at the price of a partial demonetarization of an economy whose strength had always lain in exchange.

In spite of these valiant endeavours to shore up a failing system, frontier violence continued to increase. In the fateful year of 406 a whole swarm of tribes crossed the ice-bound Rhine, forced their way into Gaul and settled where they pleased. Subsequently the Franks established a secure footing on French soil, the Alamanni settled in Alsace, the Vandals and Alans crossed Gaul and directed their footsteps into Spain and Africa, and the Burgundians established themselves in northern Gaul. In 412 the Visigoths set out from Italy and settled in the Toulouse area. In 416 an important page was turned, when the Roman authorities were forced to recognize the kingdom of the Visigoths as an autonomous mini-state – a move that marked the first serious tear in the fabric of imperial power.

Less conspicuously, however, the barbarian quest for land was dovetailing neatly with the empire's need for manpower: the Germanic tribes helped to repeople a society in the throes of depopulation. Though barbarians were moving in to settle in much larger groups than before, Rome had been sanctioning lesser settlements for some

The Porta Nigra, or "Black Gate", at Trier, now in Germany. The city was built up in the third and fourth centuries as the "Rome of the Gauls", and the centre from which the *limes* was controlled. From 460, however, it fell into Frankish hands. The gate, originally of bright sandstone, acquired its name from the build-up of grime over time.

Celtic deities were often associated with the figure three. Sometimes gods were represented in groups of three, and sometimes the gods were shown with three heads. This crude triad, dating from the third century, suggests a continuance of, or perhaps a revival of interest in, Celtic religion.

time. From the third century, in fact, the Romans had created *laeti* in depopulated areas, that is, settlements of refugees and barbarian prisoners of war. Gallo-Roman dealings with the barbarians took increasingly welcoming forms. In 358 the Salian Franks were accepted as military auxiliaries around the Rhine and Meuse estuaries: barbarians were now manning the *limes*. In 430 Franks occupying the region of Tournai and Cambrai were recognized as *foederati* ("federates"), or treaty-based allies. In 443 the Burgundians were established as "federates" in the Jura–Geneva region, and soon began to expand, taking control of most of the Lyonnais. Meanwhile the "federated" Visigoths began to piece together a massive empire in the south-west. They annexed Provence between 470 and 472, the far south-west in 472, Auvergne between 474 and 475, and then set about forcing their way into northern Spain.

In these various ways the ethnic mix of the Gallo-Roman provinces in general, and the army in particular, was being transformed. Franks were particularly successful as soldiers – one Frankish general, Silvanus, had even usurped the imperial title (in 355) – and as military veterans they could retire to land-holdings within Gaul. In the 440s the Visigoths were used to put down a major rising of the Bagaudae in the south-west. In 451 Attila the Hun was defeated near Troyes by an army which included Franks, Visigoths and Burgundians. By that time, however, it seemed that even a barbarianized

Roman empire would find it difficult to resist further barbarian advances and internal dissension. The fall of the western empire in 476 had little impact on Gaul precisely because the processes of decomposition and restructuring were already far advanced.

With imperial power challenged both without and within, Gallo-Romans lived with a growing sense of anxiety. Long before 476, there had been warning signs of a loss of confidence in Rome's capacity to cope with barbarian raiding and peasant rebels. Effectively demilitarized during the *pax romana*, towns learnt the hard way that times had changed. The raid on Lutetia (Paris) in 258, for example, led to the rapid fortification of city defences. The city walls of a great many Gaulish towns had been for prestige and ostentation rather than defence, but all this now changed. Sometimes the size of the city needed to be reduced: defensible walls were too expensive to cover the entire living area, so cities determined to fortify only a central core. The fortified heart of Saintes covered 18 hectares where the city had formerly extended over 168, and at Amiens the reduction was from 100 to 10 hectares. At Sens, Tours and Périgueux, the authorities took stones from their amphitheatres and temples to buttress the inner defences. Now exposed, some of these massive leisure facilities were invaded by rats, weeds and squatters. Ominously, too, cities began to creep up hills again. In times of prosperity, under the *pax romana*, being close to roads and rivers had been seen as essential; now more remote, but more defensible hillside sites seemed attractive. The destruction caused by prolonged raiding was often too extensive to be properly repaired, so that the seductions of city life waned fast. Since barbarian raiders made a beeline for the concentrations of movable wealth in cities, many local notables shifted away from urban centres to newly fortified rural villas, less attractive, it was hoped, to the seasonal raider.

In this context it is perhaps understandable that Celtic language and culture enjoyed a renaissance. While Eastern religions, including Christianity, made progress in the towns, the Celtic pagan gods also made something of a comeback. The social elite was far from renouncing *romanitas*. But these developments signalled that the imperial cult had, it seemed, failed to make the "eternal city" eternal.

CHAPTER 3

From Frankish Gaul to the Kingdom of West Francia

Historians conventionally characterize the period from around 500 to the establishment of the Capetian dynasty in 987 in terms of the Frankish kingdoms formed after the fall of the Roman Empire. From the late fourth century a Frank, Clovis (r. *c.* 481–511), of the Merovingian dynasty, established a dominion which, under his successors, extended beyond Roman Gaul into Germany and north Italy. Although the Merovingian dynasty's political system was in clear decline by the seventh century, Frankish control was secured by the emergence of a Carolingian dynasty. This powerful family went on to establish a western European empire which was at its furthest extent under Charlemagne (r. 768–814). On Charlemagne's death, however, decline set in again. After a three-way division of the Carolingian inheritance in the Treaty of Verdun of 843, there emerged a new western bloc, "West Francia", which was to form the historical basis for the formation of France.

FRANKS, MEROVINGIANS AND OTHERS

The process by which the Frankish Merovingian dynasty came to prevail throughout Roman Gaul was a triumph for rude martial valour – though some might call it brutal thuggery. Frankish kings were above all great warlords, who enforced their power over their subjects by all means at their disposal. They maintained armed retinues, who swore an oath of allegiance to their chieftain in return for a place in his household and a share of plunder. King Clovis, said to descend from the legendary king-deity Merowech, rooted out rival Frankish rulers on the Rhineland with a brutality subsequently – and colourfully – recorded in Gregory of Tours' chronicle, *The History of the Franks*. He also pushed forward to defeat, in 486, Syagrius, king of Soissons, possibly the last commander of an outpost of the Roman Empire, before going on to crush the Burgundians and the Visigoths in the south. Clovis established the basis of Merovingian power by making Paris his capital (in 511); by converting to orthodox Christianity (around 500); and by issuing a fundamental legal code, the Salic Law.

Clovis' work was continued by his sons, who secured Burgundy in 536, wrested Provence from the Ostrogoths in 537 and expanded into south and central Germany and northern Italy. With the exceptions of Lower Languedoc and Roussillon, which remained in the hands of first Visigoths, then Saracens, and the intractable western tip of the Armorican peninsula, the Merovingian dynasty had by the mid sixth century conquered all of Roman Gaul, as well as much of central Europe.

Rulers came and went. The practice of subdividing the kingdom among heirs meant that political arrangements varied considerably, and that only very few Merovingian rulers – such as Dagobert I, sole king from 632 to 638 – reigned over all Frankish lands.

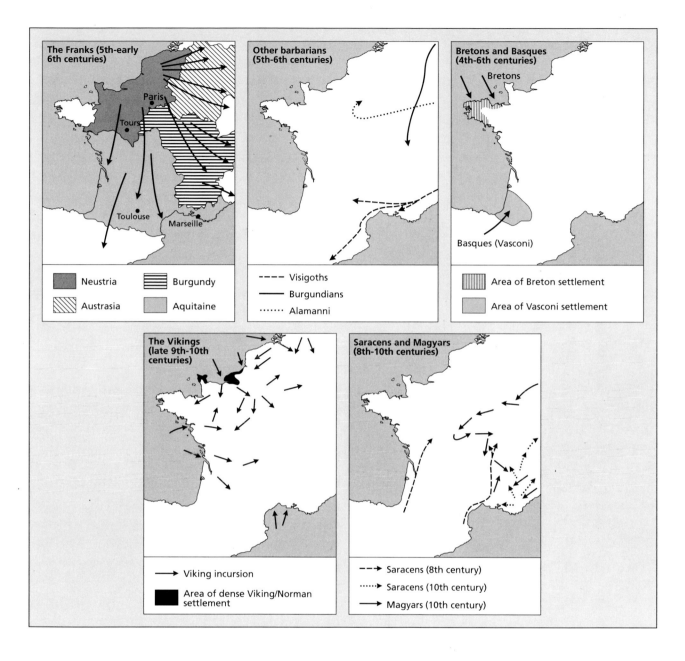

Conceived of as a broad political and cultural entity, however, Frankish power dominated the former Roman provinces of Gaul, and indeed western Europe more generally, for two-and-a-half centuries under the Merovingians, and for much the same length of time again under their Frankish Carolingian successors.

The word "France" originates in "Francia", designating the kingdoms and cultural domain of the Franks, so etymology, if nothing else, seems to reserve for the latter a special place in the formation of France and French identity. It is best, however, to resist the temptation of treating this period as merely a Frankish chapter in the unfolding story of France. Historians have perhaps been too readily convinced by the propaganda

The age of invasions. The conquest of Roman Gaul by the Franks could not prevent repeated invasions and incursions between the fifth and tenth centuries. As a result, other groupings – the Visigoths, the Burgundians, the Bretons, the Vikings – made a lasting cultural impact in many regions.

Gregory of Tours

The author of *The History of the Franks* (593–4), Gregory of Tours (538–94), our most lively and penetrating source on fifth- and sixth-century Gaul, was not a Frank by birth, but an Auvergnat. He was born into an aristocratic Gallo-Roman family of the sort on whose active support the Frank invaders heavily relied. The "Herodotus of the barbarian world" witnessed political life at close quarters: from 573 he was made Bishop of Tours, and worked closely with Merovingian rulers. He was a quirky individual – in trying to clear up his infirmities, he apparently made himself ill several

Fourteenth-century illumination of bishops Gregory of Tours and Salvius of Albi chastising Chilperic, Frankish king of Neustria.

times by drinking potions made from the dust of saints' relics. But he proved a stubborn and individualistic prelate. He

keeps a pretty straight face throughout his chronicle of Frankish garottings, murders, deceit, duplicity, corruption and personal violence. While representing Clovis as "a great man [who] became a great soldier", and clearly stressing the importance of the king's conversion to Christianity, he does not shrink from depicting a lust for personal power of almost psychotic proportions. Only occasionally does feeling break through: recording the dysentery of 580, which was especially deadly for children, he noted, "and so we lost our little ones who were so dear to us and sweet, whom we had fed and nurtured with such loving care. As I write, I wipe away my tears ..."

of the Franks, by the military successes they enjoyed, and by the fact that they were the only invading group to establish a long-lasting and influential dynasty. As a result many have overestimated the depth of Frankish influence. Significantly, it was the Latin-based Gallo-Roman language spoken by the bulk of the population, rather than Frankish German, which was the foundation of the French language. Furthermore, the character and experience of power had shifted appreciably with the fall of the Roman Empire. Roman Gaul had been an integral part of a broader imperial system, and this had had repercussions on political and cultural identity. The very phrase "civis romanus sum", available after AD 212 to every citizen of the Roman Empire, had evoked a varied set of rights and entitlements for all under Roman dominion. From the late fourth century onwards, in contrast, there was no such close association between individual identity and wider power structures. Roman Gaul was no longer part of a wider state. On the contrary, it was honeycombed by a bewilderingly diverse set of local identities, surprisingly few of which were profoundly "Frankish" in any way at all.

National histories which conflate the history of France with the chronicle of the Franks also undervalue non-Frankish barbarian and external influences. The history of the far south-west in the centuries following the fall of Rome is less the story of Frankish invasion than of the establishment of Gascon power structures; and that of Brittany, of immigration from southern England by Breton groups. Parts of what had been Roman Gaul were invaded, first time round, by Burgundians, Visigoths, Alans, Alamanni, Saxons, Huns and others, and in a second spate of invasions from the late eighth century, by Saracens, Magyars and Vikings. Each of these groupings left its own particular cultural mark, which highlighted the diversity of political and cultural identities in France in the post-Roman period.

Furthermore the Franks and the other immigrant groupings were less numerous than is often assumed. The "barbarian invasions" failed to register a seismic shift in the genetic make-up of Roman Gaul. Frankish newcomers numbered between 150,000 and 200,000 – perhaps 2 to 3 per cent of a population of maybe six to seven million. Other groupings counted even smaller contingents. The Franks were also unevenly spread throughout the country. Their influence was strongest in the north and north-east – indeed it was stronger in Belgium, the Netherlands and Luxembourg than in France. Placename evidence suggests that the further one travelled west and south from the region between the Rhine and the Somme and Meuse rivers, the less concentrated Germanic presence was. In the Midi, it was minimal. The dominance of the Franks was not based on population numbers nor on genetic impact, but was essentially political. Even then, moreover, it was limited.

The Franks' value-system was not totally alien to Gaul's erstwhile *romanitas*. As we have seen, the *limes* marking the border of formal Roman power had not been a *cordon sanitaire*, keeping Germanic and Roman cultures uncontaminated by each other. It was more akin to a garden fence, facilitating exchange and reciprocal influence. The Franks had been established on both sides of the frontier even before the "invasions". Population pressures from the east had helped force together what had formerly been a cluster of minor tribal groupings – the Salians, the Chamavi, the Bructeri, the Chattuari and others – into a kind of defensive league ascribed the title "Frank". They were easily enticed as military auxiliaries into defensive duties along the *limes*.

Roman influence on the Franks was apparent long before the period of the invasions. Roman luxury items were sought after by the Germanic tribal aristocracies. Roman political forms had also made themselves felt: the Frankish lawcode, the so-called Salic Law, was influenced by Roman precedent and composed in Latin (as were similar codes drawn up by the Visigoths and the Burgundians). This contained punishments for individuals attacking their neighbour's vines (showing that the quintessentially Roman taste for wine, rather than Germanic beer, had established itself

Far left Merovingian gold coin showing Romulus and Remus, suckling at their wolf mother. It was struck in the early seventh century at Toulouse, capital of Aquitaine, where Roman cultural influence was particularly long-lasting.

Near left Early seventh-century coin of Dagobert I, who reconstituted Frankish unity and proved to be the last Merovingian to rule personally over all Frankish lands. Mounted to be worn as a medallion rather than used as a unit of exchange, this coin testified to the post-Roman decline in mercantile activity.

among the Frankish elite from early times). Even the warlike traditions of Germanic kingship had a Roman gloss: customs such as bearing a new king aloft on warshields were borrowed from the Roman army.

The Franks never lost their fascination with the Roman inheritance in Gaul, nor their pride in being the most powerful of the Germanic successors of Roman imperium. From the conversion of Clovis, through to the coronation of Charlemagne (in 800) and beyond, the Franks tended to view themselves as having assumed the Romans' former role as God's chosen people. The ruler was God's elect, the earthly vessel of sacral power. He wore his hair long, perhaps as a magical symbol. Clovis had received a message from the eastern Emperor Anastasius saluting him as "consul" or "Augustus", and Clovis' sons and grandsons sent diplomatic representatives to Constantinople. Merovingian coins in the early seventh century depicted Romulus and Remus, while later apologists for the dynasty trumped even this, claiming that Frankish rulers were descended from refugees from Troy after its fall. They could thus claim to be the equals as much as the successors of Rome.

The long-haired kings' association with the orthodox Christianity to which Roman emperors had subscribed – a further emblem of continuity – proved one of their trump cards. By converting from paganism to orthodox Christianity, Clovis had won the lasting support of existing Gallo-Roman elites. In the south the latter felt threatened by the Arian heresy – which questioned the divinity of Jesus, and which was espoused by the Visigoths and most other German tribes – and they attempted to lure the Franks south to lend them their support. Frankish rulers came to make liberal use of the Church. Civil administrative boundaries were made to coincide with the diocesan structures established since the fourth century. Bishops played a key role in administering the south, where they often took on the post of count, the major local agency of Frankish power.

The Frankish adoption of Christianity undoubtedly strengthened the dynasty's ideological appeal. Through its monopoly of book production, training in the arts of copying and writing, collection of manuscripts and educational provision, the Church was crucially important in transmitting those Roman values with which the Frankish dynasty chose to identify. The Merovingians extended a wide range of benefits and gifts to the clergy, and from the late sixth and seventh centuries, notably, to monastic houses, whose numbers were growing fast.

Indeed generosity was an essential lubricant of Frankish governance, and the ideal Merovingian ruler was an open-handed giver of gifts. Rulers required means of rewarding their agents and followers, whether these were prominent churchmen, loyal aristocrats or the warbands on whom they depended for military victories. The distribution of booty and tribute acquired through successful military campaigning – movable wealth (gold, silver, jewellery), but also land, tax immunities and other fiscal benefits – was thus of paramount political importance.

The regime's dependence on plunder gave it a somewhat militaristic, even brutal hue. Yet the Franks would never have kept their dominions together had they relied solely on crude coercion and selective political assassination. In general they preferred accommodation to liquidation, adaptation to colonization – and, indeed, such was their numerical inferiority in most places, it was in their interest to do so. They may even have posed as liberators of peasants ground down by Roman tax demands. In the late fifth century the clerical writer Salvian of Marseille had portrayed peasants welcoming Germanic invaders, "since they cannot endure the barbarous mercilessness they find among the Romans".

Despite the more militaristic set of values conveyed by the Franks and other groups, the example of religion shows that there was substantial continuity with pre-Frankish conditions. The shift towards a system whereby troops of Germanic settlers offered protection to Gaulish town-dwellers was also less abrupt than it might appear: the latter had long experienced the presence of imperial troops of Iranian, Iberian, African or Germanic origins living amongst them. Under these enforced "hospitality" arrangements the barbarian "protectors" were either allotted a share of local taxes or else took an agreed amount of local land. Because Romans had deserted so much land there was usually enough vacant territory to be assigned to the newcomers without causing excessive friction. They and the host community were soon intermarrying – and being buried in the same cemeteries with the same funeral rites.

There was continuity in administrative structures and personnel too. Administration continued to operate within the framework of the old *civitates*, now called *pagi* (*pays*). Each area was placed under a revocable royal deputy, the count, who worked to implement the ruler's wishes, presiding over lawsuits, collecting taxes (in so far as this was possible), occasionally levying troops, supervising public works and so on. In the south local Gallo-Roman families with a prior hold on local power largely commandeered the post of count. The same was true for the post of bishop, which Frankish rulers allowed a great deal of authority. The dependence on civic and Church hierarchies stuffed with Gallo-Roman notables was a further factor aiding integration between the two communities.

Germanic kingship brought changes in notions of power. Under Rome during the early empire a hard and fast distinction had been made between military and civilian spheres, and between private and public. The situation under the Franks was completely the opposite. The Salic Law, for example, established a system in which law enforcement depended on family and kin rather than a disinterested state. There were, none the less, important factors of continuity here too. If German kingship was militaristic, charismatic and personal, Roman imperial power had developed into something not so very different by the third and fourth centuries. Moreover, barbarian law codes were not forcibly extended to the Gallo-Romans, who could choose to be judged according to Roman law if they wished. This was most common in the south, where barbarian influence was at its weakest.

The impact that these legal changes had on the position of women is not at all clear. The element of choice in law codes may have been in their favour. Some barbarian codes exemplified a respect for women's bodies: the Salic Law stipulated fines of 16 solidi for a man who pressed a woman's hand, and of 32 solidi if he touched her above

In the year 804 the Benedictine monastery of Gellone was founded at Saint-Guilhem-le-Désert in Lower Languedoc by the Austrasian aristocrat, count of Septimania, Saint William of Gellone (c. 755–812). Later *chansons de geste* were to call him William of Orange and depict him as one of Charlemagne's paladins, the heroic victor over the Saracens, who captured Nîmes by bringing in his troops hidden in wine-barrels. The founder retired from the world to his monastery, and when he died there it was said that the bells of the surrounding province rang without any hand on their ropes. The monastery became a stopping-place on

The monastery of Saint-Guilhem-le-Désert

the pilgrimage route to Santiago de Compostela in northern Spain. Wealth from this source led to extensive rebuilding from the thirteenth century, with a great deal of impressive decorative work.

Saint William was a convert to the Benedictine form of monasticism, which had originated in the work of Saint Benedict of Nursia (c. 480–547).

Reformed by Saint Benedict of Aniane (c. 750–821), and formalized in Louis the Pious' decree of 817, the rule was to be followed in all monasteries throughout the empire. It emphasized poverty, celibacy, obedience and stability – the monk was to be attached to his house as a serf to his land, and to lead his life as a full member of the community. Monks divided their day between prayer – the demands of worship were extensive – and labour (Saint Benedict of Nursia had recommended seven hours' manual work).

The cloister – an open courtyard surrounded by covered passageways – was the centre around which monastic life revolved. The main rooms and chambers of the institution led off from it – refectory, chapter-house, library, workshops and so on. Here monks walked in meditation, had their schooling, studied and perhaps copied manuscripts.

Purchased by a stonemason in the Revolution of 1789, when all Church lands were nationalized and much monastic property sold off, the monastery's buildings were pitilessly ransacked for construction materials. Elements of the cloister were found in the nineteenth century serving as vine supports in the garden of a magistrate in nearby Aniane, and they have since been reassembled in the grounds of the Metropolitan Museum of Modern Art, New York. Only the abbey church of the original institution still remains in place.

Reconstituted cloister of the abbey of Saint-Guilhem-le-Désert.

Saint Radegund (*c.* 518–87), queen of the Franks, depicted, in this tenth- or eleventh-century image, seated at the table of her husband, Clothair (r. 558–61), son of Clovis, before a table bearing bread, wine and fish. Radegund abandoned the court for an austere hermetic life.

the elbow. Yet this respect came mainly from the fact that women were viewed as prize possessions of their husbands, particularly as bearers of children. They enjoyed less legal autonomy than under Roman law, though they could control some forms of property independently. They were also more disposable now as marriage-partners: polygyny was well established – four Merovingian rulers, including Dagobert I, are known to have had more than one wife, and Charlemagne was to have four. Repudiation or divorce of a wife was easier. The Burgundian Code had it that women seeking a divorce were to be smothered in mire. Against this background of unreflective violence, women's lives could be tough: Only 40 per cent of women lived past forty, as against nearly 60 per cent of men.

The weakening of central power and the fusion of public and private spheres under the Merovingians – as under the later Carolingians – threw political power back into the lap of aristocratic families. The lack of formal state structures and the importance of the ruling family allowed women of strong character to make a real impact. One awe-struck chronicler recounted how foreigners were unable to cope with a barbarian wife settling her husband's disputes: "least of all when she swells her neck and gnashes her teeth and, poising her huge white arms, proceeds to rain punches mingled with kicks". Because there was little distinction between public and private law, women in close proximity to the reins of power within high-born families could, and did, exploit their position.

Women were also highly visible within the Church. Roughly a quarter of saints between 650 and 750 were women – an unusually high proportion. Women had tended to be among the keenest supporters of Christianity, which had a softening influence on the severe masculinity of Germanic codes. The Burgundian princess, Clotilda, had been instrumental in converting her husband Clovis to orthodox Christianity – and was canonized for her pains. The Church was more insistent on the sanctity of marriage – divorce became much harder for husbands. The Church also offered women a viable alternative to marriage, in the form of cloistered life as nuns. Nunneries spread far and wide in the sixth and seventh centuries. They were often linked to local patrician families; wealthy widows might, for example, establish them as retirement homes.

While barbarian and Gallo-Roman cultures began to fuse, the economy was changing fast. The structures of urban life remained at first broadly intact, but they functioned at a less dynamic level. Towns, immeasurably weakened from the third century, stabilized their fortunes in the sixth and seventh. By then, however, it was clear that with the breakdown of the Romans' singular administrative and tax systems the crucial influx of wealth from the East had been irrevocably reduced. Decay was accelerated by the role of militant Islam from the seventh century, which destroyed the economic and cultural unity of the Mediterranean Sea. Gaul exported very little of value to the East, so less and less came back into the Western economic circuits, except as plundered loot and coerced tribute.

Significantly, the Frankish ruler and his aristocracy preferred rural villas to city life, so towns lost much of their former zest, with the great estates now setting the economic tempo. Although towns remained administrative and ecclesiastic centres – especially in the Midi – they were no longer plugged into international networks of production and trade, and drew more heavily instead on their rural hinterlands. Long-distance, luxury-based commerce still took place: town-dwellers in Marseille, Narbonne and Bordeaux could still afford pepper, spices, drugs and silks from the Levant. Greeks, Jews and Syrians – the latter, implausibly, riding camel trains around the French interior – came to play an important role in distribution. But this was now little more than an exotic fringe activity.

Money continued to circulate; gold dried up after 700, but the more widespread availability of silver made up for this. Yet the circulation of precious metals was increasingly a byproduct of the payment of tribute and gift-exchange as a means of ensuring political loyalty and stability, rather than an index of a lively money economy. The economic centre of gravity shifted away from the Mediterranean to more rural northern

An important urban centre throughout the period of Roman rule, Arles endured numerous sieges before falling to the Visigoths in 480. Barbarian attacks had restricted the lavish scale of urban building, and the great amphitheatre was abandoned, before becoming a built-up neighbourhood, complete with parish church, in the Middle Ages.

France, where the Merovingian court and the wealthiest Frankish families were to be found. Those closest to the ruler's largesse had most to spend. That this was less and less a money economy characterized by exchange was signalled by the recurrence of famines. "Many people made bread with grape-pips or hazel-catkins," noted Gregory of Tours of the 585 famine, "while others dried the roots of ferns, pounded them and added a little flour." The Midi also suffered disproportionately from the sudden and catastrophic appearance of plagues after 542, which triggered a population decline that was not reversed until the late seventh century.

In this fluid economic situation, central political authority proved difficult to maintain. Merovingian military success had been grounded in control over armed retainers kept loyal by shares in booty and plunder. These vassals, as they came to be called, often received land grants, under conditions of service. Such benefices were conventionally viewed not as perpetual but as revocable by the donor – at least in theory. The vassals in turn would use their land base to build up their own followings of armed retainers, whom they too would reward with land and booty. Unless it was very carefully monitored, particularly to avoid benefices becoming perpetual and hereditary, this system risked parcelling out sovereignty and fragmenting the state.

Historians are wont to blame the long-haired kings of the Merovingian dynasty – whose representatives in the late sixth and early seventh centuries became known as *rois fainéants* ("do-nothing kings") – for their failure to control such centrifugal forces. The latent forces of decentralization in Merovingian France were so strong, however,

Merovingian illumination from the eighth-century manuscript "Saint Augustine on the Heptateuch". Merovingian art took some quite extraordinary forms, imaginatively mixing zoomorphic and geometrical motifs, which seem to suggest links with the eastern Mediterranean.

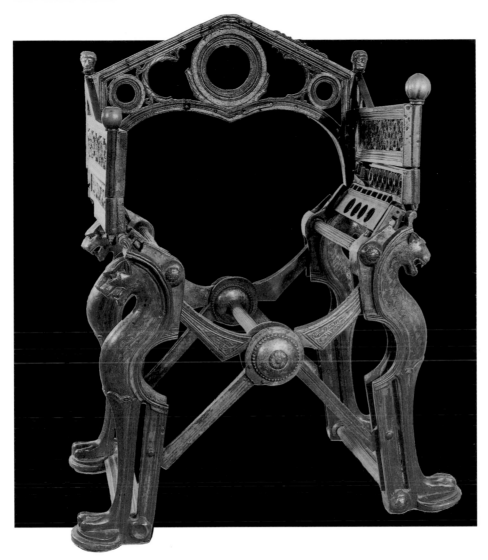

The throne of Dagobert. Added to in the ninth century, then rediscovered in the eleventh century by Abbot Suger, arch-ideologist of Capetian power, this ceremonial furnishing became a standard fixture in coronations. Napoleon made use of it when crowning himself emperor in 1804.

that the problems look structural rather than personal. Perhaps wisely, rulers tended to concentrate most of their efforts on keeping under firm dynastic control the heartlands of Frankish power, the region stretching roughly between the Seine and the Rhine, an area referred to as "Francia". These lands were often subdivided between Austrasia, located between the Rhine and the Meuse, home of the Rhineland Franks whom Clovis had subdued; and Neustria, the "New Frankish Lands" to the west, running from the Meuse to the Loire. Here the key cities were Paris (which Clovis had chosen as his capital) and Soissons.

Over the seventh century the Alamanni, the Thuringians and the Bavarians increasingly asserted their independence from this central core. Within Gaul, too, many areas began to follow suit. In Aquitaine the Visigoths, whom Clovis and his successors had conquered, now held insecurely on to Septimania, a strip of low-lying land along the Mediterranean basin through to the Rhône delta. However, they tended to be involved increasingly with the Iberian world to the south rather than with their northern

Frankish neighbours. From 700 the region came under the sway of its own duke, Eudo. Neighbouring Provence asserted its virtual independence of the north at about the same time. The character of the extreme south-west was changed by the inward drift of the Vasconi (or Basques), who migrated into the region from Spanish Navarre from the late sixth century onwards. The Franks made great, but largely unsuccessful efforts to bring the turbulent Basques under their control.

Burgundy and Brittany constituted two other areas over which the Franks found it difficult to maintain their influence. Neustrian attempts to bring Burgundy more fully within the Merovingian orbit in the early seventh century instigated a spate of revolts. Brittany exhibited similar stubbornness. Bretons had migrated from southern England into this western edge of the Armorican peninsula from the late fourth and fifth centuries onwards, possibly fleeing Saxon incursions, possibly answering a call from the Gallo-Roman authorities in Gaul to offer protection against piracy and raiding. While the rest of northern Gaul was experiencing Frankish dominance, the Armorican peninsula was effectively being re-Romanized by these Breton newcomers. Thereafter the region to the west of Vannes showed few signs of Frankish influence, and maintained a high degree of autonomy, under the rule of dukes or subkings.

The Franks, then, had perennial problems in securing the loyalty of the peripheries. What looks on paper like a major world empire running from the Atlantic to the Danube was, increasingly, a patchwork quilt of semi-autonomous and fractious chiefdoms. Even within the traditional heartlands of its power, moreover, power was slipping from the grasp of the long-haired kings. Because Merovingian domains were divided up between heirs, rival factions developed and rifts widened within the ruling elite. Chlotar II (r. 613–29), for example, achieved power only by defeating Queen Brunhild with the aid of magnates whose power, as a reward, he was duty-bound to extend.

The steward of royal domains, the so-called "mayor of the palace" became a power to be reckoned with. When, as was often the case in the seventh century, the ruler was a minor, dynasties of mayors of the palace held the reins of power. While supervising the royal income, they were able to build up their own wealth and clients. "Wealth and power were in the hands of the mayor of the palace," the chronicler Einhard later noted of this period, "who exerted ultimate authority. The king had nothing remaining him beyond the enjoyment of his title and the satisfaction of sitting on his throne with his long hair and his trailing beard there to give the impression of rule."

The Arnulfing family, descended from an adviser of Dagobert, in time built up enormous power as hereditary mayors of the palace in Austrasia. They became the largest landowners in the north, and soon outweighed in influence the different branches of the Merovingians. Increasingly called "Carolingians", because of the frequency of the name Charles ("Carolus") in the family, this dynasty would in the late seventh century overthrow and displace the Merovingians. Furthermore they would harness, albeit briefly, the strongly centrifugal forces within Frankish society in order to launch an ambitious scheme of European domination, an empire that would cover the huge swathe of land once dominated by Rome.

THE CAROLINGIANS

The rise of the Carolingians from dynastic estate managers (mayors of the palace) to imperial dynasts meant that the Merovingians had to be marginalized. In 679 the Carolingian mayor of the palace, Pepin II of Herstal, ended Merovingian royalty in Austrasia, and in 687 defeated Neustrian forces at Tertry to unite the post of mayor of the palace in Austrasia and Neustria. It was not until 751, however, that the Carolingians definitively disposed of the Merovingian line and assumed full powers themselves.

The supposed sacral power of the long-haired kings still commanded respect among the Carolingians. For all its manifest faults, the old dynasty was supposed to have a god (Merowech) among its ancestors, and the Merovingians still trailed clouds of glory as descendants of the Trojans and as heirs to Rome. Pepin of Herstal's successor, Pepin III the Short (mayor of the palace, 741–68; r. 751–68) at first seemed to accept this combination of Carolingian sword and Merovingian halo, installing the Merovingian Childeric III (r. 743–51) as ruler. In 751, however, he evidently tired of having the Merovingians as the holy figleaf hiding Carolingian power, and performed what in retrospect constituted an act of foundation for a new dynasty. Grouping together an assembly of Frankish nobles to elect him king, he then, with papal permission, had himself anointed with oil by his friend, the saintly Boniface (c. 680–754), Christianizer of German lands. In 754 Pope Stephen II repeated the act of consecration, thus giving Pepin enough sense of spiritual prestige that he could afford to pack off Childeric to end his days in a monastery. An act of usurpation, grounded in naked power, was thus overlaid by a double ceremony of election from below and religious benediction from above. The new dynasty could from the start pose as the bearer of a new social contract, and also claim to derive its power not from blood ties with a pagan deity, but from divine grace.

The Carolingians put the seal on their power by conducting a vigorously expansionist policy and they revived a booty economy, which had been beyond the means of the later Merovingians. Pepin of Herstal's illegitimate son, Charles Martel, had expanded Carolingian power into central Europe, defeating the Frisians, the Bavarians and the Saxons in a series of campaigns from 724 to 738. He had also subdued turbulently independent Aquitaine, and in 732 met and defeated at Poitiers Arab forces, which since the early years of the century had penetrated beyond the Pyrenees. Though the Arabs kept a toehold in the Narbonne region, this defeat checked further Arab expansion into western Europe.

Defeat of the infidel amplified the dynasty's religious aura and military reputation. Pepin the Short continued along the same path, forcing the Saxons, the Alamanni and the Bavarians to do homage to Childeric III, and working to bring Burgundy and Provence more securely under Merovingian/Carolingian rule. Charlemagne was to prove the most successful expansionist of them all. Emerging as sole ruler in 771, after the convenient death of his co-ruler brother Carloman (r. 768–71), Charlemagne had

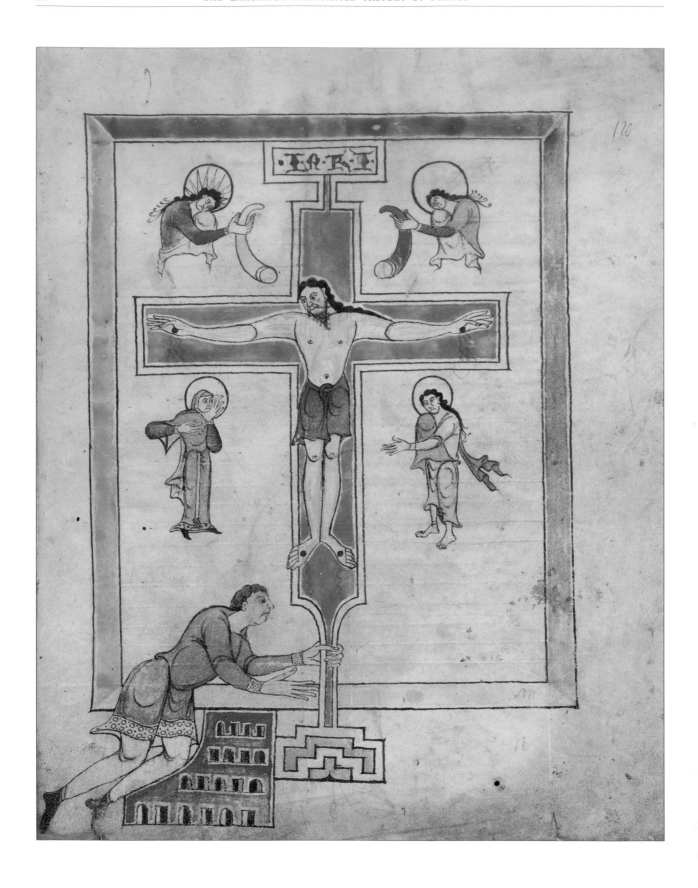

The Carolingian Renaissance

Like the later Italian Renaissance, the Renaissance which historians have located in the reign of Charlemagne and his ninth-century successors was characterized by an intense interest in the art and literature of classical antiquity. Classical Latin had to be relearnt as a language of expression, following its displacement by Germanic languages and by its evolution in West Francia into "rustic Roman". Yet whereas the Italian Renaissance was to be marked by fascination with non-Christian artistic and intellectual forms, the Carolingian Renaissance was soaked in ecclesiastical values, and was indeed largely conducted by self-consciously Latinizing churchmen.

The Carolingian Renaissance had its roots in Charlemagne's desire to act out the imperial role. Church and state overlapped very considerably. Carolingian capitularies (or edicts) multiplied the number of legal offences, and had much to say about the reform of morality. Law, it seemed, could Christianize and moralize the inhabitants of the empire, and the Church had a fundamental part to play in this mission. It provided the Carolingians with administrators, councillors, imperial agents, scholars, legal experts, teachers and ecclesiastical

This exquisite gold and bejewelled talisman, reputed to have belonged to Charlemagne, contained holy relics in its hollowed-out centre.

advisers. Churchmen were indeed the dominant figures in the Renaissance. The York-born ecclesiastic, Alcuin, who presided over the palace school – and who was noted for "anointing his throat with wine and beer to improve his teaching and make his song more melodious" – dreamt, it was said, of making the imperial court at Aachen (Aix-la-Chapelle) a new Athens.

The rescue of the classical heritage through the copying of Latin manuscripts was a central concern, and indeed most extant writings from antiquity were transcribed by the Carolingians. The codification of law, reform in handwriting and improvements in musical notation were further areas of interest. Apart from the construction of the imperial palace at Aachen – largely a copy of a church in Ravenna – few major artistic and architectural projects have survived. Carolingian art is distinguished by artefacts of a more modest scale, often displaying minute artistic workmanship. The wall paintings, jewellery, illuminated manuscripts and books that have came down to us combine classical models with the inheritance of late Roman, Byzantine, Celtic and Germanic art forms.

by the turn of the century built up a massive European empire extending over all former Frankish domains and spreading into south-eastern Europe and Italy. By entering the Italian peninsula to defeat the Lombards in 774, and assuming the mantle of king of the Lombards, Charlemagne made the Carolingians the dominant power in Europe, and he followed this up by pushing towards the Elbe and the Baltic in savage campaigns conducted against the Saxons.

The Carolingians prided themselves on campaigning with the cross as well as the sword – this was made all the more possible, because Arab power was now bottled up within the Iberian peninsula. Charlemagne also forced defeated pagan peoples to convert to Christianity. The missionary zeal of Saint Boniface in the conversion of the Germans was the velvet glove around an uncompromising iron fist: the defeats of the pagan Saxons in 782 were followed by near-genocidal massacres. In 785 Charlemagne

Opposite Detail from Louis the Pious' psalter, dating from the second quarter of the ninth century. Louis' reign was closely associated with the move for religious reform, notably of monasticism.

decreed that any Saxon refusing to be baptized or indulging in behaviour insulting to the Church was to be executed. Victor over the pagan and the infidel, the Carolingian dynasty also offered firm support to the papacy. Charlemagne's triumphs in the Italian peninsula allowed him to stabilize the position of beleaguered Pope Stephen II, as well as to carve out for him the papal states. These would remain the temporal base of the papacy right through to the nineteenth century. It was against this background that one should see the events of Christmas Day 800 when, in a ceremony in Rome which Charlemagne himself claimed not to have anticipated, Pope Leo III placed a crown on Charlemagne's head. He was thus consecrated as Emperor – the first emperor in the West since 476. Papal anointing helped to add a theocratic tinge to Carolingian power.

Charlemagne took religion seriously within his empire as well as without. He extended a strong measure of protection to the Church. Bishops played a major part in local administration, often outweighing the influence of counts. Charlemagne was also an important patron to monastic houses – not least because he saw them as counter-balancing the considerable secular power of the bishops. Of 304 major building projects undertaken in his reign, 232 were monasteries (as against seven cathedrals and sixty-five palaces). The dynasty made enormous gifts to the Church: from the years 751 to 825 Church lands in Christendom appear to have tripled, growing from 10 to about 30 per cent of the total cultivable area. The tithe, regulated by the emperor in a series of measures from 779 to 801, was to constitute a major element of Church income down to the French Revolution.

Generosity, to favoured laymen as well as to the Church, was thus a crucial ingredient of Carolingian power. It had a number of sources. The constant inflows of booty and tribute from wars were essential. There were military campaigns every year from the time of Charles Martel to Charlemagne's coronation. The treasure of the Avar Kingdom in Hungary, which Charlemagne brought back with him in 796, was fabulous. Land was a currency of power as much as gold, silver and jewellery. Territorial expansion provided new sources for giving property. The later Carolingians' capacity for generosity, notably towards the Church, had been partly based on Charles Martel's earlier confiscation of huge tracts of Church lands. After the last of the Merovingian *rois fainéants* had been deposed in 751 their confiscated lands placed huge resources at the disposal of the Carolingians. Rulers were also wont to distribute tax immunities.

Carolingian prodigality stimulated something of an economic revival. With plague dying out from the late seventh century, population grew – perhaps from 7.5 to as much as 9 million between the mid seventh and the mid eighth centuries. Monasteries which had benefited from Carolingian largesse were in a strong position to profit from the continuing eclipse of the urban sector. Indeed they often came to act as surrogate towns in their own right, amassing capital, organizing labour and facilitating exchange. Certain fairs run by monastic houses – such as those at Saint-Denis (near Paris), Corbie (near Metz), Saint-Riquier (near Amiens) and Saint-Vaast (near Arras) – achieved international prominence. Those associated with monasteries located in the suburbs of a

Purse reliquary of Pepin of Aquitaine (r. 817–38), son of Louis the Pious. Allegedly donated by Pepin to the abbey church at Conques, it shows the Virgin Mary and Saint John flanking Christ.

town – as was the case with Saint-Germain-des-Prés in Paris, Saint-Rémy at Reims and Saint-Sernin at Toulouse – even helped to revive the fortune of the adjacent town.

Economic revival could not, however, lessen the fragility of Carolingian power. It proved difficult to convert additional wealth within Carolingian society into major sources of income for the royal treasury. The monarch, who, as Christian warlord, dispensed favours with a liberal hand, still needed to secure new sources of income to operate as a generous provider of tributes. It would appear that this problem was becoming acute for Charlemagne in the last years of his reign. By about 800 he had reached a "plunder frontier" – campaigning abroad was replaced by more defensive operations to secure loyalty and conserve possessions within an already oversprawling empire. Other methods of securing support within his dominions were required.

The development of a bureaucratic style of government was a potential answer to the problem of making the empire cohere in a period when booty was in short supply. Carolingian administration had a strongly ecclesiastical flavour. Missionaries were used in Germany as the ideologists of Carolingian power, and they were quick to equate sins against God with crimes against the imperial person. But Charlemagne also viewed churchmen as able and literate administrators. The so-called Carolingian Renaissance – the revival of arts and learning – had a strongly religious flavour, and served the interests of the state bureaucracy. An innovation from 775, for example, was the systematic appointment of roving imperial administrators, the so-called *missi dominici*, on top of the routine administrative network of counts and bishops. Usually

This idealized bronze horseback figure of a Western emperor (860–70 AD) may represent Charlemagne, or else Charles the Bald, under whose reign it appears to have been made. Frankish in many attributes – long moustache, clothing, hairstyle – the figure also recalls Roman equestrian statues.

sent out in pairs, one of whom was an influential churchman, these officials were entrusted with administrative surveillance. They judged, punished, redressed wrongs, received oaths and, on occasion, raised armies. A particular responsibility was to announce and put into effect Carolingian edicts, known as capitularies. These, made at the annual assemblies of free men, were written down and formed a body of imperial statute extending to religious, moral and secular concerns. The role of the *missi dominici* was complemented by Charlemagne's own tireless travelling. Oaths of loyalty to himself, introduced from 789 and required of males over twelve years old, also had a unifying function. So, too, did acts of commendation, the special oaths of fealty which he imposed on his most powerful subjects, theoretically making them royal vassals.

The oaths, the capitularies, the *missi dominici*, the imperial tours and the use of the Church as a dynastic agent and ideologist could temporarily hold in check, but proved unable to eradicate, powerful centrifugal forces. Rulers could posture as Rome's heirs or as Christian theocrats. By the end of Charlemagne's reign, however, it was becoming increasingly apparent that the prime political cement was still booty, essential for keeping the ruler's powerful subjects and their followers happy. The shortage of scope for plunder and booty posed a problem which was to become even more acute for Charlemagne's successors.

AFTER CHARLEMAGNE

The essentially unitary nature of Carolingian power had contrasted forcefully with the weak and divisive authority of the *rois fainéants*. After Charlemagne's death, however, a new phase of dynastic division damaged the already fragile mainsprings of imperial power. In 817 Charlemagne's successor, Louis the Pious (r. 813–40), declared that on his death the empire would be split up among his heirs. This caused a wave of resentment among his children, who from 830, with the support of magnates, waged civil war – first, against their father and then, after his death in 840, among themselves. In 843 the Treaty of Verdun made formal a division of the great Carolingian empire into three parts. The imperial title resided with Lothair, who was accorded a bloc of territory, Lotharingia, stretching from the Italian peninsula to the Baltic, and containing both Aix-la-Chapelle and Rome. This was squashed between an "East Francia" under Louis the German and a western bloc, West Francia, which was placed in the hands of Charles the Bald, who ruled as king from 838 to 877 and as emperor from 875 to 877.

The term "Francia" was still sometimes given to the area from the Seine to the Lotharingian frontier, but more generally the title "West Francia" began to be used for the western chunk of the old Carolingian empire. As time went on, it became apparent that this area had clearly floated off from the more Germanic, eastern part of the dominion of the Franks, and that the rough, unfashioned trunk of future France was becoming dimly discernible. It would be quite wrong of course to read too much into this. At the level of political geography, about one-quarter of present-day France was in the late ninth century in Lotharingian or German hands, and this changed only very slowly. The division enshrined at Verdun had nothing to do with ethnic groupings. (If it had, it would presumably have separated the Basques and the Bretons, the most clearly defined ethnic groupings in the western empire, from the mixed Germano-Gallo-Roman stock prevalent elsewhere.) Rather, Verdun marked political and hence highly fragile borders, following the courses of the Meuse, Scheldt, Saône and Rhône rivers, with splendid disregard for ethnic or cultural boundaries.

Nevertheless Verdun did help to constitute a new, broader cultural division. In the Oath of Strasbourg of 842, which Charles the Bald and Louis the German had sworn just prior to Verdun, Louis the German's army had to have the oath explained to them in German, Charles the Bald's in "rustic Roman" – that degenerate form of Latin which was the basis of the French language. The dominion which the Franks had established

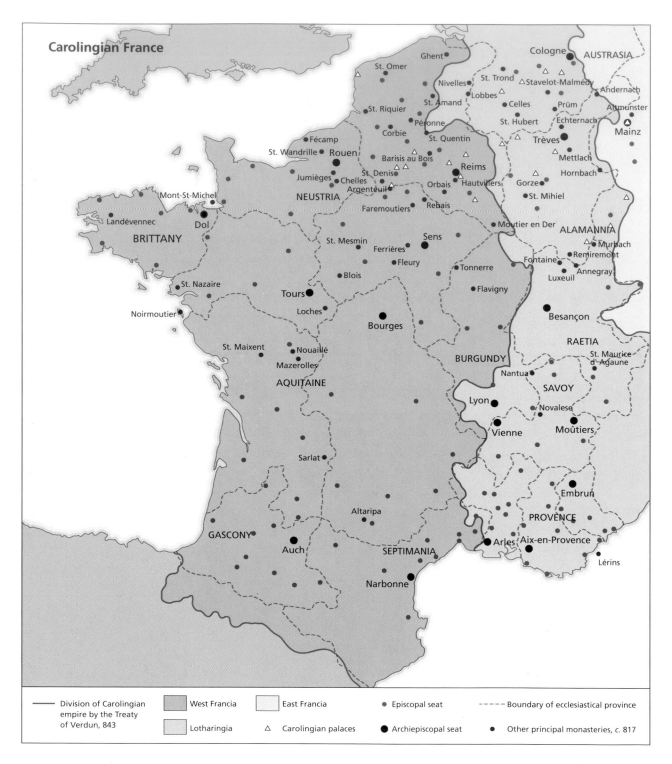

Carolingian France

AUSTRASIA

Cologne
Ghent
St. Omer
Nivelles   St. Trond   Stavelot-Malmédy
Lobbes   Andernach
St. Amand   Celles   Prüm
St. Riquier   Altmünster
Péronne   St. Hubert   Echternach
Corbie   Trèves   Mainz
Fécamp   St. Quentin   Mettlach
St. Wandrille   Rouen   Barisis au Bois   Hornbach
Jumièges   St. Denis   Reims
Chelles   Orbais   Hautvillers   Gorze
Mont-St-Michel   Argenteuil   St. Mihiel
NEUSTRIA   Rebais
Landévennec   Faremoutiers   ALAMANNIA
Dol   Moutier en Der
BRITTANY   St. Mesmin   Sens   Murbach
Ferrières   Fontaine   Remiremont
Fleury   Tonnerre   Annegray
St. Nazaire   Blois   Luxeuil
Tours   Flavigny
Noirmoutier   Loches   RAETIA
Bourges   Besançon
St. Maixent   Nouaillé   BURGUNDY   St. Maurice d'Agaune
Mazerolles   Nantua
AQUITAINE   SAVOY
Lyon   Novalese
Vienne   Moûtiers
Sarlat
Embrun
Altaripa   PROVENCE
GASCONY   Arles   Aix-en-Provence
Auch   SEPTIMANIA   Lérins
Narbonne

—— Division of Carolingian empire by the Treaty of Verdun, 843	▨ West Francia	▢ East Francia	● Episcopal seat	----- Boundary of ecclesiastical province
	▨ Lotharingia	△ Carolingian palaces	⬤ Archiepiscopal seat	• Other principal monasteries, c. 817

The trunk of future France is evident in the western bloc of the Carolingian Empire, carved up in the Treaty of Verdun of 843. As well as marking out "West Francia" from an eastern, Germanic, "East Francia", the treaty also defined the profile of an indeterminate area into which both powers would penetrate over the next millennium. The Carolingian Empire was also important for defining and consolidating the ecclesiastical and administrative framework of France's later development.

in the sixth century was slowly coming to be divided by language: by the end of the tenth century, the term "Frank" (*francus*) meant French; "Francia" was routinely distinguished from the "kingdom of the Teutons" or the "kingdom of the Germans" in the east; and kings of West Francia and Germany themselves needed translators to make themselves understood to each other.

Wide cracks, then, were opening up within the Frankish domain. Dynastic wranglings further whittled away the prestige and authority of central power. Lothair's death in 855 brought a further round of territorial reallocation; and briefly, from 881 to 887, the feeble Charles the Fat (king of West Francia 884–7) enjoyed the imperial title and ruled its entirety. His political weakness led a group of aristocrats to elect as king one of their number, Odo, a "Robertian" (that is, a descendant of the powerful count Robert the Strong). On his death, the throne passed back into the hands of a Carolingian, Charles the Simple (r. 893–922). But for the last century of Carolingian power, the throne shuttled back and forth between Carolingians and Robertians, depending on the political complexion at the time.

These dynastic squabbles took place against a darkening political atmosphere. Carolingian domains were subjected to fresh waves of attacks and looting from outside, by Saracens, Magyars and, especially, Vikings. Raiding by Saracen pirates from North Africa had begun in 793 with attacks in the Lower Languedoc area. Corsica was devastated in 806, and the whole of southern France subject to brutal raiding between 838 and 842, when the Saracens pushed up the Rhône valley to Arles. They established a permanent base at La Garde-Freinet, in the Saint-Tropez area, and they continued spasmodic raiding from here until their eviction in 972/3. It was in the tenth century, too, that the Magyar tribes from the east made destructive sorties into French territory. They had reached Germany and Italy by early in the century, and from 919 through to the late 930s made lightning strikes into France, causing widespread devastation.

The pagan Vikings, or "Norsemen", constituted by far the most serious and enduring foreign threat which Charlemagne and his successors faced. These Scandinavian seafarers had conducted piratical raids on the west coast of France and the south coast of England from the last years of the eighth century, and were soon exploring the French interior. In 844/5 they attacked cities as far from the sea as Toulouse, Tours and Paris. From 851 they wintered in France, conducting systematic raids in the southwest of the country.

The Vikings caused a great deal of destruction and economic dislocation. The Carolingians saw in them the cause of all the empire's ills: population decline, material destruction, economic disruption, a drop in political morale. Yet the empire's nobles could not really gripe, for the Vikings were only practising the arts of plunder in which the Carolingians themselves were past masters. The plunderer had become the plundered, the predator the prey. Perhaps, too, the fact that most chroniclers were clerics, and that churches and abbeys were among the pagan Vikings' prime targets for looting, has unduly prejudiced later views. The incidence of Viking attacks on most areas in France was, moreover, often highly sporadic. Picardy suffered seventeen

The Vikings

In 885 the inhabitants of Paris cowered nervously on the Île de la Cité awaiting the arrival of a massive force of Vikings, coming to sack the city and put its inhabitants to the sword. The Parisians already knew about the Danish seafaring pirates. In 845 the latter had brought their fearsome long-boats to the city, "laying waste everything on either side," a chronicler had noted, "and meeting not the least bit of resistance". Pausing only to refit their vessels with timbers hacked from the rafters of the abbey church of Saint-Germain-des-Prés, they had retraced their route up the Seine.

The exploits of these pagan seafarers – the French called them *normands* ("Norsemen") – had studded Carolingian history for a century by 885. After several decades of fitful coastal raids, from early in the ninth century they had begun to use France's extensive river system to carry plundering to the heart of the country. Emperors, then kings of West Francia, did their best to combat the scourge. From 845 Charles the Bald regularly paid out tribute to the raiders to make them withdraw. The Norsemen only came back for more. From 860 the king began a policy of barring rivers in order to inhibit inland raiding.

The Viking fleet eventually reached Paris in 885: 700 large vessels, it was said, plus a fleet of smaller craft, and an accom-panying army of 30,000 to 40,000 men either in the boats or marching along the banks. Small Parisian armed bands, led by the Robertian leader Odo, heroically defended the two bridgeheads to the island. A lengthy siege developed, with the Vikings using every form of offensive craft, including fire-boats targeted at the bridgeheads. To the Parisians, it seemed that the Christian God was on their side. A Viking warrior was struck dead on entering the tomb of Saint Germain in the abbey church. And the ghost of the saint was observed walk-ing along the ramparts at night sprinkling holy water. The saint's relics were devoutly brought to the Parisian front line. Eventually Emperor Charles the Fat arrived with an army. He preferred to negotiate rather than to fight, and, their pockets swollen with ransom, the Vikings were soon proceeding back up the Seine.

Paris was fortunate. Rape, pillage and wanton destruction were the hallmarks of these sea-borne raiders. "There is not a road," recorded one Carolingian chronicler, "that is not strewn with the bodies of slain Christians." Yet within a few decades the Viking warriors were seeking to settle down. Under the chieftain Rollo, the "Norsemen" established themselves near the estuary of the Seine in 910–11, and within a matter of generations had transformed themselves into "Normans".

The seventy metres of the Bayeux Tapestry portray the Norman duke William's conquest of England in 1066. The Normans – "Norsemen" – are, interestingly, referred to as Franks ("Franci"). Acclimatization was, it seems, complete.

assaults between 835 and 925 – which meant that the region was without raids three-quarters of the time.

Furthermore, there is a case for arguing that the impact of the raids was sometimes positive. By plundering urban and monastic centres which had stockpiled riches, the Vikings released wealth on to the open market and stimulated the economy. As with the Carolingians who preceded them, moreover, looting was only part of wider patterns of trading, bartering and gift exchange. Viking raiding had, it might be argued, a far more destructive impact on the Carolingian dynasty than on most of its subject peoples; it is important to disconnect the fate of the population of France from the fortunes of its major dynasty.

The crisis of the central power within West Francia, and more widely within the empire, was, moreover, as much internal as external. It became particularly pressing during the reign of Charles the Bald (r. 838–77), who was powerless too against Viking raids. Wealthy and powerful subjects were increasingly slipping the reins of a central power unable to ensure protection to its peoples. The Carolingians tended to fall back – as had the Merovingians before them – on the heartlands of their power between the Loire and the Scheldt. Rulers in the tenth century rarely went outside this area – in sharp contrast with Charlemagne's restless travelling. Indeed the Robertians, chosen as monarchs by northern nobles to defend against Viking attacks, were not even recognized in Brittany or south of the Loire. The *missi dominici* system broke down by the middle of the century. Capitularies ceased from 884. No national assemblies were convened after 889.

The structure of delegated royal power was also changing. The post of counts, in theory revocable at the ruler's whim, became more and more a lifetime, then a hereditary, appointment. In 877 they stopped presenting their accounts to the central government, thus marking a change in their status from state official to hereditary territorial princeling. Many of these men had in the past been awarded royal benefices (possession of royal estates). In the early days such royal gifts could in theory be withdrawn – the idea was that the servants of the crown were allowed, in return for service, to have temporary and provisional enjoyment of landed revenues, but not possession of the land itself. This distinction was increasingly lost. Magnates with extensive landed possessions began to assume the title of duke and act as royal viceroys. Indeed some began to assume regal airs, even mimicking their ruler by building up private followings whom they rewarded in kind and whom they attached to their person by similar oaths of fidelity. These forces had once been kept in check, but monarchs found it difficult to resist them now, as they had so little left to give. Local potentates developed extensive patronage networks in administration and in the Church which the Carolingian dynasty could not suppress. Favours were now bypassing the court, whence all bounty had once flowed.

Local leaders had an appeal kings could not match. The defensive needs of the period led to local magnates building fortified castles, from behind whose walls they posed as defenders of the local population from outsiders. In time they came to regard

After the Treaty of Verdun in 843, Lothair I (emperor 840–55), son of Louis the Pious, held the central strip dividing the kingdoms of West and East Francia, and retained the imperial title.

national, and even regional, authorities as outsiders just as much as Viking raiders. Under the late Roman Empire Salvian of Marseille had noted how peasants wishing to resist state tax demands and avoid rural brigandage and barbarian raiding, "put themselves under the care and protection of the powerful, [making] themselves the surrendered captives of the rich and [passing] under their jurisdictions". The Viking raids and the breakdown of central power in the ninth and tenth centuries posed a similar range of choices for many peasants. The strengthening of personal bonds between them and their lords laid the basis, as we shall see, of medieval feudalism.

The Carolingian dominion seemed to be disintegrating into smaller constituent parts, rather as it had under the *rois fainéants*. The Lotharingian middle kingdom proved highly volatile. It passed into the orbit of West Francia in the late ninth century, but shuttled back towards East Francia in the following century – anticipating the destiny of the future Lorraine as the endless bone of contention between France and her neighbour, Germany.

Most of Burgundy had passed under the control of Lothair at Verdun. In 877, however, Charles the Bald's brother-in-law, Boso of Vienne, had himself crowned king of Burgundy and Provence (the latter also originally part of Lotharingia). Boso's kingdom soon crumbled, but his son Louis was made king of Provence in 890. Factional struggles involving local groups of magnates continued into the tenth century. Rudolf II of Burgundy, for example, established in 933 the kingdom of Arles, which stretched from Basel to the Mediterranean coastline. Yet though this looked impressive in theory, in practice Rudolf and his successors were largely under the thumb of local magnates.

As well as the distinction between West and East Francia, another cultural divide appeared to be opening up in these years of disunity and decentralization, namely the rift between the north and the south. A broad band across the middle of France, from roughly the Poitou to Lake Léman, marked out two increasingly distinct cultural areas. In the north the Franks were numerically strong and their power more firmly based. This would be the area of the northern, ultimately triumphant branch of the French language known as the *langue d'oïl*, and an area where customary law prevailed. The Midi, in contrast, was the *langue d'oc*, an area where a strain of "rustic Roman" closer to classical Latin was prevalent. Here the Franks were less numerous and influential, continuity with a Roman, often urban past was more pronounced, and Roman codes formed the basis of law.

Political and cultural diversity were increasingly apparent. The chronicler Flodoard of Reims, writing early in the tenth century, noted that Gaul was composed, besides Franks, of "the Burgundians, the Aquitanians, the Normans, the Bretons, the men of Flanders, those from the land of the Goths and the Spanish march". These were indeed the dominant political units in the last century of the Carolingian dynasty. Normandy was a particularly interesting case. In 910 / 11, after unsuccessfully besieging first Paris, then Chartres, the Viking chieftain Rollo negotiated a treaty with King Charles the Simple whereby the Vikings would be allowed to settle land on the lower Seine in return for converting to Christianity and staying loyal to the dynasty. The Vikings integrated with the indigenous population, notably under Richard I, who organized the region as a hereditary Carolingian count, and his successors, who assumed the title of duke. Also in the north Baldwin "Iron Arm", after abducting and marrying the daughter of Charles the Bald, had himself created Count of the Flanders March in 879. His son Baldwin became count of Flanders, moulding the northern area into a fairly well-integrated political bloc.

The process of political fragmentation was even more extreme in the south and west. The part of Burgundy which had stayed within West Francia in the ninth century passed under independent dukes based in Autun, though in 956 the region fell temporarily into the hands of the Robertians. Aquitaine maintained its secular tradition of independence. After 887 local dynasties, counts of Poitiers, Toulouse and Auvergne, engaged in endless factional disputes for control over the region, while the Gascons, straddling the Pyrenees, managed to remain relatively aloof. "Gothia", formerly Septimania, was dominated by the counts of Toulouse, who were unable, however, to keep hold of the Spanish march.

In the west, Brittany continued to go its own way. Following a series of Carolingian attacks from 753 to 824, the Bretons agreed to do homage to the Frankish dynasty. But this meant little. Local rulers were soon calling themselves duke, and even king. To prevent expansion by the Bretons, who pushed towards the Mayenne river, the Carolingians established a march here. From the 860s on, the Lotharingian aristocrat Robert the Strong, who became count of Anjou, Touraine and Maine, and whose task included close surveillance of Viking expansion, held sway here.

The case of the Robertians is a particularly good example of the scale of disintegration taking place. Robert the Strong's control of the Anjou and Maine was extended in the late ninth century when Charles the Bald gave Robert's brother Hugh, lay abbot of Saint-Denis, control over most of Austrasia. Robert's son Odo, count of Paris and heir of his uncle Hugh, was, as we have seen, elected monarch in 888. The family renounced rule on Odo's death in 898, but they strengthened their local power within the Île-de-France. Odo's brother ruled as Robert I from 922 to 923, and Robert's son-in-law Ralph from 923 to 936. Robert I's son, Hugh the Great, helped the Carolingian Louis IV establish himself in 936, for which he was rewarded with the title, "duke of the Franks" (or "duke of Francia"). Even within Hugh the Great's territories, however, ominous divisive tendencies were unravelling Robertian power structures. The aggressive countships of Anjou, Le Mans and Blois and the emergence of independently minded castellans eroded Robertian power in the Breton march. In 987 when Hugh's son, Hugh Capet, quietly assumed the monarchical mantle, thus founding the Capetian dynasty, the political agenda of West Francia appeared to be decentralization and the fragmentation of power.

CHAPTER 4 — *The Middle Ages*

There was nothing about the condition of West Francia at the turn of the millennium which suggested its future as one of the most important states in western Europe. The new Capetian dynasty had only a tenuous hold on the assemblage of peoples and political units within the borders of a West Francia riven by major cultural divisions, and increasingly pulverized into often tiny political units. The French state might have subsequently developed on the scale of a Bavaria or a Belgium, that is, as a minor and second-rank power. Alternatively, such was its evident weakness after 987, it might have disappeared altogether and been swallowed up into some larger unit. At one stage, for example, in the late twelfth and early thirteenth centuries, it seemed possible that much of West Francia would be incorporated into an English-based "Angevin Empire". Henry, count of Anjou, had vast holdings on the Continent and was also, from 1154 to 1189, Henry II, king of England. At best, West Francia looked more like a collection of potential future states than a single, unitary one.

That "West Francia" between the year 1000 and the early fourteenth century developed into "France", a potentially front-rank power, owed a great deal to its rulers. The Capetian dynasty, after a slow start, became exceptionally adept at aggressive statecraft, extending the boundaries of its rule and increasing its hold over subject peoples. The roles of Louis VI (r. 1108–37) and Louis VII (r. 1137–80) in building up the Île-de-France as the centre of dynastic power; of Philip II Augustus (r. 1180–1223) in breaking the Angevin grip on south-western France; and then of Louis VIII (r. 1223–6) and Louis IX (r. 1226–70) in extending Capetian power in the Midi were paramount in this process. "In all of Christendom," an Italian observer noted by the early fourteenth century, "the king of France has no equal."

Moreover, the Middle Ages marked the beginnings of "France" as an ideological construct. The Capetian dynasty in particular helped to establish an idiom in which people could talk about France as a territorial unit *and* as a political community. Roman Gaul had been geographically more than the future France, and politically it formed a small part of a larger unit, the Roman Empire. West Francia was similarly only one-third of the wider community of the Franks – and it was to boot smaller than future "France". In the twelfth and thirteenth centuries the latter established itself for the first time as a key concept of political and cultural identity.

The chronicle of how the Capetian dynasty achieved what it did is, however, one aspect of a far more complex story. We need to evaluate the context of their activity, the lives of groups and peoples still often outside direct Capetian control, who were embarking on a process which would lead to "Frenchness". To do this we need to understand the workings of the feudal system and to unravel the workings of the Church in what became an "age of faith". We need to explain the mainsprings of the great economic and demographic revival which France experienced during these centuries. And we need to comprehend something of the complexity of regional life within West Francia.

Enamelled grave plate of Geoffrey, count of Anjou (1113–51), father of Henry II of England, architect of the Angevin empire. The inscription reads: "By your sword, prince, the crowd of robbers is routed and by your vigilance the Church has peace." The motto and the emblems of power convey a prince's assumption of royal attributes.

The making of Capetian France.
**Though the early Capetians
were titular kings of West
Francia, they exercised direct
power in only a tiny part of the
territory. By diplomatic guile
and increased military power,
the dynasty came to dominate
their kingdom by the advent of
the Valois line.**

THE FEUDAL LIMITS OF CAPETIAN AUTHORITY

The West Francia which fell into the hands of Hugh Capet in 987 covered roughly the
same territory as that carved out in the Treaty of Verdun in 843. It had, in Hugh Capet,
a ruler more closely identified with the territorial aspect of his rule than with his
Frankish ancestry. He could not comprehend the German spoken by the "East Franks"
(soon to be called "Germans" or "Teutons"), nor much Latin. France, if we can now
call it that (the term "West Francia" soon fell into disuse), had lost any ethnic dimension. During the Merovingian and Carolingian centuries racial particularities had

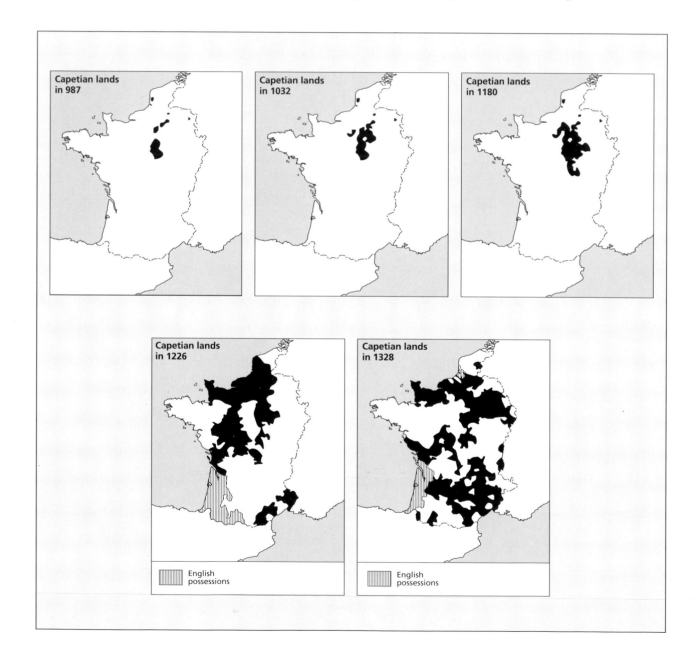

become gradually effaced, while strong regional differences came to the fore. This reflected the highly fragmented nature of the state, which by the year 1000 had split into around fifty distinct political divisions.

France in 987 was still a geographical expression. Unless we believe in the ineffable workings of some Hidden Gallic Hand, we should accept that luck played a key role in how many areas came to be bound up with France as a political and cultural entity. Some parts of West Francia were not, moreover, destined to have an enduring association with the developing French state. Flanders, for example, would follow an increasingly independent line up to its declaration of autonomy in the sixteenth century (though France would claw back parts of the region in the seventeenth century). Catalonia too formed part of the West Francian state, at least on paper, until the mid thirteenth century, when the king of France renounced his rights here. Again, the French would retrieve part of the region in the seventeenth century.

Furthermore many regions within West Francia were within the cultural orbit of other European powers. Up until the twelfth century Aquitaine and Gascony, for example, looked more to the Iberian peninsula than to the French homelands north of the Loire. For more than a century after 1066, Normandy's history belonged to England rather than France. The extension of Angevin influence similarly placed a great many areas under direct English influence. Guyenne was wholly English between 1154 and 1453; the Limousin, for over half the period. Further outside links were forged through dynastic alliance and diplomatic power-broking. In 1234, for example, the counts of Champagne became kings of Navarre, while in 1261 the count of Anjou became king of Naples.

For most of the Middle Ages, too, the eastern and south-eastern side of later France was dominated by Germany – known, from the mid ninth century, as the "Holy Roman Empire". Emperor Otto I (r. 936–73), for example, brought Alsace into Swabia, and divided Lorraine into two separate units. Flanders was built up by its counts into a powerful and strongly autonomous unit, and in 1056 they were recognized as counts of the empire. Burgundy had been divided since 843: West Francian Burgundy remained autonomous, if largely loyal to the Capetians, while eastern Burgundy passed to the emperor. Imperial Burgundy was linked to the sprawling kingdom of Arles, including Provence. For most of the Middle Ages Provence was competed over by the families of local magnates: in 1125, for example, it was split between the counts of Barcelona and Toulouse.

So the lands of the Capetians were just one, not even particularly impressive, unit in a highly complex and shifting political scene. Lands directly in the hands of Hugh Capet in 987 were probably more extensive than those of the last Carolingians, but were still pretty meagre. With the exception of territory around Montreuil on the Channel coast, they were located in the Paris area. Though the king had some possessions within Paris itself, he did not control the city, which was in the hands of minor princelings. He also had rights over a number of major abbeys, and had the right to appoint roughly one-third of French bishoprics.

As a power base this was solid, but it made a poor showing compared even with other magnates within West Francia. When in 1052, for example, the counts of Poitou merged Gascony with Aquitaine, they created a unit far larger than the Capetian lands. When in 1154 Brittany and neighbouring Normandy were brought together with Aquitaine and England, the resultant Angevin empire was bigger than the lands owing allegiance to the Capetian kings of France. Closer to home, the Capetians could also, with some justification, claim to feel encircled in 1125, when the powerful counts of Blois acquired the important county of Champagne. In the Midi the counts of Toulouse also came to dominate a massive part of southern France, stretching in the early twelfth century from the Rhône to Angoulême and from the Pyrenees to the Auvergne.

If the geography of Capetian power was patchy, so too was its consistency. Scribes occasionally portrayed the early Capetians as being "emperors in their own country". Yet their claims to sovereignty were hollow; rulers no longer passed laws, delegated power through a revocable bureaucracy or obliged free men to take obedience oaths. Their monarchical powers were less significant than their seigneurial authority. There is indeed a case for arguing that Hugh Capet and his immediate successors – Robert II the Pious (r. 996–1031), Henry I (r. 1031–60) and Philip I (r. 1060–1108) – owed their survival less to strength than to weakness. Their virtual inability to threaten the local power of territorial magnates, or to prevent them from acting alone and building up loyal followings, made the "rulers" tolerable for those who were actually more powerful.

Political authority now took the form of a confusing welter of personal ties of dependence. In theory the Capetian monarch was at the apex of a pyramid of feudal power, and the great magnates and high churchmen of the realm bound themselves to him by links of personal loyalty as his vassals. Yet these ties were of varying degrees of closeness, they operated only in West Francia and were observed as much in the breach as in the exercise. The practice, developed under the Merovingians and Carolingians, of rooting dependence in land also made the exercise of power problematic. It was quite possible for a lord to possess lands under the authority of a number of other lords: the counts of Champagne were vassals of the kings of France, for example, but also of nine other lords including the German emperor and the duke of Burgundy.

The bonds of personal loyalty and dependence were increasingly grounded in honorary titles linked to property. The creation of these "investitures" acquired classic form in the act of homage. The vassal would kneel before his lord, place his hands in his and swear an oath of fidelity on holy relics or on the Bible, thus becoming his "man". Besides property, the lord provided protection over his vassal, who in return owed his lord *consilium* ("counsel") and *auxilium* ("aid"). As "counsel" the vassal undertook to attend the court of his lord, offer him advice and bring to him disputes for arbitration and settlement. As "aid" the vassal had to agree to follow the lord to war, possibly with a retinue of armed followers, and to provide occasional financial assistance, including payment of the lord's ransom if he were captured, gifts on the wedding of his eldest daughter and so on. The military dimension of the relationship was

The girding-on of swords, part of the increasingly formalized ritual associated with the making of a knight, is illuminated in a thirteenth-century manuscript.

highly important: the grant of property was viewed as a means of enlisting the armed support of the vassal on horseback, plus possibly a retinue of knightly retainers – from Carolingian times, cavalry had become a key battlefield arm.

This arrangement permitted central control only as long as the king's vassals had reason for gratitude and awe. Under the Carolingians property granted could theoretically be taken back and rights were not absolute. By the tenth century, however, property grants were hereditary and included the wholesale transfer of judicial and political power. Chains of dependency trailed, moreover, through the whole of society. Relations of loyalty extended downwards so that the king's vassals developed hordes of their own vassals, linked to the ruler only in the most tenuous way. The great territorial princes, rather than their ruler, now administered loyalty oaths to those within their jurisdictions. Inhabitants of Burgundy, for example, swore fidelity only to their dukes.

For most French men and women, the kings of France had simply vanished. Having parcelled out their authority, and lacking military might, monarchs possessed only limited powers over their vassals. They had far less effective purchase on their vassals than the latter did on vassals of their own. It was at the lower level that the relationship invited awe and subjection. "You are my man," Count William of Poitou informed one of his vassals in the 1020s, "and your duty is to do my will. If I were to command you to do homage to a peasant, it would be your duty to obey …"

This parcelling-out of authority was taken further, moreover, because of the failure of the territorial princes to maintain power throughout their own lands. Although feudal decentralization had initially favoured the territorial princes, who shielded their dependants from direct royal power, in the ninth and tenth centuries they in turn

This eleventh-century figure from a column in the crypt of the Church of Sainte-Benigne, Dijon, shows one of the most widespread attitudes of prayer in the first millennium. It was gradually replaced by the more commonplace custom of placing the hands together – a gesture modelled on the seeking of feudal homage from a lord.

found it difficult to keep their own vassals in line. The creation of castles was originally part of the organized process by which royal authority was devolved. Once in place, however, they were used by truculent castellans and knights as a base. From there they could venture forth with gangs of mounted knights to impose their power willy-nilly on neighbouring peasants and to jostle against the power and prerogatives of their neighbours in private wars and pillaging expeditions.

The maintenance of law and order and the punishing of wrongdoers were thus becoming micro-events, far removed from the increasingly nominal authority of rulers and princes. Castellans and the knightly class in general had a good deal of leeway to impose forms of social and political organization on the land which were highly favourable to themselves. The lord's castle had provided welcome protection from the raiding of Vikings, Saracens, Magyars – and the aggression of petty seigneurs – but the price in the long run was that peasants had to accept greater subservience. The knightly class's superior military technology meant that peasants were almost powerless to resist the imposition of ever harsher feudal burdens.

As a result the legal status of the peasantry dropped. Free peasants holding land which was allodial (that is, free of seigneurial dues) became increasingly rare in the north. Most peasants were serfs who operated within the all-encompassing embrace of the manorial, or seigneurial, system. Slavery went into a slow decline; power was now lodged in land rather than bodies. Lords preferred a system whereby their serfs had their own plots of land (called tenures, or tenements), with which they could maintain themselves and their families. Yet, in return, the serfs were bound to the land and were obliged to do forced labour services on their lords' own property, known as the domain. This demarcation between domain and tenures predated Charlemagne, but developed quickly after the collapse of central authority. Peasants now took oaths which imitated vassalage. If called on, they were obliged to join their lord on foot in military expeditions or to keep watch in his castle over the campaigning months in the summer. There were other dues too, sometimes fairly eccentric, such as the obligation to beat pond-waters by night to quell the mating cries of amorous frogs, allowing their lord to sleep peacefully. Besides duties of labour, serfs also paid dues and taxes of various kinds. Lords enjoyed economic monopolies, too: they could force peasants to use the seigneurial wine-press, mill and bakery. Such rights were as remunerative to the lords as they were irksome to peasants. Lords also had judicial authority over tenements as well as domain, and could impose fines on a wide range of offences.

For most inhabitants of this France in the making, power was saddled on the horses of the knightly class. With central authority in decay from the ninth century, and with even territorial princes feeling the pinch in the tenth, the defence of the land and the meting out of justice had passed to local princelings, increasingly autonomous counts and hordes of truculent castellans. "You have so many partners and equals in the kingdom," Hincmar, bishop of Reims, had informed Charles the Bald in the late ninth century, "that you reign more in name than in reality." With power fragmenting fast, even below the level of the territorial prince, this remark was even more apt for the early Capetians.

Consecration of the main altar of the abbey church of Cluny monastery by Pope Urban II, 25 October 1095. The pope is shown to the left, while leading his priests on the right is the abbot, Saint Hugh, who in 1088 had begun work on what was then the most ambitious piece of ecclesiastical architecture in the Western world.

CHURCH AND CRUSADE

In many ways, European society in the tenth and eleventh centuries was a two-class society, formed of warriors and peasants. But when churchmen conceptualized society from the tenth century onwards, however, they added themselves as an additional order, or estate. Besides *bellatores* ("those who fight") and *laboratores* ("those who work"), they listed *oratores* ("those who pray"). The Church was thus viewed as a structural element of feudal society – and indeed it would remain one until the Revolutionaries of 1789 launched their all-out attack on feudalism. Churchmen enjoyed a place alongside the warriors rather than peasants. Only "workers" would pay taxes, and serfs could not aspire to the priesthood. The wealthiest families took the most prestigious Church appointments, which were in the gift of the great. Between one-fifth and one-third of landed property was in Church hands, and administered under feudal forms of land management. The Church collected its tithes on agricul-

"We who were Occidentals have now been made Orientals. He who was a Roman or a Frank is now a Galilean ... We have already forgotten the place of our birth". The mournful comments of a chaplain attached to the court of the kingdom of Jerusalem in the early twelfth century highlight the culture shock which many French knights experienced on their contact with the Holy Land in the Crusades.

They combated alienation in a strange land by bringing with them fragments of their own culture. In present-day Syria the mighty Krak des Chevaliers, the Parthenon of crusader castles, bears witness to this. The building of castles in stone had begun in Europe in the late tenth and early eleventh century, and the architectural lessons learnt in France – and added to by Byzantine and Arab influences – are

Krak des Chevaliers

evident in Krak's design. Some of the architectural features of the inner buildings also recall Gothic styles. In time, the architectural traffic would be two-way. The experience of the East strongly influenced European castle design.

Krak stands on a high spur and, with a network of similar castles, commands valley entrances to its south and east. Built on the site of a native fortress, which was captured in 1099 by the French knight Raymond de Saint-Gilles, the main work of fortification was done in the twelfth century, though the outer walls were completed only in the thirteenth. In 1142 the count of Tripoli handed it over to the Knight Hospitallers of Saint John, the crusad-

ing order whose members dedicated their lives to succouring the needy and fighting in the Holy Land.

"A bone in the throat of the Moslems," in the view of one Arab writer, Krak was a deterrent against Arab occupation of the region. Even Saladin forbore to lay siege to it. The castle was also – like its French parallels – a satisfying symbol of feudal power; it towered over a fertile valley "rich in every kind of produce", according to one French chronicler. The Knights constructed a windmill on its battlements, as an ostentatious reminder that it had the wherewithal to withstand any siege. Krak's eventual fall in 1271 was due to undermanning. A castle that had housed several thousand knights in the early twelfth century was defended by only a couple of hundred.

Krak des Chevaliers ("Krak of the Knights").

tural produce just as lords siphoned off their seigneurial dues and rights. Even spirituality and liturgy wore feudal livery: the practice of seeking the intercession of saints par-
alleled, and derived much of its emotional resonance from, the rituals associated with
seeking feudal protection; and the holding-together of hands in prayer replicated the
gestures of the act of homage.

Yet if the Church was dominated by feudal lords and their values, as time went on
a movement of reform developed which campaigned for greater autonomy.
Monasteries, which were among the most powerful institutions in medieval society, led
the way. Just as the administrative fabric of the territorial princedom and county was
punctured by the local authority of castellans, so broader diocesan structures were
gradually subverted by monastic organizations. Under the direct authority of the pope,
the Benedictine reform movement was launched from Cluny in Burgundy after 909,
and spawned an international institutional network that was 1,500 houses strong by
the late eleventh century. Cluniac monasteries were massive landowners, whose proud
independence enforced respect. They represented a form of piety characterized by
unparalleled prestige. Popes, princes and paupers supported them with charitable
donations. The sumptuousness of their buildings, decorations and liturgy invited
envy; the scholarship, book production and manuscript illumination in which they
engaged were famous; and common people regarded the choice saintly relics they harboured as containing unmatched holy power.

The reform movement in the Church in the late eleventh and twelfth centuries took
this independence of spirit even further. Partly, this was the work of new monastic
orders – notably the Cistercians, founded in 1098, who had 350 houses by the middle
of the twelfth century, and who counted amongst their number Saint Bernard of
Clairvaux, the greatest scholar of his age. In time, a reformed papacy played a role too.
In the Investiture Contest (1075–1112), Pope Gregory VII (pope 1073–85) humbled
the spiritual claims of the emperor, and the Gregorian reform broadened into moves
for moral reform, for the reduction of lay influence in the Church, and for centralization and reorganization in Church governance. The papacy's new-found prestige
allowed it to lead moves to standardize Church doctrine, law, teaching and organization. It patronized new orders, called Church councils, defined heresy with greater clar-
ity and endeavoured to pass beyond the disciplining of bishops to undertake the
reprimanding and even replacement of errant lay rulers. The papacy's customary troubles with the German emperor, moreover, tended to predispose it towards good relations with the kings of France: popes dubbed the king of France *rex christianissimus* –
"Most Christian King".

The increased prestige of the Church in general and the close link between the
Capetian dynasty and the papacy in particular were brilliantly illuminated in the
Crusades, which were initiated in 1095 to recover Jerusalem and the Holy Places that
had fallen into the hands of the Seljuk Turks. The idea of Christianity taking collective
action for spiritual ends had its roots in earlier moves to instil religious values into the
feudal elite. From 989, Church councils in the Midi had begun to call for bounds to be

set on the inbuilt violence and lawlessness of feudal society. In this Peace of God movement, bishops and counts saw themselves as surrogates for an essentially absent royal
authority. Protection of non-combatants (priests, but also the poor and women) was
the core of the movement's message – a message targeted at the knightly class, which
was already developing a chivalric ethos. The Truce of God movement after 1027, calling for rests from fighting during Lent and Advent and on Sundays and other holy days,
took the movement further.

Overall, the aim was not to abolish violence so much as to restrain and channel it
in directions the Church could approve. It was in much the same spirit that the Church
developed Christianized versions of the rites of passage of chivalric life. The ceremony
of dubbing and belting new knights was strongly sacramental in flavour. A priest would
bless the sword and administer an oath in which the would-be knight swore to respect
the Church, protect widows and children, love peace and observe the embryonic laws
of war. Clearly, it was not a great leap to the declaration of a just and holy war: fellow
Christians had to be protected; but the infidel was fair game for military prowess.

If the Church's elaboration of chivalric codes had aimed to restrain the violence of
the knightly caste, the declaration of the crusade displaced that violence in a way which
served Church interests – but it was also turned ably to account by the Capetian
dynasty. "Let those who until now have been moved only to fight their fellow
Christians," Urban II (pope 1088–99) is said to have proclaimed in 1095 on launch-
ing the First Crusade, "now take up arms against the infidel." The call struck a responsive chord among the French elite. Urban II, himself a Frenchman from
Châtillon-sur-Marne, launched the crusade in a council held in France (at Clermont).
It sparked a bout of enthusiasm within France, notably through the preaching of Peter
the Hermit in the Midi. No other nation took so prominent a part in the crusades over
the next two centuries. At their height perhaps half the French nobility fought in them,
or else in associated actions against the Muslim infidel in the Iberian peninsula. Several
crusades were almost wholly French operations.

In the years after the First Crusade of 1095, a European presence was gradually
established in the Holy Land; in 1291 Christendom lost its last toehold there (at Acre).
During those 200 years the Crusades were marked by moments of disillusionment and
indeed downright cynicism. Their peak was perhaps in the first third of the twelfth century. The First Crusade had led to the capture of Jerusalem and the establishment of
four Latin states in the Holy Land. But the showpiece was the kingdom of Jerusalem,
over which first, in 1099, the Lorrainer Godfrey de Bouillon, then from 1100 to 1118
his half-brother Baldwin served as kings. From the 1140s, however, a long-term decline
set in. The loss of the northern county of Edessa led to the indecisive Second Crusade
(1146–8). The capture of Jerusalem by Saladin in 1187 sparked an emotional response
in Europe. Whereas perhaps 4,500 knights had participated in the First Crusade, the
Third (1189–92) had over 150,000 men under a German emperor (Frederick II
Barbarossa), a king of England (Richard I Lionheart) and a king of France (Philip II
Augustus (r. 1180–1223). The gains were few: some minor coastal regions were

brought under crusader control, and though in 1192 Saladin agreed to allow Christian pilgrims free access to Jerusalem, the city stayed out of crusader hands.

With the exception of the Fifth Crusade (1218–21), when Jerusalem was partially reoccupied – through negotiations rather than by feats of arms – the city remained tantalizingly out of reach. Moreover, material motives, never far distant from the heart of the crusading movement, became increasingly important in strategic planning and execution. The Fourth Crusade (1202–4) ended in utter fiasco, because the crusading force was wrongly rerouted towards Constantinople, which it proceeded to put to fire and sword. The last century of the Crusades saw more and more desperate attempts to deal with the problems in the Holy Land by attacking the power-base of Egypt: "The keys to Jerusalem," it was said, "are to be found in Cairo." The campaigns ran into the sand on reaching the North African coast.

Crusading served Capetian dynastic interests well. It channelled knightly energies away from France, thereby reducing levels of internal violence. The spirit of plunder could be exercised at the expense of infidels rather than Christians, foreigners rather than the French. "Before the Christians started for the lands beyond the seas," noted the Benedictine monk Guibert de Nogent, "the kingdom of France was prey to perpetual disturbance and hostilities." The movement also helped to develop solidarity and shared values among the feudal class, and accustomed even the greatest feudal lords to a Capetian leadership which was becoming a tangible reality.

Saladin (1138–93), sultan of Egypt and Syria, from a Persian painting of c. 1180. Perhaps the most formidable of the crusaders' enemies, he preached a holy war against the infidel in order to unite the Arab peoples, but combined this with a chivalric generosity towards the weak.

THE RISE OF CAPETIAN KINGSHIP

By the end of the thirteenth century the French monarchy had come a long way since the days of the first Capetians, who had seemed at times the playthings of their more powerful magnates. Unable to count on naked coercion to have themselves obeyed – in 1100, for example, the counts of Flanders could field an army of vassals 50 per cent larger than that of the kings of France – successive Capetians were obliged to play to different strengths. In particular, they focused on one of the principal differences between them and even their most powerful subjects, namely, the sacral character of monarchy. Kings and churchmen used this as a propaganda weapon for dynastic prestige. They cleverly yoked together Merovingian and Carolingian traditions, to make of a Capetian coronation something similar to a bishop's consecration. It was a sacramental event marked – following the precedent of Pepin in 751–4 – by the monarch's anointment with holy oil. Not only did they thereby rule "by the grace of God",

The flower of French chivalry, commanded by Saint Louis, attacking and taking the Egyptian city of Damietta, during the Seventh Crusade in 1249. The crusade foundered in 1251, when Saint Louis was taken captive. He was not ransomed until 1254.

Capetian monarchs were God's anointed as David and Saul had been – royal propaganda made great play of Biblical precedents. The fleur-de-lis, associated with King Solomon, was adopted as a royal emblem.

From the time of Charles the Bald in the ninth century, Clovis' coronation in 507 in Reims had been viewed as the act of foundation of the French people, blessed by divine grace. In a further dimension of their spiritual prestige miraculous healing powers were attributed to Capetian monarchs after they had received sacred unction at Reims. From the times of the son of Hugh Capet, Robert II "the Pious", the monarch was said to be able to cure scrofula by the power of his touch. Touching for "the King's Evil" was seized on by a school of dynastic chroniclers at the Abbey of Saint-Denis. In particular Abbot Suger, close adviser of Louis VI (r. 1108–37) and Louis VII (r. 1137–80), portrayed the monarch as God's Anointed, and the French people, by artful implication, as His chosen people. Robert the Monk evoked, in almost messianic terms, "the holy race of the Franks whom God has chosen as His people and His heritage".

The idea developed of France as an entity with its own characteristics and attributes. As the dying Roland, Charlemagne's paladin, had sighed in the twelfth-century *Chanson de Roland* ("Song of Roland"), it was "sweet" France. France was seen not only in personal terms, almost as an individual, it was also thought of as being symbolized by its monarch. The Saint-Denis school dated the origins of the kingdom of the Franks from the conversion of Clovis to Christianity. It was Abbot Suger who made widespread the custom of referring to the monarch as the king of France rather than as king of the Franks. The "Most Christian king" was at one with a "most Christian people".

The sacral character of the Capetians' power, to which no feudal lord could presume, was exercised in their role as suzerain, or feudal overlord. Even the mightiest vassals chose to have the royal signature appended to their charters, implying that the prestige of the ruler at the tip of the feudal pyramid still served some remaining purpose. As the twelfth century went on, moreover, rulers showed themselves increasingly adept at using their feudal prerogatives to boost dynastic power. The right to demand forty days' military service from vassals was used in 1124, when Louis VI was threatened by a coalition between the German emperor Henry V and King Henry I of England. In this way, Louis forced the emperor to back down, marking a moral triumph that the dynasty's chroniclers were quick to flaunt. More mundanely, rulers used their role of feudal umpire in cases of disputes among vassals in order to swell their own power. For example, Philip Augustus took Montdidier and Amiens in 1185 as compensation in a case involving the count of Flanders. Rulers also confiscated the property of law-breaking vassals who failed to attend their courts to answer a case. From the late twelfth century, moreover, the king of France enjoyed sufficient prestige to be adjudged a catch for any heiress. So, in 1137, Louis VII married Eleanor, the daughter of his most prestigious vassal, the duke of Aquitaine, while in 1180, Philip Augustus married Isabelle of Hainaut, the daughter of the powerful count of Flanders.

The Capetians might have initially been little more than figureheads, but by presenting themselves as useful ones, who symbolized the interests of the whole commu-

Seal of Philip Augustus, seemingly seated on Dagobert's throne, and resplendent with fleur-de-lis, the monarchy's emblem since the mid twelfth century.

nity, they gradually built up their power as well as their prestige. They enjoyed a fair share of luck. Europe fortuitously happened to be calm in the late tenth and eleventh century, with major rival powers busy elsewhere. The Normans were bound up with England and to a lesser extent with Sicily, while the German imperial dynasty was involved in struggles with vassals, the papacy and in the Italian peninsula, and was more attracted to the open frontier to the east. The Capetians were fortunate too in that their domains were situated at the hub of a major communications network in the centre of northern France, whose soil counted among the richest and most productive in all France. They were lucky even in their marriage bed. Hugh Capet had instituted the practice of crowning the heir in a king's own lifetime, a practice which caused the atrophying of traditions of elective kingship and divisible inheritance, which had caused so much dispute in the last century of the Carolingian dynasty. But to prevent a troubled succession, an undisputed male heir was essential. Eleven successive rulers from Hugh Capet onwards managed one.

The Capetians knew how to ride their luck. They used every trick in the book – from using their powers as seigneurial overlord to outright coercion – to extend their power within and around their domains. It had become difficult to travel around Capetian domains without being attacked by rogue castellans and forced to pay tolls or ransoms. Even kings suffered this fate on occasion. Louis VI and Louis VII repressed such stubborn castellans and vassals in their domains. They brought Paris' petty seigneurs to heel and established the city as the dynasty's capital. In the eighth century, the court had been based at Clichy or (under Charlemagne) at Aix-la-Chapelle, in the ninth at Saint-Denis, and (under Charles the Bald) at Compiègne. Paris had a population of 15,000 to 20,000 under the Carolingians, but under the Capetians it grew fast, reaching between 150,000 and 200,000 by the beginning of the fourteenth century. When Philip Augustus erected a wall round the Capetian capital in 1189/90, it covered an area twenty-five times larger than the former fortifications round the Île de la Cité.

The new verve of the Capetians was further signalled by their bringing under control, in a long and protracted struggle, the powerful Anglo-Norman dynasty. In 1152, Louis VII had repudiated his wife, Eleanor of Aquitaine, who promptly married Henry Plantagenet, count of Anjou and duke of Normandy, bringing with her a province covering roughly one-third of France's total landmass. When in 1154 Henry succeeded to the English crown as Henry II, he presided over a gargantuan seaborne empire running from Bayonne to Berwick-on-Tweed. The so-called "Angevin Empire" grew even more in the 1180s, when as a result of dynastic marriage alliance Brittany passed under Plantagenet control.

The year 1159 had seen the opening hostilities in what historians have sometimes called the "First Hundred Years War" (1159–1299). The Capetians contained and then, from the last years of the twelfth century, destroyed the Angevin empire. Philip Augustus exploited his full armoury of stratagems to subvert his rivals. He encouraged Henry II's sons to conspire against their father, then plotted darkly against each of them in turn when they acceded to the crown. Though he fought alongside Richard I

Reims cathedral

The famous "smiling angel" greets the entrant to the cathedral at Reims, generally acknowledged as one of the finest Gothic monuments of the French Middle Ages. Constructed from 1211 onwards, it is a typical product of the great period of cathedral building. Chartres might have more impressive stained glass, and the architectural merits of a number of other cathedrals may surpass Reims, but Reims' profusely abundant statuary – the other main component of the Gothic style – is particularly outstanding. The product of a number of sculptors' workshops, it influenced ecclesiastical buildings from Assisi to Westminster, and from Burgos to Strasbourg.

The Capetian dynasty was closely associated with the Gothic style – and with Reims in particular. The style's

innovator and champion, Abbot Suger of Saint-Denis, was a particularly potent and imaginative propagandist of the Capetian line. The style was widely referred to as *opus francigenum* – "Franks' work". The Gothic's conquest of Europe enhanced the dynasty's ideological lustre.

Reims was, along with the Abbey of Saint-Denis and Notre-Dame cathedral, one of the three key symbolic sites associated with the Capetians. Saint-Denis was where the kings of France since Dagobert I had been buried. Paris was the home of the living monarch, who took mass at Notre-Dame. Reims, in turn, was where Capetians were made kings, and were infused with divine grace. Clovis, the first Frankish king, with whom the Capetians were proud to claim continuity, had been crowned here by Saint Rémy, archbishop of

Reims. From the ninth century, it was claimed that a dove had descended from the heavens bearing in an ampulla oil for sacred unction. Miraculously, the oil never dried up, and successive kings of France were anointed with it. At Reims, too, the king became a miracle-worker: by receiving divine unction, he could henceforth cure by his touch individuals afflicted with "the King's Evil" (that is, scrofula).

By the reign of Saint Louis, a complex web of symbolic acts and associations had hardened into a "timeless" tradition which no monarch would wish to break. Reims cathedral thus became a "site of memory" (Pierre Nora) for the dynasty and, by extension, for the king's subjects. It was to remain in use for coronations down to 1825, when the last descendant of the Capetians to reign, Charles X, was crowned here.

Left The smiling angel of Reims cathedral.

Above left This medieval illustration shows Clovis being at once baptized and anointed as a ruler, as a dove descends from heaven bearing an ampulla of sacred oil. As a result of this sacramental event at Reims, the monarch acquired the power of the "royal touch".

Above Reims cathedral, coronation church of the kings of France.

Simon de Montfort
(*c.* 1160–1218) had been a
crusader in the East before
leading the internal crusade
against the Albigensian heresy
in the Midi in 1209. Killed
while besieging Toulouse, his
tomb is located in the cathedral
of Carcassonne.

Lionheart (king of England 1189–99) in the Third Crusade, he returned early from the East to stir up Richard's French vassals against him. Aware of the Capetian threat, Richard had the massive fortress Château-Gaillard built on the approaches to his Norman lands, and in 1198/9 joined forces with Baldwin of Flanders to bring Philip under control. Philip bounced back, however, against Richard's brother and successor, John (king of England 1199–1217). In 1202, over a petty feudal dispute, Philip invoked his authority as John's suzerain to declare him a felonious vassal for failing to answer charges made against him in his court, and ordered the confiscation of his lands. He moved militarily against John, overcoming resistance at Château-Gaillard and bringing Normandy under his control in 1204. By 1206, he had won Anjou, Maine, Touraine and Brittany, as well as Poitou and the Auvergne.

The English did not give in gracefully. Capetian expansion in northern France (notably in Artois and Picardy) had provoked local hostility, and John joined the counts of Flanders and Boulogne and the German emperor in an anti-Capetian coalition. In 1214, in the Battle of Bouvines, Philip defeated the allied forces, and in the subsequent Treaty of Chinon (1214), John was forced to accept Capetian gains. Fighting rumbled on during the thirteenth century under Philip's successors, Louis VIII (r. 1223–6), Louis IX or "Saint Louis" (r. 1226–70), Philip III (r. 1270–85) and Philip IV the Fair (r. 1285–1314). The pendulum continued to swing in France's favour. In the Treaty of Paris in 1259, Henry III of England formally recognized the Capetians' annexation of all former English possessions except the Guyenne, and this was largely ratified in the Treaty of Montreuil in 1299.

Philip Augustus had broken the back of Angevin power and increased Capetian territories fourfold. His successors not only continued his work but also acted to extend the dynasty's power in the Mediterreanean south. In the sprawling lands of the powerful counts of Toulouse, heresy had taken deep root in the twelfth century. The Waldensian heretics – whose name derived from their founder, the Lyon merchant Valdes – preached forms of apostolic poverty and attacked hierarchy and wealth within the Church. More widespread was the so-called Albigensian heresy of the Cathars, centring on lands between Albi, Carcassonne and Toulouse. The Cathars believed in a form of dualism in which the material world was intrinsically evil, and only an elite of "perfects" could aspire to a life of purity. This left little room for conventional Christian belief or for the Catholic clergy. The "perfects" were widely venerated among the peasantry, while the movement's anti-clerical strain won it support from an elite irritated by the presumptions of Church power. Cistercian preaching missions led by Saint Bernard of Clairvaux had failed to nip the Cathar movement in the bud. In 1208 Pope Innocent III pronounced the Cathars more dangerous than the Saracens.

Philip Augustus was too involved with the Angevin struggle to lend open support to moves against the Cathars, but he did give tacit encouragement to a warband of marauding northern knights led by Simon de Montfort, who in 1209 attacked the count of Toulouse for protecting the heresy. This internal crusade was waged with heartless ferocity – "Kill them all," a papal legate ordered the northern knights on taking Béziers. "God will recognize His own." De Montfort assumed provisional control over the lands of the count of Toulouse, but it was Louis VIII who reaped the fruits of this vicarious northern victory. In 1224, the king purchased rights to the countship from de Montfort's heir; then in 1226 he led an expedition southwards with papal blessing, capturing Avignon *en route* and forcing all of Languedoc to acknowledge his rule. Further hostilities led to a compromise peace in 1229, organized by the young Louis IX's regent, his mother Blanche of Castile. The Venaissin county surrounding Avignon was ceded to the papacy. The Capetians retained most of Lower Languedoc for themselves, while Poitou and Auvergne were ceded to Louis IX's brother, Alphonse of Poitiers. Louis IX secured his position in the Midi in the Treaty of Corbeil with the king of Aragon in 1258: Louis renounced suzerainty over Catalonia and the Roussillon in return for Aragon's renunciation of claims in Toulouse and Provence. The area of the Spanish march, a Carolingian before a Capetian possession, had been losing touch with the rest of France since the twelfth century at least. This agreement helped to fix the limits of Capetian power on the Iberian frontier.

STATE AND SOCIETY

Both the geography and the consistency of Capetian power had been transformed between the tenth and early fourteenth centuries. The territories directly administered by the Capetians had grown enormously. Hugh Capet had enjoyed prestige as the vessel of sacral power and as feudal overlord of West Francia; Philip the Fair, by contrast, was the proud, even arrogant monarch of the most important state in western Europe. This was especially true now that, after the death of Frederick Barbarossa (emperor 1152–90), the Holy Roman Empire in eastern Europe was fragmenting under internal and external pressures.

The star of kingship had risen immeasurably high in France. Rulers still accentuated both the sacral and seigneurial sources of their power. Renewed interest in classical antiquity in the twelfth and thirteenth centuries, moreover, had led to the development of Roman Law, and a growing elaboration of the concept of sovereignty. It made of the monarch not just a feudal suzerain but also an heir of Roman *imperium*, who, as "emperor in his own country", as the phrase went, was responsible for the common good throughout the realm. From Saint Louis onwards, this included the power to legislate. That Philip II took the assumed name "Augustus" was symptomatic of the shift in the base of monarchical power. So was the monarchy's concern with coinage. Efforts to reduce the legal status of coins minted by others were supplemented in 1266 by Saint Louis' introduction of the large silver coin known as the *livre tournois*, which was to be the basis of French currency thereafter. The circulation of images of royalty prevailed over those of their mightiest subjects and was closely connected with the realm's new-found prosperity. The development of a large royal court wedded to conspicuous consumption and display also underlined changes in representations of monarchical power. The court of Philip V (r. 1316–22), for example, numbered 5,000 individuals, making it as large as a medium-sized city.

The growth of the court was part of the more general progress in state formation. The expansion of Capetian power made new bureaucratic demands: crown tax revenue grew by 80 per cent under Philip Augustus between 1180 and 1203, and as much again once the dynasty acquired Angevin possessions. Saint Louis and Philip IV, in particular, helped to develop the state's bureaucracy. Accountancy and archival procedures were improved. Clerks of the royal household were grouped into a chamber of accounts, while others specializing in judicial affairs became institutionalized as the parlement, which served as the monarch's final court of appeal. The standards of justice which the university-trained legists offered within the parlement were widely viewed as superior to those of the feudal lords. The role of the parlement was supplemented in the provinces by the network of salaried royal judicial officials, known as *baillis* (the title *sénéchal* was used in the Midi). Such officials had long been sent out spasmodically, but from 1190 they were assigned fixed places of residence. In addition, their powers – notably in supervising local administration and legal process, in representing the king and in transmitting his orders – were more carefully defined.

The extension of Capetian authority was accompanied by a number of practices which set pragmatic bounds to central power. These included the custom of bequeathing territories to the control of close relatives of the monarch in the form of "appanages", as they were known. On his death in 1226, Louis VIII made his sons appanages of Artois, Anjou, Maine, Poitou and the Auvergne. Such cessions – continued by his successors – were usually made on the understanding that the territory would revert to the crown if a line became extinct. This meant a delay of variable length. The vast sprawling appanage of the Poitou, ceded to Louis IX's brother Alphonse of Poitiers, reverted to the crown when the latter died childless in 1271. In other cases the

Royal legislation, municipal regulations and cultural interdicts aimed to keep lepers at a distance. In this fourteenth-century illumination a leper, complete with clappers to warn of his presence and begging-bowl, seeks urban alms alongside a disabled beggar.

reversion could take longer: Artois and Anjou, ceded in appanage in 1226, only reverted to the crown centuries later.

The growth of royal administration was accompanied by the revived notion of the monarch as fount of justice. This was no longer merely a feudal justice benefiting only the great and the good, but a fairer, more accessible form of justice. The memorable (and probably apocryphal) story of Saint Louis, seated under an oak tree in the forest of Vincennes, dispensing justice to all-comers, was endlessly recycled after being cited in Joinville's idealized account of the king's life. Saint Louis owed much of his repute to his saintly qualities. As well as professing a personal piety, he also acted the part of the crusader monarch both in the East and at home, where he completed the rout of the Albigensian heretics.

As this example suggests, the rise of Capetian monarchy, and its increasing emphasis on the sanctity of centralized justice, was accompanied by a growing intolerance towards a wide range of forms of dissidence and non-conformity. Like his father (who had at one stage exiled all Jews from the kingdom), Saint Louis introduced stringent anti-Semitic measures. Coercive measures were taken against lepers, too, to ensure they were placed in leper-houses. The rituals of confinement condemned sufferers from the disease to a form of living death, shutting them away from the rest of society. Sexual deviance was frowned on too. Prostitutes were more or less equated with lepers, and formally banned. (Saint Louis' successors would take a different tack, subjecting prostitutes to religious surveillance and regulation, which sometimes led to their being confined to certain areas of the city, as Jews with their ghettos.)

Sex was a particular anxiety, and the tendency was to project that anxiety on to women. Reform of the Church – notably the growing emphasis on clerical chastity – contributed to a worsening of their status. The idealization of "Woman" in courtly love literature, and in the growing cult of the Virgin Mary, centred on sexual purity rather than indulgence, and related the exception rather than the rule. For clerics now obsessed with their own chastity, women were a danger to be avoided – "sacks of shit", as one cleric charmingly put it; "mad dogs," stated another. The male-centred stance of the clerical elite may have helped to drive some women towards religious heterodoxy. Women were, it seems, particularly drawn to Catharism, which envisaged both men and women being able to achieve spiritual perfection, and a number of other, more sexually liberal sects and heresies. Women had always been excluded from warfare and the priesthood – the *bellatores* and *oratores* were uniquely masculine. They were also now excluded from the literate elite who formed the state bureaucracy and the liberal professions: indeed, the professionalization of government severely reduced the influence of highly placed females.

Church and state had combined their forces in the eleventh and twelfth centuries to construct a new matrimonial order. Marriage was a sacrament and the regular civil means of contracting alliances. The rules of feudal property-holding increasingly made of women from aristocratic backgrounds pawns on the feudal chessboard – the dowries they brought with them were seen as components of the male-administered system of inheritance. On the other hand, those who did not fit well enough into family property calculations were dispatched to nunneries. In fact, some women from within the social elite were still able to use their powers as wives, widows and mothers within the public sphere. Many, for example, simply took over all the administrative aspects of property when their men went crusading. Blanche of Castile, the mother of Saint Louis, who stood in for her son on several occasions during his reign, is a case in point. Similarly, there were many aristocratic women who still turned disadvantage to their favour, making their vocation within religious orders a spring-board for religious and sometimes political power.

Women, then, were only rarely and exceptionally allowed a voice. This contrasted all the more strikingly with men; for one of the characteristic features of state develop-

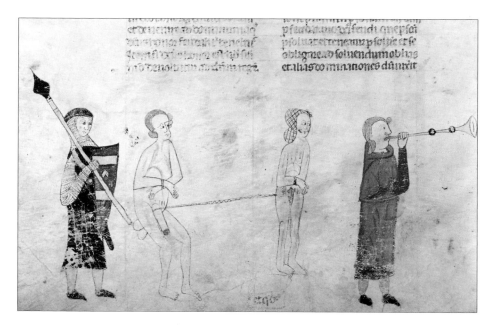

Chartered towns had extensive rights of local justice. In this folkloric case from Toulouse a pair of adulterers, chained together by their errant members, walk the streets in shame to the sound of the trumpet.

ment in this period was the rise of new methods of consultation and representation. Rulers in the past had consulted with magnates and prelates on matters of state as part of the feudal rite of *consilium*. In 1302 Philip the Fair formally convened the three estates of the realm – clergy, nobility and "Third Estate," or town representatives – specifically for this purpose. The Estates General, as it became, was France's national representative body down to 1789. A sounding-board and intelligence-gatherer of some importance, the Estates formed a pragmatic means of consulting the wider (male) political community, in order to acquire – maybe even to manufacture – consent for royal policy.

Other measures highlighted the dynasty's willingness to seek accommodation with the constituent parts of French society. The practice of consultation in the Estates General was extended by the development of provincial Estates later in the fourteenth century. Monarchs also ratified local legal custom: the codes of the Vermandois region

King Philip the Fair, depicted taking counsel. This imperious monarch was the first to consult systematically with representative bodies throughout the realm as a means of gauging opinion and seeking community approval for his acts. The lords spiritual and temporal are shown, together with their coats of arms.

and the Beauvaisis were given the seal of approval in the late thirteenth century, for example. Even from the eleventh century, the Capetians had also been profligate in granting municipal charters. In return for receiving royal protection, towns were accorded financial and judicial privileges.

The monarchy's use of these political mechanisms testified to a perceived need to keep abreast of opinion throughout the land, not just the views of feudal leaders. In 1303, for example, Philip presented for approval to the Estates the first permanent taxes of the Capetian monarchy. Levied on merchandise, but also including a substitution tax for non-performance of military service, the taxes proved difficult to collect, but they did mark an important stage in the development of relationships between state and society.

Finance was also at issue in another matter which came before early meetings of the Estates, namely, religion. The "Most Christian Kings" did not take kindly to even a pope interfering with royal prerogatives. Even the saintly Louis IX had proved staunch in the defence of the French Church, and his own rights within it. The growth in the strength of the papacy in the late thirteenth century, after the collapse of the Holy Roman Emperor's power and the conclusion of the Albigensian crusade, brought fresh strains. Relations took a turn for the worst when an attempt by Philip the Fair to increase taxes on the clergy led to violent denunciation by Pope Boniface VIII (pope 1294–1303). National and provincial Estates swung dutifully in line behind their king. The dispute got out of hand when Philip seized Boniface at Agnani, and the pope died on his hands from shock. The election in 1305 of a French pope, who in 1309 established his residence in Avignon, tipped the balance in the dynasty's favour.

Finance and religion were also intertwined in the king's attack on the Knights Templar. This crusading order had developed a lucrative sideline as international financiers, and in order to secure their wealth and contacts Philip the Fair had their leaders arrested in 1307 on certainly trumped-up charges. After a sensational show trial, he had them executed and the order dissolved, with their property passing into the royal treasury. Royal power was certainly pragmatic; it could also still be brutal.

THE "NEW SPRING": THE MEDIEVAL ECONOMY

The period from the late twelfth to the early fourteenth century, which witnessed the growth of Capetian power, produced in France, as in most of western Europe, a phase of brilliant social and economic progress, a "new spring" (G. Duby). Indeed the rate of economic expansion from 1180 to 1220 was probably unsurpassed until the eighteenth century. Climatic improvement may have made a contribution to better harvests – a warmer, less rainy long-term phase set in after about 1160 – though it was hardly a determining factor. An increased injection of precious metals into the European economy may also have played a part – imports of gold and silver from West Africa and the Near East were accompanied by the growth of silver-mining within Europe, notably in Saxony, Bohemia, Spain and even France's Massif Central. The halting of Viking, Saracen and Magyar raids helped too, since the disruption these had caused probably delayed economic growth in many areas. The Auvergne, which had been spared such raids, enjoyed boom conditions as early as the ninth and tenth centuries, while the upturn was much slower in Provence, which had been particularly severely affected by Saracen raiding.

Technological improvements were a further spur to economic growth. Not only were new methods and techniques invented, but their use became more widespread more quickly. The spread of heavier wheeled ploughs, combined with more effective methods of harnessing draught-animals, improved the productivity of arable land, especially in the north. The introduction of triennial rotation of crops probably helped here too. Windmills, pioneered in Normandy in the late twelfth century, and watermills also became more common: there were 245 of the latter in Picardy alone by about 1175, and perhaps 20,000 in France as a whole. As well as processing food, water power was put to industrial use, driving hammers or bellows, for example. The spread

The public burning, after torture, of Jacques du Molay, master of the Knights Templar, in 1314. A crusading order, whose members took monastic vows and who lived as soldiers, defending the Holy Places and guarding the rights of pilgrims, the Templars had developed skills in high finance. Their wealth and influence attracted the wrath of Philip the Fair.

of the use of the domestic spinning wheel was another factor boosting manufacturing production. Better techniques in mining and metallurgy were introduced, producing not only better arms and armour but also stronger and more resilient ploughs, agricultural implements and tools. Incremental technological innovations – the compass began to be used from the twelfth century, for example – also made for more navigable and more capacious ships.

Economic growth and diversification were closely linked to a massive rise in population. France, in its present-day frontiers, had a population of perhaps 7.5 to 9 million under Charlemagne, though this had probably fallen to about 5 or 6 million by the time Hugh Capet came to power in 987. By the time of the last Capetians, in 1328, it stood at between 18 and 21 million, perhaps 15 million of whom were directly under French kings. These figures could be compared with England's 3 to 3.5 million, or the 8 to 10 million in the Italian peninsula.

This rough tripling in population over three centuries was bound up with changes in the organization of the economy. The links were complex and reciprocal. Extra mouths gave an incentive to produce more food to peasant farmers, who, as serfs, owned their land, albeit under feudal conditions. Meanwhile extra hands, in what was still a very labour-intensive economy, allowed more to be produced. Certainly a great deal more land was brought under cultivation. Perhaps half of France's total landmass had been forest in 987; this was massively reduced. French monarchs from Philip Augustus onwards introduced surveillance measures on royal forests, suggesting that land reclamation on such a scale needed some regulation. The forms that land extension took were manifold. Some monastic orders, like the Cistercians, were specialists in colonizing large tracts of wilderness far distant from civilization. Hence Saint Norbert, founding a house at Saint-Gobain in 1120, deliberately chose "a fearful

Blanche of Castile

The daughter of Alfonso VIII of Castile, and granddaughter of Eleanor of Aquitaine, Blanche of Castile (1188–1252) was married at twelve years old in 1200 to the future Louis VIII (r. 1223–6). Her husband named her in his will as guide and adviser to their son. She served as regent from 1226 to 1234 while Louis IX (r. 1226–70) was a minor, remained close to the centre of government through to 1244, and then stood in again for her son from 1248 to 1252 when he was on crusade. She frustrated repeated attempts to foment rebellion by powerful nobles, who held that "a woman should not govern so great a thing as the kingdom of France". On occasion, she placed herself at the head of royal armies. She also ensured governmental continuity and responsible support in all her son's major administrative reforms – a son whose political achievements have eclipsed her own.

Saint Louis' chronicler Joinville emphasized Blanche's bad relations with Louis' queen, Marguerite of Provence, so that she has been regarded as the classic difficult mother-in-law. In fact Blanche placed great stress on the religious side of mothering, and took personal charge of her children's education. That her eldest son was canonized, a daughter (Isabella) beatified, and that she herself was regarded as a saint augmented the lustre of the Capetian dynasty. The chronicler who commented that she ruled as well as a man was paying her the ultimate backhanded accolade.

Blanche of Castile, with the young Louis IX at his books. From a fourteenth-century manuscript.

solitude … a fetid marshland, sterile and uncultivable heath, the home of fevers and wild beasts". Much land reclamation, however, amounted to little more than the extension of cultivation to wasteland and scrub on the margins of the village. Five-sixths of land reclaimed in Picardy, for example, took this form.

The result was a transformation of the physical character of the landscape. Bread was the staple foodstuff of nine out of ten French men and women, and farming patterns reflected this. In the north and north-east, the open-field system of cereal cultivation firmly established itself. Dwellings were often clumped together around a central hub – a form of habitation favoured by new communities that were formed in virgin territories. About 500 *villeneuves*, as the new communities were called, were created in the Paris basin. In Aquitaine, where they were called *bastides*, 600 took root. France was also endowed with over 1,000 leper houses during this period, and these frequently took the form of agricultural colonies. Reclaiming land involved draining marshes as well as chopping down trees: the construction of dike-systems for this purpose developed in Flanders, and it subsequently spread to the lower Somme, the Seine, and the marshlands of Poitou, Brittany and the Camargue. These developments put the finishing touches to the creation of the network of 30,000-odd villages within which French rural history – and indeed French history full stop – has been lived out to the present day.

The vast extension of cultivable land was not a straightforward exercise in supply and demand of land and labour. Existing structures of feudal power loomed large in the initiation and conduct of these enterprises. The days of the booty economy were passing, for the Crusades had failed to provide a long-term theatre for military pillage. The costs of military hardware spiralled upwards – the sophisticated protective mail-shirt required by knights cost the price of a farm in the late eleventh century. Many a crusader had to sell up in order to afford to campaign in the Orient. Changes in aristocratic lifestyle also provided an incentive to adapt; the round of hunts, tournaments, feasts and courtly entertainments was becoming increasingly expensive. Seigneurs, then, were motivated to make their rural power pay more. Those who failed to adapt risked losing everything, and the period saw the decline, for example, of many petty castellans who, attached to the military aspects of their status, still held out hopes of living from plunder.

The growth of agrarian productivity in the medieval period owed much, then, to the pressure which the seigneurial class put on their peasants. Wherever one looked, feudal rapaciousness was close at hand. Seigneurs might agree to marginal extensions of land, for example, on condition that peasants paid them extra levies. The more ambitious among them invited peasants to reclaim land, offering them incentives, tax privileges and exemptions from seigneurial dues – even, on occasion, livestock and tools. The prosperous seigneur now not only collected dues and taxes on all aspects of the lives of the peasants within his domains; he also exploited his control of the local millhouse, bakehouse and winepress; pastureland and forest were often under his control, too; and he regulated all aspects of economic activity in the locality. Rather than using feudal labour services as a means of having his domain land farmed, he often preferred to lease this out to local peasants under sharecropping (*métayage*) or money-rent arrangements. Other seigneurial dues and levies might be commuted to cash too. As a result, feudal lords were changing from agricultural producers in their own right to *rentiers* – receivers of rents and dues. The extensive legal rights and judicial powers that they continued to enjoy helped to ensure that they creamed off the best part of peasant surplus.

Increased seigneurial rapaciousness acted as an incentive in peasant agriculture, too, spurring innovation and diversification. Cereal productivity registered real progress. Other sectors of the rural economy also benefited. Wool became a particular area of speciality, especially as the cloth trade expanded. Lay lords and bishops were also closely involved in the development of winegrowing. Salt and metal production

Illumination of the letter Q, from a Burgundian manuscript representing the life and activities of Cistercian monks, who are shown roughly clad in brown (they later switched to white). In the early days the monastic communities were entirely self-supporting.

boomed. Though the main beneficiaries of economic expansion were drawn from the social elite, many peasants, too, enjoyed an improvement in their lot. Those in particular who produced a marketable surplus benefited enormously. Village communities proved adept at winning privileges from their lords, so the seigneurial burden may have lightened in some areas.

With the raiding and pillaging of the ninth and tenth centuries at an end, towns too could now come out of their shell. The period from 1100 to 1300 produced an urban growth more dramatic than anything since Roman times. Whereas early medieval cities had been essentially religious and military centres, they now developed above all through their economic functions. They looked to river and sea for expansion and

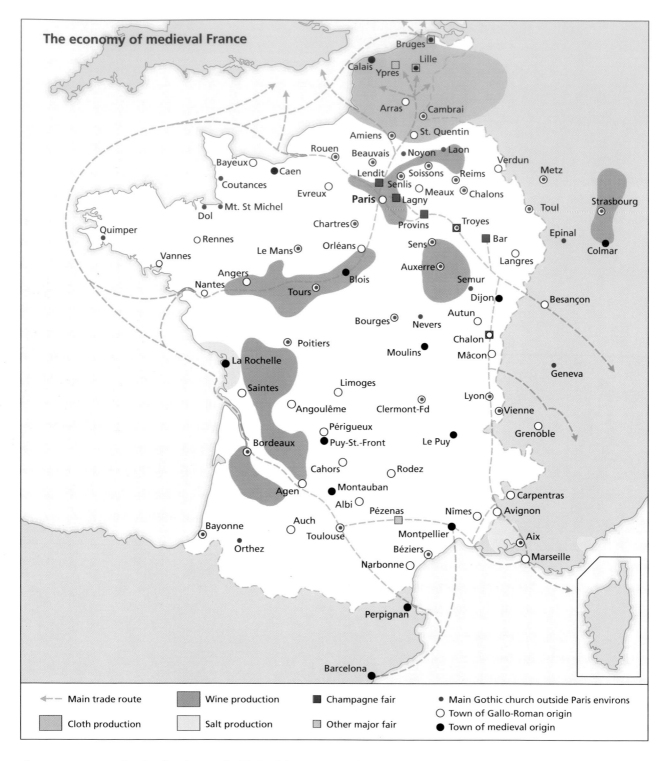

The economy of medieval France

Bruges
Calais Ypres Lille
Arras Cambrai
Amiens St. Quentin
Rouen Beauvais Noyon Laon Verdun
Bayeux Caen Lendit Soissons Reims Metz
Coutances Senlis Meaux Chalons Toul
Evreux **Paris** Lagny Strasbourg
Mt. St Michel Chartres Provins Troyes
Dol Sens Bar Epinal
Quimper Rennes Le Mans Orléans Auxerre Langres Colmar
Vannes Angers Blois Semur Dijon Besançon
Nantes Tours Autun
Bourges Nevers Chalon
Poitiers Moulins Mâcon Geneva
La Rochelle Limoges Lyon
Saintes Angoulême Clermont-Fd Vienne
Périgueux Grenoble
Bordeaux Puy-St.-Front Le Puy
Cahors Rodez
Agen Montauban
Albi Pézenas Nîmes Carpentras
Bayonne Auch Avignon
Orthez Toulouse Montpellier Aix
Béziers Marseille
Narbonne
Perpignan
Barcelona

Legend	
←--- Main trade route	• Main Gothic church outside Paris environs
Wine production	○ Town of Gallo-Roman origin
Cloth production	● Town of medieval origin
Salt production	■ Champagne fair
■ Other major fair	

The economic geography of medieval France highlighted the importance of the Paris region. Conveniently placed to benefit from the booming Champagne fairs and the cloth-making region of Flanders, it was an important grain- and wine-growing region and was also situated on major currents of commerce. The city of Paris was only the most important in a burgeoning network of medieval urban centres, most of which could trace their origins back to the Roman Empire or beyond.

wealth. Of the cities with more than 20,000 inhabitants in the thirteenth century, Paris, Ghent, Ypres, Toulouse, Strasbourg, Tours, Orléans, Lyon, Lille and Metz all commanded important waterways, while Bruges, Rouen, Saint-Omer, Montpellier, Narbonne and Bordeaux all turned resolutely towards the sea.

The feudal elite had such a powerful hold over the levers of economic power at the height of the Middle Ages that they inevitably influenced the development of towns. Lords, increasingly sensitive to market potential, realized that the presence of towns and fairs attracted wealth into the region which they could tap through tolls and other dues. The stone castles from which truculent castellans had defied authority and coerced peasants from the tenth century often came to house local markets. Patterns of castle building reveal a growing symbiosis between feudal power and mercantile exchange. Fortified walls were extended so that merchant houses and artisans' dwellings could nestle up against feudal keeps. Mercantile wealth came to be a kind of life-support system for a feudal nobility ever more alert to the high costs of the aristo-cratic lifestyle. Demand for luxury goods and services among the nobility also attracted many craftsmen to the towns that were growing up in the shadow of the castle. There, these artisans would transform the raw materials bought at the markets into desirable luxury commodities. Much the same was true in towns with resident bishops and monasteries. The upper clergy were among the most conspicuous of consumers, and made important contributions to urban development and diversification.

In this context, the old three-way division of society into "worshippers", "warriors" and "workers" was beginning to look archaic even as it became fully established. The military and ecclesiastical elites still held sway within society, but the "Third Estate" label hid a wide spectrum of existences. Social differentiation on the land had given rise to a small elite of peasant producers who were doing well by marketing their surplus. Their status contrasted with the majority of rural workers, who hardly produced enough for themselves to eat. In the towns the arrogant disdain of lay lords and prelates now had to accommodate the presence of the wealthy merchant and manufacturer. The appearance of the grasping merchant as a stock figure in medieval sermons and litera-ture reveals the growing importance of a social mobility which found no place within the fixed categories of feudal society. Other social groupings were also emerging. In par-ticular, a strong service sector was making its presence felt: churchmen, scribes, judges, medical men, property stewards, notaries – all contributed to the diversity of the urban milieu, as did the growing numbers of state officials.

Public law could accommodate these emerging social categories through the exten-sion of corporative privileges. Just as provinces were having their legal customs endorsed by the state, so towns and the economic and work-related groupings within them were accorded legal personality, and given extensive rights of self-regulation. In 1268 there were no fewer than 100 recognized guilds in the city of Paris alone. France was becoming – like its European counterparts – a *Ständestaat*, a "society of orders", in which the social tissue was composed of many corporative bodies, all with their own rights and privileges enshrined in public law.

Seal of the commune of Meulan, 1195. The collective portrait of the founding officials sits below the royal fleur-de-lis. The seal, the treasure-chest, the bell, and communal property (notably the town hall) were the four characteristic attributes of communal authority.

Although many towns had started life as the poodle of the local feudal lord, they were soon straining at the leash, and bidding to establish freedom and autonomy. Associations of town-dwellers, or "communes", bound together by an oath of fraternity rather than an act of feudal homage, petitioned the monarch for rights of self-government. The city of Le Mans was the first to make such a bid, in 1070. Lay and Church authorities often looked askance at such movements – communes were "turbulent conspiracies" in the view of one churchman, "violent and pestilential" according to another – and towns did indeed sometimes harbour heretical religious movements. Yet the feudal elite soon discovered how to turn the communes to their own account. Thibaut IV, count of Champagne in the early thirteenth century, it was said, "established communes of burghers and peasants in whom he trusted more than his own knights". The Capetians were also especially adept at using the establishment of communes as a way of extending their own authority and at the same time disadvantaging rival lords. Louis VI was known as "the father of the communes" in recognition of the large number of such municipal franchises he granted, including Laon, Beauvais, Noyon, Soissons and Reims.

This development sparked some ferocious power-struggles. In Laon in 1112, the local bourgeois seeking a municipal charter even murdered their own bishop. A "battle of the bells" sometimes ensued, with the town-hall clock, which chimed out a "time of the merchants", competing with the "time of the church" struck out by church bells (Le Goff). Tension was less acute in the cities of the Midi, which already had strong traditions of municipal institutions and where local nobles and bourgeois proved more compatible bedfellows. Brittany, in contrast, had no municipal institutions whatever before the fifteenth century. But, in general terms, such struggles demonstrated that the feudal nobility could no longer count on having everything their own way.

MONARCHY, CULTURE AND REGIONALISM

France's economic boom in the twelfth and thirteenth centuries made it seem a kind of terrestrial paradise. The country, noted the chronicler Philippe Mouskes, "abounds in woods, rivers and meadows, in virgins and in beautiful women, in good wines and in redoubtable knights". Capetian propagandists claimed that economic prosperity was a direct reflection of the new-found strength and prestige of the dynasty. They did the same for France's cultural prowess, which was increasingly expressed through the medium of the French language. Under the Merovingians and Carolingians, Latin had been the only written language of consequence in the West. As Latin ceased to be spoken, local dialects boomed. French, with its roots in Latin, was originally Francian, the popular language of peasants and artisans of the Île-de-France. Yet it came to gain a wider European significance because of Capetian power, though Latin stayed in place as the language of the Church, the law-courts and the universities.

The international standing of the French language never rivalled Latin. Nevertheless, it was the official language of the social elite in England from the Norman invasion of 1066 down to the end of the thirteenth century; and it served the same pur-

The troubadours

"It was in Languedoc", Dante later noted, "that the users of living languages were first to essay poetry." Indeed, from roughly 1100 down to 1300 (but particularly from c. 1130 to c. 1200), a vernacular lyrical poetry developed in southern France. Troubadours, who combined poetry with musicianship, were drawn from every echelon of society: from wandering minstrel-acrobats up to such nobles as William, ninth duke of Aquitaine, who was allegedly the first practitioner. There were, moreover, trobairitzes – roughly twenty female troubadours are known.

"My lady tries me and tests me so she can know how I love her." This dictum of William of Aquitaine is symptomatic of the quest of the lover and his "lady" celebrated in troubadour literature. Love is celebrated between a usually idealized woman and her champion and lover – a relationship, it has been suggested, which reflected a common social reality, what with large numbers of unpropertied knights swarming around the households of the nobility. The erotic element in the relationship evidently clashed with the ethic promoted in orthodox Church teaching. In poetry by trobairitzes, too, there is often an element of mutual sensual gratification – as, for example, with Béatrice de Die, who mourns the loss

Juggler troubadours, eleventh century. At first, the troubadour was a warrior like other courtly figures.

of her champion, and who remembers when

Naked-armed I held him tight
And pillowed on my breasts at night
I gave him joy with my caress.

The vibrancy and apparent popularity of this school of poetry testified to the dynamism of the *langue d'oc* culture of the Midi. In time, it would influence aristocratic circles in the *langue d'oïl*: Eleanor of Aquitaine and her daughter Marie de Champagne were notable channels for the lyricism of troubadour poetry into the north. They also helped to formalize it into the conventions of courtly love, which placed less emphasis on sexual gratification than on the quest for the favours of a distant, idealized lady.

The placing of women on a pedestal, linked to the adoration of the Virgin Mary, corresponds with little that we know about the status of most women in medieval society. Indeed, it may be that the development of courtly love tells us less about women than men. Women's voices are increasingly absent from the poetry, and women figure essentially as objects of male passion. Courtly love was an arena in which new versions of masculinity – chivalrous, courageous, gentlemanly – could be constructed.

pose in the Two Sicilies (the state comprising Sicily and the southernmost tip of the Italian peninsula) from the eleventh to the fifteenth century, and throughout the lives of the Frankish kingdoms in the Holy Land. By the thirteenth century, when its use in official documents highlighted its association with the dynasty, a French literature was beginning to appear. This included chronicles, such as the crusading yarns of Geoffroi de Villehardouin and Joinville's life of Saint Louis, and sundry religious works, but most famous of all was the tradition of romances in both poetry and prose. The famous "Song of Roland" (*c.*1100–25), with its Carolingian paladins, crusading heroics and chivalric ethos, was the most celebrated of the *chansons de geste*. More ambitious were the writings in the courtly love genre, whose most brilliant exponents were Guillaume

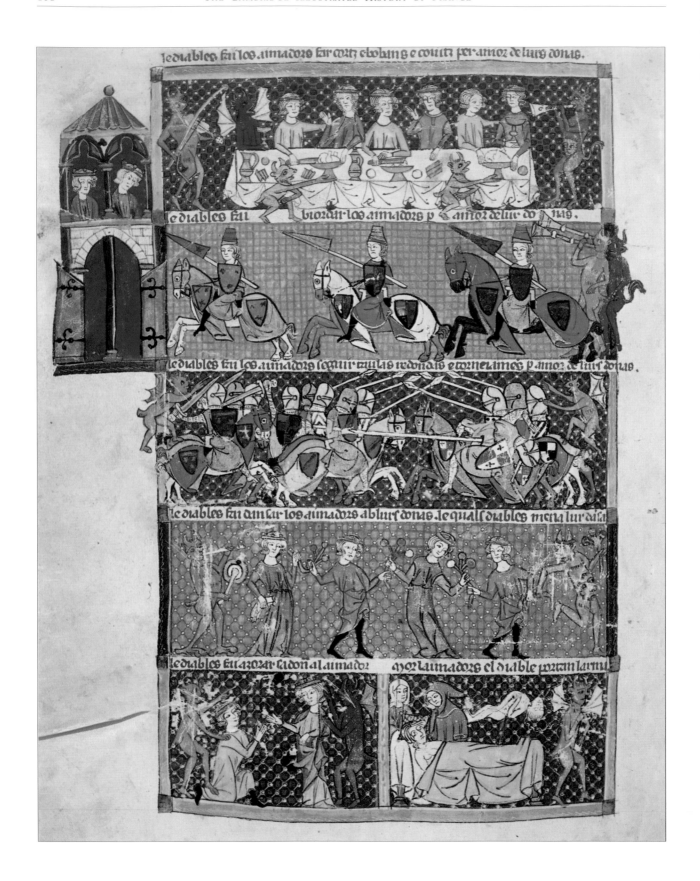

de Lorris and Jean de Meung, authors of the hugely popular mid-thirteenth-century *Roman de la Rose* ("Romance of the Rose"). French, cleric Nicolas Oresme proudly noted in the fourteenth century, had become "the noblest language in the world".

The language of the Paris region, then, was emerging as the language of French elites, if not yet the French community as a whole, which was still faithful to its distinctive languages and dialects. Paris' own intellectual prestige in the twelfth and thirteenth century played a part in this too. The largest city in western Christendom by 1300, the booming city was, in Pope Gregory IX's words, "wisdom's special workshop". Here, as in a number of other cities north of the Alps (Orléans, Chartres, Tours and so on), loose associations of individuals had, in the twelfth century, formed around teachers who were often linked with cathedral schools. These informal groupings gradually acquired the right to teach and, recognized by both pope and king, the Paris teaching community assumed corporative status as a "university". In the thirteenth century, it was divided into faculties of law, medicine and theology. Universities posed an alternative to the education conducted within monasteries. They were as good as their teachers – and Paris had the best of them, not least the brilliant and charismatic philosopher Peter Abelard, whose bold approach to theology brought to the city a cosmopolitan and boisterous student body attracted to working at what seemed to be the leading edge of knowledge.

The universities were the most brilliant product of the "Twelfth-Century Renaissance", which encompassed art, architecture, religious revival and vernacular literature as well as learning. Like its Carolingian forebear in the ninth century, the movement exemplified a revival of interest in the literature and culture of the Ancients, and in particular a fascination with the lay learning of the ancient world, which contact with Eastern and Arabic cultures had promoted. The Capetian dynasty buttressed the university movement: the development of the state bureaucracy and the opening up of law and royal service as alternative careers to the Church were important preconditions for their expansion. The Paris university's European reputation was strongest in the fields of theology and philosophy. Teachers attempted to reconcile the beliefs of Christianity with the learning of the ancient world. The Italian Thomas Aquinas, who taught here in the mid thirteenth century, provided a merger of Aristotelianism and Christian dogma that ultimately became Church orthodoxy down to the Scientific Revolution of the seventeenth century.

Gothic architecture constituted another medium in which Capetian power was expressed. Like the French tongue, it had originated as a model within the Île-de-France, and was closely associated with the dynasty. At the root of its emergence was, characteristically, royal propagandist Abbot Suger of Saint-Denis. In rebuilding the abbey church in the 1130s, he merged the pointed arch which had been in use in some Burgundian buildings with the ribbed vault derived from Anglo-Norman models. The style was used on the west front at Chartres cathedral in the 1140s, and the teams of builders employed there then moved on to Sens which, completed by the 1170s, was the first cathedral built in the Gothic style.

Opposite A folio from the *Breviari d'amor* of the Béziers monk Matfre Ermengaut (c. 1288). The text attempts to merge the eroticism of the courtly love tradition with the more spiritual love of orthodox Christianity. Demons stalk lovers (from the top downwards) in feasts, jousts, battle, dancing and courtship, and at the end (bottom right) a demon carries off the soul of the dying lover.

By then, the style was being used in a host of cathedrals – Noyon (1140–86), Senlis (1167–91), Laon (1150–1233), Chartres (in its entirety, following a fire, from the 1190s) and, from the 1160s, Notre-Dame in Paris. By the turn of the thirteenth century, the style was ranging more widely outside the Île-de-France: Amiens, Beauvais, Le Mans, Rouen, Sées, Coutances, Angers, Troyes, Reims, Strasbourg, Bourges and so on. Saint Louis' project of building the Sainte-Chapelle on the Île de la Cité in Paris to house Christ's crown of thorns gave the style a new prestige. Constructed in the 1240s the chapel exemplified the mix of architecture, sculpture and stained glass which had become the essence of the Gothic. The style also flourished in the wake of Capetian expansion in the Midi, appearing for example in Clermont, Rodez, Albi and Carcassonne, before spreading throughout Europe, from Uppsala to Famagusta.

The Capetians gained much prestige by association with the triumph of the Gothic in Europe, the growing pre-eminence of the French language, the acknowledged brilliance of Paris University, and the city's wealth and cultural élan. Yet to concentrate attention solely on Paris and the cultural developments associated with the dynasty would be to miss the economic diversity and cultural pluralism of medieval France.

France's strong economic performance in the Middle Ages can certainly not be reduced to the dynasty's achievements alone. France drew economic succour from sources of mercantile power outside its border, notably Flanders and north Italy, but also Catalonia and northern Germany, home of the powerful trading corporation, the Hanseatic League. French commerce was geared into wider European networks and trade did not follow the fleur-de-lis. The Rhine and the Rhône rivers – the one entirely outside France, the other on its margins – were key arteries of exchange for the French, as for the European economy. One of the most prosperous trading regions in France was Champagne, which from the 1130s became the junction-box connecting trading currents from Flanders and from northern Italy, the two power-houses of the medieval economy. The fairs held in succession over six weeks in the Champagne cities of Troyes, Lagny, Bar-sur-Aube and Provins developed into major international occasions of cultural as well as economic exchange. The cloth of the prime Italian and Flemish producers was present in abundance, as were goods from the Levant (spices, silks), the far North (Scandinavian timber goods, furs) and the South (Spanish leathers). In addition, exchange took place in services, notably the banking skills of Genoa, Florence and Lucca.

Many other parts of France still looked outwards to beyond national frontiers. The booming cities of French Flanders straddled the frontier with the Empire, and also linked up with the English economy: Dunkirk, for example, developed into a major port for Anglo-Flemish trade. In the south, the economic development of the Guyenne was inextricably connected to links with England through Bordeaux – the wine and salt trades were particular beneficiaries. In Lower Languedoc and Roussillon, the economy boomed under the kings of Aragon, with Perpignan emerging as a major cloth producer. The cities of the parts of eastern France under the power of the emperors also enjoyed economic prosperity. Haguenau was for a time an imperial residence, while

Opposite Poitou and the Dordogne contain a particularly fine range of Romanesque art. Notre-Dame-la-Grande in Poitiers, constructed between 1130 and 1145, has the most richly decorated façade in France. Romanesque architecture exemplified a wide range of cultural influences, and was often linked to the movements of religious revival in the tenth and eleventh centuries.

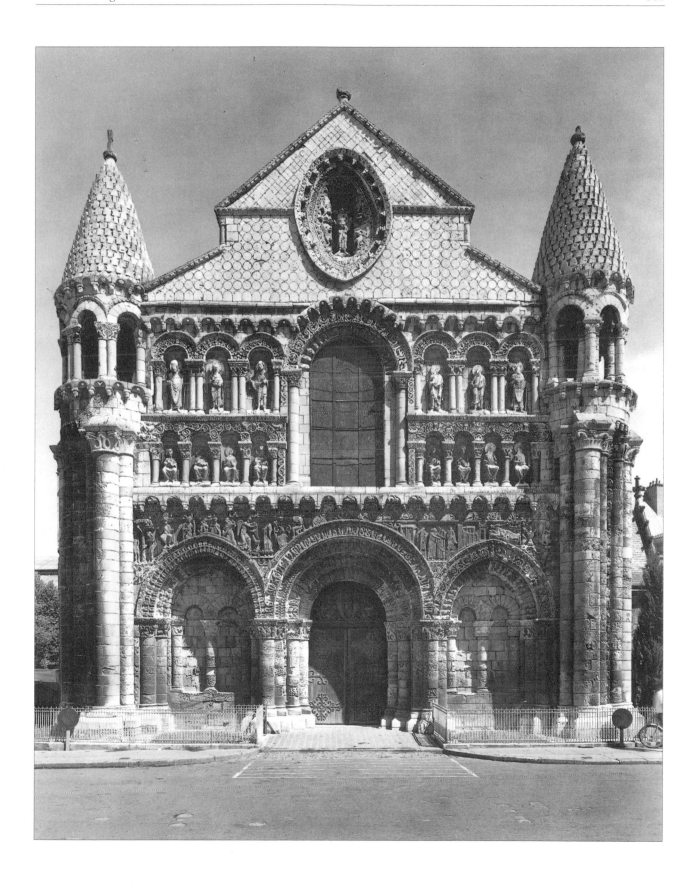

Gottfried of Strasbourg (d. 1230), here reading poetry before a princely court, was an important influence in transmitting the romance traditions of chivalric literature into Germany. The twenty thousand verses he wrote in his romance, *Tristan and Isolde*, formed the model for subsequent poetry.

Strasbourg, through trading links with central Germany and Switzerland, became a major international centre.

Diversity was the keynote in cultural development too. The French language, which prevailed in the long term, lagged behind as a form of purely literary expression. During the twelfth century more literary works were produced in France in languages and dialects other than Francian. Occitanian, the language most in evidence in the so-called *langue d'oc* in the Midi, was the medium in which an important troubadour literature developed. Languedoc and Provence witnessed the first flowering of the courtly love traditions. Although the movement did not survive the dogmatic intolerance introduced by the Albigensian crusade, it proved a strong influence on northern romance authors.

The French language had competition from inside the *langue d'oïl* as well as from the *langue d'oc*. Picard, a close relative of French, was still an important literary language, and the chronicler Froissart, for example, wrote in it. Chrétien de Troyes composed in a modified form of Champenois. In the west, Breton lays told tales of Arthur, Tristan and Isolde and the Holy Grail. In the east, Alsace enjoyed something of a cultural renaissance in the eleventh and twelfth centuries in the medium of German.

If the Capetian court stimulated the growth of culture, the same could be said of the courts of many great provincial magnates, who engaged in lively patronage of the arts.

Before the Champagne dynasty acceded to the kingdom of Navarre in 1234, the court of the counts of Champagne was a sterling patron of chivalric literature. It was here that Marie de Champagne, daughter of Eleanor of Aquitaine, commissioned the romance *Lancelot* from Chrétien de Troyes, for example – and Villehardouin and Joinville were active here too. Meanwhile the presence of the Cistercian headquarters at nearby Clairvaux stimulated a strong current of religious art and writing. Normandy was another culturally dynamic area. It had helped to proliferate the Romanesque architectural style, whose most outstanding buildings were far from the Île-de-France (notably in Burgundy and Auvergne, but also in Poitou, Périgord and Provence) and went on to play a key role in the spread of Gothic architecture. In the Midi the court of the counts of Toulouse was a centre for troubadour poetry – before it became a home for the Albigensian heresy. If Paris University retained its prime status as a centre for philosophy, other universities were active too. The medical faculty at Montpellier benefited from links with Arabic, Jewish and Greek scholarship, and developed into one of Europe's foremost centres of medical science and teaching. Universities at Toulouse (from 1229) and Avignon (1303) were also worthy of note.

There were, then, strong countervailing cultural and economic forces resisting the apparent dominance of northern, Capetian France. It was an important marker of cultural change, therefore, when, in 1328, following the death of the last Capetian, Charles IV, the succession was debated within the political elite. The claims of Edward III, king of England, to the French throne were generally resisted on the grounds that, as one writer put it, "the French did not admit without emotion the idea of being subject to England". The Capetian dynasty had constructed a notion of French identity within the political elite which benefited the French claimant to the throne, Philip, the Valois duke. Claims for the cultural unity of France were, however, to be sorely tested in the following century.

CHAPTER 5

Valois France: The Later Middle Ages and the Renaissance

The Capetian dynasty had helped to make France one of the foremost states in medieval Europe. However, all its achievements seemed in jeopardy in the centuries which followed. A great cycle of disease, famine and warfare unleashed countless problems on to the French state. In the darkest days of the Hundred Years War against England (1337–1453), the country's very viability seemed in question, and fragmentation, similar to that which Germany was undergoing, seemed possible. The dynasty survived (though it passed to the collateral Valois line), and was able once more to piece together a strong political system – one which put paid to English rivalry and consolidated its hold over French society. Soon, though, the reborn state was engaged in conflict against the Spanish and Austrian Habsburg house for European domination.

An illusory moment of brilliance – associated with the cultural stirrings of the Renaissance – was followed by conflict and division. The Reformation, instigated by Martin Luther in Germany in 1517, had the effect of splitting the religious unity of French society. Its impact was amplified by a fresh wave of civil strife, the Religious Wars (1561–98), from which the French state was lucky to emerge intact. Survival was finally achieved by a change of dynasty: the last Valois, Henry III, gave way to the first of the collateral Bourbon line, Henry IV.

FROM GOOD TIMES TO BAD

By 1328 the legendary good luck of the Capetians in their marriage bed had run out. A line of eleven uncontestable sons ground to a halt after the reign of Philip the Fair. His three children – Louis X (r. 1314–16), Philip V (r. 1316–22) and Charles IV (r. 1322–8) – ruled consecutively, but none could produce a durable male heir. The succession debate was eventually decided in favour of Philip de Valois, nephew of Philip the Fair, who took the title Philip VI (r. 1328–50).

The constitutional controversy that followed Philip de Valois' elevation to the throne illuminates the underlying drift of political priorities. There had been lawyers who argued that Edward III, Plantagenet king of England, had a superior claim – he was son of a daughter of Philip the Fair; the blood of Saint Louis ran in his veins too; and conventional laws of feudal succession would have allowed the title to be passed through a female, even if they prohibited women inheriting in their own names. But opposition to the English claim was grounded partly in an Anglophobia which highlights a growing sense of French identity among the political elite. Legal experts at court also retrospectively invoked the Salic Law of Clovis and the Franks, forbidding the transmission of kingship through females. The Salic Law had till then been little more than an antiquarian curio. From this time onwards, however, it became the basis of the kingdom's constitutional laws, and ruled out the possibility either of a reigning

King Edward III of England formally pays homage to Philip VI of France for Aquitaine. The French monarch bestows the accolade to the approval of surrounding courtiers.

queen or succession through a female. So the ushering-in of the Valois dynasty showed not just a developing sense of French political identity; it also illustrated and confirmed changes which had been taking place, as we have seen, in gender relations.

The legal case for Philip VI had proved persuasive enough for Edward III to do homage to the new French ruler in 1329. But it made the king of England pause for thought. And when Philip attempted to copy the strategy of Philip Augustus towards John of England, calling Edward a felonious vassal and attempting to confiscate his lands in the Guyenne, Edward reacted forcibly. By 1340 he had declared Philip VI a usurper and added the kingship of France to his own titles. The Hundred Years War between France and England (1337–1453) was beginning.

International warfare and dynastic dispute between Valois and Plantagenet could not have come at a worse time. By the early decades of the fourteenth century the economic cycle on which medieval prosperity had been based was coming to an end. Some of the causes of economic downturn were accidental or became more serious because they coincided. The Champagne fairs, for example, went into decline after 1310 because Italian merchants preferred to use Alpine passes and the Rhine waterway to reach the Low Countries, or else took the sea route via the straits of Gibraltar. England was also emerging in Flanders and Gascony as a commercial rival to France.

Medieval population growth had been grounded in an ability to expand food production by reclaiming land and by increasing productivity through technical and economic developments. In the thirteenth century yields were apparently reaching maximum levels for existing levels of agrarian technology. Population growth had led to cultivation of marginal lands that could not sustain intensive farming for a generation or more without exhausting the soil. Land reclamation projects continued in Lorraine down to 1330, and *bastides* were still being established in the Dauphiné in the 1370s; but projects had dried up in the Paris region, more significantly, from the

Female-headed family depicted on a fourteenth-century tax-roll from the village of Saint-Paul-les-Romans, near Valence. The high death rate meant that single-parent families were often numerous.

1230s. Population growth meant that holdings were divided up below viable levels of self-sufficiency, and peasants became increasingly dependent on the market for subsistence. Spasmodic rises in the price of bread caused a slump in demand, which had severe knock-on effects in trade and manufacturing. The famine which much of France experienced between 1315 and 1317 – when contemporaries witnessed a wave of crime and outbreaks of cannibalism – was not simply a result of bad weather; it was also a symptom of a society living too close to the margin of self-sustaining production.

Hunger bred discontent, and discontent bred rebelliousness, turbulence and the seeking of scapegoats. In 1321 there were widespread attacks on lepers, who were held to be poisoning wells in a plot hatched by the Muslim king of Granada. In the towns there was growing hostility to urban aristocrats who controlled city life and sporadic pogroms against Jews who were associated with financial chicanery. Two thousand Jews were massacred in Strasbourg in 1349. In the Flemish countryside between 1323 and 1328 there were massive peasant risings directed against manorial lords, and these were put down in a pool of peasant blood – in the Battle of Cassel in 1328, the count of Flanders killed between 12,000 and 15,000 rebels. Even this paled against the scale of repression which greeted the Jacquerie of 1358 (so called because nobles referred to their peasants as "Jacques"), when peasants in northern France attacked seigneurs and burnt down castles.

Among the outriders of social catastrophe moreover there now loomed the figure of the tax official. The *gabelle*, or salt tax, was introduced in 1341, and by the 1350s and 1360s, taxes had become a regular tug on the purse-strings of the subjects of the kings of France. Rulers also tried to balance their books by manipulating monetary values: there were no fewer than twenty-two variations imposed on coinage between 1358 and

1360. Financial policy sparked opposition. Urban anti-tax revolts erupted in the 1380s in Rouen (where the rebels of the "Harelle" jokingly elected a clothmaker their "king"), in Paris (where the "Maillotins" drove out tax officials with lead mallets), and in cities of Lower Languedoc, Picardy and Champagne.

By that time, moreover, the social landscape was darkened by the appearance of the "Black Death" – bubonic plague – after a gap of some six centuries. The disease killed probably one-third of France's population. In fact in every year for three centuries – down to the middle of the seventeenth century – there was always some locality within France which suffered an outbreak of plague. By 1450 a demographic trough had been reached: France's population had plunged from about twenty million in the 1320s to between ten and twelve million.

Population loss in this deadly pandemic caused major disruption to the workings of an economy already in crisis. In the towns the shrinkage in demand and the high costs of labour forced many industries to the wall. Labour suddenly became a scarce

A riot in Montpellier in 1379, which resulted in the death of two royal officials. High tax demands in the midst of economic difficulties sparked a rash of urban disturbances around this time.

"For in that time of death," wrote the chronicler Froissart of the years 1348–52, "there was an epidemic of plague. People died suddenly and at least a third of all the people in the world died then." Froissart's naive guess has been largely confirmed by demographers. Population losses throughout the Western world were immense. Certainly one-fifth, probably one-third and possibly one-half of Europe's population died as a result of the resurgence of bubonic

The Black Death

plague following a half-millennium during which it had not appeared in the West.

Though we may discount the legend that the disease had initially been spread by Mongols catapulting plague-ridden corpses into the besieged Crimean city of Caffa, Genoan merchants, it seems, brought the disease

back to the West from that region in late 1347. The disease killed horribly – victims suffered atrocious death agonies – and with horrible efficiency: the fatality rate of those who caught the disease was close to 100 per cent. "The plague," as the royal surgeon Ambroise Paré was later to note, "is a mad, tempestuous, monstrous, abominable, fearful, terrifying and treacherous disease. To escape its clutches is more due to God than to human agency." The best remedy endorsed by the medical professions was, on the appearance of plague, to "leave early, go far, come back late".

Extreme in its effects the disease brought extreme reactions. There were vicious pogroms aimed at Jews, who were held to be responsible for poisoning Christian wells with the disease or spreading it in some other manner. The sense of guilt it provoked produced hordes of flagellants, who wandered eastern and south-eastern France and Germany, whipping themselves and calling populations to repent for their sins. "The calamity instilled such terror in the hearts of men and women," noted the Florentine Boccaccio, "that brother abandoned brother, uncle nephew, brother sister, and often wives left their husbands ... Even fathers and mothers shunned their children."

In France, only the Béarn, parts of Picardy and the Massif Central escaped the huge loss of life of 1348–52. The chances of demographic recuperation were moreover wiped out by further visitations of the disease – notably in 1360–2, 1374 and 1382 – and there were more than a dozen particularly bad years in the fifteenth century.

The "Triumph of Death", a sixteenth-century work which recalls the enormous loss of life caused by the Black Death of 1348. Bubonic plague continued to afflict France up to 1720.

and costly commodity. Peasants and workers who survived the outbreaks of plague did well. They benefited from the drastic change in the labour market, their wages rose and their living conditions improved – meat-eating became widespread, for example. They did have to endure, however, an onslaught on their living standards by the feudal class. Some manorial lords tried to force their peasants to pay the cost of the crisis, cutting wages and increasing feudal dues. State legislation was introduced in 1351 to put a ceiling on wages. These efforts were, generally, in vain. Some seigneurs adapted by shifting out of domain farming, developing less labour-intensive pasture cultivation, converting labour service into cash payments or else offering favourable leases to peasants as a means of attracting labour. Others preferred a more atavistic approach to falling feudal profits: the extraction of plunder. The Hundred Years War might have started with the claims and counter claims of rival dynasties; but it also gained impetus as the feudal class (as well as many displaced peasants and townsmen) sought out new means of subsistence and enrichment.

Pillage was important for the English. The Black Prince, the son of Edward III, returned from a raid in the Midi in 1355, for example, bringing a thousand loot-filled wagons in his train. It was also crucial for the French. Troops from both sides carried off movable items of wealth, held individuals and communities to ransom, and frequently devastated the countryside to boot. In spells of peace too demobilized soldiers formed armed vigilante gangs – the *routiers* of the 1350s and 1360s and the *écorcheurs* of the 1420s and 1430s – which caused destruction wherever they went. Although only one year in every four or five was a year of warfare, and armies were relatively small – probably 50,000 men at the very most – the passage of troops, deserters, demobilized men and hangers-on became a barometer for the rise and fall in population. Damage was especially bad in the Massif Central, the Paris basin and Normandy. The Hundred Years constituted for Normandy a holocaust of Hiroshima proportions (Guy Bois), especially in the fifteenth century: "From Dieppe to Rouen," bemoaned one Norman city-dweller, "there is not a recognizable track left; there are no farms and, with the exception of a few bandits, no men." Throughout France roads were deserted, villages abandoned, fields and hamlets taken over by nettles and brambles, while wolves grew in numbers and in audacity.

Medieval medicine taught in the universities was essentially book medicine, based on reference to canonical texts by authors such as Galen and Hippocrates. It was utterly impotent in the face of the Black Death.

THE HUNDRED YEARS WAR

The war (1337–1453) started disastrously for the French. The French fleet was destroyed outside Bruges in 1340, and Edward III's expeditionary force meted out terrible defeats on the French at Crécy (1346) and Poitiers (1356). Troubles thickened under the impact of the Black Death, the loss of Calais to the English in 1347 and the capture of King John II "the Good" (r. 1350–64) in 1358. In the king's absence local estates in the south (*langue d'oc*) and the north (*langue d'oïl*) agitated for reforms, while in Paris Étienne Marcel led a municipal movement demanding greater autonomy. The English moreover demanded so heavy a ransom for their prize that tax pressure triggered discontent throughout France, exploding in the Jacquerie of 1358. By the Peace of Brétigny of 1360 John was obliged to agree to the loss to the English of roughly one-third of his kingdom.

The struggle was a civil war as well as a dynastic struggle. The feudal vassals of King John of France benefited from his discomfiture to extend their power. Charles "the Bad", king of Navarre, a grandson of Louis X through Louis' daughter Jeanne, who was also, as count of Evreux, a major landowner in Normandy, advanced claims to the succession and proved a constant thorn in the flesh of the Valois monarch. A war of succession to the dukedom of Brittany took place between 1341 and 1365. Charles, the pro-English pretender, emerged victorious and was soon acting as though he were independent of the kings of France. Much the same was going on in Burgundy.

The successor of John "the Good", Charles V (r. 1364–80), led a staunch recovery. The great military commander Bertrand du Guesclin relentlessly harried the English in the north and south-west, and by the late 1370s forced them back on a handful of ports. The reign of Charles VI (r. 1380–1422) was altogether more difficult. His uncles ruled selfishly and were at odds with each other during the period of his minority, and although Charles showed some signs of capacity when he acceded to full power, in 1392 he went mad and was only spasmodically rational through to the end of his reign.

The Hundred Years War. The powerful state painstakingly assembled by the Capetians (see p. 76) risked disintegration in the Hundred Years War. The Treaty of Brétigny confirmed England's role as a major rival within the kingdom. The low point of French fortunes was reached in the late 1420s, when the English king and the duke of Burgundy seemed to be working a partition of the kingdom. By 1461 the Valois dynasty had bounced back.

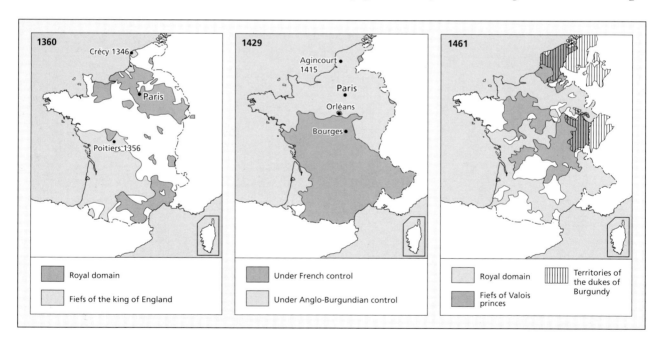

1360
Crécy 1346
Paris
Poitiers 1356

■ Royal domain
□ Fiefs of the king of England

1429
Agincourt 1415
Paris
Orléans
Bourges

■ Under French control
□ Under Anglo-Burgundian control

1461

□ Royal domain
■ Fiefs of Valois princes
▥ Territories of the dukes of Burgundy

His insanity allowed faction-fighting to worsen. The main battle lines were drawn in 1407 in the middle of a truce with England, when the Burgundian duke John "the Fearless" organized the assassination of his main rival Louis, duke of Orléans, the brother of Charles VI. The Anglo-French struggle became for a moment a side-issue to the fight between Armagnacs (as the Orléanist party were called) and Burgundians. In 1415 the English came back to the fray. Henry V (king of England 1413–22) landed in France to claim the monarchy. His defeat of the French at Agincourt in 1415 was a crushing blow, while the Armagnac assassination of John the Fearless in 1419 led the Burgundians to enter into alliance with the English. They pressurized the hapless Charles VI to give his daughter in marriage to Henry V, to disinherit his own son and to make Henry V his heir. The poor dauphin, the future Charles VII (r. 1422–61), retreated southwards, leaving most of northern France in Anglo-Burgundian hands.

French fortunes took a dramatic upturn with the appearance of the peasant girl Joan of Arc (1412–31), from Domrémy in the Lorraine. Inveigling herself into the entourage of Charles, she helped him to lift the English siege of Orléans. Newly heartened, Charles advanced on Reims, where he was crowned "by the grace of God" according to time-honoured custom – a massively important step in terms of both Charles' psychological state and the dynasty's standing. His status as monarch now fortified by this homage to tradition, he found his cause going well. He made little fuss when Joan of Arc, totem of victory at Orléans, fell into the hands of the Burgundians. They duly passed her over to the English, who had her burnt as a witch. Joan had become too closely associated with the faction in the king's entourage in favour of all-out war on the English, while Charles favoured diplomatic manoeuvrings. His diplomacy paid off, for in 1432 he won over the duke of Brittany, and in 1435 wooed back into the French camp the duke of Burgundy, Philip "the Good" (duke 1419–67).

It had proved difficult for the English to establish themselves outside the north of France. The French began to use scorched-earth tactics, destroying everything which lay in the path of the advancing armies, and this both undermined the quest for loot which drove English forces on and strained their supply lines. When in the 1420s the English endeavoured to shift from a war of plunder to one of occupation and colonization, they stimulated opposition. The restive feudal vassals of the kings of France wanted independence, not a change of ruler. The favouritism the English showed their allies caused much local resentment – "son of an Englishman" had become the gravest of insults in English Rouen – while the taxes they levied were even higher than those of the kings of France.

The rise in taxation owed much to the approximate doubling of the costs of warfare in the period. Major changes were taking place in the conduct of war. As the French learnt to their cost in the battles at Poitiers and Agincourt, which between them killed off a solid bloc of French chivalry, wars of knights were becoming a thing of the past. Knights adopted heavy plate armour rather than mail-coats so as to deflect missiles now propelled by gunpowder as well as bows. Hence infantrymen had the edge over cavalrymen, especially at close quarters, where knights' armour made them utterly immobile once they were knocked off their horses. But the eclipse of the knight owed as much to political as to military changes. The monarch could no longer rely on the feudal levy as a means of assembling a reliable army. The decline of the feudal tie meant that soldiers – even vassals – had to be paid, and paid in cash when booty was not forthcoming. Though expensive, mercenaries were not always reliable, especially if they disbanded at the end of the campaigning season to conduct pillaging raids. From 1439 Charles VII established a standing army paid out of a direct tax – the *taille*.

A portrait of Joan of Arc by an anonymous Franco-Flemish painter in a book of poems by Charles of Orléans, *c.* 1455.

Fifteenth-century carving of the arms of the city of Bordeaux under English rule. The leopards were a heraldic device associated particularly with the kings of England.

A siege in the Hundred Years War. Cannon had been present on the battlefield at Crécy in 1346, but their effectiveness as siegecraft led to a transformation of military architecture in the fifteenth century: base walls were thickened, bastions appeared on corners, and holes were made through which defensive cannon could fire.

Charles VII's standing army formed the backbone of the force that from the 1440s drove the English out of France. It was supplemented by bowmen companies (*francs-archers*) established in 1449 and by artillery. Du Guesclin had pioneered the use of the latter in the 1370s, and by the 1440s big guns had become a key contributor to battlefield tactics and siegecraft. The French operated with no fewer than 300 cannon in what was to prove the final battle of the Hundred Years War, at Castillon in 1453. The English, who had already been driven out of Normandy, evacuated the south-west, and retained only a toehold on continental Europe at Calais.

THE REHABILITATION OF THE DYNASTY

The struggle to force the English out of France proved the laboratory in which the institutions of a strong, centralized monarchy were created. In the standing army, funded by the *taille*, the Valois dynasty had developed what was to become one of the key agents of royal absolutism. The army was financed, even more significantly, without recourse to the Estates General, and was viewed as an emanation of royal sovereignty rather than as an institution freely assented to by the nation. Taxes were about obedience, not good will.

The rudiments of the administrative system of absolutism were also fixed in place in these years, and in the decades following 1453. Under Charles VII and his wily and astute successor Louis XI (r. 1461–83) the royal council took on a less feudal, more bureaucratic complexion. The monarch relied for advice on a group of professional lawyers, not merely mighty vassals. There was a greater differentiation of royal business too. Financial and judicial functions were separated. The chancellor headed the judicial arm, which was composed of a hierarchy of royal tribunals, the Paris parlement being the most important. Finance was the responsibility of a group of "generals of finance", while specialized institutions (*chambre des comptes*, *cour des aides*) also developed to deal with financial litigation and tax affairs. Local administration also underwent reform. Four major tax areas, or *généralités*, had been created in 1390, and these were gradually added to and made more sophisticated in their operations. The courts of *baillis* and *sénéchaux*, introduced in the late twelfth century, were also increased in number, and their business expanded.

Though the formal structures of the state were increasingly bureaucratic, in fact an informal system of patronage operated in counterpoint to it. This was centred on the royal court and extended into Church as well as secular affairs. By the Pragmatic Sanction of Bourges in 1438, the king of France secured a large amount of leeway in higher Church appointments and some access to Church revenues, which he now had power to tax. He still enjoyed wide rights of appointment to offices in the court, the army and the bureaucracy – though from the early sixteenth century monarchs were also organizing the sale of office, as a means of raising revenue.

The Hundred Years War and its aftermath saw the rehabilitation of a dynasty which, in 1420, had seemed on the edge of extinction. Once the English had been disposed of, however, there remained a continuing problem with regional nobles, who were resistant to the Valois bid to centralize power. The drive against the English had allowed many feudal lords to exact a price for their support. The high nobles who led the so-called Praguerie in 1440, protesting against military reforms, for example, were bought off with land. Brittany developed a high degree of independence in the early fifteenth century, and claimed to be a separate and sovereign power. It developed centralized institutions akin to those of the Valois: a more professional administration; a complex tax system; and even its own army – indeed its militia of *francs-archers* (1425) predated the French equivalent by two decades.

This portrait of Nicolas Rolin, the powerful chancellor of the dukes of Burgundy, is from the altar screen he and his wife commissioned for the new hospital they endowed at Beaune. The work of Flemish master Rogier van der Weyden, it still hangs within the hospital.

The appanage – the landed property made over to the monarch's younger sons – remained the institutional form within which much of this resistance to Valois authority took shape. The dukes of Anjou, descended from a brother of Saint Louis, were major players in the civil turbulence at the turn of the fifteenth century. "King" René, duke of Bar and Lorraine, count of Provence and titular king of Naples, as well as duke of Anjou, was one of the major figures of European diplomacy and politics in the mid fifteenth century. The main threat to Valois power, however, undoubtedly lay in Burgundy, awarded in 1363 as an appanage to Philip "the Bold" (duke 1363–1404), a son of John II. When Philip married Marguerite of Flanders, he became heir to a large bloc of Flanders and Artois, which he duly inherited in 1384. This became the basis for further expansion.

Philip's great-grandson, Charles "the Bold" (duke 1467–77), inherited what had become a strong northern and eastern power complex. It was not just the size of the Burgundian territories which made them threatening. The duchy's economic power was considerable: the region had been affected by the ravages of the Hundred Years War less than the heartlands of Valois power, while in the cities of Flanders it had massive concentrations of wealth on which to draw. It had also developed an administrative machinery quite as sophisticated that of the French kings – *bailliages*, an independent judicial system, *chambres des comptes*, local estates, a standing army and so on – while the Burgundian court was the most brilliant in Europe.

Unbridled ostentation became a battlefield on which a subtle war between the ruler and his over-mighty subjects was waged. Imitation was the sincerest form of flattery – and the surest sign of political ambition. The dukes of Brittany and the counts of Armagnac wore the gold crown normally held to be the monopoly of royalty. In Provence "King" René cultivated a similarly regal demeanour. The Valois' chivalric orders were imitated by lesser states and would-be states: the dukes of Brittany had their Order of the Ermine from 1381, while Burgundy instituted its famous Order of the Golden Fleece in 1429.

Charles the Bold aimed to resurrect a Lotharingian middle state between France and Germany and to secure imperial recognition as king of Burgundy. He failed. His defeat and death outside the walls of Nancy in 1477 killed the Burgundian dream. The French monarchy presided over the break-up of the Burgundian domains, though in the *guerre folle* ("crazy war") of 1485–8, it had to resist the efforts of ambitious princelings to turn the Burgundian débâcle to their own benefit. In the Treaty of Arras in 1482 the monarch incorporated into France the duchy of Burgundy and a number of cities along the Somme river. Marriage was also arranged between the dauphin (heir to the French crown) and Charles' daughter and heir, Marie – this so that Franche-Comté, Flanders and Artois would eventually pass into French hands.

As things turned out, the marriage never took place. The heiress married Maximilian of Austria instead, taking her landed dowry into Habsburg rather than Valois arms. Yet if this project failed, the fifteenth century witnessed considerable expansion of French power. Enduring gains in the fourteenth century had been minimal: Lyon had been

"Two hundred fat oxen, 63 fat pigs, 1,000 pounds of lard, 2,500 calves, 2,500 fat sheep, 3,600 shoulders of mutton, 11,800 small chickens, 18,640 pigeons, 3,640 swans, 2,100 peacocks, 1,668 cranes." This was just part of the fare reported to have been consumed in the colossal feasts associated with the wedding of Charles the Bold, duke of Burgundy, in 1468. Such copiousness was far from exceptional. Since the time of Philip the Bold, duke from 1363 to 1404, the Burgundian court had won a reputation across Europe for the lavishness and splendour of its activities.

The dukes were ardent cultural patrons, in architecture, painting and sculpture. Italianate Renaissance fashions had not yet made an impact in Burgundy, and the major cultural influence was from the Low Countries. Claus Sluter, master of the Burgundian school of sculpture, and painters Rogier van der Weyden and the van Eyck brothers all hailed from this part of the dukes' sprawling empire.

Court extravagance was highly self-conscious. There was a desire, first of all, to impress contemporaries – the lavish banquets laid on for visiting dignitaries and ambassadors constituted a kind of culinary diplomacy. Like the kings of France, the Burgundian dukes sponsored their own chroniclers, who presented one-sided and propagandistic accounts of their patrons' exploits. There was also a self-conscious embracing of the culture of medieval chivalry and courtly love. Poets and minstrels did not merely relate tales of Jason, Hercules, Charlemagne, Roland, Arthur, Lancelot and their ilk; painters, sculptors, tapestry-makers, goldsmiths, jewellers and artists in every medium made representations of them, employing allegory to mix these mythical figures with contemporary heroes. Clothing and decorations were especially lavish in the round of displays, tournaments, jousts, dances, plays, hunts, ceremonial entries and court entertainments. For example members of the chivalric Order of the Golden Fleece, founded in 1429 and based on the legend of Jason and the Argonauts, were at the heart of an elaborate entertainment known as The Feast of the Pheasant. Held in Lille in 1454, the banquet, whose centrepiece was a live pheasant wearing a gold necklace studded with precious stones, was the occasion when members ceremonially swore to undertake a crusade. As well as representing mythical heroes and scenes the Burgundian court also endeavoured to live them out.

Duke Philip the Good of Burgundy – recognizable by his imperious air – receives a book of poems from the Flemish romance writer Jean Wauquelin. The latter was an important figure in generating the chivalric atmosphere of the Burgundian court.

---

annexed in 1312, Montpellier in 1349, and in the same year, Dauphiné had passed under the control of the French, though it was reserved as a kind of appanage for the dauphin. Louis XI brought the province directly under royal control. The defeat of England and Charles the Bold had brought the dynasty Guyenne, Normandy and Burgundy. Appanages and other ducal lands reverted to the crown – Alençon territories in 1456 and Anjou possessions in 1473 are two such cases. In 1481 after an imbroglio concerning inheritance Provence and the duchy of Bar in Lorraine came under French control too. In 1491 Louis XI's successor, Charles VIII (r. 1483–98), beat off a challenge to the hand of Anne, duchess of Brittany, from Maximilian of Austria, now a widower. Charles' action ensured this proudly independent province a French future. Charles' early death without an heir required his cousin from the Orléanist line,

Christine de Pisan presents her poems to Isabel of Bavaria, queen of France, and wife of Charles VII. In the royal bed-chamber, wall-hangings display the French fleur-de-lis alongside the Bavarian diamond motif. The comfortable private space – panelled ceilings, shuttered windows, a carpeted floor, upholstered chairs – suggests a receptive attitude towards material comfort.

Louis XII (r. 1498–1515), to separate from his own long-standing wife and marry Charles' widow, in order to hold on to the province, which was fully incorporated into France in 1532.

A woman like Anne of Brittany was an object in the game of international power relations. This was still the lot of most elite women of this period. The example of Joan of Arc made no impression on the general run of relations between the sexes. Indeed Joan's habit of dressing like a man was more disturbing to her English judges than her spiritual claims, and the French were probably more enthusiastic about her as a dead martyr than as a living question-mark against the position of women. The feminist Christine de Pisan made as little impact. Her *City of Women* (1404) was a devastating critique of male misogyny and a disturbing analysis of how much women's supposed nature had been fashioned by the male (often clerical) imagination: "The books that so sayeth" was her refrain, "women made them not." Yet she had few disciples.

Valois acquisitions of the fifteenth century utterly transformed the shape and size of France. The incorporation of the Dauphiné and Provence, plus the as yet timid steps in Lorraine, represented the first major ruptures in the frontier settlement worked out six centuries earlier at Verdun in 843. These areas were integrated into France with a good degree of pragmatism, and respect for local autonomy was shown mainly because of the need to foster loyalty. Provinces were granted their own parlements (that is, high courts of law) – Toulouse in 1443, Grenoble in 1456, Dijon in 1477, Aix in 1501,

Rouen in 1515, Rennes in 1551, and so on – and often their own *chambres des comptes* and *cours des aides* as well. In some cases these were new institutions, in others they amounted to an official endorsement of institutions which pre-existed French control. Provinces brought under the French crown were also permitted to retain their representative assemblies, or Estates. Thus Burgundy retained its estates after incorporation in 1477, as did Dauphiné, Provence and Brittany. Royal ratification of compilations of customary law in the sixteenth century had much the same rationale. "The people of each province," the legal expert Guy Coquille was to argue, "has the right to establish laws over itself which are customs." By 1789 nearly a hundred such compilations had local force of law. On such institutions was a slowly evolving sense of regional identity based.

RENAISSANCE MONARCHY, RENAISSANCE SOCIETY

Monarchical power in the late fifteenth and sixteenth centuries was still, as it had been since 987, a mixture of feudal, holy and sovereign. What had changed, however, was the relative strength of each element, the context in which they operated and the implications they now conveyed. The ruler still liked to regard himself as the "seigneur of seigneurs" and there were ritualistic efforts at feudal style – the feudal levy was invoked even as late as 1695. The royal court and the bureaucracy had become the dynamos of power, however; the Church and the great feudal lords had been pulled in on a tighter rein; and more effective instruments of control over the provinces were evolving. Significantly the Estates General, which had originated as a means of feudal consultation, was a casualty of the strengthening of the state; it was not convened after 1484 – only a succession crisis in 1560 temporarily resuscitated it. The monarch retained his sacred aura: touching for the King's Evil (scrofula) continued. But the basis of royal power now lay in sovereignty. As Louis XI put it, "the general government and administration of the kingdom … and also of our good towns … belongs to us alone."

Public authority was now held to reside in the person of the dynast, and the crown was an expression of that sovereignty. It also came to evoke the community over which the ruler presided. "How hard and painful it is," noted the councillors of Cahors following the Treaty of Brétigny in 1360, which placed them in English hands, "to abandon one's natural lord and to receive an unknown and foreign master." The dynasty adroitly manipulated that sense of identity with the crown during the Hundred Years War and stimulated a gut hatred of the English – a point which obscured the fact that a great many inhabitants were as hostile to the demands and armies of the French state as they were of any other dynasty.

Maintaining the particular forms of the regions – local estates, parlements, customs and so on – constituted one of the duties of the sovereign. "Absolute" power, a phrase increasingly used by the dynasty's propagandists, meant not just being able to legislate, but also having to respect the "fundamental laws of the kingdom" while doing so. These basic laws were held to embrace the independence of the crown from the demands of the Holy Roman Empire and even the papacy. The medieval internation-

The château of Chambord, one of the most impressive works of art associated with the Renaissance. Constructed by Francis I between 1519 and 1547, its frontage is exceptionally wide, and it boasts no fewer than 365 chimneys. Louis XIV was a particular enthusiast for the château's charms.

alism which these embodied had had its day. The French king was "emperor in his own country". He regarded the Habsburg rulers who had acquired the imperial title in hereditary possession from the mid fifteenth century as equals rather than as superiors. The papacy counted for less too: the absolutism of the king implied the relativism of the pope. Philip the Fair had brought the papacy under his wing at Avignon from 1309, and rival popes at Rome and Avignon divided Western Christendom between them from 1378 to 1417. The efforts of Pope Pius V (pope 1504–72) to mobilize a crusade against the Turks failed ignominiously.

The spectacle of over-mighty subjects aping royal splendour impelled monarchs down the road of political ostentation, propaganda and display. A policy of calculated grandeur was developed in representations of royalty. Monarchs dressed differently and they engaged in rituals which set them apart from mere mortals. The golden fleur-de-lis, symbol of royal mercy, that rulers wore on their azure coronation robe combined with the crown, the sceptre and the great sword of state as the characteristic insignia of sovereignty. Court rituals became ever more showily splendid. Orders of chivalry – the Knights of the Star (1351) and the Order of Saint Michael (1469) – were a special focus for display.

The court's ostentatious patronage of the arts made the royal palace the heir of the medieval cathedral as the site of the finest and most sophisticated art. From the late fifteenth century the chivalric art and ideas of the Italian Renaissance penetrated the French court. The impact of fourteenth- and fifteenth-century Italy's re-evaluation of the art and learning of classical antiquity had previously been limited, partly by the Hundred Years War, though the papal court at Avignon and the court of "King" René in Provence had acted as channels for Italian influence. Francis I (r. 1515–47) was an especially keen lover of Italy, importing to France artists, painters and scholars: Benvenuto Cellini was a visitor, while Leonardo da Vinci died at Amboise in 1519. Francis I established the Collège Royal (later the Collège de France) as a beacon outside the university of the humanist scholarship pioneered in Italy. Architecture was relatively slow to be touched by Italian influence, partly because the flamboyant style of the Gothic was so dynamic. Yet Italian influence began to make itself felt in the design of the palaces of the Loire valley. The châteaux at Amboise, Blois, Chambord, Azay-le-Rideau and Chenonceaux bear witness to the success with which Italian style was implanted. Later, in the palace created by Francis from the late 1520s, the "School of Fontainebleau" – mainly Italian painters brought in for the château's decoration – had a considerable influence on native styles.

If Italy brought the French court Renaissance styles and values, the French king in return exported warfare to the Italian peninsula. The Italian Wars, which were to last from 1494 to 1559, testified to the confidence of a dynasty which had mastered its internal problems. Other states at this time were expanding and colonizing in the world beyond Europe – a world opened up by the establishment of routes to the East and the discovery of the Americas in 1492. The French-backed Jacques Cartier staked a claim in Canada in 1534, but in general the French dynasty gave more attention to the Italian peninsula than to the world outside Europe.

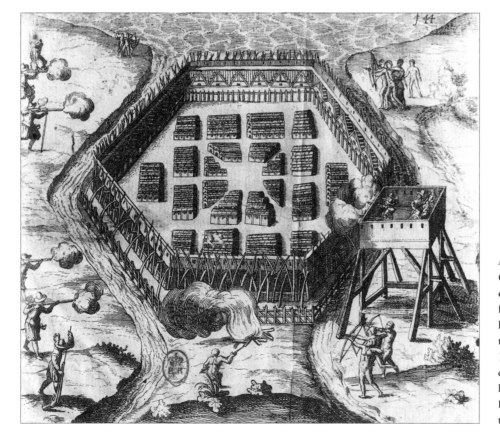

Attack on the Iroquois fort of Onondaga led by French explorer Samuel Champlain, founder of Quebec. Champlain landed in the upper reaches of the Saint Lawrence river in 1608, and in a number of expeditions joined forces with local tribes, notably the Hurons, to establish a footing in the region.

The Italian Wars acted as a channel for the aggressive tendencies of great nobles who had plagued Charles VII and Louis XI. The cause of war was a dynastic issue – the Valois claim to the kingdom of Naples championed by the young new king Charles VIII (r. 1483–98). Although the French ruler often invoked the "nation's" interests in the conduct of the wars, the French army was a mercenary force of hardened men-at-arms from Switzerland, Germany, Italy, Spain and elsewhere, as well as from France itself. The wars confirmed the close of the era of knightly warfare: the combatants were hired professional captains, or *condottieri*, now separately equipped with portable firepower. The arquebus, then the musket, joined the pike as staple battlefield arms, while the bow became a thing of the past. The big siege artillery which Charles VIII wheeled into the peninsula in 1494 enjoyed immediate success in cracking open the walls of Italian cities. Pope Julius II (pope 1503–13), rallying local powers and hiring battle-hardened Swiss troops, led the resistance. Francis I inflicted a decisive victory over the Swiss mercenary army at Marignano in 1515, however, and secured such an upper hand that the pope was obliged to sign the Concordat of Bologna in 1516, confirming the king's rights over the French Church.

The Italian Wars were coming to be about more than Italy. The peninsula became the theatre of a more general conflict that saw France in opposition to the Habsburg power lodged in the Holy Roman Empire. When the Habsburg king of Spain, Charles V, became Holy Roman Emperor in 1519 France faced the threat of encirclement – especially as Charles' dominions included the Franche-Comté and the Low Countries. The threat seemed real enough when, after defeat and capture at Pavia in 1525, Francis I was obliged to accept humiliating peace terms in the Treaty of Madrid in 1526. The French ruler fought back from this low ebb. The "Most Christian King" did not disdain alliance with German Lutheran princes and even in 1543 – for the first time in the annals of European diplomacy – the Ottoman Turks. The Treaty of Cateau-Cambrésis which brought the wars in 1559 to a close highlighted their non-Italian aspect. The French renounced any gains on the Italian peninsula, acquired Calais from the English and secured *de facto* control over the "Three Bishoprics" of Toul, Metz and Verdun in Lorraine.

There were, Louis XII was told by one of his counsellors, three things a king required in order to fight wars: "first, money; second, money; and third, money". The French state proved able to conduct these costly wars over six decades because its new structures allowed the ruler to siphon off, by means of taxes, loans and the sale of offices, a good share of the prosperity which the French economy and society had started to enjoy. The economic recovery took root in the 1450s, after the late medieval feudal crisis, and echoed a more general revival in Europe's fortunes, which the discoveries of explorers accentuated. An accurate index of recovery was population size: at a long-term low around 1450 population grew extremely rapidly from that point on, notably in the Midi. It was approaching pre-Black Death levels by the middle of the sixteenth century. France, noted Brantôme in 1572, had grown to be "as full as an egg". It helped that mortality crises had become less severe. Plagues and famines were fewer in the first

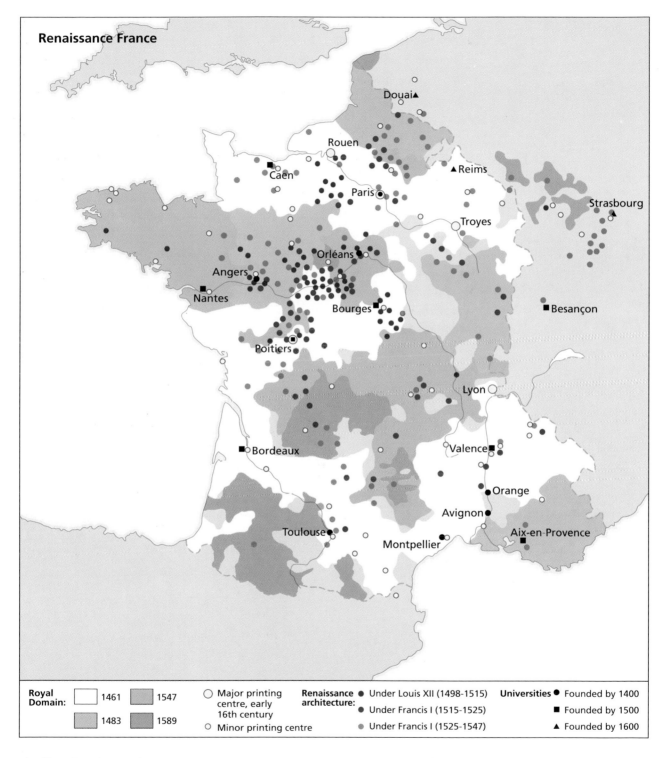

Renaissance France

Royal Domain:
☐ 1461	▨ 1547
☐ 1483	▨ 1589

○ Major printing centre, early 16th century
○ Minor printing centre

Renaissance architecture:
● Under Louis XII (1498-1515)
● Under Francis I (1515-1525)
● Under Francis I (1525-1547)

Universities
● Founded by 1400
■ Founded by 1500
▲ Founded by 1600

The fifteenth and sixteenth centuries saw the French monarchy consolidating its authority within the traditional heartlands of its power. It also durably extended its authority for the first time well beyond the line traced out at the Treaty of Verdun in 843. This was also a period of intellectual and cultural effervescence: the impact of print was combined with the growing influence of the Italian Renaissance. The Valois dynasty closely associated itself with the latter, notably in its château-building.

half of the sixteenth century, whilst from the 1490s war was conducted outside, rather than within, French frontiers.

Population growth was closely linked to agrarian recovery. Growth in output was achieved less by improvement in productivity than by extending cultivable land after the disasters of the Black Death and the Hundred Years War – nettles and brambles were cut back, scrubland cleared, the margins reduced. The spread of two high-yield crops furthered growth after 1600: peasants in the west began to sow buckwheat, while in the south a wonder-crop from the New World – maize – allowed more mouths to be fed on the same amount of land. The shift away from medieval manorial farming to peasant-based agriculture provided a more receptive context for increased production. Semi-independent peasant families had a keener incentive than oppressed serfs to produce more for an expanding market for foodstuffs.

The demographic disasters of the late fourteenth and early fifteenth century seem to have been particularly severe in the towns and cities: Limoges was said to be down to its last five inhabitants in 1435. By the late fifteenth century towns were booming again. Paris had grown to well over a quarter of a million by 1550. Between 1500 and 1600 Rouen grew from 40,000 to 75,000, Lyon from 40,000 to 58,000, Bordeaux from 25,000 to 35,000. Towns acquired a broader manufacturing base, and waves of urban building were a testament to new levels of wealth. Many nobles now built town resi-

The Île de la Cité and the Left Bank, from a mid sixteenth-century map of Paris. Notre Dame cathedral overlooks two bridges, one of which is built over by the great Parisian hospital, the Hôtel-Dieu. The Sorbonne is visible to the right, in the "Quarter of the Schools" or – because of the scholarly *lingua franca* – the "Latin Quarter".

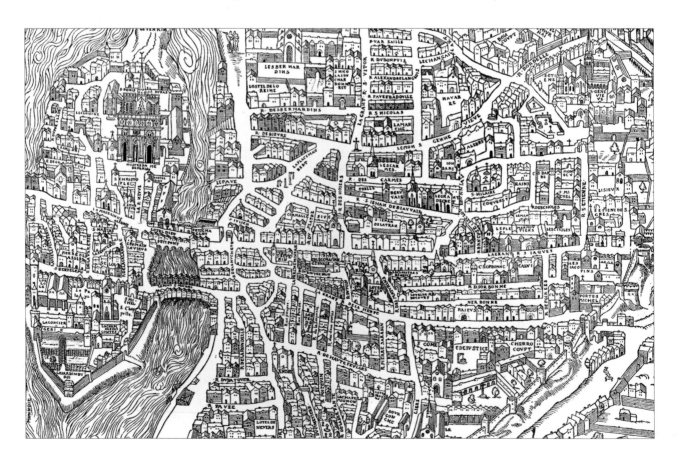

dences and participated in urban cultural life. Port cities did especially well, notably those which had formerly been controlled by enemies or rivals of the Valois dynasty – Marseille, Rouen, Bordeaux, Nantes – and which now passed fully into the kingdom. Saint-Malo, La Rochelle and newly created Le Havre also prospered. In the south-east, Lyon was a particularly dynamic and cosmopolitan centre; its situation close to the Italian and Swiss frontiers brought it a colourful blend of Flemish, Swiss, German and Italian immigrants, enticed by its very active fairs and its prowess in the banking and manufacturing spheres.

As well as enjoying more intense economic exchange within a much enlarged zone of activity, western Europe began to experience something of a communications revolution from the late fifteenth century. Print marked the greatest advance in human communications since the advent of writing. Pioneered by craftsman John Gutenberg in Mainz in 1450 the use of movable type and the printing press derived its significance from a range of supplementary innovations from the thirteenth century – the manufacturing of paper, the development of ink, the use of woodblock printing and the invention of eye-glasses. The first print shop in France was established in Paris in 1470 (though there was one in German-speaking Strasbourg from 1458) and by 1490 there were nine in France as a whole, and three times as many by the turn of the century. Books produced in the more dynamic publishing centres of the Rhineland and Italy also circulated in abundance. In the first half of the sixteenth century Paris built up a reputation as one of Europe's foremost publishing centres, while cosmopolitan Lyon also enjoyed a European reputation.

Print, a cheaper, more profuse and more manageable form than manuscript, created a new market for books. Reading circles were expanded far beyond the savants and scholars of the manuscript age, helped by the development of postal services from Louis XI's reign. There was a shift in the language of communication too. Joachim du Bellay's *Defence and Illustration of the French Language* (1549) reflected the change in readership and legitimized French as a means of learned and polite debate alongside, and sometimes over, Latin. The poets of the Pléiade (du Bellay, Ronsard, Jodelle and others), writing in mid century, established the basis of French as a resource for poetic expression. The extraordinary writings of François Rabelais highlighted the language's richness and diversity. Print also allowed the Bible to be made far more widely available in the vernacular. Occitanian, Picard and other languages and dialects which had spawned a literature in the Middle Ages were now in disarray, and remained largely spoken languages. The Edict of Villers-Cotterets in 1539, which made French the language of all legal and official documents, demonstrated that French was now the language of power as well as of literary expression.

It would be wrong to overestimate the impact of these economic and cultural changes on French society. Despite the prestige of French as a written language it would long remain a minority spoken language in France. Even in the 1790s one French person in four could not speak French and as many could not conduct a lengthy conversation in it. Breton, German, Spanish, Basque, along with Occitanian

Rabelais

A Franciscan, then Benedictine monk, who ended his life as curé at Meudon on the outskirts of Paris, François Rabelais (1494–1553) transcended his Church career in his extraordinarily profuse and multifaceted writings on Gargantua and Pantagruel, published from the 1530s onwards. Probably more important than the Church was his training as a doctor in the highly regarded Montpellier University. The irreverent laughter and black body humour that mark his writings have much of the perennial medical student about them – as do the good cheer, toilet jokes, recurrent inebriation

Frontispiece from a volume in Rabelais' Pantagruel and Gargantua series.

and relentless womanizing celebrated within them. All these qualities helped to win Rabelais a lasting reputation as a drunkard and buffoon.

If he was a buffoon, he was, however, an immensely erudite one. His works link up with medieval farces and theatre, but also exemplify many of the concerns of the Renaissance. Stays in Paris and Montpellier and visits to Italy put him closely in touch with humanism. He was the first to teach the Greek classics in Greek at Montpellier University. The swarming and inventive burlesquerie of his works teems with verbal fireworks and abstruse puns and language-games. And his black humour sustains an endless satire and commentary on current follies.

and numerous dialects and patois, still held sway in many areas, especially among the peasantry, urban workers and women. Similarly, for all the importance of the world discoveries, the boom in international commerce and the revolution in communications, four-fifths of French men and women found marriage partners within a radius of fifteen miles of their birthplace (and a great many in the same village). In addition perhaps 90 to 95 per cent of all their business and economic exchanges took place within a radius of between fifteen and twenty-five miles. For the great mass of the French people the Renaissance was about fixity and stability as much as fluidity and exchange.

Perhaps more important than cultural innovation in sparking change was a new economic fact of life – namely inflation. Its roots lay in the growth in demand caused by population outstripping resources, plus the import of precious metals from the New World. Writing in 1566 the humanist Jean Bodin reckoned that the price of commodities had increased tenfold over the previous century. He exaggerated: though grain increased by 700 per cent over the century as a whole, the overall rate was only between 2 and 3 per cent a year. Though this seems pitifully low compared with twentieth-century experiences, in the context of early modern society it acted as an economic test to which all had to apply their minds, and which produced both winners and losers.

For the commercially adept, inflation generated profit. The century was rife with success stories, as the expanding waistlines of the urbanized nobility and the commercial, manufacturing and professional bourgeoisie bore witness. On the land, seigneurs who had commuted their rents to money payments that did not adjust to inflation lost out, while those who levied rents in kind or who adjusted their rents in line with inflation stood a chance of doing well. Peasants who produced for the expanding market for foodstuffs also made their fortunes, and these *coqs de village,* or peasants-made-good, increasingly lorded it over their fellows. On the other hand, pressure on land caused by population growth led to holdings being split up below the level of self-sufficiency, and small peasants were forced to purchase their daily bread on a seller's market. Wages failed to keep pace with prices, causing a long-term impoverishment of the lower ranks of rural society, detectable in a marked decline in meat-eating. Similarly in the towns all individuals on a fixed salary – be they domestic skivvies or university professors – risked deterioration in their living standards. The poorer urban labourers and craftsmen suffered most, though. Town governments became increasingly anxious about the problem of open distress presented on the streets of the city by hordes of disinherited peasants, unemployed workers and ne'er-do-wells. From the 1520s they instituted programmes of poor relief, providing alms for those adjudged "deserving" paupers, punishment for the "undeserving" and work, where possible, for the unemployed. These were inadequate to meet the scale of the problem, and contemporaries widely blamed the pauper hordes for plague outbreaks and for urban riots. These problems constituted the downside of a period of economic growth.

Although for many the threat from below seemed to risk spoiling the splendours of Renaissance society, it was divisions within the social elite which brought the days of optimism to an end. The signing of the Treaty of Cateau-Cambrésis saw the return within French frontiers of a warlike nobility. For two generations they had channelled their aggression into the Italian peninsula, but their reappearance heralded the return of civil strife, in the Wars of Religion.

Detail of the frontispiece from Sébastien Gryphe, *La Police de l'Aulmosne de Lyon,* 1539. The early sixteenth century witnessed widespread municipal reorganization of poor relief. Here the city notables of Lyon make distributions to the ranks of the poor and the needy.

THE WARS OF RELIGION: FROM VALOIS TO BOURBON

The death of Henry II (r. 1547–59) in a jousting accident opened a lengthy period of Valois weakness. This was not to end until a new dynasty, the Bourbons, had become fully established. Henry II's heir, the sickly Francis II (r. 1559–60), did not last long, and the succession passed over the next fifteen years to his younger brothers, first the minor Charles IX (r. 1560–74), then the much-slandered Henry III (r. 1574–89). The period from 1560 was dominated by the Florentine widow of Henry II, Catherine de Medici (1519–89), who served as regent down to 1574 and who remained a force in court politics through to her death in 1589. Domination by a woman and a foreigner – in a state which increasingly prized French identity and afforded women little space within the public sphere – aggravated serious weakness in the dynasty.

As was usual in such times, government became the plaything of noble families, each enormously wealthy and influential in its own right and each enjoying extensive provincial support. The nobility more or less monopolized high office in all branches of the state – finance, justice, the armed services, the Church – and were the main beneficiaries of royal generosity. They held the lion's share of land and dominated rural society via the continuing system of seigneurial privileges (dues, economic monopolies, judicial prerogatives and so on). Patronage and clientage constituted an important cement for the power of the great, who built up wedges of support among the provincial nobility, to whom they were often related. A chivalric/feudal ethos of service bound patron and retinue together in a potentially threatening relationship for the state – it entailed military support, even against the monarch. In return patrons, through influence on the royal council, aimed to secure gifts, pensions and offices as ways of maintaining their network of patronage. The family problems of the Valois dynasty allowed the destructive aspects of these perennial features of noble life to emerge more strongly.

So, who were the key players in this aristocratic struggle for dominance? The Guise family, which claimed descent from Charlemagne, was perhaps the most turbulent and influential of these power blocs. There were two generations of the family involved in the Religious Wars (1561–98). François, one of the greatest military commanders of the day, and his brother Charles, Cardinal de Lorraine, the richest prelate in France, secured key posts on the Regency Council established by Catherine de Medici in 1559. The sons of François – Henry, duke of Guise, Louis, cardinal of Guise, and Charles, duke of Mayenne – were dominant in the later stages of the wars. The Montmorency dynasty, "first barons of Christendom" in their own estimation, were rivals to the Guise long before 1559. One of the clan, Protestant Gaspard de Coligny, won the regent's ear in the late 1560s and early 1570s. Finally inheritance, marriage and luck had by the fifteenth century made the Bourbon dynasty perhaps the last of the great feudal potentates. When Jeanne d'Albret, niece of Francis I, and queen of the tiny French principality of Navarre, had married Antoine, duke of Bourbon-Vendôme, she ensured the merger of two massive feudal inheritances into a single unit. Their son Henry, king of

Suzanne Gaudry, witch

Suzanne Gaudry, a native of Flanders, was executed by the court of Mons ...

On this same day [27 June 1652], being at the place of torture. The prisoner [Suzanne Gaudry], being strapped down, was admonished to maintain herself in her first confession [of witchcraft] ...

– Said that she denies everything she has said ...

– Feeling herself being strapped down, says that she is not a witch, while struggling to cry.

– Told that ... she declared herself to be a witch without any threat.

– Says that she confessed it and that she is not a witch, and being a little stretched [on the rack] screams ceaselessly that she is not a witch ...

Being more tightly stretched upon the torture-rack, urged to maintain her confessions.

– Said that it was true she is a witch and that she would maintain her confessions ...

The sickening records of witch-trials show their victims being subjected to stringent cross-examination and judicial torture. Under the so-called inquisitorial method of judicial procedure now in force in most of Continental Europe, no punishment could be pronounced without a confession.

This inquisitorial method of trial produced throughout Europe between the late fifteenth and late seventeenth century perhaps as many as 100,000 executions. Northern and eastern France, along with the Low Countries, Switzerland and west Germany, provided the bulk of the cases. Four-fifths of those executed for witchcraft were, like Suzanne Gaudry, women. This predominance can be explained, in part, by the fact that women were often engaged in white magic, the composing of herbal remedies and the like, which became confused by ardent examining judges with full-scale witchcraft, including signing a pact with the Devil. More importantly the image of a witch that most people held in their minds – lustful, vindictive, swayed by passions, impervious to reason – was not far removed from the more general views of women held by clergy and the elite.

The spirit of religious intolerance at large in Europe in the sixteenth century provided a particularly fruitful setting for large-scale persecution. The trials fell in number in the seventeenth century as religious passions dimmed.

Public burning in 1634 of the parish priest Urbain Grandier, convicted of having bewitched the nuns of a convent in Loudun.

Navarre (1553–1610), was a major player in the dynastic struggle from the late 1560s – and would ultimately succeed Henry III as Henry IV, king of France (r. 1589–1610).

The clash of dynasts was exacerbated by four factors. First, clients clustered around patrons, requiring pensions, gifts and favours in return for their support, and often pushing for military solutions to problems. Second, each side tended to look to foreign powers for support. Philip II of Spain gave armed support to the Guise cause, while Elizabeth's England and the Low Countries also interfered. Third, the death in 1584

Anonymous late sixteenth-century oil-painting portrait of the three Guise brothers, champions of the extreme Catholic cause in the last decades of the sixteenth century. Henry de Lorraine (1550–88) is shown in the centre, with the Cardinal de Lorraine (1555–88) on his right and the duke de Mayenne (1554–1611) on the left.

of Henry III's younger brother, the duke of Alençon, meant that in the absence of a child from Henry's III's marriage there was no direct heir. There were a number of rival claimants. The Guises, for example, with their Carolingian forebears, could even claim (some said with justice) that Hugh Capet had been a usurper! The person with the best legal claim was one of the competing dynasts, Henry of Navarre. This seemed bad enough. But to make matters worse Henry was a Protestant. Religion was the fourth – and most important – factor inflaming the dynastic squabbles in the Religious Wars.

In some ways the civil wars of the late sixteenth century were an old story; what made them new was religion. Struggle between king and nobles, centre and periphery, became inextricably connected with the new religious division between Catholics and Protestants (also known as Huguenots) which had emerged out of the Reformation. Coligny and some of the Montmorency clan were Protestants, as were Henry of Navarre and a number of other Bourbons, while the Guises were the champions of Catholicism.

The Reformation, which began in Martin Luther's Germany in 1517, was to split Christendom apart. The spread of the Lutheran message would have been unthinkable without the greater ease of communications in post-Gutenberg Europe. It was, significantly, the "Affair of the Placards" in 1534, when broadsheets denouncing the Mass were posted all round Paris, that had pushed the royal government into a policy of overt repression of Protestantism. A small number of Lutherans had been burnt at the stake from 1523 onwards, and from 1540 trials proliferated. Henry II intensified the repression: a sinisterly named *chambre ardente* ("burning chamber") was created in the parlement of Paris in 1547 to consider cases of heresy; the death penalty was decreed for Lutheran beliefs in 1551; and in the same year the Jesuits, zealous agents of the Counter-Reformation, were allowed to establish a college in Paris.

Hostility towards Protestantism was part of a more general spirit of intolerance abroad at this time, which mocked the humane views of the Renaissance. Attacks on

Waldensian heretics in the Alpine valleys in the 1540s caused over 3,000 deaths. The so-called "witch-craze" was in full swing too. Numerous individuals were burnt at the stake for alleged membership of a diabolical counter-religion. Most of these were women, and women were also at issue in the attacks on organized prostitution which began in the early sixteenth century. The Council of Trent (1545–63) also marked a shift in the Catholic establishment's view of Protestantism – towards a more aggressive approach. The increasingly bitter religious struggles were inflamed by print, which spread prejudice and bigotry as well as humane or civilized values. Both Catholics and Protestants made full use of the resources of print – in the form of broadsheets, posters, engravings, books, pamphlets – to complement the spoken word (sermons, debates, plays, trials) and visual propaganda (religious ceremonies, processions, festivals).

French Protestantism eventually followed a Calvinist rather than a Lutheran road. Jean Calvin was born in Noyon, near Compiègne, and studied in Paris before realizing that the intolerant atmosphere of the capital ill suited his views. In 1541 he settled in Geneva, which became the Rome of organized Protestantism, sending out missionaries to spread the word throughout France and western Europe. Calvin's *Institutions*, which had appeared in Latin in 1536, were issued in French in 1541, and became the basis of Calvinist theology. By the late 1550s a broad national structure was emerging. The new faith was genuinely popular and nationwide. It had won perhaps up to half of France's nobility and a third of the bourgeoisie, and was scattered throughout France, with particularly strong outposts in the south, the south-west, the Poitou and Normandy, as well as in Alsace and Lorraine. It tended to be more urban than rural –

Procession de la Ligue sur la Place de Grève (1590) by Bunel. In 1590 the Catholic League's supporters in Paris, in the form of 1,300 fully armed monks, paraded before a papal legate to show their resolve to fight the Huguenots.

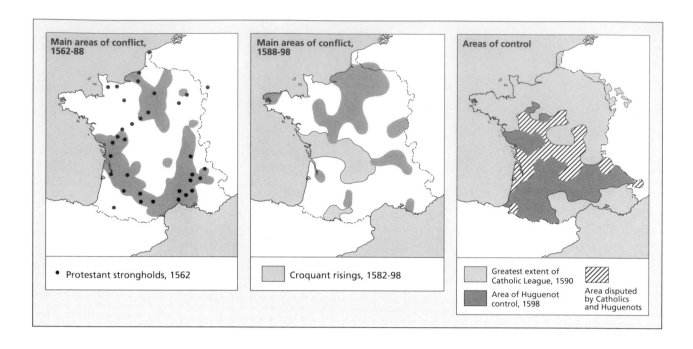

The Wars of Religion. Religious conflict in the early decades of the Wars of Religion (left) was often located within an inverted crescent-shaped area running from La Rochelle in the west southwards through Aquitaine and Lower Languedoc, and up the river Rhône to the north of Lyon in the east. Here Huguenot nobles such as the Montmorency had their strongholds, but townships and (especially) universities in this area had also become hotbeds of the Calvinist faith. The struggle in the 1580s and 1590s (centre) concentrated on the north and on the Paris region, where the Catholic League was most dominant (right).

though the peasants of the Cévennes were to prove the doughtiest of Huguenots. In addition Protestantism attracted women; its emphasis on spiritual and intellectual growth for all believers had a special appeal. Some educated court women were initially sympathetic to the reformed faith, which also came to attract many women from humbler backgrounds.

With some 2,150 churches, numbering between one and two million individuals, French Calvinism posed a difficult problem for the failing Valois dynasty. It was simply too big for the government to adopt the strategy towards Protestantism found in most of southern Europe (Spain, the Italian states), that is, liquidation. On the other hand it was not strong enough for the "north European solution" adopted in some German states to be viable – namely Protestant takeover of the state apparatus. The royal family (after some vacillation), key courtiers, the senior law courts (notably the parlements) and the capital city all proved staunchly Catholic. When the crown veered towards religious toleration, these groupings tugged it backwards by failing to operate royal policy.

Religious and political tensions came swiftly to the surface in the regency period. In the Amboise conspiracy of 1560 Huguenots made a bid to kidnap the young Francis II, in order to remove him from the influence of the senior Guise brothers. The move scuppered the valiant efforts of Chancellor Michel de l'Hospital, in the Colloquium of Poissy, to work out conditions of compromise between the two Churches. The concession of freedom of worship was fragile indeed, especially once a line of blood marking out the two sides had been drawn. In 1562 François de Guise, coming across a community of Huguenots worshipping at Vassy, sent in his troops and caused the death of over a hundred individuals, many of them women.

Between 1562 and 1598 a sombre procession of eight religious wars, punctuated by eight truces, shook the state (1562–3; 1567–8; 1569–70; 1573–4; 1576; 1577; 1579–80; 1585–98). Below the surface of high politics moreover a sickening cycle of confessional violence and slaughter was enacted at grassroots level throughout France. At first the lines of force of the struggle were based on the cities, but these soon aligned themselves with "protectors" drawn from the high aristocracy. Catherine de Medici tried with ever-decreasing success to remain above the conflict, and she came resoundingly down in the Catholic camp in 1572 in the infamous "Saint Bartholomew's Massacre". She connived in the murder of prominent Protestants, including Coligny, who had gathered in Paris for the marriage of the king's sister, Marguerite, to Henry of Navarre, but then matters got out of hand. Perhaps 3,000 Huguenots were butchered in Paris and a further 8,000 killed subsequently in provincial cities. Henry of Navarre converted to Catholicism in Paris, but renounced the faith when safely out of the capital, an action which won him papal disqualification as heir to the throne.

With Henry of Navarre seemingly unacceptable to Catholics, and with no living Valois heir in evidence, the struggle took an increasingly desperate turn. Protestants dug themselves in behind sturdy ramparts in those cities where they held the reins of government, and formed self-defence networks. Extreme Catholics, spurred on by the Guise brothers, formed the Catholic League, whose aggressively anti-Protestant policies and increasingly radical constitutional theories brought them into more and more open opposition to Henry III. In 1588 Henry III's attempt to rally Paris away from support for the Guises led to the pro-Guise "Day of the Barricades". When Henry III in desperation had the Guise brothers assassinated at Blois, the "Council of Sixteen" governing Paris called for "tyrannicide" and organized a kind of religious Terror, while the duke of Mayenne formed northern cities into a Catholic municipal league. Boxed in, Henry III allied with Henry of Navarre to besiege Paris. A fanatical supporter of the League, Jacques Clément, assassinated him, however, and Henry of Navarre was forced to lift the siege, to general Parisian rejoicing.

Henry III's death in 1589 seemed likely to break the French state asunder. On his death-bed he recognized as his heir Henry of Navarre, the rightful claimant by Salic Law, who at once took the title Henry IV. Ultra-Catholics rejected him, proposing a number of other candidates and eliciting Spanish military aid. They played their cards badly, however. There was no obvious single candidate around whom to rally, while the social extremism of the League in Paris, where the "Sixteen" arrested and executed members of the Paris parlement, alienated much solid bourgeois support. The Catholic League exuded a crude spirit of municipal democracy, but Henry IV could increasingly count on moderate Catholics – the so-called *politiques* – who were willing to make room for Protestantism if this meant the return of social harmony and an end to killing. "O Paris," bemoaned a *politique* pamphlet issued in Paris, "which is no longer Paris, but rather a dark cavern of wild beasts, a citadel of Spaniards, Walloons and Neapolitans, a refuge and a sure retreat for robbers, murderers and assassins …"

Henry IV's struggle for his kingdom was a tough one. His decision to convert to Catholicism in 1593 won support and buttressed the *politique* position. Having

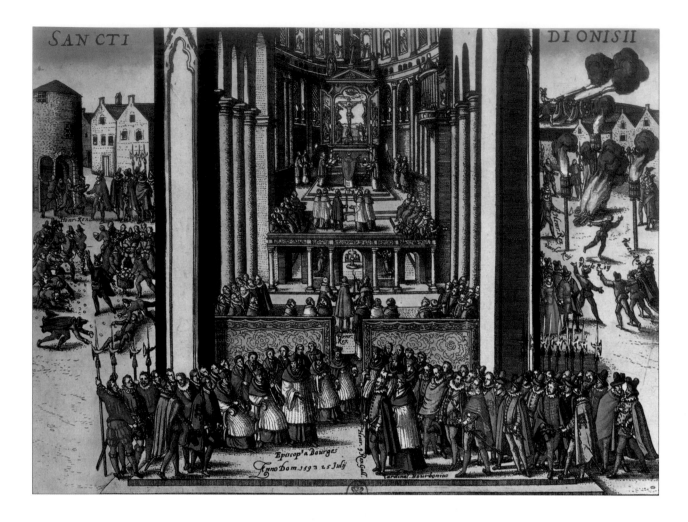

SANCTI

DIONISII

This engraving, designed for a German audience, shows Henry IV receiving mass at Saint-Denis and abjuring his Protestant faith. The picture is a kind of comic strip, with the monarch appearing in a number of places – distributing alms to the left, for example – as well as inside the church.

famously, in his own words, adjudged Paris "worth a Mass", he entered the city in 1594. Opposition was gradually unravelling and Henry spent the next four years threatening, negotiating with and buying the support of the rebels. His Edict of Nantes, issued in 1598, was a classic compromise between the two sides. Freedom of conscience and equality of rights were roundly declared, but Protestants were allowed to worship only in select locations where they had a strong community. In addition they were permitted to retain their ramparts as a guarantee of religious autonomy in 151 *places de sûreté*.

The Edict of Nantes looks far more reasonable to subsequent historians than it did to most contemporaries: the pope roundly declared it "the worst edict imaginable"; the parlements were especially concerned with the constitutional implications of the act, and the Rouen parlement only finally gave its assent as late as 1609. Even many Huguenots, whose numbers had fallen from two to less than one million, were wary. Assassination plots aimed at the king – about twenty in the course of his reign – continued unabated. The Edict was given a chance to work, however, by Henry's signing the Treaty of Vervins in 1598 with Philip II of Spain, thereby ending foreign involvement in France's civil strife. Vervins endorsed the basic positions of the 1559 Cateau-Cambrésis Treaty. France had, almost miraculously, come through forty years of civil strife without enduring significant territorial losses to greedy neighbours.

Yet if the political structures stood fast, the economy was in a lamentable state. Trade was languishing and manufacturing output was probably down by half. The wars had not been another Hundred Years War: deaths were limited and population levels overall stagnated rather than fell markedly. War, famine and disease did, however, have some impact. Population losses were severe in areas where military activity had been intense. The wars coincided too with an apparent worsening of the climate: a "Little Ice Age" set in around 1550 (and would last to the middle of the nineteenth century), characterized by cold and wet winters. This led to a string of severe harvest failures and periods of high prices (notably in 1563, 1565–6, 1573–7, 1586, 1590–2 and 1596–7). To make matters worse, there was a resurgence of plague in the 1580s and 1590s. These catastrophes, combined with continued state tax demands, triggered discontent. There was a major peasant rising – the so-called "Croquants" – in 1594/5 in the south-west, and other such disturbances in Normandy and Brittany.

The triumph of Henry IV in ending the Wars of Religion demonstrated that French society had turned away, if only temporarily, from the aim of constructing a unitary Catholic state. The price would have been enormous bloodshed and social turbulence. There was now a new political landscape grounded in hopes for social tranquillity, and French men and women must have waited nervously to see what peace and the new dynasty would bring.

CHAPTER 6

From Counter-Reformation to Enlightenment

The change of dynasty, from Valois to Bourbon, seemed initially to make little impression on the scale and impact of the regime's problems and on accompanying social and economic tensions. In some senses the spirit of the Wars of Religion was not wholly played out until the Fronde (1648–52), a combination of state bankruptcy, civil war and popular uprising. Yet beneath the surface major structural changes were taking place, notably through the "cardinal ministers" Richelieu and Mazarin, who dominated the king's council from 1624 through to 1661, when Louis XIV assumed full power. It was thanks largely to his predecessors that the "Sun King" was able to dominate European international relations from the 1680s through to his death in 1715. He did so, however, only by landing his successors with very considerable financial, economic and political problems.

If the period witnessed the progressive deterioration of the political climate in the run-up to the Revolution of 1789, it also contained two remarkable cultural movements: the Counter-Reformation, which had a massive effect on the social life and *mentalités* of the French people; and the Enlightenment of the eighteenth century, a diverse intellectual and cultural movement with its roots in the economic prosperity of the period. The Enlightenment would have a part to play, moreover, in changes in attitudes towards religion and government which had a major impact in 1789.

THE COUNTER-REFORMATION

France's change of dynasty, from Valois to Bourbon, marked a notable defeat for intolerant ultra-Catholicism. Religious tolerance was championed by a monarch whose tenure was still fragile. Indeed it was not until 1607 that Henry IV felt safe enough in his possession of the crown to authorize the amalgamation into France of his power-base in the Béarn. It was one of the ironies of the seventeenth century that the monarchy's growing fame as the most powerful and prestigious in Europe was accompanied by a revival of Catholicism and an intolerance of religious dissidence. Beginning with Henry's successor Louis XIII (r. 1610–43), the backlash reached its apotheosis in the Edict of Fontainebleau of 1685. By this, Louis XIV (r. 1643–1715) formally revoked the Edict of Nantes of 1598 and re-established Catholicism as the sole authorized religion.

The pathway towards Fontainebleau opened up soon after Henry IV's assassination in 1610 at the hands of a fanatical Catholic extremist. The first Bourbon's early adherence to Protestantism was a guarantee that he would resist backsliding towards an ultra-Catholicism still tarnished by unsavoury memories of the Catholic League. Louis XIII, in contrast, had been born (in 1601) a Catholic, he dedicated his reign to the Virgin Mary, and his youthful marriage to the daughter of the king of Spain, Anne of

Austria, sealed an alliance with the Habsburgs. In 1620 the decision of Louis XIII, influenced by his favourite the duke de Luynes, to enforce the precepts of the Edict of Nantes in still Protestant Béarn (where the Huguenots enjoyed a monopoly of religious worship) sparked off widespread armed opposition in the Midi. The monarch stood firm over what he took to be an attempt to set up a state within a state, and in the Peace of Montpellier in 1622 reduced Protestant garrison towns to two – Montauban and La Rochelle. Further Huguenot revolts in the 1620s climaxed in 1627, when the duke de Rohan led armed insurrection in Languedoc, while the mayor of La Rochelle made an alliance with the English, against whom Louis XIII had just declared war. La Rochelle, despite English aid, fell to a siege conducted by Louis XIII in 1628 that reduced the city by starvation from 30,000 to around 6,000 inhabitants. The Peace of Alès in 1629 reaffirmed the religious tolerance of 1598, but rights of assembly and garrison towns were withdrawn.

The decision at Alès to deal mercifully with the Huguenot rebels paid dividends for the crown, in that French Protestants now became almost more royalist than the king, and gave up dabbling in politics. The military and political threat of Protestantism had been effectively neutralized. The dynasty's decision to ally with Protestant princes

Colbert Presents Louis XIV to the Members of the Royal Academy of Sciences in 1667 by Henri Testelin. This totally fictitious scene dates from 1667, the king not actually visiting the Academy until 1682. Designed to reflect his glory, the Academy also served the role of state scientific and technological consultative agency.

VOICY LEGRAND
ROY
LOVIS XIIII.

IL donne Audiance, iusques au plus pauure de ses suiets, pour terminer promptement leurs procez & differans.
Salomon, s'assit sur le Throsne, pour Iuger ces deux pauures femmes, qui plaidoient à qui seroit l'Enfant.
Nostre Monarque l'imite parfaitement, & nos grands Rois & Empereurs, Charles-Magne, entreaultres, & Louis Auguste.
Ils donnoient des Audiances publiques comme luy, ils s'y estoient obliges par loy expresse, & l'auoient fait publier par tout le Royaume.
DE AVDIENTIA REGIS.

Royal propaganda, showing Louis XIV hearing the petitions of the poor. The text compares him to Solomon, Charlemagne and Saint Louis. In spite of appearances, Louis presided over the erosion of the country's representative institutions – the Estates General did not meet in his reign, and many provincial estates fell into abeyance.

against Austria and Spain in the Thirty Years War (1618–48) seemed to buttress the Huguenot position. Yet the situation was far from stable. In particular Catholicism was undergoing a process of rebirth in the aftermath of the Council of Trent (1545–63). The council had crystallized Catholic doctrine around anti-Protestant positions, while also inaugurating a battle for souls. The Church was to bring orthodox piety to the masses who, it was increasingly apparent, were often ignorant of Catholic doctrine and vulnerable to conversion to Protestantism. Though its precepts were never accepted as state law by the Bourbons, the spirit of Trent infiltrated the French Church from the late sixteenth century onwards.

From the 1650s Louis XIV's personal hostility towards Protestantism also weakened the Huguenot position. After 1659 he forbade national synods from meeting, while provincial synods began to be harassed. Between 600 and 700 churches (or "temples") were demolished – probably the greatest campaign of architectural destruction before the French Revolution. Restrictions on Protestant entry into the professions and the guilds tightened. In 1676 a Conversion Fund was established which granted small sums to Protestants who renounced their faith. But where bribery failed, coercion was tried. State officials began to force Protestants to pay supplements on tax, and from 1681 soldiers in the Poitou were billeted on Protestant families. The latter practice, soon known as *dragonnades*, was introduced with some glee in the Languedoc, where the brutality of the soldiery produced tens of thousands of "conversions" – of a sincerity one can rightly doubt. The spectacle was enough to persuade Louis XIV that a full-scale attempt to crush Protestantism was in order. In 1685 the revocation of the Edict of Nantes was decreed. Protestant pastors were to leave France and Protestant worship was forbidden.

The Edict of Fontainebleau was greeted with an astonishing measure of national and international enthusiasm. Yet Louis' wager that the Protestants could be easily brought over proved disastrously wrong. Armed resistance was soon crushed, but extensive repression was required, causing mass emigration, supported by pastors whose watchword was "Leave Babylon". Perhaps 200,000 to 250,000 individuals – roughly a quarter of all French Huguenots – many of them professional people and skilled workers, left France to join the ranks of France's economic competitors England, the Netherlands and Germany. The repression provoked the War of the Camisards (1702–4) in the Cévennes, where Calvinist peasants conducted crude but effective guerrilla operations against the state.

Protestantism went underground, and the period of the *Désert* ("wilderness") began. Ironically Louis XIV was on his deathbed in 1715 when the first national synod of the survivor churches was held in the Cévennes, foreshadowing the revival of secret national organization throughout the eighteenth century. When, on the eve of the Revolution in 1788, many of the strictures of 1685 were lifted, the Protestant Church stood at some 600,000 members.

Eradication of Protestantism was only one of the objectives of the revived Catholic Church in the seventeenth century. The Counter-Reformation had its roots in a broad-based reform movement that predated Luther and Calvin. It endeavoured to remove ignorance as well as doctrinal error, and to spread principles of godliness so as to produce a Catholicization, even a Christianization, of society. Prominent in this movement were laypeople committed to these new principles who were seeking to bring about, through the quest for Christian perfection in the world, a "reformation of manners" every bit as thorough-going as that preached by puritans. Later wickedly satirized for hypocrisy in Molière's *Tartuffe* (1664), the *dévots* (the "devout"), as they were called, operated at both national and local levels, and were particularly active between the 1630s and early 1660s under the aegis of the Company of the Holy Sacrament.

Founded by the saintly duke de Ventadour in the late 1620s, the Company of the Holy Sacrament comprised a network of activist clerics and laymen, drawn from the upper reaches of the high nobility and state bureaucracy in Paris and the cream of local society in the provinces. Operating under a cloak of secrecy, the company numbered over fifty branches, co-ordinated from Paris. Activists were in the vanguard of the campaign to reduce Protestant rights at local level prior to the Revocation of the Edict of Nantes. But they were also engaged in an enormously varied range of charitable tasks – assisting the poor, visiting prisoners, redeeming prostitutes, reforming hospitals, educating the children of the poor, clamping down on profanity during religious holi-

The Camisards

I had several inspirations by which I was told to prepare to take up arms to fight with my brothers against our persecutors, that I would bring iron and fire against the priests of the Roman Church and that I would burn their altars ... At dusk ... we set out for Saint-André-de-Lancize to carry out another order uttered by my mouth, which was to put to death the priest of the locality, to burn his house, to topple the altar and to set fire to the church ...

This account given by Abraham Mazel, one of the earliest leaders of the Protestant Camisard rebels who resisted Louis XIV's imposition of Catholicism in 1685, goes on to recount how the church was indeed burned down and the priest murdered. Such atrocities were common currency in this period of civil and religious strife, which took the form of open insurrection in the Cévennes – the southern foothills of the Massif Central – between 1702 and 1704. The *dragonnades* of royal troops in the 1680s had forced Protestant pastors out of France, leaving their flocks demoralized and leaderless. An epidemic of prophesying and speaking with tongues by (largely peasant) children and adults had pushed the movement in a millenarian direction: the end of the world seemed nigh.

The decision of the local intendant to

meet resistance with stern repression escalated the conflict. The Camisards – so named because they made *camisades* (night attacks) or else because they fought in peasant shirts, or camisoles – followed their leaders' inspirations blindly. They went into conflict against battle-hardened troops singing psalms (a form of psychological warfare which could be effective). The success of the operations owed much, however, to the mountainous and moorland terrain in

the Cévennes, which regular troops found difficult to negotiate. The Camisards might have been an even greater threat had they managed, as was planned on several occasions, to link up militarily with their fellow Protestants from England. The open insurrection was unravelled by a mixture of toughness and conciliation and ended in 1704, but guerrilla operations rumbled on spasmodically for a decade. The Cévennes would be one of the strongholds of the clandestine Protestant Church that re-emerged after the death of Louis XIV in 1715.

A Huguenot is forced to sign his conversion to Catholicism.

days and festivals, repressing folkloric practices more pagan than Christian and so on. A whole spate of new charitable foundations – hospitals, foundlings' homes, prostitutes' reformatories, charity schools and the like – was their enduring monument.

Though the national organization of the Company of the Holy Sacrament was broken up by Mazarin in 1661, local activists continued their moralizing and charitable works long afterwards. The *dévots* aimed to make universal a notion of piety in tune with society's alleged moral and spiritual needs. This line was also characteristic of the post-Trent work of the new orders and a revitalized secular (or non-monastic) clergy. A new model of pious activism was evident in the religious orders which emerged after Trent. Pastoral care rather than mysticism was the key. Imaginative and dynamic organizers stepped forwards, such as Cardinal Pierre de Bérulle, founder of the Oratorian teaching order in France; Saint François de Sales, co-founder of the Order of the Visitation and author of the *Introduction à la vie dévote* (1608), one of the best-sellers of post-Trent godliness; and Saint Vincent de Paul, founder of the Lazarist missionary order and the nursing community the Daughters of Charity. These French bodies worked in co-operation with international organizations such as the Jesuits, whose schools educated the children of the elite. The pastoral urge was exemplified in the mission. It was directed at the heathen, but it also embraced the poor within French society, whose needs the Church felt it was failing to meet. The Lazarists and the Eudistes of Saint Jean Eudes, for example, specialized in rural missions.

A notable feature of the Counter-Reformation missionary endeavour was the activities of numerous women of a similarly pragmatic and pastoral bent – like Saint Jeanne de Chantal, co-founder of the Visitandines, or Saint Louise de Marillac, co-founder of the Daughters of Charity. Female education was a particular concern: the Ursulines took in middle- and upper-class boarders, while hosts of new female teaching orders catered for poor children. Similar female orders were also engaged in poor relief. The prototype here was the Daughters of Charity of Saints Vincent de Paul and Louise de Marillac (founded 1633), who pioneered the practice of engaging religious women in the affairs of the world. This move created high levels of patient care in hospitals and charitable institutions, which became, at the same time, enveloped in an evangelical aura. Many similar communities followed in their train, and achieved a silent takeover of the institutions of poor relief. Court figures and other wealthy women patronized such bodies and supplied the financial backing for the various teaching and charitable enterprises of the period.

Louis XIV was charitable too – albeit in a more pragmatic way. The veterans' hospital, the Invalides, which he founded in 1670, was designed to prevent ex-soldiers causing havoc in civil society as much as it was to reward them for good service. It formed part of a more general campaign to confine the poor and other social groups perceived as dangerous. Louis helped to establish the national network of *hôpitaux généraux* ("general hospitals"), initially with the support of the Company of the Holy Sacrament. They not only confined the poor, providing shelter for the needy, but also meted out correction for the dissident and work-shy. A host of repressive royal edicts, notably in the 1680s, when the anti-Protestant campaign was reaching its peak, targeted for confinement gypsies, vagrants, lunatics, alleged witches, prostitutes, delinquent children and other supposedly deviant groups. Nearly two hundred such institutions were created from the 1650s onwards. The 100,000 individuals they confined were, however, only a small proportion of the targeted groups.

The objectives which the monarch set for the revitalized secular clergy emerging in this age of religious reform were double-edged. As the "great confinement of the poor" (M. Foucault) suggests, the king required them to instil social discipline as well as spiritual orthodoxy. The Council of Trent had urged the creation of seminaries to produce more worthy priests, and from the 1620s and 1630s French bishops began to establish diocesan seminaries for ecclesiastical training. These became efficient at mass-

The "Great Confinement" extended to prostitutes and paupers, and in their case often resulted in transportation to the French colony of Louisiana. Here, in 1687, Paris prostitutes and brothel-keepers – several of whom are named – embark for New Orleans from the Paris Hôpital Général. Tender farewells to their lovers are contrasted with the more bitter remarks reserved for surgeon and apothecary (shown bearing leech and enema-syringe), presumably for their attentions during treatment for venereal disease.

producing a properly educated, well-tested, zealous and pastorally concerned parish priest. Rates of formal illiteracy, ecclesiastical absenteeism, pluralism and ignorance plummeted. The *bons curés*, or good parish priests, passed on an orthodox set of beliefs. Their task was to produce at parish level a good, God-fearing Christian – and for the state, a docile and obedient subject.

There is moreover a great deal of evidence to suggest that these Counter-Reformation shock-troops did have an impact on their flocks. In particular the astonishing fall in illegitimacy and pre-bridal conceptions – fewer than five children in a hundred were born out of wedlock in most rural areas by the turn of the eighteenth century – suggests that the preaching of godliness did not take place in a void, but that the hoped-for Christianization of social *mores* was fairly effective. The late seventeenth-century decline in provincial rioting and social turbulence commonplace a century earlier may also be linked to the wider diffusion of a more effective and zealous secular clergy, able to police political as well as religious opinions.

The Catholic Church paid a price, however, for such close links with the state. In particular it risked losing its autonomy and having its agenda set by state concerns. When ecclesiastical opinion threatened too much independence, the monarch did not hold back from acting against it. The king had the archbishop of Paris arrested and thrown in prison in 1652 (admittedly it was the arch-intriguer, the Cardinal de Retz). Throughout his reign he also proved the scourge of Jansenism, a puritanical form of

Catholicism which, he felt, inclined its practitioners towards political dissidence. Nor did he refrain from taking on the pope as well as the French Church in his determination to establish his prerogatives. Indeed at one moment in the 1680s he looked close to leading the French Church into secession from Rome.

THE MAKING OF ABSOLUTISM

"Royal authority is sacred … God established kings as his ministers and reigns through them over the nation … The royal throne is not the throne of a man but the throne of God himself." The words of Bishop Bossuet underline the organic links now connecting Church and an increasingly absolutist state. The language of absolutism was not of course new, linking with Roman law conceptions of sovereignty that had been revived in the thirteenth century. It had gained currency in the Wars of Religion, when a strong monarchy could be presented as the only viable alternative to anarchy. Political discourse then became more emphatic about the need for unquestioning obedience to the king's wishes and suspicious of checks on his power. For the humanist Jean Bodin, writing in the aftermath of the Saint Bartholomew's Eve Massacre, "a king is responsible only to God and his conscience". The bluff, no-nonsense Henry IV had followed the dictates of his conscience, converting to Catholicism in order to benefit his people. He fought hard to establish an atmosphere of tolerance in the face of doubting parlements and established authorities – and finally he was able to deliver a version of royalty from which Louis XIV (via Louis XIII) could benefit. However, the latter refurbished it with a sacred aura. This Louis, notwithstanding Divine Right theory, might not be a saint nor think himself divine. Yet as his cousin, the Grande Mademoiselle, sardonically remarked of him, "he is God".

The new form of absolutism embodied by Louis XIV was not achieved without difficulty. The assassination of Henry IV in 1610 produced a period of regency, under Marie de Medici. Monarchy was always weak in a regency, a point highlighted by the calling of an Estates General in 1614 to enlist community support. Marie de Medici seemed, however, to squander the confidence she enjoyed as Henry IV's widow, entrusting power to an unpopular Italian *arriviste* Concino Concini and his wife Leonora Galigaï, whose influence triggered a spate of noble revolts. Louis XIII marked his coming-of-age in 1617 by having Concini brutally murdered, executing his wife and dispatching Marie de Medici into exile.

From the early 1620s a new figure emerged in the king's councils: Armand Jean du Plessis, bishop of Luçon, who became Cardinal de Richelieu in 1622. Richelieu was not only effective principal minister for two decades (from 1624 to 1642), but also bequeathed to Louis XIII and the young Louis XIV a successor, Giulio Mazarini. Originally a papal diplomat, from the early 1630s Mazarini came into the service of Richelieu, who made him cardinal. Cardinal Jules Mazarin would serve as principal minister until his death in 1661. The political predominance of the two "cardinal ministers" from 1624 down to 1661 was immensely important in the establishment of the absolute monarchy. Building on the legacy of Henry IV, they first came to terms with

the turbulent legacy of the Religious Wars, crushing, as we have seen, the pretensions of Protestantism to rank as a state within a state, and also muzzling the turbulent high nobility; but secondly they also reduced the influence of representative bodies and established the institutional framework of centralized monarchy.

Richelieu is sometimes credited with almost superhuman powers of foresight in the creation of absolutism. Nothing could be further from the truth. The absolutist model emerged piecemeal and fortuitously from a welter of complex and contradictory circumstances. At the heart of change moreover was the unpredictability of war. Richelieu feared that a strong Habsburg power would use the Thirty Years War (1618–48) as a means of encircling France and establishing a grip over Europe. He therefore made an anti-Austrian and anti-Spanish position the basis of his foreign policy, even though this entailed allying with, and granting financial aid to, Protestant powers.

In 1635 Richelieu entered the war. It went badly almost at once. In 1636 when Corbie in Picardy fell, with imperial cavalry outriders skirting Paris, there seemed a real threat of massive Spanish invasion from the Low Countries. The military threat was contained with some difficulty, and by 1639/40 the war started going the French way. The brilliant victory achieved by the prince de Condé over the Spanish at Rocroi in 1643 was followed by further victories and gradual French advance on the northern front, as well as occupation of Roussillon and Catalonia in the south. These efforts were crowned with success in the Treaty of Westphalia of 1648: the *de facto* French annexation of the "Three Bishoprics" (Metz, Toul, Verdun) since 1552 was confirmed in international law; the French also acquired a good part of Alsace. War with the Spanish Habsburgs continued after 1648 and was only concluded by the Treaty of the Pyrenees in 1659. By this, Roussillon and part of the Cerdagne in the south were acquired, while France also gained a string of land advancing the frontier northwards between Gravelines on the English Channel to Thionville on the Moselle, and including most of Artois and Picardy.

These victories had only been achieved by the transformation of the French army and major shifts in the character of government and administration. The French army, though occasionally reaching a force of 50,000, had rarely surpassed 20,000 to 30,000 in the sixteenth century, and in the early 1630s stood at around 20,000. Defeat at Corbie galvanized the state into desperate measures. By the late 1630s by dint of press-ganging, call-ups and the purchase of foreign mercenary forces, nearly 100,000 men were in the field. Numbers continued to grow, with army strength reaching a quarter of a million men after the 1650s.

This "military revolution" in army size (M. Roberts) entailed a massive shift towards centralized and bureaucratic government. The cardinal ministers performed a coup on the royal council, removing feudal dignitaries who felt they had a place as of right and replacing them with their own *créatures* – loyal, dependable and administratively effective men, willing to subordinate their own opinions to the will of their master. The personnel of the council was increasingly bureaucratized. Business was handled by secretaries of state and subordinate *maîtres des requêtes* ("masters of requests"). The

Opposite Besides his role in central government Richelieu, here portrayed by Philippe de Champaigne, also played an important role as a Counter-Reformation prelate. Bishop of Luçon from 1606 and cardinal from 1622, he conducted intensive missionary work within his diocese against Huguenots.

latter were the seed plot from which ministers drew intendants, agents whom they sent into the provinces from the 1620s to supervise the state machine. Though such officials had been used by earlier monarchs, it was under Richelieu that they became integral to government, reducing the freedom of old noble families to build up power bases in the provinces. Their powers were extended – from 1642, for example, they were given wide-ranging powers over the assessment and collection of the main direct tax, the *taille*. Intendants began to be detailed to each *généralité*, or tax constituency, and they were also attached to the armies, where they supervised the high command and checked on discipline and supply.

This administrative revolution, prompted by the needs of war, was highly unpopular, coming as it did on top of high war-costs. Tax levels increased threefold between 1630 and 1648 – the rise was particularly marked around 1635 – and another 50 per cent through to the end of the seventeenth century. This was combined moreover with a range of other financial stratagems: lowering the value of government stocks, special tax demands, loans, devaluations and the like. A favourite recourse was the sale of offices, or posts, in the financial and judicial bureaucracy. Henry IV's introduction in 1604 of the so-called Paulette – a tax on office which made the office hereditable – marked an important stage in the state's manipulation of venal (that is, purchasable) offices. Whereas office had been one of the prizes with which high nobles had rewarded clients in the Wars of Religion, state control gave office-holders a stake in the stability of government, rather than its destabilization. The state also valued the system for giving it additional sources of income, as well as providing the bureaucrats it required. There had been some 12,000 such office-holders in the sixteenth century; by 1650 there were approximately 50,000. State income from this source quadrupled between the 1610s and the 1640s.

The sale of offices on this scale, however, produced problems. The most important offices bore tax exemptions, so that a major increase in the number reduced the state's tax base. The system risked administrators viewing their offices as private property rather than public functions, while over-supply reduced the market value of offices, so that previous buyers resented their investment being whittled away. The use of intendants, who aimed to make the bureaucracy work more efficiently, caused resentment too, and they were viewed as interfering in private property. The role of intendants in the armies produced hostility from commanders and generals. The old nobility "of the Sword" resented the rise of a new nobility "of the Robe", who held the plum positions in the bureaucracy and seemed now to rule the roost. Henry IV had been generous in giving pensions and hand-outs to financially distressed provincial gentry, but by the 1630s the state did not have the cash in hand with which to be generous. War was pushing the state towards a corner: it was losing the instinctual support of the nobility, the most influential class within society, yet was also arousing the opposition of its own servants. State revenue demands triggered a seemingly endless round of riots, rebellions and revolts. Every year from the 1610s to 1648 there was an outbreak of popular turbulence over tax policy somewhere in France. At times, as with the "Croquant"

Anonymous seventeenth-century engraving depicting the horrors of war. In the Thirty Years War (1618–48) a rapacious soldiery dependent on living off the land caused enormous damage to the civilian population, notably in eastern France.

uprising between the Loire and the Garonne in 1636 (probably the greatest peasant uprising since the Jacquerie of 1358), or that of the "Nu-Pieds" ("Bare-Feet") in Normandy in 1639, these swelled into massive peasant revolts.

Government had to learn how to live with unpopularity in this period. There were numerous assassination plots aimed at Richelieu, for example. His opponents are sometimes represented as backward-looking egotists playing a game of "outs" versus "ins", yet in fact there was a strong policy difference between the two sides, which was particularly apparent in moves to replace the cardinal minister in 1630. The Marillac brothers – Michel, keeper of the seals, and the military commander Louis – became the core of opposition to Richelieu's policies. Connected with *dévot* circles who opposed France's alliance with Protestant princes, and who wished to ally with the Catholic Habsburgs to crush Protestantism throughout Europe, they also had the support of the king's younger brother, the meddlesome Gaston of Orléans, and the king's mother, Marie de Medici. The social distress caused by dearth in 1629/30 gave additional arguments in favour of steering away from Richelieu's pro-war and centralization policies. In a famous incident in 1630 it seemed that Louis XIII accepted the Marillac view and that Richelieu was in disgrace. The king, however, suddenly changed his mind and stuck by Richelieu. The so-called "Day of the Dupes" consolidated Richelieu's hold on power, and allowed him to go on to eliminate the opposition: Michel de Marillac was decapitated for treason, his brother Louis exiled.

The foundations of absolutism were challenged again after Richelieu's death in 1642, most notably in the Fronde (1648–52). Named after a children's catapult

Mazarin, the principal minister of Regent Anne of Austria, is depicted here in comic-book style in an episode during the Fronde (1648–52). Forced into exile in 1651, he bids the teenage Louis XIV farewell (top left), leaves Paris (top right), but pauses at Le Havre to release from prison his former political rivals, led by the Prince de Condé (bottom left). As he leaves the kingdom, the ghost of the assassinated Concini looms up before him. The relaxation of government censorship during the Fronde saw the mass production of political pamphlets, the "Mazarinades".

(*fronde*) this civil war was far less frivolous than its name suggests. The military operations of the war wreaked enormous damage on areas affected – notably in the Paris basin and round Bordeaux. What was at stake in it moreover was the whole administrative revolution associated with the cardinal ministers. War with Austria had come to an end in 1648. This made the additional financial demands that Mazarin (Richelieu's successor) wished to impose, in order to continue the struggle against Spain, seem pointless. The parlement of Paris argued, with some justification, that the extraordinary rise in the state's tax demands was unconstitutional in a period of regency – Louis XIV was still a minor, and government was in the hands of his mother, Anne of Austria, and Mazarin, both of them foreigners.

In 1648 the parlement, combining support from the old "Sword" nobility wishing to remove Mazarin with popular discontent over tax demands, temporarily forced the state to backtrack on its administrative revolution. Intendants were recalled and declared unconstitutional and Mazarin himself was exiled (on three separate occasions through to 1652). At one time, the young Louis XIV in the Louvre palace seemed a prisoner of the Paris mob. It proved impossible, however, for the "Robe" and "Sword"

nobilities to hold together and to establish the basis for a more moderate, less centralized state, and by 1652 Mazarin and Anne of Austria were back in the driving seat. Troubles grumbled on, however, throughout the 1650s: the arrest of Cardinal de Retz triggered the so-called "Ecclesiastical Fronde" in Paris; the parlement continued to criticize the government's constitutional position; and there were tempestuous assemblies of warlike gentry in the provinces and popular tax revolts down to 1661, when Louis XIV (r. 1643–1715) assumed control of the government.

The state prevailed in the long run partly because of its superiority in organized violence. In the sixteenth century noble dynasts raising the standard of revolt in the provinces had recruited armed followings, held together by patronage and kinship, which were a match for royal armies. By the 1640s and 1650s, however, no noble dynast could compete with the big post-"Military Revolution" army controlled by the state, which could be used systematically for internal policing. Richelieu had not shirked from using internal violence in the pursuit of his aims. He had a Montmorency executed for daring to defy his prohibition on aristocratic duelling. Other state enemies were executed or imprisoned, notably in the Bastille. The leading Jansenist, Abbé Saint-Cyran, for example, was kept in prison from 1638 to 1643.

Yet the changes wrought by the cardinal ministers were not brought about solely by force. They also devised more persuasive means of winning support for the new style of government. They were careful to prevent representative bodies becoming platforms for opposition to royal policies. The Estates General was never recalled after 1614 (until the crisis years of 1788/9). Another pseudo-national representative body, the Assembly of Notables was not convened again after 1626. The Assembly of the Clergy

Cyrano de Bergerac

Cyrano de Bergerac (1619–55) was a far more brilliant and multifaceted character than the long-nosed swashbuckler and letter-writing romantic of Edmond Rostand's play (1897) and recent fame. A minor nobleman and army officer, notorious for his duelling and his boastfulness, he was also something of an intellectual firebrand, who made original and unusual contributions to literary and scientific fields.

Linked from the 1630s with Parisian *libertins* (free-thinkers), he forged a materialistic philosophy out of contacts and conflicts with Gassendi, Descartes and others. He was also passionately involved in the debates arising from the Scientific Revolution. Given the increasingly close censorship which Richelieu

was imposing on intellectual life, his most daring work could only be published posthumously, and in abridged form. To the rationalism of the new science he brought a baroque fantasy. His *State and Empire of the Moon* (1657) and *State and Empire of the Sun* (1661) could be – and have been – read as predictions of space travel and early classics of science fiction. Yet they also disseminated ideas and debates on contemporary astronomy and physics, and contained some characteristically bravura passages attacking belief in miracles and witchcraft.

Space travel *à la* Cyrano de Bergerac. Engraving from a 1709 edition of his "State and Empire of the Moon".

was placed under close surveillance. Provincial estates which showed signs of dissidence were not reconvened (Dauphiné after 1628, Normandy after 1655 and so on). After the Fronde, the parlements had their rights to pose constitutional arguments against royal edicts severely reduced, to prevent them from becoming a lightning-rod for opposition.

Opinion was not only repressed, it was also shaped and manipulated. Richelieu's censorship drove out of France the greatest thinker of the age, René Descartes, whose *Discourse on Method* was published in 1637. Richelieu used paid hacks as government propagandists and hired a bevy of polemical pamphleteers. He permitted the colourful Montpellier physician and impresario, Théophraste Renaudot, to establish in 1631 the first national newspaper, the *Gazette*, which specialized in propaganda quite as much as official news. Richelieu's patronage of literary men was marked by the foundation of the *Académie française* in 1635, to uphold the purity of the French language. He and Mazarin also encouraged and patronized dramatists, painters and architects who flattered their, and the dynasty's, glory. Louis XIV would take the political uses of artistic patronage to new heights.

LOUIS XIV'S ABSOLUTISM

On the death of Mazarin in 1661, Louis XIV decided not to appoint a principal minister, but to govern by himself. This was to put the final icing on a cake whose ingredients had been so painstakingly blended by the cardinal ministers. It represented the high point of centralized government: the king's ministers reported separately to the king. For those with ambitions above their station the imprisonment and ruin he meted out in 1661 to his over-confident finance minister Nicolas Fouquet served as a deterrent. He prized loyalty and efficiency in his ministers, making use of a body of able bureaucrats left him by Mazarin, not least Jean-Baptiste Colbert. The council of state was further streamlined. In the provinces intendants were made fixtures – the last *généralité* to receive a permanent appointment was Brittany in 1689 – and they were flanked by *sub-délégués* (sub-delegates) acting under their orders. Efforts were made under Colbert to produce national criminal, civil and commercial codes. Municipal authorities were more closely supervised from above. Paris, whose turbulence during the Fronde Louis XIV had felt at first hand, was in 1667 put under a lieutenant-general of police, a minister-ranking appointment, whose job was to reduce crime and engage in urban development, while in the provinces a mounted national police constabulary, the *maréchaussée*, was organized. The spread of a network of poorhouses-*cum*-workhouses throughout the kingdom marked an important gesture towards a national poor-relief policy, and also formed an effective agency of social control.

By acting as his own principal minister, Louis XIV cut the ground from under the feet of all but the tamest political opposition. Opponents of royal policy from 1624 to 1661 had been able to adopt the polite fiction that they were "rescuing" the king from his ministers; this was no longer plausible. The brutal repression of peasant revolt in the Boulonnais in 1670, or the punishments meted out to rebels by the historical d'Artagnan (1611–73) in Languedoc in 1670, highlighted the equation between opposition and treason. For arch-ideologist of absolutism Bishop Bossuet, "However bad a prince might be, the revolt of his subjects is always more criminal."

The absolute nature of royal power was closely linked with the development of patriarchal authority within the family. The way the state developed had a direct impact on the everyday lives of men and women. Both Protestants and the Catholic "godly" emphasized the time-honoured place of the family in women's lives. The old adage *aut maritus aut murus* – "either a husband or a cloister" – could no longer apply to Protestant women, for whom no nunneries existed. The Council of Trent had stressed the importance of cloistering female religious communities and groupings – or at least of giving those who operated in the world, such as the Daughters of Charity, a spiritual armour-plating against the desires of the flesh. In the name of female sexual purity both Protestants and Catholics directed campaigns against organized prostitution and any form of sexual deviance.

A young Louis XIV, costumed as Apollo for the ballet *Fêtes de Bacchus*, performed in 1651.

The state supported these campaigns, amplifying the role of the family head in controlling and policing the behaviour of female members. Just as the poor and deviants were to be confined in state poorhouses, so women and children would be confined within the power of the family. Between around 1550 and 1700 a whole range of measures was introduced to strengthen the legal powers of the paterfamilias, often justified using the same language of absolute sovereignty that Bourbon propagandists used about the monarch. "Marriages," an edict of 1666 stated, "are the fecund sources from which the strength and grandeur of states are derived." The father's power was upheld in civil rather than church courts and concerned all aspects of relations between the sexes (choice of partner, rights over property and inheritance, marital separation and so on). The state pushed the courts to act in favour of greater male control over subordinate females. In 1684 fathers were permitted to use *lettres de cachet* (royal warrants bypassing the courts) to put away in prisons or convents those they adjudged guilty of infringing conventional sexual morality or family honour. This "Family–State Compact" (Sarah Hanley) led to the sovereign himself being conceptualized in more paternal terms: "The king," one lawyer stated, "is the husband and political spouse of the public interest."

If the family was restructured to bolster the power of the state, governments also proved adept at using arts and letters to the same effect. The aim was for the king to be "dazzling and magnificent", as Bossuet put it, so as "to make the peoples respect him". Urbanization was one area of concern. Henry IV had used building projects in Paris to attract attention to his power. For example, he completed the Pont-Neuf, the first bridge in Paris to span the whole of the Seine – an equestrian statue of him was later placed in the middle – and started the Place Royale (now the Place des Vosges). As Louis XIV's faithful minister Colbert reminded him, "Your Majesty knows that, in the absence of striking actions of war, nothing more marks the greatness and the spirit of princes than buildings." Louis XIV rose to the occasion: the Louvre was brilliantly revamped; the Place Louis-le-Grand (now Place Vendôme) and Place des Victoires were created; boulevards were developed on the lines of the old fortress walls; and the Invalides, the Observatory and much else besides were constructed. Under pressure of these urban initiatives the city grew beyond half a million individuals. Even this, however, was eclipsed by Louis' development of the palace of Versailles, where he moved his court in 1682.

Versailles would be widely copied by aspiring absolutist monarchs throughout Europe, from Potsdam to Hampton Court and from Scandinavia to Naples. Yet bricks and mortar were only one aspect of the way the palace operated as an ideological mechanism of absolute power. It was the centre of a kind of "theatre state" in which the main actor, the monarch himself, performed a range of power rituals. The way of life in the palace – an ostentatiously large household, the ritualization of public space, the theatre of daily life, down to the mundanities of getting up, eating meals and going to bed – were emulated by nobles and rival monarchs as statements about power. The metaphor of the sun – an ever-present motif in the art at Versailles – was used in order to make the "Sun King" the point from which all power and vision radiated. The rectilinear angles of classicism converged on the eye of the ruler. So much wealth and prestige now clustered around the court that even the highest nobility felt obliged to reside there. Louis XIV had built a gilded cage in which the turbulent warriors of the Wars of Religion became the foppish courtiers of the Sun King.

Just as classical symmetries had converted unpromising swampland into the might-

"Carrousel" – a courtly and chivalric entertainment – held in Paris to celebrate the engagement of Louis XIII with the Habsburg princess, Anne of Austria in 1612. The event was staged in the fashionable Place Royale, now the Place des Vosges. This building development had been started by Henry IV in 1604.

iest palace in Europe, so the court aimed to domesticate and "classicize" culture. The early decades of Louis XIV's reign mark two of the most fertile periods of French literary history, and most of its major figures – Corneille, Racine, Molière, La Rochefoucauld, La Bruyère and La Fontaine – received state pensions, which Colbert had systematized. Symptomatically Louis took both painters and historians on his military campaigns with him, for he wished to control representations of his power. A whole range of media were used to glorify monarchy – portraits, histories, medals and coins, court ballets (Louis was his own *premier danseur* down to 1679), equestrian statues, triumphal arches, formal entries, ceremonies of touching for the "King's Evil", all added to the lustre of Louis XIV. The Comédie française, the French national theatre, was established in 1680. Louis XIV took Richelieu's idea of the academy, and applied it to specific branches of learning and culture: an Academy of Dance was established

Madame de Sévigné, patient

"After salvation," Madame de Sévigné confided to a cousin, "I count health as of primordial importance." However, how could health be guaranteed in an age whose doctors were satirized so ruthlessly by the dramatist Molière and when, it was generally reckoned, doctors killed off as many patients as they cured?

The correspondence of archletter-writer and court aristocrat Marie de Rabutin-Chantal, marquise de Sévigné (1626–96), provides us with a particularly full account of one woman's response to this fateful question. The importance she attached to sickness is underlined by her tendency to be most prodigal in health advice to those she loved most, notably her adored daughter, Madame de Grignan.

Madame de Sévigné displayed a fashionable disdain for medical men, grounded in a good knowledge of Molière's classics. The favoured remedy for a multitude of ills among Parisian physicians was bleedings – yet because of her small veins, which were difficult of access, Madame de Sévigné was a poor bleeder. The most highly

A surgeon prepares a lady's arm for a phlebotomy (bleeding).

regarded practitioners of the court and the capital passed under her consideration. So did high-flown surgeons such as Félix, who had made his name and his fortune for successfully operating upon Louis XIV for an anal fistula; fashionable male midwives like Joubert; and a host of apothecaries, recommending everything from powdered snake to shrimps' eyes or essence of human urine. She was an endless consumer of "waters" of every kind: emerald, chicken, Queen of Hungary's water, gunpowder, and so on. She was also a denizen of spa towns such as Vichy and Alise Sainte-Reine.

Like many at court Madame de Sévigné also displayed a liberal attitude towards irregular practitioners. Some of these had hit upon remedies of lasting value – like the Englishman "Chevalier" Talbot, famous for his support of quinine. But outright quacks also received her custom, including sundry Capuchin monks praising the virtues of different panaceas. Remedies from folklore – like those preached by Madame de Fouquet, mother of Louis XIV's notorious finance minister – also provided her with advice she generally regarded as sage.

Versailles

"Versailles: the most wretched of places, without view, without woods, without water, without soil; for all there is shifting sands and marshes, consequently without air, which cannot be good there."

The acidulous comment of the duc de Saint-Simon, the most disdainful of the chroniclers of Louis XIV's court at Versailles, was not without foundation. The site was poor – its marshiness fostered malaria, which between 1661 and 1682 caused huge numbers of deaths among workers attached to the building works. During this time what had been little more than a cosy hunting lodge for Louis XIV's father, Louis XIII, was transformed into one of the most massive architectural statements of political power in French history.

Louis himself was particularly attached to the site. He hated Paris since the dark days of the Fronde (1648–52), when as a boy he had been kept prisoner by rumbustious Parisian subjects in the Tuileries palace. He attracted the foremost practitioners of the day to make the new palace the site of artistic superlatives: the garden designer Le Nôtre, the painter Charles Le Brun, the architects Le Vau and Mansart, the water engineers the Francine brothers. The king diverted over 5 per cent of state income in the 1670s and 1680s to pay for the constructions. On military campaigns he fretted about the state of his orange groves and tapestries. And he even wrote a kind of guidebook to the palace gardens.

"I entrust to you the most precious thing in the world, my renown." Louis' comment to members of his academy of fine arts highlights the political issue at stake. Versailles was to be about dynastic self-glorification, not just private pleasures. By making his high nobles and ministers reside there as courtiers, moreover, Louis gave himself a perpetual audience. Ambassadors were received there, festivals and pageants held, paupers were touched for the "King's Evil" – the palace served as a visual amplifier for Louis' personal glory.

Above Louis XIV in the gardens of Versailles, 1713–14, by Jean-Baptiste Martin. The king is foregrounded, with his courtiers, against the Apollo fountain – the sun god in the service of the Sun King – and the grand canal.

Left The Hall of Mirrors at Versailles.

in 1661, followed by Academies of Inscriptions (1662), Sciences (1666), Architecture (1671) and Music (1672). The academies set standards of taste, as if under direction from the king, and organized learning from above.

The state's action was important in bringing major scientific changes into the public sphere. Western learning was undergoing what historians have called a Scientific Revolution in the seventeenth century. Advances in astronomy, associated with Kepler and Galileo, led to a new conception of the universe as centred round the sun rather than the earth. William Harvey's work on circulation of the blood challenged the most hallowed presuppositions of medical science. There were important advances in physics, chemistry, biology and so on. Inductive, scientific reasoning threw down a challenge to a theory of knowledge based essentially on divine revelation and Church authority. Yet such work was often the product only of small international cliques of scientists, who also had to contend with the occasional opposition of the authorities – Galileo was harassed by the Church for his views. The French state, by creating a network of academies under which science could be practised in relative freedom, with moderate levels of funding and with government backing, gave a considerable boost to the practice of science. The Scientific Revolution served the monarchy well – the heliocentric universe reflected the glories of the Sun King.

The promotion of grandeur at home was part of a more general quest for glory – *la gloire* – on the battlefield. The focus of French expansionism shifted away from the Italian peninsula, where Habsburg rivalry had been countered in the fifteenth and sixteenth centuries, notably towards the northern and eastern frontiers. A string of major wars – the War of Devolution (1667–8), the Dutch War (1672–8), the War of the League of Augsburg (1689–97) and the War of Spanish Succession (1701–13) – were conducted to execute royal aims.

Had Louis XIV died in the 1680s, his reputation would have stood extremely high. In addition to the gains made in 1648 and 1659 he had by then expanded on the northern front, notably by acquiring Flanders (1678) and, in the east, taking Franche-Comté (1678) and Strasbourg (1681). These gains were part of an on-going process of "reunion", whereby the ruler endeavoured to annex the dependent territories of cities and seigneuries brought under French power in the previous generation. He was also engaged in colonial expansion. Unfortunately, perhaps, Louis survived to carry his ambitions further, and met with almost complete failure beyond this point: his "reunion" policy broke down in 1697; his support for the Stuart dynasty in England came to nothing; his attempt to link the Spanish and French monarchies after 1702 was a flop; and at the Treaty of Utrecht in 1713 he also had to accept colonial losses in North America.

This fruitless cycle of warfare after the 1680s was, moreover, enormously expensive. By the turn of the eighteenth century France was fighting on several land fronts in Europe as well as in the colonies and at sea. Colbert had expanded the French navy from some 18 ships to 276 in 1683, and their maintenance was extremely costly. Under war ministers Le Tellier and his son Louvois the army grew to over 400,000 men, and did at least keep the direct impact of warfare beyond French borders. Massive fortification by the great military engineer Vauban secured the northern and eastern fronts. All this was achieved at great cost to the economy. The public debt increased tenfold between 1683 and 1715. Offices were sold in profusion and taxes increased. A poll tax (*capitation*) was introduced in 1695 and a "tenth tax" (*dixième*) in 1710 to stave off impending financial disaster.

That Louis XIV sustained war on this scale and for this length of time testified to the strength of the state structures built up by the cardinal ministers. It was also the fruit of policies followed throughout the century to develop the economy. These policies – often lumped together by historians under the name of mercantilism – aimed to organize imports and exports in order to produce trade balances that would swell the state's coffers with bullion. Louis built on the work of his predecessors. Henry IV's ministers Sully and Richelieu had engaged in a programme of improvements in communications and fostered luxury industries (silk, tapestries, glass). Louis XIV's minister Colbert achieved the most in this field. The Canal du Midi (1665–81), linking the Atlantic with the Mediterranean, ranked among the most impressive pieces of civil engineering before the age of industrialization. Support was provided to high-quality manufacture – of tapestries, glass, fine cloth, ironwork and so on – for which France acquired a world reputation. An aggressive tariffs policy was adopted from 1667. Trading companies were established – notably the East Indies Company in 1664 – and given extensive support to carve out a larger share of European and colonial trade. The renovated navy aided in the founding of new colonies. Modest settlements began in the Caribbean islands, Canada was organized as the province of New France, and a colony was founded in Louisiana. Trading stations also formed in West Africa and in India. The new-found wealth of the ports of Nantes, Bordeaux, Brest and Saint-Malo were clear evidence of the uplifting effect of these colonial ventures on the home economy.

Such successes were not enough, however, to compensate for the trauma which war was visiting on the economy from the 1690s through to the death of Louis XIV in 1715. The loss of Huguenot skilled workers through the state's policy of religious intolerance worsened matters, while spells of bad weather in 1693/4 and 1709/10 produced perhaps the last true famines in French history. War was building up a massive financial burden, all to very little avail, as the disappointing provisions of the Treaty of Utrecht in 1713 made clear. "All France," complained Fénelon on the eve of Louis' death, "is just one great desolate hospital lacking provisions."

THE AGE OF ENLIGHTENMENT

The death of Louis XIV in 1715 and the succession of his young great-grandson Louis XV, who had been born in 1710, could stand as a parable about the underlying realities of power. Louis XIV had postured as an absolute ruler, but he could not control posterity; his will was annulled by the parlement of Paris, which installed his enemy, the duke of Orléans, as regent. Louis had done his utmost to control opinion, but there was almost open rejoicing on the news of his death, and his reputation plummeted

Opposite The anatomy theatre of the Paris School of Surgery, constructed between 1769 and 1775 by Gondoin. French surgery won European renown in the eighteenth century, and elite surgeons rivalled the prestige of leading physicians. The combination of applied science and public utility won surgeons the support of enlightened opinion.

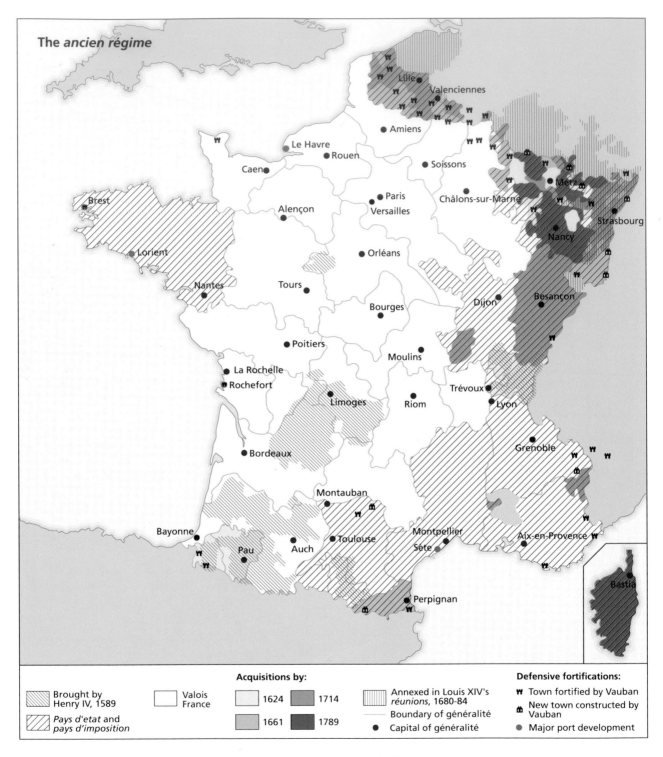

The *ancien régime*

Brest • Lorient • Nantes • Caen • Le Havre • Rouen • Alençon • Amiens • Soissons • Paris • Versailles • Châlons-sur-Marne • Lille • Valenciennes • Metz • Strasbourg • Nancy • Orléans • Tours • Bourges • Dijon • Besançon • Poitiers • La Rochelle • Rochefort • Limoges • Moulins • Riom • Trévoux • Lyon • Bordeaux • Grenoble • Montauban • Bayonne • Pau • Auch • Toulouse • Montpellier • Sète • Aix-en-Provence • Perpignan • Bastia

Acquisitions by:

Brought by Henry IV, 1589

Pays d'etat and *pays d'imposition*

Valois France

1624   1714

1661   1789

Annexed in Louis XIV's *réunions*, 1680-84

Boundary of généralité

● Capital of généralité

Defensive fortifications:

♜ Town fortified by Vauban

♖ New town constructed by Vauban

● Major port development

The "Grand Siècle" saw the significant extension of French territory on the north and north-eastern frontiers. Fortified by Louis XIV's engineer Vauban, this represented a permanent addition to French power. The period also saw the extension of key royal officials, the *intendants*, throughout the provinces, and the *généralité* became the base unit of administration. France was still divided between a central core and peripheral areas that were less firmly controlled from the centre.

before he was cold in his grave. He had aimed to annihilate the power of the nobility: yet the regency government saw the parlement of Paris given back its powers to remonstrate against royal edicts, and aristocrats were soon competing for a place on the royal council in a way that recalled the days of the Fronde.

The monarchy was eventually able to bring its high nobles under some degree of control. Yet neither Louis XV (r. 1715–74) nor Louis XVI (r. 1774–92) was able to recapture the dynastic glories of Louis XIV. They ran the formidable administrative machine instituted by Richelieu and Mazarin and perfected by Louis XIV, making marginal improvements here and there. But they no way affected its basic structure or its social basis in the aristocracy. Bureaucratic standards were improved. State aid to trade and industry continued, and from the 1760s government policy reflected the writings of the "physiocrats" (Quesnay, Mirabeau *père*, Turgot, and others), who urged state support for the rural interest. The intendancy system was streamlined, and intendants now launched a wide range of social and economic improvements. The police forces operated smoothly – deceptively smoothly perhaps, in the light of the events of 1789. Despite sporadic problems with Jansenists, the state was still able to use the clergy as administrative and moralizing agents at grassroots level. Science policy was also developed. The Academy of Sciences was now supplemented by a wide range of other state-supported institutions. The royal botanical gardens in Paris began to operate as a scientific institution, and was headed from 1739 by the great naturalist Buffon. The *Ponts et Chaussées* department, founded in 1726, concentrated on civil engineering.

This detail from Antoine Watteau's *Gersaint's Shopsign* (1721) shows a portrait of Louis XIV being packed away at the end of his reign, while the owner invites customers to examine a painting in Watteau's rococo style. The image of the Sun King was finally in eclipse.

Frontispiece of Abbé Coyer's *La Noblesse commerçante* ("The Business Nobility") of 1756. Coyer argued that nobles should abandon their hallowed disdain for trade and industry. Though many nobles were active entrepreneurs by the end of the century, the bulk of the country gentry were more financially dependent on their privileges than their industry.

Academies were established for surgery (1731), the navy (1752), agriculture (1761) and medicine (1778). In addition, government aid was behind numerous other scientific and utilitarian enterprises, including military schools, veterinarian institutes, smallpox inoculation campaigns and the like.

If the reigns of Louis XV and Louis XVI extended the parameters of absolute power, they made surprisingly little impact on the territorial framework within which that power was exercised. They failed to expand France's frontiers in major ways. The most important acquisition – Lorraine, in 1766 – was gained by diplomatic manoeuvrings rather than force of arms. It was effectively sold to the French by its last ruler, Louis XV's father-in-law Stanislas Leczinski. Corsica, which came to the French throne in 1768, was in fact given away for nothing by the Genoans, who had become tired of coping with the island's perennial turbulence.

These were small rewards when set against the effort and expense of maintaining massive armed forces in Europe. Historians have sometimes seen the period from 1688 to 1815 as a "Second Hundred Years War" between France and Britain. Unlike the first it was a truly world affair, with the two states competing not solely in Europe but also at sea and in the African, Asian and American continents. There was, however, no Joan of Arc this time, and the French came off very much the worse.

France was losing its former grip on Europe too. The newly emergent eastern powers – Prussia and Russia, but also a regenerated Austria – carved up Poland. They managed to erase it from the European map in three partitions (1772/3, 1793, 1795) without France being able to lift a finger to prevent it. In the Seven Years War (1756–63) France suffered humiliating losses at England's hands: Canada was ceded to England, Louisiana to Spain; most Caribbean islands passed into English hands, as did all West African trading stations except Gorée. France, by contrast, was left with only a handful of outposts on the Indian subcontinent. France got partial revenge by joining England's rebel colonies in the War of American Independence (1778–83), when it had the satisfaction of seeing England lose the "Thirteen Colonies". In the Treaty of Versailles in 1783 the French also retrieved Senegal and a number of West Indian islands. Even so, the balance over the century was very much in England's favour.

While the state waned, the economy waxed strong. It was extremely fortunate, and unintended, that the schemes of Louis XV's finance minister, the Scot John Law, had helped to write off many of the debts incurred in Louis XIV's wars. Law's had been a "boom or bust" strategy for economic growth, based on a national bank issuing paper banknotes, and linked with colonial expansion. Ill thought-out and attacked by speculators, it collapsed in epic fashion in 1720. Yet because the backlog of debts was effectively written off with the help of worthless paper notes, the "bust" helped create the preconditions of "boom", especially in colonial enterprise. Although it took some time for the fact to sink in to contemporaries, France was embarking from the 1720s and 1730s on a new cycle of growth, as dynamic as anything since the thirteenth century.

Economic growth was built on demographic expansion. Population levels, artificially depressed at the turn of the century through war and bad harvests, rose by a third

While surgery and medical science made great strides in the eighteenth century, there was still widespread recourse to prayer as a means of seeking health. This 1741 statuettte of Saint Roch, patron saint of plague, shows a continuing anxiety about bubonic plague long after the final outbreaks of the disease.

between 1700 and 1789, growing from 21.5 million to an unparalleled 28.6 million. The growth was mostly due to the reduction of crisis mortality. War, famine and plague were no longer playing their traditional roles as demographic levellers. With one or two tiny exceptions war was conducted outside French frontiers. Plague lost its fatal edge. Most places in France suffered their last outbreak in the 1650s and 1660s. The disease's final appearance in Marseille in 1720, though it claimed the lives of half the city's 90,000 population, was restricted to the Provence region. The famines of 1709/10 closed a cycle too. There were still bad harvests and high bread prices thereafter, but these caused hunger rather than death by starvation.

The role played by the state in lifting these demographic scourges should not be underestimated. Louis XIV's wars had created defensible frontiers and an army which no longer needed to live off the land. Such measures as the erection of *cordons sanitaires* around affected areas played a major part in preventing plague sweeping widely through the country. Governments also proved adept at famine relief, working through intendants to keep areas lacking bread properly supplied. More important in reducing explosive death rates were improvements in the production and marketing of food-stuffs, especially grain (for bread remained the staple diet of the majority of the population). Food production increased by about 40 per cent over the eighteenth century. This was because of improvements in productivity in some places, notably in the north and north-east, where modern scientific farming methods were introduced after 1750. Greater diversity in food production also made agrarian society less vulnerable to bad weather. Maize-growing, for instance, made great strides in the south, while the potato – still largely scorned as pig-food despite Louis XVI's valiant propaganda in serving it to his courtiers – spread in poorer areas in the centre and east.

Population growth acted as an incentive to increased food production, but essential too – for the food had to reach the consumer swiftly and cheaply – were improvements in marketing and distribution. The building and refurbishment of canals and roads cut journey times and helped form regional and even national markets for staple food-stuffs. Trade boomed as a consequence. European trade increased fourfold, and even this was put in the shade by the tenfold increase in the volume of colonial trade, oper-ating through ports on the Atlantic seaboard such as Bordeaux, Nantes, La Rochelle, Saint-Malo, plus the Mediterranean city of Marseille. Slaves, sugar and other colonial produce were the key commodities here, and they helped to foster industries in the port hinterlands based on refining and processing many of these products.

Buoyant profits made the port cities the home of a dynamic bourgeoisie, with whom local nobles were often only too keen to marry their daughters and make business alliances. The entrepreneurial class included a good many nobles. The system of venal office allowed wealthy commoners to buy their way into the nobility and this facilitated a greater integration of the social elite. Colbert in 1669 had allowed nobles to engage in maritime trade without losing their privileges, while in 1701 this exemption had been extended to wholesale trade. Nobles were particularly well represented in the mining and metallurgical industries – they controlled about a quarter of the country's land-surface. They also invested in farming improvement, though probably a majority preferred to concentrate their efforts on increasing seigneurial dues rather than on improving agricultural productivity.

Though some of the most enterprising capitalists of the eighteenth century enjoyed noble status, the weight of economic advance was borne on the sturdy shoulders of the bourgeoisie. The latter grew in numbers from 700,000 in 1700 to around 2.3 million by 1789, attesting to the class's vitality. The lists of belongings left behind them after death reveal a material life of great comfort and some modest luxury. The class was highly diverse, comprising not only merchants and manufacturers but also members of the liberal professions. These did particularly well out of the boom in the demand for legal, medical, administrative, carrying and other services. On the land a minority of the peasantry benefited from the improved marketing conditions and higher food prices. Any peasant who grew enough grain for himself and his family and who could manage to get the surplus into a cart and along to the local market stood to make significant gains. While the majority of country-dwellers found it hard to make ends meet, big peasants grew fat and started mimicking the lifestyles of the bourgeoisie.

Over the eighteenth century France's rate of growth in many sectors of the economy surpassed those of an England on the eve of its Industrial Revolution. Yet the state, for all its administrative efficiency, proved singularly inept at harnessing this new-found wealth in order to keep governments solvent. Faced with ever more expensive wars the state deficit grew, and grew faster the more the century wore on.

Below left In his *The Social Contract* (1762) Genevan-born Jean-Jacques Rousseau called into question the "enlightened" belief in progress and human perfectibility. His best-selling novels and other writings won him enormous popularity as a lover of solitary walks and mountain scenery. His love of "nature" included a firm emphasis on women remaining within the family and an attack on female "bluestockings". The nineteenth-century ideology of "separate spheres" owed much to him.

Below The famous transvestite, the Chevalier d'Eon, in masonic costume, *c.* 1780.

Finance minister Machault d'Arnouville attempted to recoup some of the costs of France's involvement in the War of Austrian Succession (1740–8) by introducing the "twentieth" (*vingtième*) – or 5 per cent tax – on all revenues in 1749. This stimulated a furore among the clergy and nobility over their tax privileges. The nobles claimed (with implausible reference to antique tradition) to have the right to pay only the "blood tax" on the field of battle, while the clergy felt they should tax themselves. The campaign against government tax reform was adroitly conducted by the parlement of Paris, which was now priding itself on representing the wishes of the nation. A further *vingtième*, bringing up the tax level to 10 per cent, was added in 1756, to help fund the Seven Years War, and a third in 1760. Since the state was at war, this was perhaps less contentious than the decision to continue to demand two *vingtièmes* after the end of hostilities. Louis

Jean Huber's engraving, *The Philosophers at Supper, c.* 1750. Voltaire, with his arm raised, presumably to speak, presides over the dinner table of a fashionable salon. Also recognizable are Diderot (to his right), d'Alembert (side-view, on the left) and Condorcet (back facing).

XV was determined to overcome the increasingly open criticism of his tax policies in the parlement. Accordingly, he instructed the chancellor, Maupeou, to introduce sweeping judicial reforms to deprive the parlements of their claimed political role. The crisis which ensued was going the government's way when Louis XV died, and his successor, as a pledge towards national unity, decided to dismiss Maupeou and recall the parlements. The new king would live to rue this act, for the parlement would soon lead opposition to the crown's attempts to solve its financial problems in the late 1780s.

The French state in the eighteenth century was, then, failing to come to terms with nagging political and financial problems within a changing economic environment. The century was also arguably one of the most brilliant in French history, in which the impact of the country on European and world affairs was probably as deep as at any other time. Ironically this greatness was not based on the absolutism which Louis XIV had so carefully constructed. Rather, it had its roots in an optimistic and reformist movement of ideas – the Enlightenment – which to a great extent developed on the margins of, and sometimes in open hostility to, the French state. The Sun King, in the person of Louis XIV, had been the source of cultural radiance; yet it was writers and intellectuals, often drawn from relatively humble backgrounds, who set the tone of the *siècle des lumières* – "the age of lights".

The Enlightenment was an immensely diverse and pluralistic cultural phenomenon. Like the Scientific Revolution of the seventeenth century, to which it paid handsome tribute, it stressed the application of human reason and, wherever appropriate, scientific method. Whereas the thinkers of the seventeenth century had concentrated their efforts on the "hard" sciences (physics, astronomy, medicine and so on), the emphasis was now on the whole of social life as a field for rational enquiry and, wherever feasible, improvement.

The writers of the Enlightenment – the *philosophes*, as they called themselves – made up in daring what they lacked in originality. Montesquieu wittily satirized court society in his *Persian Letters* (1721), but went on, in his massively erudite *Spirit of the Laws* (1748), to propose a liberal vision of politics. Voltaire, for his part, lived his whole life as a social critique. His witty and wickedly satirical accounts of social, religious and political misdeeds won him a bout of imprisonment and periods of exile. Finally he secured a home, or "bolthole", as he called it, near enough to the Swiss frontier to be able to escape if his writings got him into trouble. His ultimately successful campaign to clear Jean Calas, a Protestant tortured and executed in 1762 by the parlement of Toulouse for allegedly killing his son to prevent him converting to Catholicism, was an outstanding example of Enlightenment rationality and tolerance, and showed up established religious and judicial institutions in a sombre light.

Diderot was no less daring in his way. The *Encyclopedia* (1751–72), which he edited in thirty-five volumes, represented the bible of the Enlightenment, an attempt to survey methodically material and social worlds in a spirit of sharp rationality. Writing to Voltaire, he noted:

> This shall be our device: no quarter for the superstitious, the fanatical, the ignorant, or for fools, malefactors or tyrants. I would like to see our brethren united in zeal for truth, goodness and beauty … It is not enough for us to know more than Christians: we must show that we are better, and that science has done more for humankind than divine or sufficient grace.

Such intellectual and political daring was essential, for the *philosophes* operated on the interstices of a publishing world subject to rigorous censorship. The Bastille was used more systematically to imprison writers and impound "dangerous" writings than at any other time. Newspapers had no brief to provide political news; the *Gazette* provided the news the government saw fit to print. The frequent recourse of the *philosophes* to allegory and fiction – Voltaire's most telling genre was the short story, or *conte* – show this determination to beat the censor, and to be read widely. Though the Church establishment often found the *philosophes*' scientific rationalism difficult to stomach, the anti-clericalism of Enlightenment thinkers was often a strategic means of implicitly

Madame Geoffrin was fully at her ease ... she had the good sense to talk only on those matters about which she knew something and, for everything else, to give their head to people who knew more than she ... The brightest, most animated and most amusing man within this society was d'Alembert. Having spent his morning deciphering algebra or solving problems in dynamics or astronomy, he left his study like a schoolboy leaves the classroom, asking only to enjoy himself ... Whether it was Madame Geoffrin's intention, or whether it was the natural effect of the pleasantness and brilliance that the meetings of these writers gave her home, there was not a prince, a minister nor a man or woman of renown who did not have the ambition of being invited for one of these dinners ...

The salon of Madame Geoffrin (1699–1777), on the fashionable rue Saint-Honoré in Paris, was from the 1730s one of the most brilliant and renowned of literary salons. Here artists and literati mingled with court nobles,

A soirée *chez* Madame Geoffrin

high state officials, wealthy bourgeois and visiting dignitaries to discuss, to debate and to engage in polite social intercourse.

Merit rather than birth was the key to admission to these gatherings: Madame Geoffrin famously turned down the marshal de Richelieu on the grounds of lack of distinction. Wit, urbanity, artistic ability and *politesse* ensured entrée, not genealogy. Madame Geoffrin's visitors were indeed highly distinguished: d'Alembert, Fontenelle, Montesquieu, Voltaire, Helvétius and Marmontel among the *philosophes* and, among the socially distinguished, Gustavus III of Sweden, the future Catherine the Great of Russia and Stanislas Poniatowski, former king of Poland.

The salon became an instrument of intellectual, and thereby political, power. It was said that to enter the Académie française, for example, one had first to receive the approval of the

salon of Madame de Lambert. Salons also had a powerful impact over public taste: Madame Geoffrin's salon was said to be important in winning critical acclaim for new artistic and literary works. The "Czarina of Paris", as she was called, was thus an important disseminator of Enlightenment values and shaper of public opinion.

The influence of the salons was probably declining from the 1770s as new organs of sociability and opinion-forming developed (masonic lodges, clubs and so on). The dominance of women became a target of criticism. The salonnières were seen as aristocratic bluestockings, who rendered politics and politicians effeminate. This misogynist attack was launched from within the Enlightenment. Writer and political theorist Jean-Jacques Rousseau's view, that women should be excluded from politics and should stay at home and bring up children, was influential right across the political spectrum. The ideology of "separate spheres" would be taken further in the Revolutionary and Napoleonic periods.

Une Soirée chez Madame Geoffrin, 1812. A. G. Lemonnier's painting depicts the first reading of Voltaire's play, *The Orphan from China* (1753–4).

attacking a political establishment wedded to the established Church. It also found an audience among a population increasingly indifferent to religion. The zealous piety of the seventeenth century was giving way among the literate classes to a more materialistic, urbane set of attitudes. Religious enthusiasm was increasingly seen as poor form.

What was important about the *philosophes* was not simply that they said what they did, but that they were listened to – and listened to by ever increasing numbers. Economic growth and widening social mobility were accompanied by broader and more varied cultural activity. The literacy rate doubled over the century, and though the national figures were still only roughly 50 per cent for men and 25 per cent for women, these averages disguised much higher rates in the major cities. The scientists of the previous century had spoken to hundreds of fellow scientists; the "light" spread by the *philosophes* reached a much wider audience. The folio volumes of the *Encyclopedia* or Buffon's *Natural History* reached thousands of readers, while Voltaire's *contes* or the moralizing novels of Jean-Jacques Rousseau were read by hundreds of thousands. Publishing was indeed one of the most dynamic sectors of the economy, and the traditional book trade diversified into periodicals, journals and ephemera of all sorts.

If the press led the way as a place of cultural and intellectual exchange, other institutions followed. Scientific discussion took place in the numerous provincial academies which developed over the century. At a more mundane level coffee-houses, reading rooms and masonic lodges became centres of sociability in which ideas of all sorts could be tested and exchanged. Salons, often presided over by witty and intelligent women, were also a forum for polite intellectual exchange.

A new public sphere was opening up for the discussion of ideas. Under Louis XIV the court regarded itself as the sole generator of sane ideas and public taste. Politics was to take place, it has been said, only in the head of the absolute ruler (K. Baker), and public affairs were generally seen as the preserve of the courtier, the minister and the diplomat. But economic and cultural change transformed the limits and the elitist character of public space. The literate and polite elites could now engage in discussion and debate. Contemporaries began to perceive public opinion as a political force that was impossible to ignore. For the Swiss Jacques Necker, Louis XVI's finance minister in the late 1770s, public opinion constituted "an invisible power that, without treasury, guard or army, gives its laws to the city, the court and even the palaces of kings …"

To hear the monarch talk, one would think that the rules of absolutism had been carved in bronze: "The entire public order emanates from me," Louis XV icily informed the Paris parlement in 1766. "The rights and interests of the nation whom you dare to make a separate body from the monarch rest solely in my hands." Or again Louis XVI, when questioned in the parlement on whether an edict was constitutional: "It is legal, because I wish it." Yet things had changed. By the eve of the French Revolution, for all the absolutist bluster, even the French king was in thrall to public opinion. The court, whether it liked it or not, was having to give ground to the coffee-house as the arbitrator in public issues. Economic growth and the Enlightenment paved the way for the political Revolution of 1789.

CHAPTER 7

The Revolution and Beyond

> But 'twas a time when Europe was rejoiced
> France standing on the top of golden hours
> And human nature seeming born again.

The English poet William Wordsworth later recalled the spring-like optimism which the Revolution of 1789 sent reverberating throughout Europe. As with the Eastern European revolutions two centuries later, in 1989/90, the change was as unexpected as it was impressive. The basis of the crisis which created the events of 1789 was evident only in retrospect – revolution was a new word in the lexicon of international affairs. It took on, moreover, a strongly French flavour. Between the late eighteenth and the middle of the nineteenth century, France experienced four different styles of monarchy (before 1789, 1789–92, 1815–30, 1830–48), two republics (1792–1804, 1848–52) and two empires (1804–15, 1852–70). The period contained seven revolutions or major *coups d'état* (1789, 1792, 1794, 1799, 1830, 1848, 1851) and a great deal of incidental political violence to boot. Despite being the European state with the strongest revolutionary tradition, France nevertheless, remained a society that revolved around a dominant elite of wealthy bourgeois and landowners. In this way the volatility of the political moment was balanced by firm elements of continuity.

1789: THE "GREAT REVOLUTION"

Social, economic and demographic change in the eighteenth century had brought benefits and advantages – but drawbacks too. The long-term rise in grain prices had boosted profits for farmers who produced a surplus for the market. But such individuals were proportionately fewer; population growth meant that there was not enough land to go around for self-sufficiency. The increased numbers of peasants dependent on rural work joined with landless urban workers to form an army of labour that even an expanding economy could not painlessly absorb. Over the century wages failed to keep pace with price rises, putting pressure on the majority's living standards. The pressure could be borne in normal times through a variety of strategems – working harder, wives and children taking paid employment, scraping by on less money, turning to petty crime (theft, poaching, prostitution, and so on). But the poor's "economy of makeshifts" (Olwen Hufton) was put to the test year in, year out.

From the 1770s, moreover, times were increasingly bad. Boom years in the middle decades of the century gave way to recession from early in the reign of Louis XVI (r. 1774–92). That recession hurt many among the social elite. Many noble and bourgeois landowners had taken advantage of rising food prices to experiment with new agricultural techniques in order to maximize productivity. However, rather than changing the existing seigneurial system, with its complex network of rights and dues, they preferred to work within it. This meant that when recession hit they were in a strong position to make their peasants bear the brunt, reducing wages, increasing dues and rents, and introducing changes (such as enclosures) which reduced labour costs.

Peasants were less cushioned than their social betters. Seigneurial dues and tithes to the Church made a proportionately larger dent in their incomes, even at the best of times. In 1775 in the so-called "Flour War" protesting crowds of peasants and urban consumers rioted over grain shortages. Other peasants had switched to wine production by mid century, only to see prices slump as a result of over-production. Matters were aggravated by a massive outbreak of cattle plague which caused havoc to livestock herds. Industry too suffered from a downturn in production. Levels of petty crime and vagrancy rose sharply. The fabric of *ancien régime* society looked increasingly taut. To cap it all, appalling harvests in 1787 and 1788 sent bread prices spiralling upwards. The price of the standard loaf of bread, which was the staple foodstuff of most French people, was at its highest point in the eighteenth century in the middle of July 1789. This was precisely the moment at which contemporaries came to date the opening of the Revolution, as the Bastille – since the fourteenth century a harsh symbol of royal power – was stormed by an angry Parisian mob.

We should be wary, however, of assuming a knee-jerk reaction between high prices and popular revolution. We must understand 1789 in the context of the state's financial and political problems as well as of the economic crisis. After the miserably expensive Seven Years War (1756–63) the government had sought to pursue its rivalry with Great Britain. This it did not only by refitting the largest army in Europe, but also by building up a fleet to match the Royal Navy at sea and in the colonies. The policy had its first success in the American War of Independence (1778–83), when France's alliance with the American rebels led to a victorious outcome, sealed by colonial gains. Such noble army officers as the marquis de Lafayette, who had fought alongside George Washington, returned to France full of the experience. For the state to support both a massive army and a strong navy proved beyond the government's capabilities. After all, none of its rivals attempted such a feat. It was only achieved by dint of extensive borrowing. Servicing the national debt was consuming more than half the state's tax income by the 1780s.

The government had a severe credit problem. The Protestant banker Jacques Necker, whom Louis XVI made his finance minister in 1777, had financed the American War without raising taxes – an achievement without precedent in the annals of the early modern state. When he fell from power in 1781 as a result of court intrigues, he published a self-justification, the *Compte Rendu au Roi*, which purported to show the state's finances in a rosy condition. Yet he had done this only by excluding from his account "extraordinary" (notably war) expenditure. His successor Calonne soon found himself facing state bankruptcy. In desperation he convened a hand-picked Assembly of Notables – a body which had not met since 1626 – to justify the introduction in peacetime of a new land tax which would bail out the state. Many refused to believe his account of the distressing state of government finance, which

Sketch of a bourgeois couple from the parish of Sadournin in Gascony attired in their Sunday best, drawn from the local land-register for 1772. The man's studied gentility and his wife's lace, shoes and fan mark them out as representatives of an increasingly consumerist urban lifestyle outside the cities.

Combat de Baune

Louis Mandrin (*c.* 1725–55), smuggler *extraordinaire*, deserted from the army before taking to a life of crime. His exploits before his capture and execution – bringing in untaxed tobacco, and cheap textiles, and fighting pitched battles against soldiers and excise men to do so – could be represented as a struggle to bring consumer goods to an increasingly consumerist audience. Voltaire and others tended to overlook his gratuitous brutality and to amplify his posthumous reputation as a "social bandit" who took from the rich to give to the poor.

flatly contradicted Necker's widely believed *Compte Rendu*. In addition Calonne's plan was widely seen as a measure aimed at increasing the power of the monarchy and the clique of parasitic aristocrats who were kept immune from economic difficulties by the oxygen of court sinecures, favours and pensions.

The government's problems were as much about credibility as about credit. Public opinion – now, as we have seen, a force to be reckoned with – was skilfully mobilized on everything relating to taxation by the parlement, which claimed to defend the interests of the "nation". Although court extravagance actually accounted for a tiny proportion of state expenditure, it was widely blamed for all difficulties. The secrecy and favouritism of court life were seen as running counter to interests of the "nation". This seemed all the more scandalous because the king was increasingly dependent on the

The theories of Austrian scientist/charlatan Franz-Anton Mesmer on "animal magnetism" were highly popular in fashionable society in the 1780s. Mesmerist sessions, in which hypnotist techniques were practised, were widely satirized for the way they took sexual advantage of gullible women.

"nation" for the loans he needed to keep the ship of state afloat. The monarchy's financial needs were too extensive to be met by the social elite alone; they required the aid of international money markets and the pocket-books of the middling as well as the upper classes. Yet just at the moment when the needs of the state seemed to demand a broadening of its social base, the monarchy was increasingly identified with aristocratic parasites. High nobles selfishly profited from the growing weakness of the monarchy. Reforming ministers found themselves victimized by court intrigue. Nobles acted to strengthen their hold on Church, army and state administration. The Ségur Ordinance of 1781, for example, restricted high rank in the army to the oldest "Sword" nobility.

In 1788 the government accepted that there was no way out of its financial dilemma except to consult the nation, in the form of the Estates General, last convened in 1614.

In the Tennis Court Oath of 20 June 1789 deputies of the Third Estate, sensing a royal attack, met informally in a tennis court in Versailles to swear not to disband until the basis of a new constitution had been established. This famous depiction of the scene, from the School of Jacques-Louis David, highlights the solemn drama of the occasion.

Most of the nobility, including the parlements, which had hitherto led opposition to "ministerial despotism", assumed that this body would meet according to the forms of 1614, when it had been manipulated by the nobility and the high clergy. They reckoned without the deep change in political mentality wrought by the Enlightenment, and the social and economic changes that had benefited groups outside charmed aristocratic circles. The assembly of the Estates General released the pent-up energies of "public opinion". Just to meet separately, as would normally be the case, as three separate "orders" or "estates" (clergy, nobility, and Third Estate) seemed an archaic relic out of tune with the times – all the more so because it threatened to allow delegations of the clergy and nobility the chance to squander this peerless opportunity for reform. "What is the Third Estate?" asked the Abbé Siéyès in a famous pamphlet of the same name in early 1789; only to answer, "EVERYTHING. What has it been in the political order until now? NOTHING. What is it asking to become? SOMETHING."

The financial crisis of the state was, then, generating a new political discourse. That

Rights of Man, rights of women

The Declaration of the Rights of Man of 26 August 1789 has proved an enormously influential political text. Its mixture of civil and political rights – individual freedom of speech, assembly and religious opinions, but also freedom from arbitrary government – has provided the blueprint for modern liberal culture. The Declaration is a key source of the United Nations' Universal Declaration on Human Rights.

Since 1789 the scope of the freedoms covered by the Rights of Man has varied. In the 1790s, for example, domestic servants, who were seen as lacking the necessary economic independence, were never fully enfranchised. The 1789 Declaration also coexisted quite happily with the institution of slavery – though to its credit the National Convention in 1794 would abolish slavery and the slave trade outright (temporarily at least). Women too were outside the parameters of the Rights of Man. The playwright Olympe de Gouges produced a pamphlet, *The Rights of Woman* (1791), demanding the extension of rights across the gender divide: "A woman has the right to mount the scaffold: she must also have the right to mount the tribune." Such views failed to make an impression on a revolutionary culture increasingly wedded to an ideology of separate spheres for the sexes. Law, politics and the economy were the male domain, whereas women were confined to a private sphere of sexual virtue, obedience and maternity.

Ironically de Gouges went before the Revolutionary Tribunal for treason in 1793 and mounted the scaffold herself. Women would get the vote in France only after World War II. For more than a century and a half after 1789 the political Rights of Man were confined in France to Men of the masculine sex.

Men rather than women dominated new Revolutionary rituals. In this gouache by Lesueur, women look on decorously and decoratively as their menfolk raise the liberty tree.

discourse – critical of the so-called "privileged orders" and demanding consultation with the "nation" – was, moreover, being heard throughout the land. When censorship was relaxed from July 1788 a flood of political pamphlets and newspapers was unleashed throughout France. The process of election to the Estates General, moreover, involved parish meetings and the drawing-up of *cahiers des doléances* ("books of grievances"). In these, under the influence of the spiralling cost of bread, the new political language fused with the hunger and anger of the poorer classes to produce an early revolutionary fervor. By the time the Estates met in May 1789, it was apparent that this was not going to be a replay of the Fronde, restricted to the political agendas of the high aristocracy, but a much broader and more challenging phenomenon.

It was Louis XVI's frightened attempt to turn back the clock that triggered revolution. Although he eventually agreed to convert the Estates General into a National Assembly charged with framing a new constitution for France, from late June 1789 he began to organize a *coup d'état* aimed at dismissing the Estates General. The next step would be to assume control in conjunction with a now compliant nobility. The city of Paris erupted into insurrection, with the storming of the Bastille. "It is a revolt, then?"

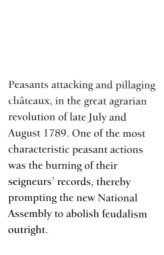

Peasants attacking and pillaging châteaux, in the great agrarian revolution of late July and August 1789. One of the most characteristic peasant actions was the burning of their seigneurs' records, thereby prompting the new National Assembly to abolish feudalism outright.

commented the king on hearing the news from Paris, only to be told coolly, "No, Sire, it is a revolution." The king backed down, and the new Assembly set about building a new constitution.

The entire constitutional landscape had changed. The king now ruled by the will of the people, not by the grace of God. Sovereignty no longer resided in the body of the dynast, but in the people. The "fundamental laws of the kingdom" were clearly insufficient to contain the implications of popular sovereignty. The nation was now made up of citizens with rights, not privately sanctioned groups with privileges. Ironically privilege had once been viewed as a bulwark against royal tyranny and as synonymous with freedom. Now it was a dirty word. It contrasted with the "rights" which all men – not just a select few – were adjudged to have, and which were enshrined in the Declaration of the Rights of Man.

The political crisis of the late summer sent shockwaves throughout the countryside. A (totally unfounded) "Great Fear" that the nobility had hired gangs of brigands who were touring the countryside destroying the harvest and frustrating any hopes of reform mobilized the peasantry into direct action against their seigneurs. Châteaux were attacked, estate managers harassed, seigneurial and feudal records burned. The new National Assembly, on 4 August 1789, not only endorsed peasant revolution by formally abolishing "feudalism". Led by enthusiastic liberal nobles like Lafayette, the assembly also extended the latter term to a wide range of *ancien régime* practices (the Church tithe, venality of office, and so on). These were added to the funeral pyre of what was already being called the "*ancien régime*" – "the former regime". The foundations of a new political culture were being laid.

FROM MONARCHY TO REPUBLIC

The Revolution was about words. Old hate-words ("privilege", "feudalism", and so on) contrasted with terms newly infused with Revolutionary meanings – "citizen", for example, and "nation", to say nothing of the Revolutionary triad "liberty", "equality" and "fraternity", which formed the building blocks of the newly emergent political culture. Terms destined for a long future were either forged, or received a markedly modern twist: "Left" and "Right", for example, "Terror", "terrorist", "bureaucrat", "conscription", "vandalism", "to revolutionize" and "to centralize".

If the Revolution was about words, it was also about symbols. From the earliest days politics saturated daily life. The Bastille, symbol of royal despotism, was transformed into a symbol of the people in arms, and found its way on to flags, wallpaper, shop-signs, pocket-knives, fans, buttons, book covers and all the bric-à-brac of everyday life. The tricolour flag was created when Louis XVI visited Paris following the fall of the Bastille, and Parisians added the Bourbon white to the city's heraldic colours of red and blue as a symbol of unity. The motif was, within hours, being worn in cockades as an emblem of patriotic virtue. The red cap too – mimicking the Phrygian bonnet, which in antiquity emancipated slaves had worn – became another Revolutionary passe-partout. To wear a white cockade, or to dress in overly elaborate aristocratic dress, was viewed as making a counter-revolutionary political statement. A subtle symbolic repertoire evolved as the Revolution unfolded, often involving collective activities. The

The Demolition of the Bastille by Pierre-Antoine Demachy. As soon as the Bastille was captured, the order was given to demolish it. The erasure of a symbol of royal despotism created welcome jobs for the unemployed and hungry workers of the Faubourg Saint-Antoine, the eastern neighbourhood in Paris in which the Bastille was situated.

The unity and indivisibility of France, pronounced on the day the republic was ratified, have proved the basis for state centralization to the present day. The picture depicts some of the most widely circulated emblems of patriotism: the red cap, the tricolour cockade and the fasces (representing justice).

planting of liberty trees became the occasion for revolutionary festivals to evolve, while political clubs such as the Jacobins developed as focal points for patriotic sociability, ritual and debate.

The reforms introduced by the National Assembly between 1789 and 1791 were about substance as well as symbols, and rank among the most impressive and most creative in French history. A constitutional monarchy was set in place. It was as if a decision had been made to make the past a blank sheet. Root-and-branch administrative reform led to the dissolution of the ancient provinces, within which French history had hitherto taken place. They were replaced by some eighty-three departments, which constituted – and still constitute – the basis of all forms of administration (financial, judicial, religious, military, and so on). Careers within the administration were opened up to all. A system of election extended to clergy and judiciary as well as those in political life, while high offices of state were no longer reserved for an exclusive caste. The so-called "career open to talent" had been established.

Careers tended to be most open to bourgeois talents. Although the universalistic language of 1789 was meant to apply to everyone, few members of the lower orders made it to the top. The bourgeoisie tended to hog the Revolutionary gains, although that other collective agent of 1789, the peasantry, now freed from tithes and seigneurial dues, also did well. The restriction of the vote to property-owners favoured the bourgeoisie and the bigger peasants, who also benefited most from the Revolutionary land settlement. The state had extricated itself from imminent bankruptcy in 1789 by nationalizing Church property – between 6 and 10 per cent of cultivable land. Sold off in lots this property rounded out the fortunes of the urban bourgeoisie and larger peasantry. Although some agrarian collective rights were maintained, property rights were now viewed as absolute. All internal tolls and customs-posts, which before 1789 made levies on the movement of goods, were abolished, allowing the formation of a truly open, national market. The spirit of *laissez-faire*, *laissez-passer* prevailed. In accordance with this, state interventionism in trade and industry was cut back, benefiting bourgeois employers, but having more mixed effects for workers. Guilds and workers' associations were also prohibited – trade unions were not made legal until 1884 – though bosses' cartels were not so easily abolished.

Economic liberalism was accompanied by the institution of the freedoms inscribed in the Rights of Man. Religious tolerance was permitted: its extension to Jews made France a world pioneer of Jewish rights. Habeas corpus was introduced, freedom of speech upheld, and freedom of the press championed. The press in particular was to prove one of the distinctive features of Revolutionary political culture. A vast number of newspapers, journals and pamphlets appeared, and readership mushroomed in size: in the mid 1790s, possibly one French adult in four or five read the Revolutionary press. Politics, so long excluded by *ancien régime* censorship, was suddenly news. The Revolutionary press acted as a channel and amplifier for a new, Revolutionary political language. It was in the pages of the Revolutionary press that a new breed of radical politician – Marat, for example – established its reputation.

Marat, "Friend of the People"

Jean-Paul Marat (1743–93) was typical of a set of late Enlightenment petty intellectuals to whom the Revolution gave a chance to make a new career. Until 1789 Marat's career was a failure, lived out in the curious shadowy world of Parisian hack-writers and "Grub Street" authors. Trained as a physician in France and Britain he tried to make an impact as a radical scientist in the late 1770s and early 1780s; but his attacks on Newtonianism flopped and failed to win him recognition. His political writings, notably his libertarian *Chains of Slavery* (1774), also failed to ignite the public. By the 1780s he was bitterly blaming the intellectual establishment for conspiring to frustrate his career.

Marat made himself a front-rank revolutionary through the political press. His radical *Ami du peuple* ("Friend of the People") from September 1789 became one of the most notoriously radical news-sheets. Like other political journalists – Hébert, with his populist *Père Duchène*, or Camille Desmoulins, with his *Vieux Cordelier* – he came to be associated with the title of his newspaper. The "Friend of the People" called not only for radical and democratic reforms, but also preached the spilling of the blood of aristocrats, royalists and priests who stood in the way of reform. His pre-Revolutionary experiences had made him an expert in denunciation. His precociously republican, terroristic message was too extreme for fellow citizens in the liberal phase of the Revolution up to 1792, but seemed prophetic thereafter. Marat played a part in the grisly September Massacres of 1792, when vigilante gangs murdered several thousand prisoners in Parisian gaols.

Marat was a more effective political journalist than politician. When he was eventually elected to the National

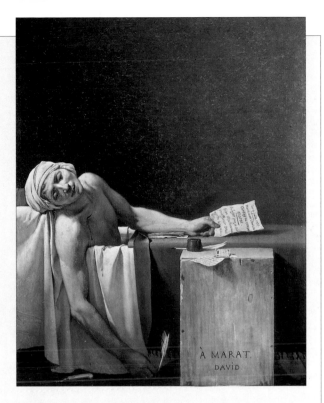

The Dead Marat (1793) by Jacques-Louis David.

Convention in 1792 he proved oddly ineffectual and was easily marginalized. His fame was given an added boost, however, by his death. He was already in the final stages of a terminal skin condition, when in July 1794 the young Charlotte Corday assassinated him in his bath. Marat, in whom Corday saw the essence of Parisian extremism, became a martyr of the Revolutionary cause; his bust was venerated among radicals throughout the land, and his ashes were interred in the Pantheon, the shrine for national heroes created by the revolutionaries.

Newspapers not only conveyed and reflected political events, they also shaped them. The Revolutionary press crystallized the lines of division and adversity within the nation. In the early days political culture was diverse and decentralizing. The principle of election gave local communities far more sway over their daily lives than had ever been the case before. The incorporation of the personal freedoms stimulated a hubbub of different, often divergent voices. Yet the Revolution's discourse on itself – as voiced in the National Assembly and as echoed through the pages of the press – stressed unity in progressively more strident tones. Far from the nation's defeat of tyranny having ushered in a golden age, it soon became apparent that severe social, economic and political problems remained. The huffy emigration of many high nobles ruined many of the luxury trades, while political instability put the sugar islands in the Caribbean in a state of open rebellion. The undoubted malevolence of the Revolution's enemies at home and abroad fuelled a search for scapegoats. The gap between the expectation of prosperous social tranquillity and the altogether more sober reality was filled by the language of conspiracy. Hence, problems were ascribed to secret counter-revolutionary plots by noble exiles, foreign powers, hostile courtiers, embittered clerics and a whole range of bogeymen and bogeywomen, including (unfortunately for them) the king and the queen.

From the earliest days Louis XVI, well meaning but desperately weak, proved incapable of playing the part of constitutional monarch written for him in the Revolutionary script. To refashion himself from miracle-working absolutist ruler into liberal constitutional monarch proved beyond his powers, especially when he was so ill advised by the grudge-bearing Marie-Antoinette. In June 1791 the royal pair fled from Paris in the direction of the German frontier. Brought back ignominiously from Varennes Louis recovered his status, but not for long. He failed to commit himself wholeheartedly to the Revolutionary cause even after France went to war with Austria in April 1792. Their crisis came when news arrived in Paris that Verdun, the last fortress on the Austrian army's line of march towards Paris, was about to fall. At this, a crowd was assembled by the *sans-culottes* – as their enemies called the popular street radicals who distinguished themselves by not wearing the knee-breeches of gentility. On 10 August 1792 the king was overthrown, and on 21 September a constitutional Convention, elected by universal male suffrage, proclaimed a republic that was to be "one and indivisible".

The Nation in Arms constituted the foundation myth of the First Republic. The patriotic pike of the *sans-culotte* had overturned royalty. On 21 September 1792, as the

Revolution, religion and politics. The religious division marked out by responses to the oath on the Civil Constitution of the Clergy in 1791 has proved one of the most influential guides to France's religious and political geography. The areas that rejected the oath broadly remained centres of Catholic observance and support for the Right until the late twentieth century. Many of these areas were on the periphery. However, some outlying areas – such as those centred on lower Provence and Languedoc and the Bordeaux area – have been traditionally more committed both to republican values and anti-clericalism.

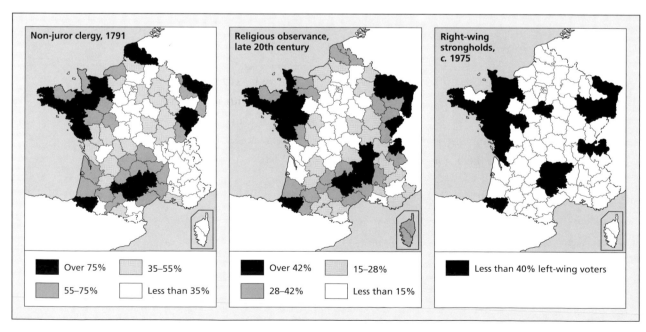

The "War Song for the Army of the Rhine" composed by Rouget de l'Isle in 1792 was adopted by the volunteers from Marseille marching north to depose the king on 10 August and then to proceed to the front. "The Marseillaise", as it came to be called, was adopted as national anthem in 1795, but was dropped from 1815 onwards. It was readopted in 1879.

republic was being declared in Paris, volunteers fought alongside the heavy artillery of the regular army, defeating the Austrian and Prussian armies in the cannonade of Valmy. "This is the beginning of a new epoch in history," the German writer Goethe, who was present at the battle, told his comrades, "and you can claim to have witnessed it." The French commander celebrated the victory not with a solemn Te Deum but with a marching song penned by Rouget de l'Isle for Marseille volunteers on their way to Paris and then the northern front. "Aux armes, citoyens! Formez vos bataillons!" As its chorus indicates "The Marseillaise" was, from the beginning, the battle hymn of the French republic.

Pugnacity was essential if the republic was to be kept "one and indivisible". By early 1793 France was at war with most of the rest of Europe, and was also experiencing counter-revolutionary insurrections, notably in the west. In this crisis there developed a number of fault-lines – notably over religion, social radicalism and political centralization – which threatened to tear the state apart. They were also to mark enduring points of fracture within the political nation well into the twentieth century.

The nationalization of Church property had made thoroughgoing reform of the Church inevitable. The reorganization of Church structures in the Civil Constitution

Chouans and Vendéans

While the Revolution of 1789 gave France a new political culture, the lineaments of which are still in place, it also stimulated powerful opposition forces that were to prove influential in modern France. The deepest and most enduring oppositional forces were located in the west, home of the Chouans and the Vendée rebels. In the course of the 1790s as many as 150,000 to 200,000 executions took place in the region, and the total number of deaths in the ongoing civil wars approached half a million.

The preconditions of rebellion had been laid by the Civil Constitution of the Clergy, for the west was hyper-Catholic and resented religious reforms. Finally, open insurrection was triggered by the state's conscription demands in February 1793. The Revolution did not seem worth fighting for. Though peasants had been freed from seigneurial dues, new state taxes made a worse dent on peasant budgets here, and the reform of the Church removed an important charitable safety-net. The local nobility were slow to pick up on the potential of the insurrection – they preferred warfare between gentle-

men to guerrilla operations. However, by the summer of 1793 a full-scale "Church and King" revolt was under way in the Vendée department and its environs.

The new republic was finding it difficult enough to cope with foreign war at this time, and revolt in the west seemed like a stab in the back. Matters came to a head after power on the Committee of Public Safety (the war cabinet) was centralized and terroristic policies were introduced. A powerful repressive riposte was soon being visited upon the west. A decree of 1 August 1793 envisaged the total destruction of the rebellious areas. Some historians have viewed the ensuing bloodbath as a genocide – and certainly women and children as well as male combatants were often indiscriminately slaughtered. However, this both exaggerates the scale of repression and understates the two-way character of the violence. Hideous atrocities were certainly committed on both sides.

Terror contained the insurrection in the west by early 1794. But it proved more difficult to quell less formal operations. Just as the Camisard rebels against Louis XIV in the early 1700s had made good use of their Cévenol moorlands, the *bocage* in the west – the landscape of hedgerow and wooded cover – provided an excellent terrain for guerrilla operations. The area in the triangle between Lorient, Le Mans and Saint-Brieuc became the home of the Chouans (the name probably derived from *chat-huant* (screech-owl), the imitation of whose cry served as nocturnal signal among the rebels). Occasional threats of a link-up with *émigré* troops and British landings were only the tip of an iceberg which consisted of endless vendettas against revolutionary officials, banditry, highway robbery and political assassination.

Though the area was brought more firmly under control by Napoleon, the reputation of the west among republicans as the home of dyed-in-the-wool reactionaries and primitive barbarians proved more long-lasting.

of the Clergy (July 1790) won a great deal of clerical support, but also much frank hostility. An oath of allegiance to this act turned into a kind of national opinion poll on the Revolution, as parishes pressurized their priests into voting either for or against. A rough fifty/fifty split between "jurors" (those who swore the vote) and "non-jurors" (those who refused) emerged, plus the geographical profile of "two Frances". Areas which rejected the oath – most notably in the west and north – would remain in favour of Church and tradition, and vote right wing in elections down to the Fourth Republic. In contrast those regions accepting the oath tended to be, and to remain, anti-clerical and republican. That non-jurors were associated with counter-revolution in these war years etched the line of division ever deeper. "Church and king" peasants, notably in the Vendée department in the west, took up arms against the republic in 1793. Their uprising, fuelled by opposition to religious reform but also by antagonism towards new taxes and other Revolutionary demands, was put down in a sea of blood.

If religion was in dispute in the foundation years of the republic, also at issue under the pressure of war were key questions of social class and political radicalism. The

Opposite "If I advance, follow me; if I retreat, kill me; if I die, avenge me." The words of Henri de La Rochejaquelein (1772–93), the young noble who was first to serve as commander-in-chief of the Vendée rebels, typify the intransigence of royalists in the west. He died in fighting outside Nantes, but was immortalized in this 1817 painting by Pierre-Narcisse Guérin.

Lafitte del.

Fresca sculp.

PLUVIOSE

$\frac{21}{22}$ Janvier. *Le Soleil est au Signe du Verseau*
Obs. Ast.

Sous un léger tissu s'achemine au Boccage.
La Nymphe au doux Nectar apportant son trousseau,
Bravant Pluie et Hiver, brûlante en ce bel âge
Des feux qui vont l'unir à son cher Pastoureau.

Année Commune	Lever du Soleil	Coucher du Soleil	Soleil sur l'horison
Paris	4.34	4.26	8.34
Rome	7.13	4.47	9.34
Madrid	7.4	4.51	9.42

1er du Mois	Lever du Soleil	Coucher du Soleil	Soleil sur l'horison
Londres	7.43	4.17	8.34
Petersbourg	8.32	3.28	6.56
Vienne	7.34	4.26	8.52

A Paris chez l'Auteur, rue de Sorbonne N.º 389.   Déposé à la Bibliothèque Nationale.

political elite split between Jacobin deputies in the Convention, who favoured victory even at the cost of alliance with the lower classes, and those who expressed qualms at such a strategy. If the republic in mid 1793 was to be saved, "we must rally the people". So spoke the deceptively mild-mannered Jacobin lawyer from Arras, Maximilien Robespierre, darling of the Paris *sans-culottes*. But moderate deputies in the Convention, the Girondins, feared mob rule if too many concessions were made to the Parisian street radicals. The Jacobins prevailed; a *sans-culotte* purge rid the Convention of Girondin leaders and the Jacobins took over the Committee of Public Safety, the war cabinet directing the war effort. To enlist popular support in Paris and the provinces, they introduced a wide range of radical measures: incomes and price-fixing policies were established; the final vestiges of feudalism were removed; slavery was abolished both at home and abroad; radical divorce legislation was confirmed; and an embryonic welfare state sketched out. That this strategy was successful could be seen when virtual national conscription – the *levée en masse* – was introduced in August 1793. This act, which brought three-quarters of a million men under arms, and increased the total size of the army and its support services to over a million individuals, was a precursor of the mass warfare of the twentieth century. The Revolution was perceived to be worth fighting for; national politics saturated every town and village in an entirely new way.

Political centralization was the third major fault line opened up in republican culture in these years. The Girondins, who had resisted Jacobin populist reforms on the grounds that they infringed the rights of property and the liberal freedoms of 1789, opposed the centralizing thrust of the Jacobins' strategy on much the same grounds. The most ruthless kind of centralization (the very word, significantly, dates from the Revolution) was needed to put the social radicalism of the Jacobins into effect. Terror was made "the order of the day": the Committee of Public Safety was given sweeping powers, a Revolutionary Tribunal was set up in Paris, while mass executions were conducted in civil war zones throughout France. Though fewer than 3,000 individuals were executed in Paris, the national body-count ran to several hundreds of thousands. Perhaps half a million individuals were also imprisoned as "suspects" during the reign of Terror in 1793/4. Another 130,000 to 150,000 individuals emigrated. The victims were drawn from all classes, though the privileged classes of the *ancien régime* were treated particularly harshly.

However unpalatable the fact might be, the Terror saved the republic. Girondin hostility to social radicalism, centralization and repression seemed wilfully squeamish – and not just to extreme Jacobins like Robespierre, Danton and Marat. Many moderate deputies also placed the survival of the republic above rigid respect for decentralized powers and liberal freedoms. The Committee of Public Safety's war minister Lazare Carnot, the "Organizer of Victory", held right-wing, virtually royalist opinions. The Jacobins branded the Girondins, their rivals in the Convention, as guilty of "federalism" – that is, wishing to dilute the Committee of Public Safety's policies of radical centralization – and equated their opposition with outright treason and counter-revolution.

Opposite A month from Louis Lafitte's version of the Revolutionary calendar, introduced in 1793. The Revolutionaries believed that their actions marked an inaugural date in the history of humanity, not just of the French. Their calendar was dated to start on 21 September 1792 – the day the republic was proclaimed. All prior and particularly Christian associations were dropped in favour of names derived from nature. Pluviôse was the "rainy month" (from "pluie", meaning rain) and lasted from late January to late February.

The prefects introduced by Napoleon in 1800 were in some respects the heirs of Charlemagne's *missi dominici* and the *ancien régime*'s intendants. In other respects they were the forerunners of the modern bureaucrat – professional, steeped in theoretical and practical training, utterly obedient and single-mindedly loyal.

The republic survived its infant traumas, but Jacobinism did not have long to crow about the victory of anti-clericalism, social radicalism and political centralization. The very success of the Committee of Public Safety undermined the Jacobin position. Internal counter-revolution and federalism were routed, and by spring 1794, French armies were forcing foreign troops out of France. The case for relaxing the Terror seemed strong, yet Robespierre and his colleagues on the Committee of Public Safety intensified repression, even executing former allies such as Danton who were now calling for greater clemency. The populist dislike of the established Church seemed to be driving the Jacobins in a millenarian, or prophetic, direction, towards an unrealizable "Republic of Virtue". A Revolutionary calendar was set up, the metric system was devised and new forms of popular religion were developed, notably Robespierre's favoured Cult of the Supreme Being. It all proved too much for the solid phalanx of bourgeois deputies in the Convention, who rebelled. On 27 July 1794 – 9 Thermidor Year II under the Revolutionary calendar – Robespierre and his allies were overthrown by a conspiracy hatched in the Convention.

The pendulum now swung almost at once away from the policies with which the Committee of Public Safety had been associated. Surviving Girondins returned to the Convention, demobilized the *sans-culotte* movement, dismantled the key institutions of Terror and set about introducing as much decentralization as was consistent with winning the war against Europe. A new constitutional regime was devised – the Directory (1795–9) – which attempted to build on the liberal ideas of the 1789 to 1791 period. It proved difficult, however, to keep the new regime within the rule of law; greater freedom benefited the opponents of the regime, both on the Left and on the Right. A subversive movement based on the early communistic ideas of Gracchus Babeuf was defeated in 1796. On the Right, vigilante royalist gangs in the Midi operated a ruthless "White Terror" against former Jacobin supporters, the Catholic Church made a strong comeback and constitutional royalists made big gains in the elections. The supporters of the Directory survived by turning themselves into a self-perpetuating political elite. They fixed elections, manipulated the polls to retain a grip on power and endlessly zigzagged from Right to Left in order to remain strong enough to continue the war against Europe.

By the late 1790s a new and worrying phenomenon was emerging from the war, in the shape of a group of political generals. Pichegru and Moreau, for example, were linked to the royalists. Hoche, a stable-lad under the *ancien régime*, and living embodiment of the Revolution's "career open to talents", was viewed as a Jacobin. So too in his early days was the young Corsican general, Napoleon Buonaparte – the Italianate "u" was dropped only in the late 1790s – who gained credit with the Right by suppressing a rioting mob in Paris in September 1795 "with a whiff of grapeshot". Bonaparte won a brilliant reputation in campaigns in northern Italy in 1796/7, which shifted the balance of European power in France's favour. His decision to pursue the struggle against Britain in the Near East led to the Egyptian campaign of 1798/9. When his plans went awry there, he returned to France to discover the Directory engaged in

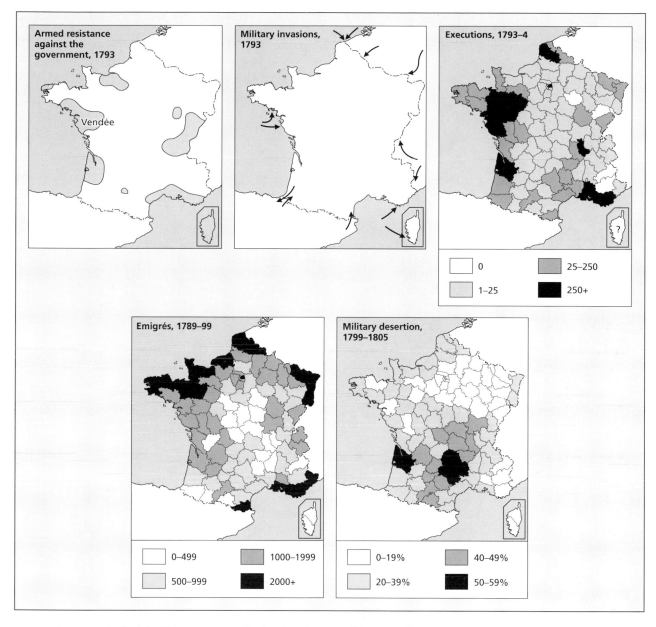

The impact of Terror. The Terror provoked a variety of regional responses. Executions for political offences tended to be concentrated in areas hit by civil and foreign war. The frontiers produced larger proportions of émigrés, while the map of military desertion highlighted a traditional north-east versus south-west split.

yet another round of crisis. He was approached to head a *coup d'état* aimed at securing the gains of 1789 without returning to the terrible days of 1793/4. He did so – but on his own terms. His *coup d'état* of 2 November 1799 (18 Brumaire Year VIII under the Revolutionary calendar) overthrew the Directory and created a new regime, the Consulate, over which he held unchallengeable power. The French Revolution seemed to have fallen into the hands of a Corsican adventurer.

NAPOLEONIC FRANCE

Although there was a strongly militaristic aspect to his rule, Napoleon – first as Consul, then from 1804 as Emperor – offered not so much military dictatorship as strongly

Jacques-Louis David's evocation (*c.* 1800) of the young Napoleon crossing the Alps on his way to military glory in Italy in 1796–7. The artistic style has shifted from Classical to Romantic – and does some injustices to history: Bonaparte is known to have crossed the Saint-Bernard pass seated on a mule, docile but more footsure than David's champing steed.

authoritarian personal rule. The First Empire was another instance of that strong strain of centralized power inherent in French history whose most recent manifestation had been in the Reign of Terror. "From Clovis to the Committee of Public Safety," he noted, with that immodesty which has ever since attracted megalomaniacs to his name, "I embrace it all."

As the quotation suggests, to a considerable extent Napoleon built on the achievement of the Revolution, even as he prided himself on offering an alternative to it grounded in French traditions. "I am the Revolution," he claimed – while also arguing simultaneously, "The Revolution is over." He endorsed the Revolutionary land settlement involving the sale of Church lands, which gave all peasant and bourgeois purchasers a vested interest in supporting the regime. Financial stability was helped, too, by the foundation of the Bank of France in 1803. The tax system was simplified and

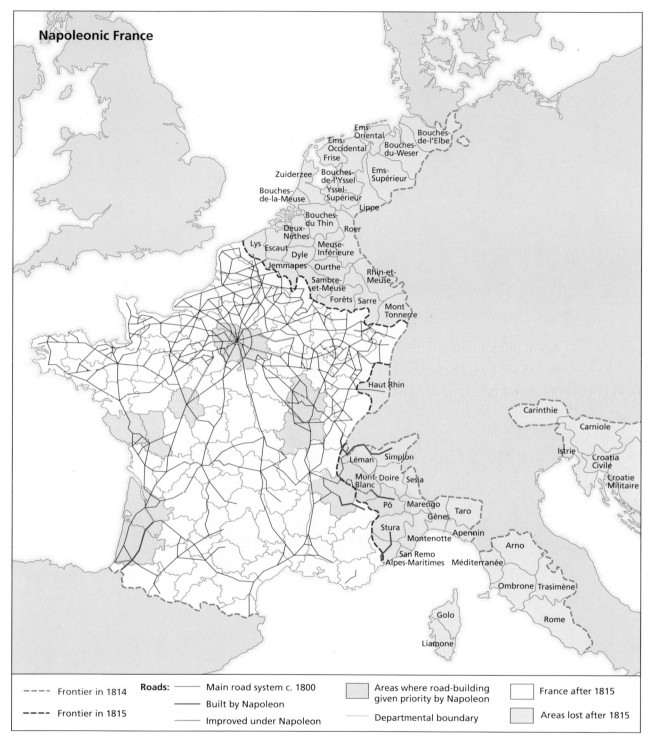

Napoleonic France

Ems-Oriental
Ems-Occidental
Frise
Bouches-de-l'Elbe
Bouches-du-Weser
Zuiderzee
Bouches-de-l'Yssel
Ems-Supérieur
Bouches-de-la-Meuse
Yssel-Supérieur
Lippe
Bouches-du-Thin
Roer
Deux-Nèthes
Lys
Escaut
Meuse-Inférieure
Dyle
Jemmapes
Ourthe
Rhin-et-Meuse
Sambre-et-Meuse
Forêts
Sarre
Mont Tonnerre
Haut Rhin
Carinthie
Carniole
Istrie
Croatia Civile
Croatie Militaire
Léman
Simplon
Mont-Blanc
Doire
Sesia
Pô
Marengo
Taro
Gênes
Apennin
Arno
Stura
Montenotte
San Remo
Alpes-Maritimes
Méditerranée
Ombrone
Trasimène
Golo
Rome
Liamone

	Roads:				
- - - Frontier in 1814	—— Main road system c. 1800	Areas where road-building given priority by Napoleon	France after 1815
- - - Frontier in 1815	—— Built by Napoleon	—— Departmental boundary	Areas lost after 1815
	—— Improved under Napoleon		

Napoleonic France was the hub of a sprawling European system of power, very little of which lasted beyond 1815. The Napoleonic regime was, however, important in exposing many areas on France's borders to the institutions and reforms of the Revolutionary era (abolition of feudalism, legal reforms, etc.). Improvements in communications aimed at closer integration of economically (and often politically) backward areas. The base unit of power was the department, now headed by a prefect.

made more efficient along lines sketched out in the 1790s. The administrative reforms of the Revolutionary decades were also maintained, though in an authoritarian twist in 1800 each department was endowed with a Napoleonic nominee, the prefect. The prefects were essentially updated and streamlined versions of the intendants of the *ancien régime*. Within their constituencies they acted as petty emperors to ensure the imperial will was carried out. This reinforcement of the principle of authority was mirrored in the field of liberal freedoms: imprisonment without trial, a refined version of *lettres de cachet*, was introduced, overriding habeas corpus provisions. Napoleon reimposed strict censorship, which also recalled the *ancien régime*. Once the herald of Revolutionary politics, the newspaper no longer had a place in the hierarchical and repressive world of the First Empire: over a thousand new titles had appeared in the decade after 1789; by 1811 only four had full governmental authorization.

As the decline of journalism indicates, colourful political hyperactivity gave way to an altogether paler version of public life after 1799. "If the press is not bridled," Napoleon commented, "I shall not remain three days in power." Politics became little more than a façade, especially after Napoleon assumed the imperial title. Significantly, Revolutionary insignia had to make way for the emblems of personal empire. The tricolour survived, but Napoleon's head now appeared on coins, and he bore a sceptre like a Capetian. The pike, symbol of popular sovereignty and the Nation in Arms, was replaced by the imperial eagle. There were elected representative bodies; but they were toothless. Most legislative work was done by imperial decree – and done in volume. Over fifteen years Napoleon was personally responsible for 80,000 letters and decrees. Political opponents were either deprived a platform or sent into exile. Propaganda was developed as a fine art. Marshal Berthier's terse assessment of Napoleon on the field of battle – "Nobody knows his thoughts and our duty is to obey" – applied as much in civilian life. As his interior minister Chaptal was later to remark, "He wanted valets, not advisers."

The "valets" were well rewarded for their pains. The streamlined spirit of Napoleon's administration did not obscure the links of patronage and sheer corruption which ran through the regime. The *légion d'honneur* was created as a means of ensuring political loyalty, but this was only the tip of a very considerable iceberg of favours, gifts and concessions. Titles were bestowed, a court aristocracy was formed, a strict social hierarchy re-established. The sober egalitarianism of the Revolutionary assemblies gave way to a naked love of ostentation and grandeur, which painters, sculptors, authors and decorative artists were commissioned to celebrate. Jacques-Louis David, for example – once a follower of Robespierre, and the pageant-master of revolutionary festivals under the Terror – now turned admiring portraitist of the emperor.

This blend of Revolutionary rationalism and authoritarian principle was epitomized in the famous *Code Napoléon*, or Civil Code, issued in 1804. The product of endless committee meetings throughout the Revolutionary decade, the code was brought to completion under Napoleon's chairmanship. Equality before the law and the "career open to talents" were preserved, but one could detect the hierarchical hand of

"A stoppage to a stride over the globe." From the late 1790s English hostility to the young victor of the Italian campaigns was expressed in numerous satirical cartoons. French expansion had to be checked by "little Johnny Bull".

Napoleon in the way in which the family was made the base unit of social organization. Under the influence of Roman law, the paterfamilias's authority put the rights of women in the shade.

Women had played a larger role in public affairs in the Revolutionary decade – organizing clubs, getting involved in direct action, publishing and reading up on political events – than in any rebellion of early modern Europe. Yet the ideology of separate spheres which had evolved in the Enlightenment had also had an important effect. Radical politicians had criticized such women as Marie-Antoinette for "feminizing" and corrupting politics under the monarchy. Even the Jacobins had attacked women's clubs as a left-wing deviation, preferring women to stay at home and bring up good patriots. Napoleon endorsed this view, and in the Code reduced women's status to that of minors. Given the patriarchal cast of mind of the political elite, it is hardly surprising that many women took refuge in religion. In fact the number of nuns rose tenfold between 1815 and the 1870s. Catholicism, through education, charitable good works and even personal vocation, provided a space for women outside the private sphere.

Other measures worked in much the same way. Imprisonment without trial was used like *lettres de cachet* under the *ancien régime* to incarcerate errant wives, daughters and other family members. Family law in the Revolutionary decade had been made egalitarian and gender-blind; under Napoleon daughters' rights were systematically diminished. Rather generous welfare provisions for war-widows, the aged and even unmarried mothers were brought to an end. The liberal divorce laws of the 1790s, which had provided battered and abandoned wives with a means of improving their legal position, were altered in ways which disadvantaged women. Provision for female education was in poorer shape in 1815 than it had been in 1789; it was almost wholly under the Church, since the state only concerned itself with the teaching of boys. The *lycées*, founded by Napoleon for secondary schooling, aimed essentially at reproducing a male social and bureaucratic elite. The Napoleonic regime was bad news for women, and it would take generations for them even to begin to recover or improve on their lot.

"The weakness of women's brains," Napoleon claimed, "and the mobility of their ideas mean that their social destiny can only be achieved through religion". The rehabilitation of religion after a decade of ardent anti-clericalism was viewed as serving the interests of the family, as well as society at large. In Christianity Napoleon claimed to see "not the mystery of the incarnation, but the mystery of social order", and he smirked that he would convert to Islam were it politically expedient. The Concordat he signed with the pope in 1801 was an immensely important buttress of the regime's power. It implied papal recognition of the nationalization of church property in 1789, and weakened the position of "Church and King" opponents of the regime. Catholicism was reestablished as "the religion of the majority of Frenchmen", and brought under the authority of the state. (This, incidentally, did not prevent the emperor from according Protestants and Jews state endorsement and funding.) Every effort was made to have bishops act as "prefects in purple", parish priests as "mayors in black".

The First Empire was able to restore a great deal of the social harmony lost in the Revolutionary decade. The priesthood was reincorporated into the nation and religious minorities were placated. Exiled aristocrats now returned to vie with rising bourgeois for their place in the imperial sun. Napoleon lost France's overseas possessions, an outcome that had been hastened in the West Indies by his attempt to reintroduce slavery. But the warfare which Napoleon conducted so relentlessly in Europe produced an empire which only Charlemagne had rivalled: 130 departments were ruled from Paris; numerous satellite and allied kingdoms dotted the map; members of his family were scattered liberally among European crowned heads; and only Britain remained irredeemably hostile. In the late 1790s warfare had ceased to be about ensuring national defence and become a matter of naked expansionism. It was Napoleon's genius to have turned the Carolingian-style quest for plunder into a political buttress for his regime. By constantly expanding the area of his direct influence and by consistently directing the costs of warfare (in the form of higher taxes and conscription) on conquered territories, he was able to conduct war without imposing high taxes within France and without ruinous state borrowing. The "Continental System" he developed provided the framework for the semi-colonial exploitation of much of Europe. In the process he ruthlessly subordinated the economic interests of conquered territories to French needs. Napoleon thus made conquered Europe pay the price of France's warfare, and

kept the population within French frontiers cushioned and prosperous. As he observed, he "would rather face 20,000 soldiers on the field of battle than 2,000 workers on the streets of Lyon".

So the Napoleonic regime cleverly balanced domestic stability with external aggression. "If only it lasts," commented Napoleon's mother, at seeing her proud son the arbiter of the continent, and her other children the backbone of the European ruling class. It didn't. By 1810 the regime was running into severe problems. Most of Europe had been brought under French control, but Europe's strongest economic power,

François Gérard's painting of the coronation of Charles X in 1825. The lush spirituality and phoney archaism of the gestures highlight the still close links between Romanticism in art and the Right. Chateaubriand was among the most enthusiastic supporters of the event.

Britain, held out and subverted Napoleon's economic dominion. There were signs that Napoleon had, like Charlemagne before him, reached the plunder frontier, and could not expand further without logistically and politically over-extending himself. From 1808 the Peninsular War in Spain proved a running sore. Quarrels with the pope led to a French takeover of the papal states in 1809, an action which lost the regime a great deal of Catholic support. The Continental System began to collapse. For the first time since 1794 the brunt of war costs was shouldered by France, in the form of higher taxes and heavy conscription demands. These came, moreover, just as a severe economic crisis occurred, forcing bread prices up and causing bankruptcies and mass unemployment in industry.

Napoleon's attempt to regain the strategic initiative – the Moscow campaign of 1812–13 – proved a catastrophe. He was defeated militarily, lost an army of half a million men, and found himself faced with a coalition of European powers finally putting co-operation before mutual rivalries. Further defeats followed, in Germany in 1813 and inside France itself in 1814. Napoleon was deposed at the end of 1814 and sent to the tiny Italian island of Elba. Returning to France unexpectedly in 1815, he promised a new liberal constitution and engaged in a frenetic flurry of activity. A liberal Napoleon sounded like a contradiction, however, and he failed to convince a nation sick of his demands. His "Hundred Days" ended ignominiously on the battlefield at Waterloo. This time he really had come to the end of the line.

FROM RESTORATION TO REPUBLIC

With Napoleon shipped off to spend his last days on the barren wastes of St Helena in the South Atlantic, the Napoleonic empire was dismantled. Power in France, now reduced to its 1792 frontiers, passed back to the Bourbon dynasty, in the person of Louis XVI's brother, Louis XVIII. ("Louis XVII", Louis XVI's son, had died in prison in 1795 without ruling.) The "Legitimist" dynasty, brought back "in the baggage-train of the Allies", seemed set to re-establish the natural order so rudely interrupted by Jacobins, *sans-culottes* and power-crazed generals. Yet this wish to put back the clock to before 1789 showed an astonishing lack of sensitivity; after all, 1789 and its aftermath had revolved around this very question of the legitimacy of power. It would prove difficult to dismantle the "nation" constructed in the workshop of Revolution. The period since 1789 had created new forms of political legitimization alongside Bourbon "Legitimism". The "natural" ruling class was no longer so natural. For the next half century France would live through the clash and competition of alternative forms of legitimacy, each heir to competing political cultures and each with its own language, symbols and constituencies.

In this over-charged atmosphere apparently trivial political gestures took on a disproportionate importance. Bourbons and Bonapartists, for example, rejected the republican allure of the "The Marseillaise". Similarly the Bourbons won the undying hatred of republicans and Bonapartists for reinstating the dynasty's white as the national flag. The Bourbons' ferocious attachment to their ancestral white crippled

their chances of recovering power after 1830. Louis-Philippe (r. 1830–48) acted with
more sensitivity in reinstating the tricolour and "The Marseillaise" – though he
offended republicans by not celebrating 14 July, the anniversary of the storming of the
Bastille, as a national holiday. As that keen observer of French politics, Karl Marx,
pointed out, just as the Revolutionaries of 1789 and 1794 had taken their models from
classical Greece and Rome, the generation of 1848, "drawing its poetry from the past",
styled themselves on the Dantons, the Marats, the Robespierres – and the Bonapartes
– of the Revolutionary decade. Throughout the nineteenth century politicians viewed
their future through a rear-view mirror.

Yet if political life seemed dangerously volatile, there were countervailing forces
within French society that served to contain conflict and to ensure a high degree of continuity. Equality before the law and the "career open to talent" ensured that the professional classes and the bureaucracy provided stability in social life. Individual
prefects came and went, but the institution of the prefect remained, as steady as a rock.
The administrative achievements of the period from 1789 to 1815 – the departments,
new courts, the tax system, the Bank of France – remained intact too, while the *Code
Napoléon* provided the framework for the transmission of property and civil rights
throughout the century and beyond.

Below the cut and thrust of Parisian politics those social groups which had done
best out of the Revolution – notably the bourgeoisie, the professional classes and the
bureaucracy plus the wealthier peasants – formed a solid backbone to social life. In this
respect it makes sense to talk of the Revolution of 1789 as having brought about a
"bourgeois revolution". The clergy and the nobility, who had lost most in the
Revolutionary years, could now prosper only if they adapted to the new social landscape. Even the restored Bourbons had not dared to reinstate them as self-policing
ancien régime "orders" with distinctive privileges. They lost their pre-Revolutionary
right to the lion's share of state patronage. The clergy had to accept the loss of its lands,
as did those many noble exiles who had had their property expropriated: the nobility's
share of the national land-surface fell from 25 to 20 per cent between 1789 and 1815.
The Restoration monarchy failed to reverse the long-term decline in noble influence.

High politics was increasingly the province of professional men and bourgeois, not
the high nobles who had monopolized office prior to 1789. Restoration monarchs
Louis XVIII (r. 1815–24) and Charles X (r. 1824–30) did their best to swing things in
the aristocracy's favour. They chose nobles to become their ministers, infiltrating them
into the best administrative, military and religious posts, and endeavouring to forge a
new union of "throne and altar". Such efforts only aroused resentment. The further the
Bourbons strayed from the broad outlines of the Revolutionary settlement, the more
vulnerable they became. Louis XVIII declared himself unwilling to be "king of two
peoples", issued a Constitutional Charter similar enough to the 1791 Constitution to
elicit solid support and chose moderate and conciliatory advisers. Hardline supporters
of the Bourbons, the "Ultras", were more royalist than Louis XVIII himself, and were
gaining in influence even before his brother Charles X ascended the throne in 1824.

Eugène Delacroix's *The 28th July: Liberty Leading the People* (1830), commemorating one of the "Trois Glorieuses", showed that Romanticism had moved from the Right to the Left. A mixture of allegorical and realistic elements this painting was shown in the 1831 Salon.

Charles X, a converted libertine who had found piety late in life, played his cards spectacularly badly. Impervious to how much religious gestures had lost their power to enchant, he organized a traditionalist coronation at Reims, including a ceremony of touching for the King's Evil. Such symbolism looked embarrassingly fake and outmoded, as did the sacrilege law of 1825 introducing the death penalty for blasphemy. Even a cowed and surprisingly quiet opposition found these attempts to resurrect the divine right of kings too much to stomach. But it was not until 1829/30, in the context of bad harvests, high prices and business failures, that their protests began to arouse greater support. Charles X's attempt to bridle the press and to rule as if by the grace of God rather than the wish of the people assumed the shape of a royalist *coup d'état*. The regime found it had few friends when three days of insurrection in Paris – "*Les Trois Glorieuses*" (27–29 July 1830) – forced the monarch to abdicate.

While radicals and conservative governments throughout Europe felt there was a real possibility of the days of 1794 being replayed, political operators among the Bourbons' liberal opponents moved swiftly to circumvent the possibility of a reign of terror or a Bonapartist autocracy. The monarchy was allowed to continue – but in fresh hands. To cheering Parisian crowds the ageing Lafayette, "Hero of the Two Worlds", bestowed the throne on the duke of Orléans, Louis-Philippe, descendant of a branch of the Bourbon dynasty. During the Terror his father had been unable to escape the guillotine, despite dubbing himself "Philip Equality" and voting for the death of Louis XVI. The new king had served in the Revolutionary armies of the 1790s and embraced a moderate and liberal version of the Revolutionary heritage.

The "citizen king" would preside over a "bourgeois monarchy". Louis-Philippe prided himself on being able to balance the "excesses of popular power" with the "abuses of royal power". Charles X had tried to heal the sick like a saint; Louis-Philippe carried an umbrella. Charles X had sought to subvert liberal freedoms; Louis-Philippe vigorously endorsed them. So censorship was reduced, the property franchise lightened and the elected assembly allowed to initiate laws. This was no social revolution, however. The electorate was expanded – but hardly spectacularly: still only a quarter of a million landowners had the vote. Rather, the boundaries of the ruling class had been broadened to include a greater influx of lawyers, businessmen, middling landowners and financiers. The bourgeois monarchy encouraged an interchange between the financial, manufacturing, professional, agrarian and political branches of the bourgeoisie. The flavour of the new regime was redolent not of the aristocratic salon or the elegant country house, but rather the stock-exchange, the business premises and the wealthy bourgeois private residence.

The Revolutionary and Napoleonic periods had equipped France with an unmatched array of legal and administrative structures adapted to capitalist development – abolition of feudalism, a unified home market, national legal codes, uniform weights and measures, equality before the law, a national bank and so on. Yet while the Industrial Revolution steamed ahead in neighbouring Britain, France lagged some way behind. This was partly because of France's poor natural supply of coal and iron ore, but crucial too was the major realignment required of the French economy after the events between 1789 to 1815. In those years colonial trade, the most dynamic sector of the *ancien régime* economy, had been crippled. The colonial empire that France had struggled to develop in the eighteenth century was effectively wiped out. There were attempts to build a new world empire after 1815. The conquest of Algeria was begun in 1830, while there were further gains under Louis-Philippe in West Africa, Madagascar and the South Seas (Tahiti, for example, was colonized). Yet France after 1800 had a far more continental, land-based economy than prior to 1789. Indeed the

Slave revolts

Saint-Domingue (present-day Haiti) had been the most significant element in France's booming colonial trade in the eighteenth century. The success of the West Indian colony stemmed from sugar plantations that were worked by black slaves. But in the 1790s it became the site of a black liberation movement. This owed little to France itself: the first slave protests in 1790 and 1791 were put down in a pool of black blood. The National Assembly's abolition of slavery in early 1794 was, moreover, the acceptance of a *fait accompli*: since 1793 slave armies led by Toussaint l'Ouverture had taken control of the colony along with the neighbouring ex-Spanish colony of Santo Domingo.

Toussaint was the dominant leader on the island in the mid and late 1790s. A slave himself, who had been emancipated in his thirties in 1777, he was both idolized by the blacks and respected by the whites. He attempted to work har-

moniously with the white community in order to restore the island's prosperity, but the situation was far from stable. A complex game unravelled that included the French, black radicals, and British troops in the Caribbean. Toussaint's insistence that he was French and by 1800 a loyal Bonapartist was not enough to prevent his capture, deportation to mainland France and imprisonment. Napoleon sought to re-establish slavery as the basis for the island's economic recovery: "A white myself," he is alleged to have said, "I am on the side of the whites."

"By overthrowing me," Toussaint wrote to Napoleon, "you have only cut down the trunk of the tree of liberty of Saint-Domingue. Its roots will grow back, for they are many and deep." He was vindicated. Though he died in a French gaol, his black opponents in the colony were able – with the help of yellow fever – to put paid to French armed forces and in 1804 to establish Saint-Domingue as an independent black state.

Toussaint l'Ouverture. He owed his second name to the ferocity with which he made an opening ("ouverture") in the ranks of the enemy in battle.

Revolutionary and Napoleonic Wars had caused the centre of gravity of the economy to shift from the Atlantic seaboard to the eastern and northern frontier. The big ports which had benefited from France's colonial dominion and trade in the eighteenth century – Bordeaux, Rouen, La Rochelle, Saint-Malo, Le Havre and others – declined in influence and wealth, while such eastern cities as Strasbourg and Lyon saw their prosperity grow. In the north, cities close to the coal belt also started to expand.

The Revolutionary land settlement also had a major impact on the pattern of economic growth after 1800. Most peasants now prioritized self-sufficiency above all else. The long-term drop in agricultural prices after 1817 and the damage done to foreign trade by colonial losses gave them a disincentive to sell their produce on the open market. The "traditionalism" and "archaism" for which their urban contemporaries condemned peasants were thus a rational response to a difficult economic environment. Temporary or seasonal migration was another strategy for survival. The most backward areas – the Massif Central, the Alps and Pyrenees – provided the most mobile of populations, sending out hordes of harvesters, ditch-diggers, servants, pedlars, schoolteachers and entertainers (the prize possession in the inventories of many Pyrenean peasants was a fairground bear), whose earnings helped prop up family budgets.

Ironically this peasantry, which contemporaries saw as archaic and backward-looking, was adopting that most "modern" of forms of behaviour: systematic birth control. Before the nineteenth century France, like every other European society, had had high birth- and death-rates. The death-rate started to fall, as we have seen, in the eighteenth century, and would continue to do so throughout the nineteenth century. Improved nutrition was the key here, though medical advances such as smallpox vaccination (after 1798) also had an impact. From 1800, however, while France's European rivals continued to be marked by high fertility, its birth-rates plummeted: from nearly 40 live births per thousand population before 1750, the rate fell to 32 per thousand in the early Restoration, and then to 26 per thousand by mid century. The causes of this silent sexual revolution taking place in peasant beds may relate to the growth of religious indifference which distanced peasants from the precepts of the Church. More significant, however, was the introduction of partible inheritance by the Napoleonic Code, which provided motivation for peasants to limit family size. Peasants, then, adopted birth control – largely *coitus interruptus*, it would appear – so as to prevent having to split up their lands among numerous heirs, and so that their land could stay large enough to ensure continuing self-sufficiency for the next generation.

France was still overwhelmingly an agricultural and small-town society. A far higher proportion of its population lived on the land than any of its competitors. In Britain

The railway became a satisfying social metaphor. An admiring family of prosperous bourgeois watch a locomotive, representing engineering feats (tunnel, bridge), social mixing (the passengers), speed and scientific progress. In the background loom the symbols of France which need to be changed: a château, a windmill, a church, and a peasant driving a mule.

From the mid eighteenth century, a dynasty of Koechlins had pioneered light cotton manufacturing in the independent imperial city of Mulhouse. Incorporated into France in 1798, the city became one of France's leading textiles centres in the nineteenth century.

the moment when urban population outstripped country-dwellers came in the 1830s. In Italy it was in the 1870s; in Germany around 1900; in the United States of America in the 1920s. Yet in France this moment occurred as late as the 1930s. For most of the nineteenth century between two-thirds and three-quarters of the population still lived on the land. Indeed nearly half of France's departments experienced an all-time maximum of rural population between the 1830s and the 1870s. With some exceptions, moreover, the towns cut only a modest figure. Paris grew fast, doubling between 1800 and 1850, and there was impressive growth in industrial cities like Lyon, Lille and Mulhouse. More characteristic, however, was the town of around 10,000 inhabitants, whose stuffy atmosphere was captured in the novels of Stendhal and Balzac. The social mood of the early nineteenth century was set by the notables who dominated these centres: landowners (including many nobles, whose influence at local level outweighed their prominence on the national stage), *rentiers* and the professional classes.

Hence the social and demographic setting predisposed France, even with its framework of rational institutions, to an industrialization process which would be protracted, steady and solid rather than sudden or spectacular. Mechanization was slower in France than in Britain – with its large pools of out-workers France had fewer labour bottlenecks acting as an incentive to mechanize. However, France was still far ahead of the pack among Britain's economic rivals in continental Europe, and remained the second biggest exporter of manufactured goods through to 1870. Whereas Britain's exports were mass-produced middle-quality items, France specialized in the luxury and skilled finished goods (silk, gloves, porcelain, and so on) in which it traditionally had a reputation.

There were important moves in the 1830s and 1840s, moreover, to improve the infrastructure of the economy, laying down the bases of future growth. Road and canal building was accompanied by the beginnings of investment in railways. An important law in 1842 provided a partnership between the state and business for railway development. A dense rail network, centred on Paris, was already emerging by the fall of the July Monarchy in 1848. Despite France's somewhat sleepy appearance, there was a good deal of exchange and communications. The country had 7,000 fairs a year, on top of 3,000 weekly markets. The emergence of a body of commercial travellers from the 1820s, and the development of advertising in the press, also highlighted communication and exchange.

This balanced economic development muffled the growing pains of industrialization. The latter imposed strains on the working classes which did not, however, approach the appalling levels characteristic in Victorian Britain. The fact that most peasants stayed on the land cushioned cities from the emergence of a massive urban under-class. Yet conditions were still grim. The Romantic painter Delacroix portrayed workers and bourgeois in arms together on the barricades of "*Les Trois Glorieuses*" of 1830; but the bourgeoisie soon distanced themselves from their former allies, both in politics and in social policy. Calls for a radical republic were silenced. A rising of impoverished silk-workers in Lyon in 1831 was pitilessly repressed. Social concern for the condition of the poor was rejected in favour of a *laissez-faire* attitude. Supporters of the regime attacked any talk of industrial legislation, calling factories "sanctuaries as sacred as a father's house". "Whatever the lot of the workers is," a trade minister opined in 1833, "it is not the manufacturer's responsibility to improve it." Nor apparently was it the government's. In the cities inadequate provision of decent housing, water, sanitation and job opportunities produced desperately unhealthy conditions. In Mulhouse the new-born baby of a bourgeois had a life expectancy of over thirty years; that of a weaver, of four. Cholera reared its head after 1832, causing havoc among city populations; some 143,000 people died in the 1853/4 outbreak alone, which seemed a dreadful warning of the perils of urbanization.

Grim conditions among the poor produced some response from the Right. The priest Felicité-Robert Lamennais preached a "social Catholicism" in tune with the times, while Charles Ozanam created a network of Societies of Saint-Vincent-de-Paul, which practised imaginative forms of philanthropy. Though the Right remained alert to the political potential of charity as a means of winning mass support, most fellow-Catholics in the elite dreamed primarily of a return to the *ancien régime* rather than adapting to industrial society. Yet even though industrial workers found the call from the Right unappealing, the Revolutionary traditions of 1789 seemed to have been

Flora Tristan

"The proletariat of the proletariat." "The most oppressed man can oppress one being, his wife." These views of women espoused by the Utopian socialist Flora Tristan (1803–44) were grounded in her own experiences. The illegitimate child of a Peruvian seigneur and a French migrant to Spain, she married young and returned to France in 1816, just as the liberal divorce laws introduced in the Revolution had been repealed by the Restoration government.

Good fortune alone brought an end to the hard treatment she suffered from her husband: after trying to shoot her in the street, he was declared insane and their marriage repealed. By then Tristan had developed close links with activist women among followers of the socialists Saint-Simon and Fourier. In the 1830s she also visited working-class neighbourhoods in Britain, and her

Promenades in London (1842) bears comparison with Engels' *The Condition of the Working Class* as a poignant testament to the deprivation inherent in the working-class experience.

Fearlessly energetic, she toured widely, speaking to socialist and working-class groups in the name of women's rights. Her preaching the need for women and workers to make common cause fell, however, on stony ground. Workers found her patronizing, and many socialists were as sexist as the reactionaries. Even many women who breached female social codes – such as the woman novelist Georges Sand, whose bohemian lifestyle and trouser-wearing shocked the bourgeoisie – were anti-feminist. Flora lived and died as an outsider; her *Testament of a Pariah, or Women's Emancipation*, was published posthumously in 1846.

---

hedged in by an upper bourgeois elite impervious to urban distress. New radical traditions developed as a result. With the tricolour associated with Orléanist "bankocracy" rather than "democracy", new symbols appeared. At Lyon in 1831 the black flag of anarchism was unfurled. On the barricades of the 1830s and 1840s the red flag, which would become the symbol of the international workers' movement, also made an appearance.

A wide range of radical and socialist views began to be expressed, often linking the urban working classes with disenchanted fractions of the bourgeoisie. They developed a critique of capitalism that was grounded in the often divergent radical traditions of the 1790s. The socialist Louis Blanc, for example, preached a moderate creed based on universal suffrage and social reform. The anarchist Proudhon, in contrast, rejected the state as an agency for change and advocated forms of mutual co-operation between workers. These marginal authors were read: the cheap brochures they produced circulated widely, while such socialist newspapers as *La Ruche populaire* ("The Popular Hive") and *L'Atelier* ("The Workshop") also spread the word. Educational levels were moreover still rising. The Guizot law of 1833, establishing a primary school in every commune, was important in boosting literacy levels.

In time the cultural movement of Romanticism came to add a certain glamour to some of these opposition forces. Though a movement of revolt against conventional values, Romanticism under the Restoration, in the hands of Chateaubriand and

Bonald, had had a politically conservative edge. Indeed it was most concerned with the rejection of classicism in art. By the end of the 1820s a new generation shifted the Romantic gaze more to the political left. This included Eugène Delacroix in art, Victor Hugo in theatre and other writings, and Stendhal, whose admiration for Napoleon was based on a cult of individualism, energy and heroism. The bohemian wing of the Romantic movement – strong in student circles on the Parisian Left Bank – also formulated an indirect critique of the drab materialism of life under the "bourgeois monarch". Such bohemianism was primarily designed to shock – hence the sensation which the poet Nerval caused in polite society when he paraded through the Tuileries gardens with a lobster on a leash. (When asked why, his reply, "It does not bark, and knows the secrets of the deep", displayed a certain, impeccably absurdist logic.)

By 1848 the middle-of-the-road monarchy of Louis-Philippe would find few supporters. The intelligentsia seemed at odds with everything the regime represented. The Right was still wedded to *ancien régime* values, while the Left was developing new political traditions of its own. Even in the political centre the middling bourgeoisie felt distanced from the highly elitist character of the regime and their criticisms gathered pace from the mid 1840s on, as the economy took a downturn.

THE SECOND REPUBLIC

Lacking the crumbling glamour of the Bourbons, or the tawdry grandeur of the Bonaparte inheritance, the Orléanists found it difficult to make their image of solid, bourgeois centrism attractive even to many of their own kind – let alone the peasants, nobles and workers who made up the majority of the population. From the middle of the 1840s economic difficulties began to take hold. These came in time-honoured fashion, starting with bad harvests and leading on, via high food prices and a slump in demand for manufactured goods, into an industrial crisis, bankruptcies and unemployment. The regime's fragile popularity collapsed.

Among the educated classes discontent crystallized around the call for an extension of the right to vote. Political public meetings were forbidden, so the campaign was "fronted" by public banquets held in major cities. In Paris a banquet in February 1848 suddenly flared up into a political demonstration, and the descendants of the *sans-culottes* of 1794 took to the streets and formed barricades. A panicking Louis-Philippe abdicated, and a Provisional Government of journalists, liberal politicians and lawyers was swiftly formed in Paris and immediately declared a republic.

"When France catches a cold," noted the Austrian chancellor Metternich, "the rest of Europe sneezes." As if to prove his point, the February revolution helped to spark off a host of rebellions and revolutions throughout Europe. The early history of the Second Republic (1848–52) was, then, lived out against a background of rebellious activity, with fellow revolutionaries looking to France for the kind of military aid which the armies of the 1790s had provided. In Paris too the political actors seemed to be playing out a drama scripted in the Great Revolution. The political enemy was no

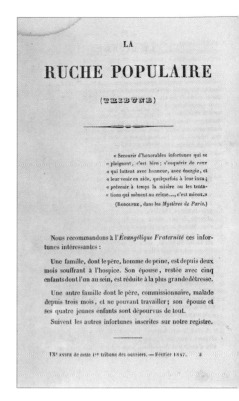

Front page from *La Ruche populaire* ("The Popular Hive"), February 1847. The July Monarchy saw the appearance of large numbers of newspapers and journals of different political hues, but written both for and by peasants and workers.

The barricades of February 1848 became a meeting point for the patriotic forces of republicanism and progress: soldiers, citizens and children overcame the paid military lackeys of the monarchy. This is very noticeably a male world: women were relegated to the private sphere under reformist republicanism as well as monarchism.

longer the *ancien régime* aristocracy, as in 1789, but rather the "bourgeois aristocracy" who were profiting handsomely from the new set-up – the "absolute bourgeoisie" rather than the absolute monarch. The struggle was not now between orders or estates, as in 1789, but between classes. "The three orders", Balzac noted, "have been replaced by what we call classes. We have lettered classes, industrial classes, upper classes, middle classes etc." Tocqueville, witnessing the unravelling of the political crisis of 1848, declared that it was "not a political struggle, but a struggle of class against class, a sort of servile war …".

Conflict revolved around the kind of republic this Second Republic should aspire to be. Paris street radicals supported the socialist Louis Blanc, who was elected to the Provisional Government, and whose influence led to the establishment of national workshops, which played an important role in soaking up some of Paris's acute unemployment problem. Such gestures were resented by moderates throughout the country, who were apprehensive at the influence of Paris radicals. The latter were alleged to want to institute a "social republic", to replay the Terror, and to establish a centralizing, anti-clerical dictatorship over the "backward", "fanatical" and "Girondin" provinces. A red scare mobilized moderate and right-wing opinion throughout the country. Conflict came into the open in June 1848, when the government closed down the national workshops, leading Parisian radicals to take to the streets. There, in spite of the barricades, they were cut to pieces by troops led by General Cavaignac. Some 50,000 individuals took part in these "June Days": 1,500 were killed, 12,000 arrested and some 5,000 subsequently deported.

In the blood of the June Days, the red scare was exorcized. Even by then the political landscape had been transformed by elections which returned fewer than 100 socialists, as against over 500 moderate republicans and about 200 monarchists. The single key factor in this rightward shift had been the introduction of universal male suffrage, under which the electorate grew from a quarter of a million to about nine million. The new, peasant vote more than counterbalanced the radicalism of the Parisian workers' movement. There was also a twist in the tail. A new president was elected under the same conditions in December 1848, and the victor – with 5.7 million out of 7 million votes cast – was Louis Bonaparte, nephew of the Great Man. The royalists were too split to pose a viable alternative – and the Bourbon pretender, the comte de Chambord, whom Charles X had chosen as his successor under the title Henry V, was too intransigent. The republicans also proved ineffectual, as they emerged painfully from the fratricidal struggle of the June Days. It seemed that the largely peasant electorate, alienated from the republic by continuing economic hardship, remembered the Bonaparte name with some fondness. Napoleon had endorsed the Revolutionary land settlement, and his reign was associated – with all the inaccuracy of nostalgia – with low taxes and French *gloire*.

Louis Bonaparte proved an imperial cuckoo in the republican nest. Widely viewed as a buffoon he had succeeded as Bonapartist pretender in 1832 when Napoleon's son, the so-called "Napoleon II", had died childless. His record prior to 1848 – a couple of Bonapartist "insurrections" that had ended in fiasco, and some woolly liberal ideas – made him massively underestimated by the political classes. Realizing that under the 1848 constitution the president was elected for a four-year mandate only, he worked ferociously hard to build up a powerful image and a solid backing. On 2 December 1851 he organized a *coup d'état* and had himself made president for life – a decision he had ratified in a national referendum. Exactly a year later he followed up this gesture by having himself appointed emperor – a title he assumed as Napoleon III. Though borne to power originally in a flood of peasant votes, his seizure of power in 1851 prompted a strong left-wing protest in the countryside, notably in the south and southwest. The radical and socialist Left had had some success in spreading propaganda in rural areas. To mop up the discontent, martial law was declared in thirty-two departments: nearly 27,000 individuals were arrested and at least 10,000 of these were deported. The "peasant emperor" had come to power in the face of the last great peasant uprising in French history.

CHAPTER 8

From the Second Empire to World War I

NAPOLEON III AND THE SECOND EMPIRE

"I am prepared to be baptized with the waters of universal suffrage, but I do not intend to live with my feet in a puddle." Napoleon III's – perhaps apocryphal – remark captures the mix of democracy and authoritarianism which was to mark his reign. He prided himself on standing above the hurly-burly of politics, transcending Left and Right, and being responsible not to the elected legislature – the new constitution rendered his parliaments toothless – but to the people. The latter, however, he neglected to consult, except for a handful of referendums stage-managed by his bureaucrats. Meanwhile he kept the press carefully shackled. Though he paraded progressive views on workers and peasants, he had established himself in power on a wave of panic among the propertied classes caused by the 1848 June Days. Furthermore he had repressed popular protest against his 1851 *coup d'état* with exemplary violence.

The Left was cowed and silent, but still represented a frightening bogey-figure in the imaginations of the majority of the political nation. Symptomatically Napoleon had supported the 1850 Falloux Law, which gave religious schools greater freedom to operate – the number of teaching monks and nuns increased eightfold and fourfold respectively during his reign. Even a free-thinker like the liberal politician Adolphe Thiers thought that the Church had a role to play in keeping "the vile multitude" on the paths of virtue. Napoleon's interior minister even forbade teachers from wearing beards, which were taken as an unmistakable sign of anarchist opinions. The Second Empire was the regime which saw in 1857 both *Les Fleurs du Mal* of poet Charles Baudelaire and *Madame Bovary*, Gustave Flaubert's great novel, brought to court for outraging public decency.

As it turned out, a regime which shaped up to be drably authoritarian and socially backward-looking emerged as a period of dynamism and prosperity. Historians still debate the extent to which the regime's successes were a personal achievement of "Napoleon the Little", as Victor Hugo dubbed him. Some major achievements can clearly be laid at his door. The transformation of Paris conducted by his appointee, Baron Haussmann, is a case in point. It was, however, immensely lucky that his coming to power coincided with a major turn-round in the economic situation. Boosted by a gold boom based in Californian and Australian mines, world trade was thriving. A period of low prices, which had lasted since 1817, ended in 1851, providing a stimulus to enterprise. By the end of the Second Empire in 1870 the value of industrial production had doubled.

A major shift to steam-power took place. Mechanized horsepower in industry quintupled, to a level higher than in all the other countries of continental Europe put

Napoleon III in full military dress poses on a pouf for an equestrian portrait. Photography has the unlooked-for effect of puncturing the pomposity of even the most ardent self-publicist.

together. Cotton production – though hit in the 1860s by the drop in imports of raw cotton caused by the American Civil War – was still second only to Britain's. There was a quintupling, too, in the kilometrage of railway track. Trains carried half of internal trade in 1870 where in 1850 they had carried one-tenth. The rail boom kick-started the coal and metallurgical industries, and boosted exchange; the volume of trade tripled, helped latterly by a free-trade treaty signed with Britain in 1860. The national rail network was dense and reliable enough, and prices sufficiently buoyant, to encourage farmers to come out of their shells and abandon self-sufficiency to produce for the market. The wine-growers of Lower Languedoc made their fortune by supplying the Parisian market, and were soon avidly adopting the trappings of bourgeois respectability. There were peasant homes here which now boasted two grand pianos.

Economic prosperity also owed much to the development of banks, which offered credit more widely than ever before. The emperor, whose partnership with private capital had started the rail boom, played a key role in establishing a modern banking system. He provided the framework within which private capital could be sunk into a network of banks: the Comptoir d'Escompte (1848), the Crédit Foncier (1852), the Crédit Lyonnais (1863) and the Société Générale (1864). The circulation of banknotes – now issued in handier small denominations – increased fivefold. Savers now deposited with credit institutions rather than adding to the family hoard under the bed, and this allowed banks to play a major part in financing national growth.

The Haussmannization of Paris

Paris is the heart of France. Let us put all our efforts into embellishing this great city. Let us open new roads, make populous neighbourhoods which lack light and air more healthy, and let benevolent light penetrate everywhere within our walls.

Napoleon III's call for the modernization of the city of Paris was implemented by Baron Haussmann, prefect of the Seine department from 1853 to 1869. Balzac's Paris – crumbling with age, slum-ridden, insanitary, prone to cholera epidemics, over-crowded – was to be brought up to date. Some rejected the changes on aesthetic grounds; the anarchist activist Proudhon denounced "the new, monotonous and tiring city of M. Haussmann". There were also many on the Left who felt that there was a hidden political agenda involved in the change – namely, the destruction of the old workers' neigh-

Napoleon III and Empress Eugénie lay the foundation stone for the new opera house, in the company of Prefect Haussmann.

Cholera, embodied as a rag-picker, protests to Hausmann that the modernization of Paris is costing him his home.

bourhoods that had fostered the radicals and *sans-culottes* of the Parisian revolutionary tradition. Barricades and boulevards could not coexist.

Modernization was part of a more general process of making the city the showcase of the imperial regime. Prestige building integrated into the new street plan included the Opéra, the Bibliothèque Nationale, extensions to the Louvre palace, the iron buildings of Les Halles (the city market), plus the development of open leisure spaces (Bois de Vincennes, Bois de Boulogne, and so on). Such changes also had the power of example: right up to World War I a great many major cities followed in the tracks of "Haussmannization" and "boulevardization".

Modernization also involved making Paris the economic motor of the country as a whole. The fact that Paris was the hub of a new railway network under-

lined Napoleon's commitment. Just as railways acted to unify the national market and energize the national economy, so the new boulevards and broad avenues, driven through the jungle of narrow medieval streets, were to connect up and produce a more integrated urban society and economy. In practice the changes also had the effect of introducing greater social distance between the classes. Classes had traditionally been integrated vertically in the city: first- and second-floor rooms were occupied by the bourgeoisie, the top floor and garret by the poor. Haussmannization brought about a new differentiation, between richer and poorer areas. The inner city became more middle-class, while workers were pushed outwards to a proletarian "red belt" encompassing the city. Haussmann had not solved social and political problems, merely displaced them.

"The Empire means peace," Napoleon had proclaimed in 1852. Yet although it never rivalled the systematic aggressiveness of the First Empire, the Second Empire did have a strongly militaristic strain, which Napoleon fitfully disguised behind a pacifistic rhetoric. The emperor dispensed with the timidity which had marked French foreign policy in preceding decades, establishing a worldwide presence. He doubled French colonial holdings most notably in Indo-China, central and West Africa and the Pacific, and prepared France for the scramble for colonies which would take place after 1880. The new banking institutions also stimulated foreign investment worldwide. The Suez Canal, opened in 1869 by Napoleon's wife, Empress Eugénie, was the achievement of a French man, Ferdinand de Lesseps, and had been largely financed from the savings of the nation's bourgeoisie. Yet Napoleon was unable to wrest the initiative in world trade and colonization from Britain. And his ill-conceived plan to establish an empire in Mexico in the 1860s resulted in a humiliating fiasco.

Manet's depiction of the slaughter meted out in the Paris Commune of 1871.

He did little better in Europe. Though his acquisition of Nice and Savoy (from neighbouring Piedmont-Sardinia) in 1859 marked the only major extension of French frontiers between Waterloo and the present day, he received little credit for an achievement that was overshadowed by his failures. The biggest of these proved to be his inability to master the rising tide of nationalism in Europe, notably in Italy and Germany. His acquisition of Nice and Savoy was achieved in exchange for giving military assistance to Piedmont in forcing through Italian unification against Austria. He got the worst of both worlds, though, upsetting Catholics by allowing the forcible incorporation of the papal states into the new Italy, yet alienating liberals by later sending French troops to defend the pope in the Vatican. On the European stage he was also easily outplayed by Prussia's Bismarck, and an attempt to trade French neutrality in the Austro-Prussian War of 1866 rebounded disastrously on him. He had hoped to be rewarded by the acquisition of Luxembourg for his neutrality at a moment when Prussia was establishing primacy in central Europe, and creating a German national state. He was humiliatingly snubbed, and found himself threatened by two new nation states.

And humiliation did now count; for public opinion was re-emerging as a political force in the 1860s. The authoritarian days of the 1850s had given way to a period of experimentation with liberal reform. Press censorship was relaxed; the circulation of Parisian newspapers, which had stood at 50,000 in 1830, reached 700,000 by 1868. Laws on public meetings were progressively weakened, too, and in 1864 the right to strike (though not yet to organize or to picket) was authorized. Radicalism grew steadily in the workplace – in the 1860s French workers were to form the largest national delegation to the First International. A republican opposition also began to coalesce – its adherents were mostly those who rejected socialism but planned liberal reforms, spiced with the doctrinaire anti-clericalism which was becoming a conventional attribute of French republicanism. Napoleon permitted ministers to have greater responsibility for their decrees to parliament and also introduced a number of measures which allowed the Chamber of Deputies to assume greater autonomy.

As a result discontent with the regime grew quickly, especially as the economy was experiencing a rather bumpier ride in the 1860s than in the golden days of the 1850s. Meanwhile Napoleon's increasingly fraught and reckless foreign policy was also attracting criticism. The opposition parties won 40 per cent of the popular vote in elections in 1869. When plans to become a fully parliamentary regime were put to the voters in a referendum in May 1870, they won a massive five-to-one majority. These changes could have proved a significant test of the democratic credentials of what had begun as an essentially authoritarian regime. The constitutional experiment was, however, still-born; by the end of the year the Second Empire had ignominiously fallen.

The collapse was military and diplomatic. Army reforms in the 1860s had not produced the looked-for improvements in military organization and morale, with the result that once Napoleon took to the field, he found his troops outmanoeuvred by the superbly effective Prussian fighting machine that Bismarck had assembled. Holed up in Sedan with nearly 100,000 troops Napoleon surrendered, and was sent to prison in

Germany. He never returned to France. The scale of the defeat led politicians in Paris to declare the end of the regime and to install a provisional government. They would be obliged to sign a humiliating peace, by which France surrendered the provinces of Alsace and Lorraine to the new German state. Hence the regime which had gained Nice and Savoy would be associated with a territorial loss greater than France had experienced since the Hundred Years War. The incoming regime would have to cope with continued political division, as well as the humiliation and economic damage caused by the loss of two strong and prosperous northern provinces.

THE COMMUNE AND THE POLITICS OF THE THIRD REPUBLIC

The Third Republic was born with France in trauma. The omens, when set against the volatility and brevity of regimes since 1789, were not good. Even the regime's midwife – Adolphe Thiers, who headed the provisional government, and was the first president – gave the infant republic little chance of survival. In the event the Third Republic was to last until 1940, making it the most enduring regime in modern French history. And indeed, although its history between the two world wars was to be troubled, the regime's prestige up to the peace treaties at the end of the World War I was extremely high. By then it had achieved its main foreign policy objective – the reconquest of Alsace and Lorraine. It had presided over extensive colonial expansion. It had maintained enviable financial stability. It had brought considerable material progress to the majority of French people. And it had been associated with a cultural life as rich and varied as that of any other period in French history: Cézanne, Monet and Matisse in painting; Auguste Rodin in sculpture; Zola and Proust in literature; Verlaine, Rimbaud and Mallarmé in poetry; Debussy in music; Pasteur in medical science; the Curies in physics; Poincaré in mathematics; Bergson in philosophy; Charcot in neurology; and Durkheim in sociology, to name only some of the most outstanding figures.

There was little in 1870 and 1871 to suggest the achievements to come. War continued after the overthrow of Napoleon III, with Paris endeavouring to hold out against a Prussian siege. The charismatic young politician Léon Gambetta escaped by balloon from a city whose inhabitants were reduced to eating rats; but his attempts to raise an army in the south were in vain. In January 1871 the provisional government capitulated, signing a peace treaty which ratified the loss of Alsace-Lorraine and imposed a war indemnity of 5 million francs, obliging France to suffer the humiliation of a German occupying army until the sum was forthcoming. Paris smarted under the blow, and elected a municipal government, which, in the spirit of national defence of 1792, took on the title of "the Commune". This time, however, there was to be no replay of history. Thiers established himself in Versailles, his position buttressed by a newly elected monarchist majority in parliament, and undertook a new siege of Paris, in which the Commune was introducing radical social legislation and calling for the prosecution of the war. With German occupying troops watching with grim fascination, a bloody dance of death ensued. Thiers' troops penetrated the city towards the end of May and began a ferociously brutal conquest of the city. The Revolutionary Tribunal

Madame Curie

Marie Curie, née Sklodowska (1867–1934), was among the most outstanding of a wave of French scientists with worldwide reputations, whose careers illuminated the intellectual history of the Third Republic. Born in Poland, and entering France in 1891, she pursued a brilliant student career before working in the scientific team of the physicist Pierre Curie, whom she came to marry in 1895. Röntgen had just discovered X-rays, and Madame Curie worked to find compounds of substances besides uranium which produced them. By 1898 she had discovered the element radium, which she and her husband succeeded in isolating in 1902. They were jointly awarded the Nobel Prize for physics in 1903.

Madame Curie continued to work in the same field after the death of her husband in 1906, and was awarded a second Nobel Prize in 1911. She was particularly interested in the use of radium in medicine. In World War I she personally supervised the provision of portable X-ray equipment for French troops. Though she had been refused admission to the Academy of Sciences in 1908 – presumably because of her gender – she received a full measure of state support after the war. After her death her work was carried forward by her daughter Irène Joliot-Curie.

The popular press played an important role in publicizing the "patriotic" science of the Curies. In 1994 President Mitterrand announced the transfer of her remains into the Pantheon.

M. ET Mᵐᵉ CURIE DANS LEUR LABORATOIRE

---

between 1792 and 1794 had accounted for fewer than 3,000 deaths; in a single week anti-Commune justice meted out on the streets of Paris accounted for between 25,000 and 30,000 deaths by summary execution, with over 40,000 Parisians taken prisoner. Hostages taken by the Commune, including the archbishop of Paris, were shot. Fires swept through the city, burning down the Tuileries palace, the Hôtel de Ville and other public buildings.

The searing memory of the Commune affected both Left and Right. It formed a myth whose heroic resonance the Marxist Left would long exploit. The Right constructed a different myth, of Paris as hotbed of sedition, home of red revolutionaries, wild anarchists and crazed women (the *pétroleuses* – female petrol-bomb throwers alleged to have started the city's fires – had a particularly blood-curdling impact on the bourgeois psyche). Even though the Haussmann reforms were already transforming the social composition of the city, forcing workers into the "red suburbs", and producing a conservative inner city, the Commune served as justification for outright reaction. Paris was kept under siege conditions until 1876. In contrast with France's other 38,000 communes, it was denied the right to have a mayor – a refusal that lasted until 1976. Only in 1879 did amnesties begin to be given to those Communards imprisoned in 1871.

With the Commune utterly discrediting and dividing the Left, the Right enjoyed a political field day. The monarchist majority in the new assembly triumphantly assumed that they constituted a kind of antechamber to a revived monarchy. This

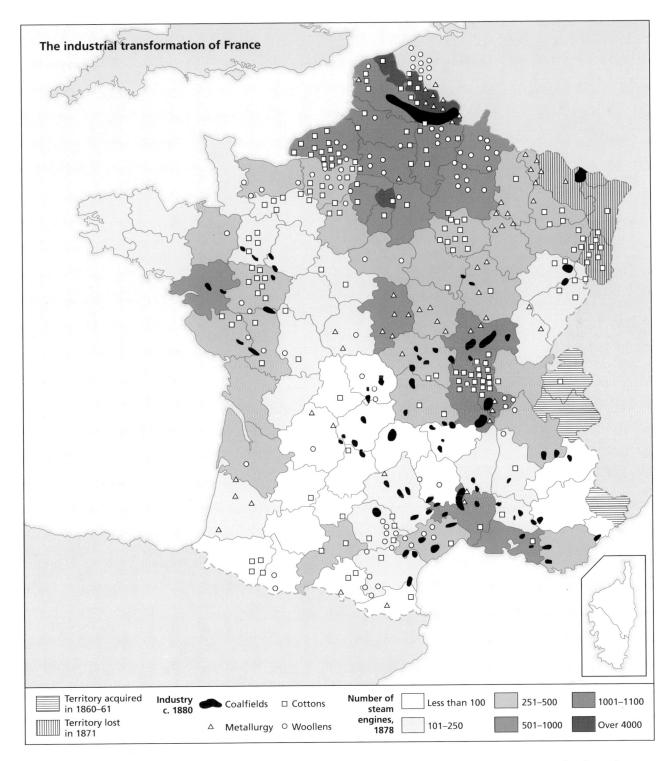

The industrial transformation of France

| Territory acquired in 1860–61 | **Industry c. 1880** | Coalfields | □ Cottons | **Number of steam engines, 1878** | Less than 100 | 251–500 | 1001–1100 |
| Territory lost in 1871 | | △ Metallurgy | ○ Woollens | | 101–250 | 501–1000 | Over 4000 |

While the political geography of France changed little after 1815 the country's industrial geography was transformed, highlighting the importance of local supplies of coal and the acceptance of steam power. While new industrial heartlands evolved in the far north, the east and the Lyonnais, many areas of traditional manufacturing – such as the woollen industries in Languedoc – failed to adapt. A contrast was opening up between a "modern" north and east and an "archaic" south and west.

The building of the new opera house (in the background) necessitated extensive house clearance in the surrounding neighbourhoods. Space around the opera house was thought necessary for security reasons, in the light of the Orsini bomb attempt on Napoleon's life in 1858 at the old, crowded opera house on the Rue Le Peletier.

proved ill-founded. The Right were as divided as the Left. The Bonapartists were temporarily in disgrace, and though they were gaining electoral victories by the mid 1870s, the death in 1879 of the Bonapartist pretender by a Zulu spear in southern Africa reduced their political credibility. The monarchists were moreover as split – and as out of touch – as ever. The crusty old Legitimist pretender, the childless comte de Chambord, refused to accept the tricolour, and though his Orléanist rival, the comte de Paris, had fewer scruples, he had fewer supporters too. Royalism was moreover tied in with the most dyed-in-the-wool backwardness of the Catholic Church. The papacy had gradually become the key rallying-point for rejection of change and modernity. A strongly mystical doctrinal strain prevailed, best characterized by the recent adoption of the doctrine of the Immaculate Conception and by the cult inspired by the Marian visions of Saint Bernadette at Lourdes in 1858. Pope Pius IX's Syllabus of Errors of 1864, wherein he attacked rationalism, freedom of speech, religious toleration, socialism and the cult of science, was given even greater impact by the acceptance of the doctrine of papal infallibility in 1870. Catholics rejected not only the political forms and limited social aims of the republic, they also condemned most aspects of modern life to boot.

With the political spectrum so widely divided, the republic survived as – in the words of Thiers, who served as president down to 1873 – the regime which "divides us the least". His successor Marshal MacMahon was an outright monarchist, and he appointed as his principal minister the duke de Broglie, whose great-grandfather had commanded the army in July 1789, when Louis XVI had tried to snatch back power from the National Assembly. Even under the "Republic of Dukes" the Right played its cards spectacularly badly, and republicanism quietly installed itself bit by bit. In 1875 the Assembly passed (albeit only by a single vote) a constitutional act which established a two-chamber legislature, and which made the president electable by the Assembly rather than by the voters. MacMahon was bypassed by events and in 1879, with the republicans starting to win more seats in the Assembly, he was replaced as president by the veteran Jules Grévy, whose very mediocrity was a bulwark against a monarchist regime. By 1900 monarchism was well on its way to becoming a mild eccentricity. From time to time alarm bells would ring. In the late 1880s, in particular, the populist demagoguery of General Boulanger, who as war minister had tuned up the military machine for a war of revenge against Germany, threatened a Bonapartist-style anti-parliamentary *coup d'état*. He too missed his moment, and the "Republic of Republicans" survived.

The men responsible for keeping the republican ship of state afloat in these choppy political waters were moderates. Gambetta, who died young in 1882, was the most seductive of a set of largely grey mediocrities. The new constitution produced a series of weak presidents and governmental instability – there were some sixty governments between 1870 and 1914. Yet in an important sense this volatility was only an optical illusion, one which applied to much of post-Revolutionary politics. The surface froth of changing ministries in fact hid a deeper continuity among the political class as a whole, who were drawn from similar backgrounds and who held similar views. In the early years moderate republicans – or "Opportunists" – dominated ministerial posts, joining forces with the slightly more progressive Radicals whenever the republic seemed under threat from the Right, and providing a greater degree of stability than initially met the eye. Though their attachment to the republic was paramount, Opportunists and Radicals distanced themselves from the extremist, Communard tradition and prided themselves on representing the interests of bourgeois France. The parliament now acted as the mouthpiece for what Gambetta called "new social strata" – merchants, provincial businessmen, state functionaries, doctors, lawyers and journalists. This class was a rung down from the financial and business elites who had dominated national politics since 1830.

Universal male suffrage also allowed the largest social grouping within France, the peasantry, to maintain an influence on policy. It proved difficult to keep the peasants happy. An agrarian depression set in during the 1870s and lasted through to the turn of the century. The import of grain by steamship from the United States proved strong competition for French farmers. Boom times among wine-growers evaporated, with an epidemic of the phylloxera disease ravaging vineyards throughout France. Towns grew in strength, producing a "ruralization" of the countryside, with employment there becoming based wholly on agrarian activities. Some peasants left the land – in some areas the trickle became a flood, especially from the Alps, the Massif Central and Aquitaine. Others turned to more extremist politics. In the wake of French nationalism regional nationalisms began to be developed by local intelligentsias. The writer Mistral, for example, helped develop an Occitanian nationalism – which developed an

Prototype postage stamps (not released) of the opportunistic General Boulanger – a form of publicity to which few could aspire. Stamps had been introduced, and their sale in tobacconists' authorized, in 1849.

anti-republican attachment to the Church and the far Right. Elsewhere traditionalist "white" areas turned "red" under social and economic pressures, so that radical peasants could now link up with urban workers against the political centre.

The Opportunists held essentially liberal views; laws in the 1880s ensured freedom of speech and assembly, for example. But even they bowed to peasant pressure when they reintroduced a degree of agrarian protectionism – notably in the Méline laws of 1892 – to mollify rural areas. They were less prepared to pacify the proletariat. Although they legalized trade unions in 1884, they tended to deny the existence of a "social question". Measures of social security were lamentably slow to develop in France, especially in comparison with Great Britain and with Bismarck's Germany. By 1914 achievement in social reform was slight: a ten-hour day for women and children from 1900; eight-hour shifts in the mines from 1905; a mandatory one day of rest in seven from 1906; optional (and under-used) social insurance measures from 1910. As a consequence, mutual aid societies were highly developed, containing over two million workers by 1914.

Disregarding social reform, Opportunist politicians prized a unifying republican ideology. Significantly, in 1879, "The Marseillaise" became the national anthem, while in 1880 Bastille Day (14 July) was agreed as a national holiday. The town-halls of France were equipped with busts of Marianne, a symbol of the republic since the 1790s which emphasized unity rather than division, and which was often modelled on the statue unveiled in the Place de la République in Paris in 1883. Opportunist politicians also drew on republican mythology in a heightened emphasis on anti-clerical policies. Gambetta's cry, "Le cléricalisme, voilà l'ennemi!" was sufficiently rooted in the republican tradition to find allies on the Left without the need to accommodate radical social reform. Education became the battlefield on which the struggle was fought: the children of Marianne had to be rescued from the divisive and vengeful clutches of a backward-looking, anti-republican Church. In legislation between 1881 and 1886, sponsored by Jules Ferry, free public primary education was introduced for children between six and thirteen years old; all children between those ages were to attend either a lay or a religious school; public secondary education for girls was put on a proper footing for the first time; and generous provision was made for teacher training and school building. These important laws were supplemented by more specifically anti-clerical measures: the repeal of the Falloux Laws of 1850, which had given religious teaching communities greater freedom to operate; the removal of churchmen from the councils of universities (which were also reformed and expanded); a ban on Church institutions offering university degrees; and so on.

Ferry's "schools without God" were bitterly opposed by churchmen, who too easily saw them as the work of Protestants and freemasons, both of which groups were strong supporters of the republic. Yet despite their contested beginnings the schools proved one of the most enduring cultural achievements of the early Third Republic. Village schoolhouses still stand as monuments to the republican values of the late nineteenth century. Schoolteachers came to represent an alternative cultural focus to the parish priest, and proved the republic's most ardent supporters: the death-rate among school-teacher volunteers in the trenches of World War I (roughly one-fifth) was higher than in any other social group.

Lay schooling was seen as a means of removing children from the Church, but also from the noxious influence of women. Anti-clericalism was very much a male province – orthodox conformity was far more widespread among women. As a result they came to be seen as handmaidens of the Church's mission to turn young minds to God. The lay schools aimed to instil metropolitan and masculine values. Petty bourgeois virtues

Third Republic history school textbook. Strong hints of hostility towards German "barbarian" pillagers in the guise of Clovis' Franks blend uneasily with an awareness of the role of the Franks in the development of the French nation.

of hard work, reward for merit, reliability, thrift and respect for property were preached. The loss of Alsace and Lorraine, moreover, stimulated a kind of muscular nationalism. Physical training and sport could ensure that the fight for the integrity of France might yet be won on the playing-fields of, say, Palavas-les-Flots. History teaching preached a cult of the fatherland and its defence. In textbooks "patriotic" figures such as du Guesclin, Joan of Arc, Philip Augustus and even Robespierre enjoyed prominence, while scorn was reserved for the Merovingians, who had proved constitutionally incapable of maintaining their kingdom's integrity – and who were kings to boot.

To many who attended them, however, these schools must have appeared as colonial as well as republican institutions. The metropolitan bourgeois values they promoted were foreign to many peasants, workers and women. Despite the universalist and meritocratic assumptions behind the Ferry legislation these three groups did markedly worse in the classroom, and this made the school a means of social control as much as of career mobility. This was truer the further southwards and westwards one went from the capital city. Social commentators were already remarking on the existence of "two Frances" on either side of a line joining Saint-Malo and Geneva. To the south and west of this line populations were shorter in stature, less well-fed, less highly educated, more prone to violent crime and more likely to evade taxes and desert from the army. Research in the 1860s suggested that in roughly one-quarter of French communes – most of these in this south-western bloc – French was still not spoken. Law-courts in Provence, Brittany and the Limousin were still having to use interpreters in order to deal with the testimony of peasant "natives". On the eve of the 1789 Revolution half of men and three-quarters of women had been unable to sign their names. In the early years of the Third Republic, the comparable figures were one-quarter and one-third.

The "two Frances". Economic and industrial change (p. 219) was highlighting the profile of "two Frances". The division between north and east on the one hand and south and west on the other was cultural as well as economic. The north and east had far more impressive levels of literacy (centre) – a fact that owed something to the enduring presence of non-French languages in the south and west (left). The divergence was attitudinal as well as linguistic: the north and east found it easier to accept that emblem of modern life and personal freedom, the bicycle (right).

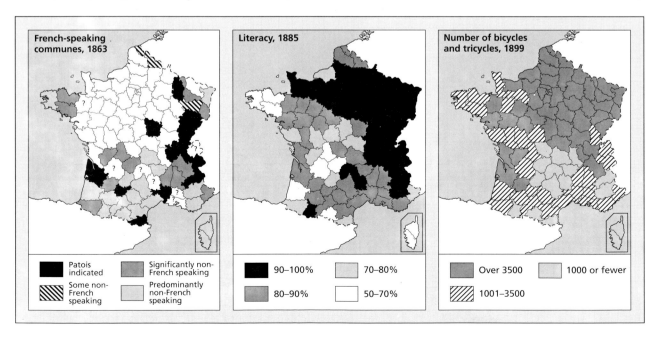

One of the avowed aims of lay schooling was to remedy these defects, and to acculturate those parts of France resistant to bourgeois metropolitan culture. A prominent tactic here was the emphasis on the French language as the sole means of communication within the school. Though this approach infuriated the regionalist intelligentsias, the latter failed to find mass support. Illiteracy was equated with inability to speak French, ignorance with anti-republicanism. The Opportunists linked up with the rhetoric of the 1790s revolutionaries, for whom French had been "the language of liberty", while "the mass of corrupted dialects" represented "the vestiges of feudalism". Speech, like the republic, had to become "one and indivisible" if brutalized peasants were to be brought back within the pale of civilization. Children who broke into their native idioms within school walls were humiliated and punished. National conscription, introduced from 1872, proved an important supplementary means of linguistic control. The marked reduction in levels of illiteracy – by the early 1900s less than 10 per cent of conscripts were unable to sign their names – demonstrates the success of this programme of cultural assimilation.

The "civilizing mission" of the politicians of the Third Republic also found fertile terrain in the colonies. Though some opposed colonial ventures as a diversion from the essential task of winning back Alsace-Lorraine from the Germans, the years down to 1914 saw France increase its overseas holdings tenfold – the empire extended to three million square miles and contained fifty million inhabitants. France participated in the "scramble for Africa", building up spheres of interest in East and central Africa and strengthening its hold on the north. Indo-China was effectively colonized and gains were made in the Pacific and Indian Oceans. Significantly it was the arch-educationalist Jules Ferry who was the crucial figure in acquiring control of these regions. Ferry once commented that the only aspect of the empire to arouse French passions was the belly-dance. However, though he bemoaned his fellow-citizens' lack of enthusiasm for these new arenas of domination, he helped establish France as the world's second imperial power, behind Britain.

THE NEW MATERIALISM OF THE *BELLE EPOQUE*

In 1889 an International Exhibition was held in Paris, the crowning glory of which was the iron tower erected by the Burgundian engineer Gustave Eiffel. Standing at over 300 metres, the tallest metal structure in the world, and illuminated at its inauguration by over 20,000 gas lights, the Eiffel tower symbolized the Third Republic's attachment to its revolutionary heritage. Opened in the centenary year of the Revolution of 1789 by Eiffel planting a tricolour flag on its summit, it was a secular riposte to the building of the basilica of the Sacré-Coeur, which ardent clericalists had erected at Montmartre to atone for the death of the archbishop of Paris in the Commune of 1871. With its modernistic design and electric elevators the tower illustrated the Third Republic's respect for science and technology. And it also exemplified a new craze for mass entertainment – hundreds of thousands of visitors flocked in within months of its opening – and a flagrant, somewhat self-indulgent materialism.

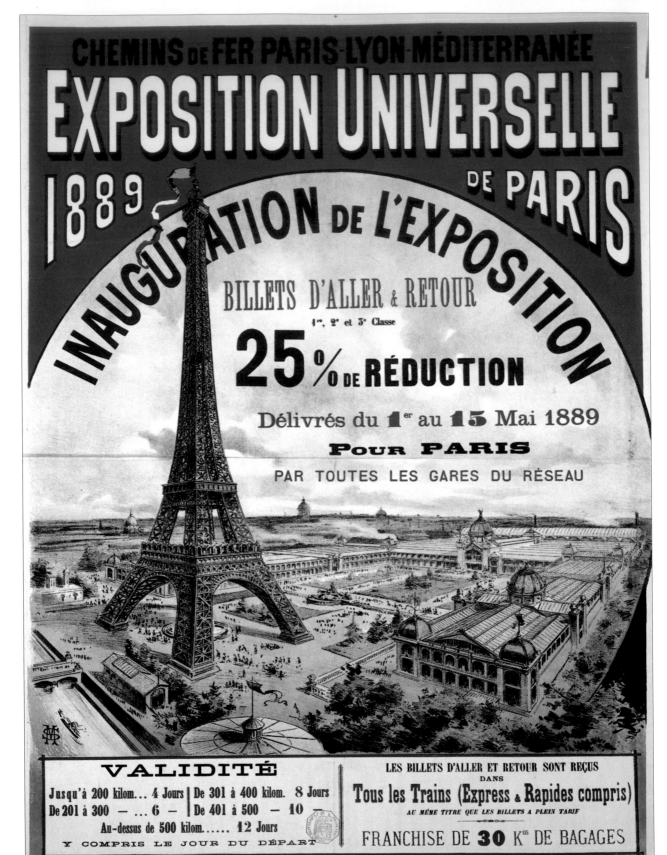

This advertisement for Menier chocolate by Firmin Bouisset (1892) pays unwitting testimony to the progress of female literacy in the *belle époque*. The period saw posters take off as a brilliant new art form.

The first half-century of the Third Republic saw massive shifts in the material culture of most French men and women. The writer Charles Péguy, commenting on the eve of World War I, estimated that France had changed more since he was at school in the 1880s than it had since the time of the Romans. Material improvement was grounded in the continuing progress of industrialization. France's economy continued its slow and steady expansion. Overall France was slipping from second to, by 1914, fourth greatest industrial world power, yet this still represented considerable growth. On top of the already impressive increases seen during the Second Empire, industrial output tripled and national income doubled. Growth was fastest in the period after 1896 and in particular in the decade before the outbreak of war. Steam-power increased sevenfold in industry from the 1880s, and this was used in the progressive iron, chemistry and automobile industries, which were the key sectors of this second phase of the industrialization process. The electricity industry also developed, including hydro-electric power. Peugeot, which had originally made its money in textiles, switched to bicycles, then to automobiles by 1914. Along with Renault, Citroën and others the automobile industry was second only to that of the United States, and produced twice as many cars as Great Britain. Already Michelin was making its name in the rubber industry, servicing motor cars, while Blériot's famous

Opposite Poster for the 1889 Universal Exhibition held in Paris. The Eiffel tower, an engineering triumph, and here bedecked by a tricolour pennant, was the star attraction. Most of the other exhibition buildings were subsequently demolished.

flight over the Channel in 1909 also signalled France's pioneering role in the aeroplane industry.

As the latter examples suggest, improvements were especially marked in the communications sector of the economy. The so-called "Freycinet Plan", launched in 1878, set about improving communications in all parts of France. The plan broke with the custom of having the rail network centred on Paris, for example, and the increase in rail kilometrage from 24,000 to over 64,000 between 1881 and 1914 included a great many branch lines extending into formerly quite untouched areas. Canal building and improvement doubled the volume of goods carried by water over the same period, while massive road construction also helped to integrate and extend the national market. From the 1890s trams came into wide use in cities, while in Paris the metro system was introduced in 1900. Personal mobility was also increased by the spread of bicycles, which numbered 375,000 in 1898 and 3.5 million in 1914. These changes in the distribution and communications sectors of the economy caused a major shift in employment patterns: one-fifth of workers had been employed in this sector in 1850, but by World War I the figure had risen to nearly one-third.

This reflected changes in other forms of communication, too. The electric telegraph was being used from the 1850s and was able to convey intercontinental messages from the 1860s. The telephone made large strides too: public booths were introduced in the 1880s. The total number of telephones rose from some 12,000 in 1889 to over 300,000 by 1913. In 1878 the telegraph services were combined with the postal services and in 1889 the PTT (*Postes, Télégraphes et Téléphones*) was formed to combine the three services. The village postman became a standard figure – his daily round would take him the equivalent of seven times round the globe in his career! In 1911 it was a French man who initiated the world's first air-mail service.

The output of the printing presses was also revolutionized, helped by the growth of literacy and the rise of larger middle- and lower-class readerships. As newspapers entered the mass age, costs continued to fall because of the growth of advertising and technological improvements (the advent of the rotary press from the 1860s, the linotype from 1880s and so on). The number of Parisian daily newspapers had doubled in the July Monarchy and quintupled under the Second Empire; it rose fivefold again up to 1914, which still marks the high-point in French newspaper-readership. The provincial dailies followed this upward trend. Circulation had rarely exceeded 10,000 to 20,000 before the middle of the nineteenth century. *Le Petit Journal* in the 1860s was the first to aim for a mass audience, cramming its pages with crime stories, serialized novels and human-interest items, and soon managed one-third of a million copies – over one million by the 1890s. The advertisement was another form of communication to develop fast. The liberal bill-sticking law of 1881 allowed the wall-poster to come of age as an art form as well as a means of communication and persuasion: wines, liqueurs, patent medicines and all forms of entertainment were among the most widely peddled items.

These changes in patterns of communications marked the rise of the mass consumer. This was evident in diet, where there were changes, especially from the 1890s,

Au Bon Marché

The vestibule [was] changed into an Oriental salon. From the doorway it was a marvel, a surprise that ravished them all ... From the ceiling were suspended rugs from Smyrna with complicated patterns that stood out from the red background. Then, from the four sides, curtains were hung: curtains of Karamanie and Syria, zebra-striped in green, yellow and vermilion; curtains from Diarbekir, more common, rough to the touch, like shepherds' tunics; and still more rugs ... strange flowerings of peonies and palms, fantasy released in a garden of dreams.

This description of a Parisian department store in Emile Zola's novel *Au Bonheur des Dames* (1883) captures well how exotica were used to sell goods in this new mode of retailing. Art and reality sustained fruitful interactions: Zola based his description on Paris' first great department store, Au Bon Marché, founded in 1852. But within a couple of decades department stores and displays were being deliberately modelled on Zola's inspired imaginings. However, even the largest and grandest of newcomers – notably La Samaritaine (1869) and Galeries Lafayette (1895) – were far behind the annual turnover of Au Bon Marché, which until World War I was the biggest department store in the world.

The roots of the department stores' popularity were economic: they offered a wider selection of products at lower prices, and their practice of setting fixed prices made a pleasing break from the need to haggle. Their emergence also testified to a new prosperity among a mass clientele. Yet it was the novelty and wonder of shopping within these cathedrals of consumption that completed the allure. Browsing, mingling anonymously with crowds of like-minded consumers, window-shopping, impulse buying – all created a quite new experience of commodity consumption, to which entrepreneurs responded with ever more fantasy and flamboyance.

The grand staircase of the Paris Bon Marché.

in both the quantity and the quality of food consumed by the average person. From the middle of the nineteenth century down to World War I consumption of those great staples, bread and wine, increased by 50 per cent. More marked, however, were rises in other constituents of popular diet: meat, beer and cider consumption doubled; other alcohol tripled; and sugar and coffee quadrupled. The diversification of national tastes even helped to check the rural exodus by allowing farmers to specialize – the fruit and vegetables grown on the lower Rhône, for example, revitalized the region. More scientific farming techniques – mechanical harvesters, for example, or chemical fertilizers, which vastly increased productivity – also allowed farmers who had emerged from the pre-1896 agrarian depression to adapt successfully to new patterns of consumption.

French men and women had more money in their pockets. Real wages rose 50 per cent for urban workers in the last two decades before 1914. To meet the demand for consumers' ready money, the number of bank branches quintupled. New forms of retailing made clear how much lifestyles were being transformed. Most notable, perhaps, were the big department stores springing up in the major cities, supplemented

Poster (*c.* 1900) celebrating the virtues of Papillon cycles. Children catch butterflies ("papillons"), while a young woman celebrates the new-found independence a bicycle affords by leaving her groom at the altar.

by catalogue buying through the post. Universal exhibitions – held in Paris in 1855, 1867, 1878 and 1900 as well as in 1889 – helped to stimulate a concern for novelty and fashion. Women's fashion became a matter of popular, not just elite, concern, and was helped by the rise of the sewing machine from the mid century onwards. Six million women's corsets were in circulation in the 1870s. Bourgeois comforts spread downwards in society: running water, decent sanitation, gas and electricity transformed the character of home life for the comfortably-off.

The *belle époque*, as this period came to be called, is particularly associated with the rise of new forms of mass entertainment. The music hall had its heyday. The Moulin Rouge, haunt of Toulouse-Lautrec and a fashionable *demi-monde*, opened in Montmartre in 1889 – and soon gave the world the can-can. Other enduring entertainment centres (the Folies Bergères, Olympia, the Casino de Paris) were also established at this time. Tourism developed as a leisure industry: Deauville became Parisians' weekend jaunt, while the Côte d'Azur became a fashionable resort in the Midi. Cheap swift transportation revived the medieval pilgrimage as a form of mass leisure. Half a million visitors passed through Lourdes each year, with over 1.5 million coming in 1908, the fiftieth anniversary of Saint Bernadette's visions. Sport too developed as a form of mass leisure and entertainment: soccer, rugby, gymnastics and rowing developed national organizations, while in cycling the famous Tour de France started in 1903. Sport won approval for toning up the nation for forthcoming anti-German conflict. Nationalism was so rife in sport that even the idealistically internationalist aims of Pierre de Courbertin, who convened the first Olympic Games of the modern era in 1896, ended up as part of a chauvinistic desire "to show the Boches".

France's economic growth may not have matched that of its trade rivals, then, but the experience was still extremely positive. Wealth was filtering through to the general populace – not least because demographic growth was still very slow. The population grew from 36.1 to 39.6 million between 1871 and 1911 – a rise of less than 10 per cent – while Germany's population mushroomed by 50 per cent from 41.1 to 64.9 million over the same period. The death-rate had continued to fall – the development of bacteriological theory by Louis Pasteur helped here, as did improvements in public health

Scientific lecture on the evils of alcoholism in the Fresnes Prison in 1903. The "disciplinary society" (M. Foucault) exemplified in penitentiary institutions stressed surveillance, bodily control and the training of individual consciences. Alcoholism was seen as the seedbed of vice and crime.

and sanitation. *Belle époque* babies had twice the life expectancy at birth of their ances-tors under Louis XIV. Yet the birth-rate in France had also continued to drop, and dipped from 26.1 births per thousand population in the 1860s to 18.8 per thousand on the eve of the war (Germany's was still nearly 30 per thousand). This slow growth inevitably resulted in an ageing population which, it was feared, lacked the vitality of its Teutonic neighbour.

Population fears fuelled an anxiety, common in periods marked by improvements in popular living standards and lifestyles, of decadence and even racial degeneration. Reactionary analysts of crowd behaviour found "scientific" proof of the irrationality and insanity of mass politics and cultural pursuits. Syphilis and alcoholism were blamed for wreaking catastrophic damage on French racial stock. Lesbianism, sodomy and sexual perversion were painstakingly logged as symptoms of national decline. Every form of mass leisure found its critics. The improbably named Dr Ludovic O'Fallowell, for example, sternly condemned cycling for producing "genital satisfac-tion and voluptuous sensations" among lady riders. Catholic thinkers railed against the *capotes anglaises* – the English would refer to these new by-products of the vulcan-ization of rubber as "French letters" – which looked set to make sex a leisure activity rather than the fleeting prelude to childrearing. Perhaps what was particularly galling was the way in which mass culture was subverting the normal categories of social order. The *belle époque* saw many of the peasantry, the working classes and the lower middle classes having access to and using for their own benefits some of the social, eco-nomic and cultural gains formerly reserved for the elite.

POLITICAL AND SOCIAL CONFLICT

Despite the name, all in the *belle époque* was far from sweetness and light. Tension and conflict played in tantalizing counterpoint to frivolity, consumerism and pleasure-seeking. In the event the *belle époque* would run on discordantly into the horrors and anguish of World War I.

Late nineteenth-century birth control technology. *Coitus interruptus*, the standby of the Frenchman since the early nineteenth century, was being overtaken by new devices: the condom and the pessary. "Neo-Malthusian" groups diffused large numbers of tracts and brochures on the new methods.

International tension was a staple of French public life throughout this period. The smart to the national psyche caused by the loss of Alsace-Lorraine was never totally erased. Franco-German rivalry poisoned a system of international relations which had managed since Waterloo to solve conflicts without a full-scale European war. With the newly united Germany emerging as the major political and economic force of Europe, a subtle balance of power between the major states started to break down. A clear sign of this was the slow emergence of two armed camps in Europe, bound together by defensive and sometimes offensive alliance. The Dual Alliance, signed by Germany and Austria in 1879, was extended into a Triple Alliance by the addition of Italy in 1882. Suspicion, fear and the wish for revenge had left France rather isolated among the Great Powers until the 1890s. As late as 1898 a chance colonial incident at Fashoda in the Sudan had nearly tipped France into armed conflict against Britain, which was in fact an obvious candidate for friendship and alliance. Closer links with autocratic Russia in the 1890s were, however, gradually extended to Britain and in 1905 an Anglo-French *Entente Cordiale* was agreed. Colonial expansion, which could have served as an alternative outlet for French aggression, served only to heighten tensions and resentments, especially as Germany's militarism grew more rampant. Several years prior to 1914 European affairs were like a powder keg awaiting a match.

The call for national revenge – *la revanche* – spilled over into internal affairs. In one of the more surprising political reversals of the period the Left began to move away from a call for *la revanche*, while the Right developed a hyper-nationalistic ideology. The popular writer Paul Déroulède formed a League of Patriots, which acted as a political pressure-group and street-fighting militia. In 1899 Déroulède even came close to initiating a *coup d'état* during the funeral of President Félix Faure. The skilful journalist Charles Maurras also developed an extra parliamentary right-wing populism, which the politicians found difficult to deal with. Maurras' newspaper and political grouping, *L'Action française*, even accepted the tricolour – a highly significant symbolic gesture – and engaged in thuggish street violence. This new "patriotic" Right developed a chauvinistic critique of a corrupt centrist politics dominated, it was alleged, by Protestants, Jews, freemasons and "aliens".

Sufficient evidence could be cobbled together to give some credence to this xenophobic programme. Idealistic concern with the defence of the republic among both Opportunists and Radicals was overlaid with a more day-to-day concern with personal enrichment. In the so-called "Wilson Affair" of 1888 the son-in-law of President Jules Grévy was found to be secretly selling political honours to the highest bidders. In the "Panama Scandal" of 1892 large numbers of republican deputies (including the prominent Radical politician Georges Clemenceau) were found to have accepted bribes to hush up corruption in the affairs of Ferdinand de Lesseps' Panama Company. As for the cast-list of alleged villains Protestants were indeed disproportionately represented among the Opportunists and Radicals. So too were freemasons, for masonry provided a form of political sociability linking local and national power-bases. Immigration, notably from Italy and Spain, had brought into being a community of

Alfred Dreyfus

Alfred Dreyfus was one of those unassuming individuals whose name becomes so over-used in debate and polemic that our understanding of the person behind the symbol is lost. Besides Dreyfus the Affair, there was also Dreyfus the man – and the latter is quite as illuminating about facets of the Third Republic as the former.

The youngest of seven children, Dreyfus was born in Mulhouse into an assimilated Jewish family, who owned a successful textiles business. He left his home city when it was taken over by the Germans after the Franco-Prussian War in 1871. After coming to school in Paris, he chose a military career, training in the prestigious Ecole Polytechnique, and was eventually assigned to the general staff in 1892.

His conviction for treason for alleged clandestine activities in this post did not shake his patriotic attachment to France, which was typical among long-established Jews. France had, in the Revolutionary and Napoleonic period, been the first country to afford Jews some degree of civic equality. Many Jews, fleeing Czarist and East European repression, emigrated to France in the last decades of the nineteenth century, which swelled the size of the Jewish community from 50,000 to 100,000 by 1914. The influx stimulated a visceral anti-Semitism among many French people. They resented not only the religion of the newcomers but also their cultural and ethnic identity, which was far more pronounced than that of established Jews. It was to cries of "Dirty Jew" and "Down with Jews" from the watching crowds that Dreyfus was formally stripped of his military rank in a ceremony of December 1894. Dreyfus' own reaction was characteristic: "I am innocent! Long live France! Long live the army!"

Dreyfus' health was ruined by the four years of penal servitude he spent on the former leper colony of Devil's Island in Guyana from 1894 to 1898. Only finally cleared and pardoned in 1906, he was forced by bad health into early retirement a year later. However, he rejoined the army in 1914, rising to the rank of lieutenant-colonel and receiving the *Légion d'honneur*.

Ten years after his death in 1936 (which was scarcely noticed) the reactionary and vigorously anti-Semitic Marshal Pétain was convicted for his leading role in the Vichy government. "It is Dreyfus' revenge!" he cried from the dock, when sentence was passed. The comment showed how far adrift the name had come from it modest and quietly patriotic bearer.

The political nation was divided by the Dreyfus Affair into two violently opposing camps. Improved print technology allowed political propaganda to reach out widely within *belle époque* society.

over one million foreigners, making up some 10 per cent of the total workforce. They too were an easy target for racist scapegoating.

The charge which the populist Right aimed against Jewish influence upon the affairs of the republic had its roots in a deep-seated anti-Semitism long a feature of the Right. It owed a good deal, however, to the Dreyfus Affair. In 1894 a Jewish army officer, Alfred Dreyfus, had been dismissed and deported to the French penal colony in Guyana for allegedly passing classified military information to the Germans. The story became amplified into the greatest political *cause célèbre* of the Third Republic, as a result of consistent attempts within the military general staff to organize a cover-up. The amplifying agent was the new mass press. The writer Emile Zola in 1898 published in the radical newspaper *L'Aurore* an open letter, under the title "*J'accuse*" ("I accuse"), to the president of the republic. In it he attacked the army cover-up and went on to assert Dreyfus' innocence. Zola ended up in temporary exile for his pains, but from 1898 a League of the Rights of Man grouped together intellectuals on the Left calling for Dreyfus' exoneration. Lining up against them were "anti-Dreyfusards", encouraged by the new-Right and pro-Church politicians who seized on the affair as a stick with which to beat the republic. Dreyfus' pardon in 1899, supplemented in 1906, might have been thought to have ended the matter; but by then the battle-lines had been drawn and the two sides had entrenched themselves.

The governments of the early 1900s, now ultra-sensitized to the threat from the Right, seized the initiative and lurched into a campaign targeting the Church establishment. In line with their general outlook on republican values they concentrated their attack on the question of schooling. In 1900 the Assumptionist teaching order, which had been particularly prominent in attacks on Dreyfus, was dissolved, and in 1901 it was decreed that all teaching orders had to be authorized by the state. In 1904 religious congregations were prohibited from teaching, a step which was followed next year by the formal separation of Church and state. An era of lay–religious relations, inaugurated by Napoleon's Concordat of 1801, was thus brought to a close. Thousands of religious schools were shut down – about one-third of all primary and one-quarter of secondary schools. The republic's attempts to wind up these establishments smoothly were poisoned by the intransigent opposition of the pope. His predecessor had in the 1890s encouraged Catholics to countenance *le ralliement* – acceptance of the republic. Dreyfus and the anti-clerical decrees of the early 1900s ended this, and effectively scuppered the emergence of a strongly pro-Catholic political party that accepted the framework and institutions of the republic.

The Dreyfus Affair had, then, shifted the centre of gravity of politics as well as coarsened its tone. The Right was split between the traditional elites determined at all costs to defend the Church and the extra-parliamentary forces of *Action française* and its ilk. A Catholic supporter of the republic would remain a rare bird among the political elite. Marianne, symbol of the republic, remained *la gueuse* ("the whore") in right-wing parlance. Catholic voters were, however, less intransigent – and possibly less traumatized by the Dreyfus Affair. Some indeed even drifted away from adherence to the Church.

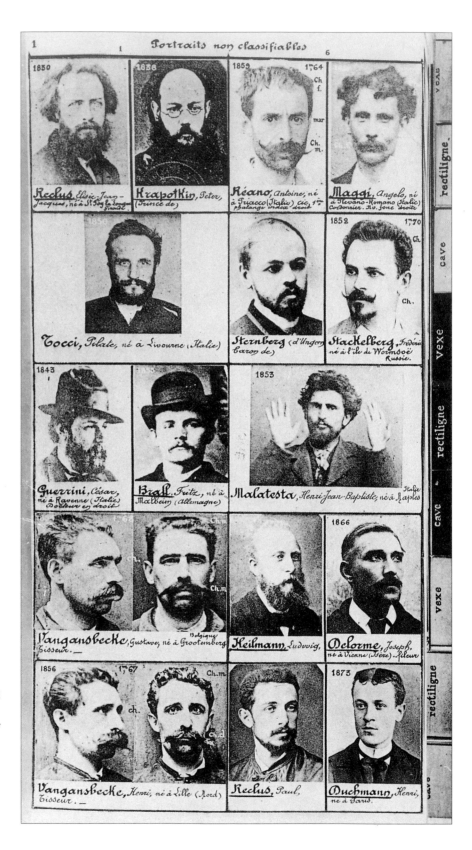

Photography was by 1900 being used routinely to help in police work. This cosmopolitan gallery of anarchist suspects was sent to border-guards in an attempt to catch those responsible for the bomb outrage in the Chamber of Deputies in December 1893.

In Limoges, for example, the number of children not baptized rose from 2 to 40 per cent between 1905 and 1914, while the number of civil marriages increased from 14 to 60 per cent. Religious inflexibility was, then, having the counter-productive effect of distancing practising Catholics from the precepts of the Church, and adding to the already large numbers of the effectively non-Christian. The Catholic masses also seem to have gone further than their leaders, and voted for established parties – particularly the Opportunists. This shifted the Opportunists to the Right, allowing the Radicals to emerge at the fulcrum of Third Republic coalition politics, with anti-clericalism acting as a party cement. This brought in its train a limited degree of political stability: there were only two cabinets between 1899 and 1905 – something of a record for the Third Republic.

By concentrating their attentions to the Right and against the Church, however, the Radicals left themselves vulnerable from the Left. The arrogant indifference of the Radicals and Opportunists to "the social question" left ample room for class conflict to develop. Even though many farmers enjoyed the fruits of overall economic expansion, there was misery on the land, especially in the south and west, where small-scale peasant farming was still the rule. Poverty drove many into exile to the cities and radicalized whole areas. In the Midi competition from cheap Algerian wine in the aftermath of recovery from phylloxera brought about a wine glut, which sparked off the Winegrowers' Revolt of 1907. A mutiny of regular troops at Béziers made the emergency all the more acute.

The chic surface appearances of towns hid a netherworld of misery and distress in workplaces and workers' suburbs. Social protection for workers came late if at all, and was poorly enforced. Zola's famous novel *Germinal* (1885), set in a northern mining town under the Second Empire, portrayed conditions which beggared belief among the well-to-do, but which had scarcely changed under the Third Republic. A twelve-hour day was the rule throughout industry in the late nineteenth century, though this was falling towards ten hours by 1914. Although cholera had thankfully disappeared, levels of mortality and disease were far higher among urban workers than their social betters or their own European counterparts. Child mortality had fallen dramatically by the end of the nineteenth century, but still registered massive social differences – in the expanding poor neighbourhoods of Paris it was double that of the richest areas in the city. The First Republic had given the labouring classes land; the Second, the vote; and the Third was providing schools, railways and mass culture. But there was still much which clamoured to be done.

The voice of social protest was, however, surprisingly muted. The Opportunists and Radicals, who made capital from divisions on the Right prior to the Dreyfus Affair, also benefited from deep fissures on the Left among socialists and working-class activists. The Commune had had a double-edged effect. If it was inspirational to some, its repression had crushed the Parisian militant cadres, and it also alienated many workers from seeking allies on the parliamentary Left. An anarchist movement developed. Versed in "propaganda by the deed", it engaged in a series of outrages, especially in the early 1890s. A bomb was lobbed into the Chamber of Deputies in 1893, and President Sadi Carnot (grandson of the famous "Organizer of Victory" in 1793/4) was assassinated in 1894. Although these incidents won little mass support, they were symptomatic of a more general suspicion concerning the parliamentary pathway towards socialism. The sphere of worker activity had been widened by the legalization of strikes in 1864 and trade unions in 1884. Union activity divorced from the political sphere attracted many workers. At local level the emergence of the *Bourses du Travail* – local trades councils and labour exchanges – provided the focus for militancy. Many militants gave preference to direct action and the doctrines of revolutionary syndicalism, arguing for a general strike which would lead to a collapse of government and the installation of a workers' state. The national trades congress the CGT (*Confédération Générale du Travail*), which met for the first time in 1896, was generally antagonistic to parliamentary manoeuvrings. It seemed confirmed in its views by the toughness, even viciousness, with which Radical ministries treated mass strikes, especially from 1906 to 1910. Radical minister Clemenceau gloried in the title of *le premier flic de France* ("France's top cop") and brutally put down strike action.

Militant workers were in demand from many organizations. The CGT, which represented only one worker in six, found itself vying with an overtly political socialist Left which was also fundamentally split. There were five main socialist groupings by the 1880s. The most authentically Marxist of these – Jules Guesde's Workers Party, or POF (*Parti ouvrier français*) – scorned electoral politics as feeble reformism. They were, at best, "schools for socialism", which could educate workers in the futility of parliamentarism. Guesde also disdained as "gas and water socialism" the call to implement socialist policies at local level – a policy advocated by rival Paul Brousse's French Socialist Party (*Parti socialiste français*).

It was difficult for socialism to make headway at national level. Socialists won a few seats in the 1880s and around forty in the 1893 elections. But it was the southern deputy Jean Jaurès who helped to mould these socialist factions into a respectable political force. An Opportunist deputy in 1885, he evolved towards socialism in the 1890s, and in 1905 brought the various strands together into the "French Section of the Worker's International" or SFIO (*Section française de l'Internationale ouvrière*). In 1906 the Socialists polled nearly a million votes and had fifty-one deputies elected, and these figures rose to 1.5 million votes and about a hundred deputies in 1914.

As international tensions mounted, this Socialist advance was made doubly problematic given the proudly proclaimed internationalism of the French Left. While the extra-parliamentary Right was draping itself in the tricolour, the Left had developed strong strains of anti-nationalism, anti-militarism and pacifism. They had strongly criticized the decision in 1913 to extend the period of conscription from two years to three, and in the same year the CGT specifically resolved that its members should not fight if war broke out. Jaurès too distrusted the apparent rush towards war – though his influence was removed at the crucial moment in 1914 when he was assassinated by a right-wing fanatic. Yet though the future of the republic in 1914 seemed to hang

The Winegrowing Crisis from *Le Petit Journal*, 9 June 1907. A crooked (that is, teetotal) businessman comes under attack, as protesting peasants march under the tricolour.

uncertainly on the resolution of this political tension, it was not the Jaurès murder but another assassination which gripped the minds of the French public in 1914. News of the worsening international crisis was driven off the front pages of the national newspapers by a sensational murder trial. The editor of *Le Figaro*, Gaston Calmette, had allegedly been shot and killed by the wife of prominent Radical politician Joseph Caillaux, after the newspaper's character assassination of her husband.

In this fateful summer of 1914 the trial of Madame Caillaux brought to the front of the reading public's mind another source of tension during the *belle époque* – namely, the "woman question". The "woman question" was to a large extent a "man question". A cult of masculinity had emerged under the Third Republic, linked with a sense of national shame after the loss of Alsace-Lorraine. Muscular – especially sporting – chauvinism was accompanied by an almost pathological penchant for private violence in the form of the duel. The duel allowed individual male honour to be settled by violence pending collective resort to the battlefield in the settlement of national honour. So prevalent was the code of honour among the political and social elite that it sucked in the most unlikely of duellists, from the pacifistic (Jaurès) to the effete (Proust). Prominent politicians became hardened habitués of the field of honour: Clemenceau fought in twenty-two duels. This hyper-masculine behaviour implied a crisis in relations with women, as well as a problem over the frontiers of the state.

Women's role in society was still very largely determined by the patriarchal rigidities of the Napoleonic Code. Women belonged in the private sphere, as angels of the home, rather than in the public sphere of politics, business and the law. Women were unable to vote, hold public office, act as witnesses in civil acts, serve on juries or take a job without their husband's consent. Their property was under the stewardship of their husbands, to whom they owed obedience (husbands legally owed their wives "protection" only). Adultery was for women a crime, for their husbands a misdemeanour. There was, it is true, some improvement in their status under the Third Republic. Most of the reforms were marginal and piecemeal, such as the right proclaimed in 1897 for married women to dispose of their own earnings. The reintroduction of divorce in 1884 was another step in the same direction. But it was symptomatic of the scale of the problem that the feminist call for women's suffrage never attracted

The late nineteenth century was the zenith of the French spas: they numbered over one thousand. Enghien-les-Bains offered treatment for respiratory ailments and also for rheumatoid and arthritic complaints. Improved railways allowed the ailing Parisian bourgeoisie to restore their health on a day-visit basis by train. For those who overnighted, there was an exciting array of worldly attractions, including a casino.

widespread support, and indeed was often viewed as ridiculous. Representations of women in news, advertisements and literature stressed that the social role of women lay in rearing children, engaging in charitable acts and in serving their husband's needs. The wifely and motherly "good woman", restricted to the privacy of her husband's home, contrasted with the "bad" or "public woman" – the prostitute – who was subjected to close, often humiliating, medical and police surveillance.

There was another side, of course, to this renewed stress on the notion of female domesticity. It applied far more, first of all, to bourgeois women than to peasants or workers. Women had a secure niche within the labour market. On the land it was still an unthinking reflex for women to labour on the family farm. Official statistics on the eve of the war showed that nearly 40 per cent of adult women were engaged in work outside the home – a higher proportion than in any other European country. Women's work was mostly in menial, poorly paid employment – domestic service, clothesmaking in sweatshops, clerical employment and primary teaching. What caused more anxiety among Third Republic males was that bourgeois women were beginning to enter the public sphere – notably those professions from which the bulk of politicians were drawn. Women had gained access to universities from the late 1860s, and by 1914 made up 10 per cent of university students. Secondary education for women had also been extended under the Ferry laws of the 1880s. From the 1880s small numbers of women had secured full medical training, and in 1914, 3 per cent of practising physicians were female. In 1900 the first woman joined the Paris bar.

Changes towards greater female independence – often linked to the greater availability of divorce – had a far bigger impact on male views than mere statistics can suggest. The mood of national decline and disgrace was heightened by women's increased emancipation, as well as the rise of working-class organizations and mass culture. One can now understand why Madame Caillaux's case pushed international news off the front pages of the newspapers: a woman with a smoking gun in her hand in a question of male honour was a disturbing icon of female power. The trial endeavoured to find a solution to the case which met with the requirements of domestic ideology. She was found innocent, mainly on the assumption that premeditated murder was so unbecoming for a lady from the leisured class that she must be adjudged temporarily insane. It was none the less a reminder of the depths of division and tension within a *belle époque* society now embarking on war.

CHAPTER 9

France in Transition: World War I to the Liberation

A chance assassination on 28 June 1914 – the killing in Sarajevo of Archduke Franz Ferdinand of Austria by a Serbian gunman – triggered Europe's lumbering machinery of war into action. Within a matter of weeks the two armed camps, which had spent the previous two decades sabre-rattling, were officially at war. (One of the penalties of the system of military alliance that had bound the nations of the two armed camps together was that a single such incident would entail the widening of the conflict to all partners.) The Triple Entente powers – France, Russia and Great Britain, along with Belgium – faced the central powers (Germany and Austria). Cheering French crowds saw their troops off to the front from the Parisian railway termini to cries of "Berlin by Christmas!" They were to be bitterly disappointed. What strategic analysts had assumed would be a brief encounter turned into the horrifying drudgery of four years of total warfare, which inflicted deep wounds on every aspect of French life.

France emerged victorious from the struggle. Achieving every *revanchiste*'s dream, it even won back the provinces of Alsace and Lorraine lost to Germany in 1871, as well as considerably increasing its colonial possessions at Germany's expense. But it was a pyrrhic victory. The strains imposed by the war were so severe that France was never to be the same again. World War I and its aftermath were to prove a rude awakening indeed from the illusions of the *belle époque*. Internationally France had now to acknowledge the constraints of growing American power and, by the 1930s, of a resurgent Germany. In population terms France had passed irremediably from its former prime position: one European in six had been French under Napoleon; after 1918 the figure was one in twelve or thirteen, and the situation was worsening. Economically the next two decades were to provide a mixture of modest advances – and notable retreats: in 1939 national wealth stood roughly where it had in 1914. Others had made more progress. Socially no major changes occurred, as those in positions of power clung insecurely and anxiously to their places in the face of social unrest. That government was controlled by interest groups attracted bitter criticism from Left and Right. Down to 1939, when a new war with Germany put the country to a further test, France was a stalemate society, seemingly locked within infernal circles of its own making. Crushing and humiliating defeat in mid 1940 saw France's Third Republic, the longest-lasting of all regimes since the French Revolution, come to an inglorious end. The country underwent a spell of authoritarian, traditionalist rule by Pétain's *Etat français* ("French state"), under the watchful surveillance of a German occupying army.

THE IMPACT OF WORLD WAR I

Social and political division had been an integral part of the *fin de siècle*. It therefore came as something of a shock that France went to war in the summer of 1914 a united nation. President Poincaré evoked a spirit of "sacred union", urging the shelving of political, religious and social differences. The Socialist deputies in the chamber voted for war credits – and they were not deterred even when leader Jean Jaurès was assassinated on 31 July by a right-wing fanatic. By the end of August two Socialists (one of them the old Marxist warhorse Jules Guesde) had joined a cabinet reflecting every shade of the political spectrum. The war was also accepted, apparently joyfully, outside the political nation too. The trade unions failed to live up to the pacifistic sentiments which they had earlier voiced. The army general staff had expected draft evasion rates of over 10 per cent; in fact the level settled down at little over 1 per cent. It was as if groups lacking a voice within the political nation had integrated themselves into the Third Republic without the elites being aware of it.

Socialist deputy Jean Jaurès seen speaking at a rally in 1913 against the increase in the term of conscription. Jaurès was suspicious of professional armies, favouring defensive, patriotic forces. A brilliant journalist, historian and political thinker, Jaurès was also a powerful orator. The photograph was touched up with red at the time to underline the revolutionary nature of the gathering.

The realities of war did not take long to reveal themselves. By Christmas 1914 a battle-front of over 700 kilometres of trenches had been established from Switzerland to the Channel. Military strategists, who had anticipated a war of lightning mobility, were proved devastatingly half-right: railways brought men swiftly to the front; but as soon as they got there, troops became bogged down and immobile. Technical change had rendered warfare defensive rather than offensive. The machine-gunner, properly dug in, could resist heavy artillery bombardment and still have a vast advantage over exposed advancing troops. Trench warfare became the currency of conflict. Complex networks of trenches, stretching back two to three miles, were constructed among con-

The "Miracle of the Marne"

"Soldiers! Your country's survival waits upon the outcome of this battle ... Retreat would be unforgivable!" Generals make this kind of speech fairly frequently. In the case of Joffre's address to his men at the beginning of the Battle of the Marne (4–10 September 1914) he was speaking with full seriousness.

Both sides had adopted an aggressive opening gambit to the war on the western front. Joffre launched the French into the Lorraine – and was soon held up by stout resistance. For their part the Germans had adopted a variant of the so-called "Schlieffen Plan", which involved a strike through Belgium followed by a wheeling action to encircle Paris. The aim was to force the French out of the war within six weeks.

The violation of Belgium's neutrality brought in the British on the French and Belgian side, while the Germans also sent troops against the Russians. German strength was thus less imposing than it might have been. Nevertheless they forced the French back across the Marne river and towards Paris. German troops were twenty to twenty-five miles from the capital in the first days of September. In a famous gesture Joffre requisitioned a thousand taxi drivers from the Paris region to drive additional volunteers to the front. Joffre pushed forward, driving the exhausted German forces back across the river. He had managed the "Miracle of the Marne": Paris was safe, the line of trenches began to form, and German hopes for a swift end to the war were firmly frustrated. In a sense the war was now ready to begin.

Requisitioned Paris taxis and cars line up outside the Invalides on 29 August 1914 in readiness to transport troops to the western front.

Surreal trench landscape with tanks.

crete fortifications and forests of barbed wire, creating, under the impact of heavy shelling, sublunar landscapes forever etched on the imaginations of combatants.

Unfortunately the generals on both sides failed to think through the consequences of these changes. Shielded from the worst of the fighting themselves – HQ was doggedly in the rear – and still wedded to outdated notions of offensive warfare, they had few qualms about sending the best and brightest of a generation to be cut down by battlefield fire. Gallantry and élan had little impact on barbed wire, the spade and the bullet. Casualties were enormous: 600,000 Frenchmen died in 1915 alone. In 1916 the Germans determined to concentrate their attack on the fortress of Verdun, whose loss they adjudged the French would find politically impossible. Indeed no French general or politician brought up on the story of national defence in 1792 could hope to survive the loss of this historic fortress. The Battle of Verdun lasted from 21 February 1916 – when Germany launched the greatest artillery bombardment in the history of the world hitherto – to 18 December. The French commander, Philippe Pétain, won a massive reputation by managing to hold on – albeit at enormous cost (400,000 Allied casualties, as against maybe half a million German deaths). Morale was severely tested by these bloodlettings. A further futile and costly offensive in 1917 sparked off mutinies among regiments. Pétain restored order with a mixture of firmness (twenty-seven shootings, nearly 3,000 prison sentences) and moderation.

The mutinies sounded a warning note in Paris, where politicians were as bankrupt of ideas as their generals. They lasted less long, too: in true Third Republic fashion there were four different administrations between 1914 and 1917. Attempts to break the deadlock on the western front by initiatives elsewhere – as with the disastrous Dardanelles expedition of 1915 – were unsuccessful. Only towards the end did politicians and their commanders come to find ways of breaking the defensive deadlock. Aeroplanes were employed (though mainly in reconnaissance and minor bombing raids), while tanks eventually overcame an initial tendency to get stuck in the mud and were being used effectively by 1918. The technological innovation exploited by most – in defiance of the Hague Convention of 1899 – was chemical warfare. The "poisonous cloud" (particularly mustard gas) was responsible for tens of thousands of French deaths, and numerous German casualties too. Politicians pinned most hope, off the battlefield, on the effects of the naval blockade on Germany. Despite the best efforts of German U-boats, the Allies' naval superiority made economic conditions for civilians within Germany far worse than those endured by the French.

"Let's hope they hold out," a famous cartoon has one front-line soldier saying to

J.L. Ruffe's woodblock print depicts *La Grogne* – grumbling – which became increasingly prevalent among French troops following the mass battlefield slaughters of 1916 and 1917. Regimental mutinies ensued.

another. "Who?" "The civilians!" World War I was fought on two fronts, the civilian and the military. In a mass war, dependent on conscript armies, maintaining morale in the country as a whole becomes a major objective. Propaganda was a key part of government strategy. Newspaper editors soon got the hang of news management. The war was represented as a defence against "Teuton barbarism", often painted in luridly racist colours, and the French *poilu* – or foot-slogger – was portrayed as endlessly resourceful, patriotic and cheerful. Life in the trenches, it appeared, was not so bad – some even had central heating according to press reports. "The burst of shells, the shrapnel … so many jokes!" one newspaper had a front-liner say. Another recorded how such men "looked forward to the offensive as to a holiday. They were so happy, they laughed, they joked." Censorship ensured that news on the scale of the defeats of 1914/15 was much restricted. There was also a good deal of reticence over the widespread nature of shell-shock. Generals thought it "unmanly", while doctors found it difficult to accept that hardened male troops could experience "feminine" hysteria.

The press became less gung-ho as the war went on. Soldiers on leave will have spread a rather different story about trench warfare – the cold, the wet, the shelling, the nervous tension, the rotting flesh of corpses, the seeming futility … Refugees from the war-zones – no fewer than ten departments were partly or wholly behind German lines from 1914 onwards – will also have rectified some of the propaganda. In Paris aerial attacks by Zeppelins in 1915 and poundings by the German super-gun "Big Bertha" in 1918 gave civilians a small flavour of the front: 600 Parisians died from enemy action. Living conditions worsened under pressure from the financial and logistical demands of engaging in mass warfare. Unemployment rose at first as a result of industry's switch to war production. There was marked inflation and the disappearance of some goods of prime necessity. Queuing became a mundane reality. Price controls were introduced in 1916 and rationing had to be started in 1918.

The demands of war forced the government to become far more interventionist in economic matters than it had ever been. Generous allowances for families of soldiers made the hard facts of war on the battle- and home-fronts easier to bear. Price-fixing and rationing showed concern to keep the civilian consumer as happy as possible, too. On the supply side key industries such as railways, iron and steel and shipping experienced the full range of government action – planning production, enforcing industrial relations, allocating labour and so on. To cope with these new areas of involvement, the state bureaucracy mushroomed in size, growing by a quarter in a mere four years.

Morale did not crack – but it came close. A political crisis in 1917, fuelled by military failures, army mutinies, divisions within the political elite, plus a wave of strikes in key industries, brought Clemenceau to the centre of the political stage. Offering "Just war, war, nothing but war", he assumed semi-dictatorial powers and stiffened the war effort for a final push. The struggle was nicely poised. The Bolshevik Revolution in 1917 had effectively taken the Russians out of the war, yet the United States had come in on the Allied side. With troops withdrawn from the eastern front, German commander Ludendorff made a final offensive in 1918, where since the 1917 mutinies the British had been taking a fuller load. It made sense for the Germans to attack before American reinforcements could make their presence felt. This last push was all the more important as political revolution was breaking out in the German cities and the position of their allies worsening in the Balkans, Syria and Italy. But Ludendorff failed, his troops were driven back, and on 11 November 1918 the Germans agreed to the signing of an armistice.

THE AFTERMATH OF WORLD WAR I

The task of reconstruction which faced the French in 1918 was dauntingly immense. With the Treaty of Versailles in 1919 the lost provinces of Alsace and Lorraine were reincorporated into France, bringing 1.7 million men and women into a society long characterized by population stagnation. Even this was not enough. The country had lost 1.3 million soldiers in the war, the highest proportion of deaths of any of the major warring nations. There were three million disabled, about one-third of whom were permanent invalids. Some 200,000 civilians had died in the fighting, while – as if all this was not enough – a virulent epidemic of Spanish influenza caused 166,000 deaths in 1918 and 1919. The birth rate had slumped during the war, though rampant illegitimacy helped to compensate for negligible fertility levels within marriage. As author Drieu la Rochelle later remarked, French men were "mean with their sperm, but not with their blood". The ninety departments of France in 1919 contained 39 million inhabitants – where the eighty-seven departments of 1914 had contained 39.5 million.

The name-laden war memorials of every town and village in France bear witness to the scale of this dreadful haemorrhage. Only one of France's 38,000 communes did not lose someone to the war. Its impact was especially severe in the ten occupied departments: the Aisne lost nearly two-thirds of its population, and five others roughly a half. Material damage was at its worst here, too. Ploughed up by endless shelling and irrigated by the ooze of decaying corpses, much agricultural land here had become entirely infertile. Overall the war had caused the destruction of nearly a million buildings, plus endless kilometres of railway track and roadway, numerous bridges, much industrial plant and so on. The body count of war included nearly a million sheep, as many cattle and half a million horses.

Not only was France's economic infrastructure enormously damaged, its capacity to rebuild had also been severely affected. Casualty number one was the franc. Solid as a rock since 1801 it had taken the Battle of Waterloo and the Commune in its stride, but proved unable to cope with the demands of mass warfare. Propped up by the state it was worth four-fifths of its value during the war, but in the aftermath it fell through the floor. It had lost half its value by 1919, four-fifths by 1920. The government's ability to support the franc was affected by the enormous debts it had contracted during the war. Although income tax was belatedly introduced in 1916, it was a timid measure, full of loopholes, and covered only one-third of the costs of the war. The rest was met by the government liquidating its gold reserves and massive foreign investments, and by borrowing, especially from the United States. Only a doubling of indirect taxes, and a tripling of direct taxes after 1920, helped to fund repayment.

The impact of the war on the social, demographic and moral fibre of France explains why the French call for security was so strident in the war's aftermath. Clemenceau's idle dream that a buffer state might be erected on the Rhine between France and Germany – like a post-Carolingian Lotharingia – had little chance of success. Yet it seemed important to hem in Germany, by a territorial buffer in the west, and by alliance with Germany's neighbour-states in the east. Restricting Germany's economic potential was another key element, whether by partition or by exacting financial reparations, which would provide the economic leverage for French reconstruction.

Though hampered by Britain and the United States, Clemenceau was nevertheless able to make some effective settlements. He managed to secure the return of Alsace-Lorraine; a fifteen-year protectorate by the newly formed League of Nations of the coal-rich Saarland; and the demilitarization of the Rhineland. The German army was to be reduced to 100,000 men. And Germany – now governed by the Weimar Republic – was to accept war guilt and to make financial reparations.

The quest for security explains much of the apparent French intransigence towards Germany in the inter-war period. The Versailles Treaties which the allies had negotiated were rejected by the United States Senate, so that the achievement of collective security through the League of Nations was hobbled from the start. The French occupied

Queues outside the Paris Opera – not for tickets but for coal rations. By the last two years of the war, morale on the home front was wearing thin, and 1917 saw a resurgence of strikes.

the Rhineland for a short time in 1923 in an attempt to force Germany to step up its reparations schedule. This pressure led to the 1924 Dawes Plan for repayments, but difficulties continued. Even the Locarno Treaties of 1925, by which France, Germany and other powers committed themselves to mutual respect of existing frontiers failed to convince the French that its eastern frontier was secure – especially given the growing influence of right-wing parties, *revanchiste* in their turn, in the Weimar Republic. It was in this charged atmosphere that the decision was made in 1929 to build the Maginot Line – a highly modern, supposedly impregnable defensive structure on the eastern frontier, from Switzerland to Montmédy, near Verdun.

The work of economic reconstruction depended on recovering war costs from Germany. Yet, though the reparations slowed to a trickle, the French economy did extremely well in the decade following the Versailles Treaties. The switch from war to peace production was far from straightforward – in 1918 war industries were employing 1.7 million workers, who did not adapt easily to peacetime production. In addition German occupation of the north had disrupted the economic life in this traditional homeland of heavy industry. Recovery was helped by the modernization of much French industry under wartime conditions. New principles of "scientific" management, such as Taylorism, had made important industries leaner and stronger than they had been in 1914. Iron and steel did particularly well – but so, too, did the key secondary industries of rubber, automobiles, aeroplanes, petro-chemicals and electrical equipment. The French aircraft industry was a world leader during the war, though it slipped behind the United States soon afterwards. By 1924 overall industrial production had reached 1914 levels. The growth of consumer demand after the hardships of war helped in this, as did the lowered value of the franc.

The French economy was growing faster in the early 1920s than that of any of its

Populationist postcard message aimed at the troops and their families, and sent from Verdun in 1917. Such propaganda failed to stir the demobilized footsloggers into action: the birth rate stayed low throughout the inter-war period. The issuing of condoms within the army probably aggravated matters.

A French lesson in Alsace, now reincorporated into France. The postcard, dispatched in 1918, bears the message, "France is our fatherland." Smiling children seem to go together with the tricolour.

competitors. By 1929 industrial production was up 40 per cent and foreign trade up 66 per cent on 1913 figures. France's population, in contrast, was far less dynamic. With much of the adult male population of marriageable age in their graves the basis for demographic recovery was poor. The government responded to labour shortage by attracting immigrants, especially from Italy, Spain and Poland – with a smattering of White Russians, Belgians and other groups. There were roughly a million foreigners resident in France before World War I, but half a million entered during the war, and the inflow continued apace over the 1920s. France became (after the United States) Europe's melting-pot, containing some 2.5 million foreigners by the mid 1930s – nearly 10 per cent of the adult population.

Governments, then, tried to deal with the country's demographic problems partly by mobilizing immigrants into the workforce. Conversely they also acted to *de*mobilize women and to return them from the workplace to the hearth, and hopefully to encourage them into procreation. The war had provided a powerful stimulus to female labour, notably in war industries, but also in white-collar jobs. The wartime press had habituated the public to the idea of women bus-drivers, munitions workers, blast-furnace workers and riveters. Though their wages were still only a fraction of male workers', women probably enjoyed a higher living standard than ever before. This caused male resentment, even among the politically progressive.

Women munitions workers during World War I. Women in the war industries took industrial action in 1917, mainly over high prices.

Rather like the immigrant groups women made surprisingly little impact on political life. Socialist prime minister Léon Blum would later bring three women into his Popular Front cabinet in 1936. They were not permitted to vote, however, any more than other women, and the Left was to do precious little for women as a group. Radicals and Socialists feared that enfranchised women would vote for the pro-Church parties. Bills to give women the vote failed to secure parliamentary backing in 1919, 1929, 1932 and 1935. Female educational provision improved, but boys from bourgeois homes dominated secondary and higher education, to the detriment of all women and working-class males.

More generally the spirit of the Napoleonic Code still hovered over the "woman question". When a law was introduced in 1917 to limit the working week to five and a half days in the clothing trade, this was widely viewed as a means of allowing women garment-workers the chance to do their family shopping on Saturdays. It was only in 1938 that women were made legal majors – prior to this date a wife needed her husband's permission for something as trivial as acquiring a passport. Even then the assumption was that women would be better off having babies to rally France's drooping population. In 1920 the sale of contraceptives was prohibited, and tough new laws introduced against female abortionists, the so-called "*faiseuses d'anges*" ("angel-makers"). In the same year the state threw its support behind celebration of Mother's Day and introduced state medals for fertility (bronze for mothers of five children, silver for those with eight, gold for those who broke the barrier of ten offspring).

If women suffered in relative silence – the women's movement was dormant and divided throughout the inter-war period – the same could not be said for their male counterparts. The working classes still endured poor working and living conditions.

The eight-hour day was secured in 1919, but rates of adult male disease and mortality remained significantly worse in France than in countries with a similar economic and social structure, and social insurance measures still lagged way behind the rest of Europe. Real wages in 1918 were nearly a fifth lower than they had been in 1914, and though they jerked upwards during the 1920s, they had returned to 1914 levels in 1930. Inflation also hit members of the lower middle classes. Prime Minister Raymond Poincaré stabilized the franc in 1926, but this was achieved only by pegging the currency at one-fifth of its pre-war level. This might have helped export performance; but it crippled the budgets of those living off pensions and fixed incomes. On the land, too, the situation was far from good. The peasants had suffered a high proportion of war deaths. Though some peasants had done well from the added demand for their products under wartime conditions, the return to normality did not favour them. The continuing trickle of a rural exodus towards the towns highlighted the difficulties of the agrarian economy, but also the relative weakness of the demand for industrial labour. There was some improvement in productivity: whereas in 1914 a farmer fed 4.2 persons, by the 1930s this figure was 5.1. Yet the comparable rise in the United States was from 10.2 to 14.8. In the world scales French farming was increasingly inefficient.

THE THIRD REPUBLIC IN QUESTION

Despite the economic recovery after 1918, which lasted down to the end of the decade, post-war France was the home of a range of discontents. This was hardly surprising, given the social, economic and demographic strains of the *après-guerre*. The old Third Republic game of ministerial musical chairs continued. Indeed there would be forty governments in the two decades down to 1940, the shortest-lived lasting a matter of three days. The dominant political grouping was still the Radical party, but this had now grown fat and gone to seed – a description which also applied to many of its members. Its pre-war radicalism had evaporated under the impact of the Bolshevik Revolution of 1917, and it now tended to spice its traditional anti-Church stance with support for the petty bourgeoisie, artisans and shopkeepers. In 1919 after an election fought on the basis of a red scare (anyone to the Left of the Radicals was depicted as "a man with a knife between his teeth") they formed a government with the Right.

After voters' growing disillusionment with the Right, the Left's electoral success in 1924 found the Radicals switching their support to form the so-called "Cartel of the Left". Yet the fate of the government highlighted the difficulty of achieving structural reforms. Edouard Herriot, prime minister from 1924 to 1926, found himself in the downward spiral of an economic and financial crisis. The flight of capital left the franc undefended and the government clueless. The return of a Centre–Right coalition in 1926 restored business confidence, but created on the Left a deep-seated certainty that a *mur d'argent* ("wall of money") would always stand in the way of left-wing governments. Particular hostility was shown towards the "200 Families" – the 200 biggest shareholders in the Bank of France, who allegedly had a nefarious influence on the money markets and the political system.

The Surrealist Manifesto

SURREALISM (noun) Psychic automatism by which it is proposed to express, whether verbally, or in writing, or in any other manner, the real functioning of mind. Dictation of thought, in the absence of any control by reason, beyond aesthetic or moral considerations.

(Philos.) Surrealism is based on a belief in the superior reality of certain associations, neglected hitherto, on the all-powerfulness of dream, and of the disinterested play of thought.

These somewhat opaque definitions were offered by the poet André Breton, proclaimed leader of the new surrealist movement, in the Surrealist Manifesto of 1924. They highlight the importance in poetry and art of dreams and forms of action which bypass normal rational procedures. Breton, exposed to nervous disorders when working as a medical orderly in World War I, had been influenced by the writings of Freud, but wished to tap into the subconscious for reasons other than to seek out symptoms of psychic malaise. Rather, he wished to discover the basis of new forms of artistic expression – notably in the form of "automatic writing", or spontaneous, dream-based compositions.

Through the manifesto Breton was setting out a programme for the artistic development of the poets associated with him – Paul Eluard, Louis Aragon, Robert Desnos, Philippe Soupault – as well as a number of artists, including Picasso, André Masson, Man Ray and Max Ernst. But also the surrealists came to prominence as their original inspiration, the Dada movement, was running out of steam. A nihilistic movement, led originally by Romanian-born Tristan Tzara, Dadaism had its roots in a sense of rejection of the bourgeois values which seemed to accept the slaughter of World War I. Having developed in Zurich, then Paris, Dada aimed to subvert conventional values by systematic provocation on all fronts. One of its famous moments, for example, was the presentation by Marcel Duchamp of a urinal (with the title, *Fountain*) as an artwork for exhibition, which caused a tremendous scandal.

Breton wanted to go beyond wild playfulness to form a movement which, while retaining Dada's iconoclasm, could have a positive impact on the parameters of human imagination and experience. The wish to bring about change led the surrealists to form alliances with, first, the Communist Party and then, from the mid 1930s, with Trotskyists.

Although surrealism's political projects ran into the sand in World War II, by then it had had a major impact on French poetry as well as on artistic expression. The surrealist vision has been one of the most profound influences on twentieth-century art and – not least through its adoption by advertising agencies from the 1960s – on everyday life.

Photograph of leading Surrealists, their portraits grouped around a painting by Magritte, published in *La Révolution Surréaliste*, no. 12, in 1929, as the group was issuing a Second Surrealist Manifesto. Besides poets (Breton, Aragon, Eluard, Peret), the group includes artists (Dali, Tanguy, Arp, Ernst, Magritte) as well as film-maker Luis Buñuel.

Politicians were viewed as being in the pockets of businessmen. Though popular perceptions were rather jaundiced about "hard-faced men who had done well out of the war", employers emerged with their morale and ambitions high. A Lyon chemical manufacturer had noted with satisfaction during the war that "It is for the industrialist that people fight. It is he who will later gain the economic victory", and something of this spirit was detectable after 1918. Employers became better organized than before; a national confederation of industrialists was founded in 1919, and industrial associations were common. These groups acted as powerful pressure-groups and lobbies in the political arena.

French society was riven with social tensions. Radical change of any kind seemed fraught with difficulties and the cards remained heavily stacked in the favour of the social elite and the business classes. In these circumstances it is hardly surprising that the political establishment came increasingly under attack. Indeed it is remarkable that the regime was able to absorb so much criticism and to continue to function effectively. A lingering sense of despair was partly attributable to the impact of mass warfare. Henri Barbusse's anti-war *Le Feu* (1916) was a best-seller, and pacifism grew deep roots, especially through the veterans' associations which developed after 1918. Movements of political provocation and subversive rejection of bourgeois values also prospered in intellectual circles. In the art world notable examples were the Dada movement, which began during the war, and the surrealist movement, which developed out of it in the 1920s. Jean-Paul Sartre's novel *La Nausée* (1938) was a late-flowering bloom of much the same anti-bourgeois disgust. The yearning for a new kind of society took many participants in these movements towards left-wing politics. Others drifted into the ranks of the extreme Right. Maurras' still-influential *Action française* gave house-room to many young disenchanted right-wing authors. The novelists Drieu la Rochelle and the rabidly anti-Semitic Céline were among others drawn to a critique of contemporary society from the far Right.

Where artistic movements of revolt and rejection did not embrace left- or right-wing politics, they often led their participants towards individualistic hedonism. Victor Margueritte's much condemned (and therefore much read) novel, *La Garçonne* ("Bachelor Girl"), in 1922 described a bohemian female existence laced with free love and lesbianism. The book created a moral panic among the strait-laced. The sexual overtones of short hair, short skirts and flat chests were endlessly (often pruriently) debated. Though there was much about such works which was in the (bourgeois) tradition of shocking the bourgeoisie, they also reflected ideological changes and conflicts within society. Male wartime mortality had spurred an increase in the numbers of independent women, with unmarried and widowed middle-class women now entering the labour force in large numbers. Three years after the war, 42 per cent of adult women were still in gainful employment, and they comprised two-fifths of the total labour-force. The fuzziness in the boundaries between the sexes – highlighted in the debate on shell-shock (it seemed contradictory to talk of male hysterical illness) – had not therefore been erased by the return to peacetime "normality". Evidently women with

Having one's hair cut short was to the 1920s what bra-burning would be to the 1960s. It was held to proclaim a new spirit of independence among women, though critics feared the advent of a "civilization without sexes" (M. L. Roberts). Cloche hats – sometimes likened to soldiers' helmets – bold cosmetics and costume jewellery completed the effect.

Listening to the radio was at first an upper-class practice. Other examples of the new technology to make an impact on bourgeois homes in the inter-war period included washing machines, vacuum cleaners, floor-polishers, telephones and record-players.

money in their pockets were resisting the drive to return them to the hearthside and the bedroom.

Such changes were integral to the emergence of a more materialist and consumerist mass culture. Catholic prelates wrung their hands at the decline in religious fervour: less than one in ten industrial workers was a Christian, it was claimed, and the working classes preferred going to the cinema to attending church. French cinema had enjoyed a golden age prior to World War I, and indeed it retained much of its vitality in the inter-war years: there were 250 million box-office tickets sold in 1933 alone. Cinema, radio (from the 1920s) and gramophone records (especially from the 1930s) spread more widely the cultural fads of the Parisian elites. Jazz, for example, became a national phenomenon rather than the passing craze of the Parisian nightclub circuit; a dancer and singer like Josephine Baker could become a national star.

Traditional media also did very well in the inter-war years. France was one of the great newspaper-buying nations, and the press showed a sensitivity to the changing character of mass demand. Photo-journalism and comic books emerged, and a sports press flourished, reflecting the general public's growing attachment to spectator sports. A fashion press developed, too – the appearance of *Marie-Claire* in 1937 was a landmark, helping couturiers like Coco Chanel to bring female fashion out of the bourgeois salon and into the high streets. When personal advice columns cropped up in the press religious guardians feared the replacement of the Catholic confessional by the agony aunt, in an age of too much sex and shopping.

These were developments with which the stolid political elite was almost completely out of touch. The major politicians were an increasingly aged set with their roots in the *belle époque* rather than the jazz age. Symptomatic of the lack of perception was the serious misjudging by the "Cartel of the Left" in 1924 of the relevance of anticlericalism as a live political issue. Their attempt to rally support by an attack on the Church was a damp squib. Religion, so hated by pre-war radicals, was a question of apathy rather than hostility for increasing numbers. The Catholic elites, moreover, had shown signs of tardily rallying to the republic. Catholic priests had served in the trenches in World War I. Diplomatic relations were restored with the Vatican in 1921, and in 1924 issues outstanding from the separation of Church and state in 1905 were settled amicably. The republic's stance on contraception and abortion won Catholic approval. Though some cardinals and bishops kept alive the flame of sublime antago-

Josephine Baker

Josephine Baker. Is she a man? Is she a woman? Her lips are painted black, her skin is banana-coloured, her hair, which is short, is stuck to her head as if her hair were dressed with caviar, her voice is piercing, she is driven by a perpetual trembling, her body twists like that of a snake, or, more exactly, it seems to be a saxophone in movement, and the sounds of the orchestra seem to issue from her.

This account of the black jazz and dancing star neatly captures the astonished, disturbed reaction which Josephine Baker appears to have aroused in her male audiences. Appearing when still in her teens in *La Revue nègre*, which opened in Paris in 1925, Baker, whether naked or semi-naked, had stouter members of the middle classes muttering darkly about the "decline of the West". Her slicked-down hairstyle created a new French verb, "*bakerfixer*", one of a horde of Americanisms brought in by the jazz craze of the 1920s (*up-to-date*, *un jazz band*, *un cocktail*, *le jazz hot*, and so on).

Often accompanied by a pet leopard or with a snake curled around her neck Baker played the role of exotic foreign superstar to the hilt. She won an enduring affection in the French musical public, which lasted to her death in 1975. Her reputation was amplified by her participation in the Resistance during World War II, at a time when many French stars were compromising themselves with the Germans.

nism towards the republic, their flocks were becoming more sanguine. There was a Catholic trade union – with 300,000 members by the late 1930s – and from the 1920s an attempt at creating a Christian Democrat political party. The Church was simply no longer the convenient bogey-figure which Radical politicians had loved to invoke.

The growth of extremism underlined the bad odour in which conventional politics was increasingly held. The influence of Fascism and Nazism was not negligible, but the emergence of the extra-parliamentary Right had deep roots in French history. Maurras' *Action française* – 60,000 strong in 1934 – had been founded in 1898 after all. However, its support for Church and King looked increasingly quixotic given the movement's rejection by both the pope (in 1926) and the Legitimist pretender (in 1937). A host of what were usually referred to as "fascist leagues" also developed, often flanked with paramilitary action groups on the lines of *Action française*'s *camelots du roi*. They were strongly critical of the failings of the Third Republic and increasingly exasperated by the conventional Right. Most threatening of all seemed the *Croix de Feu* ("Flaming Cross") movement of ex-veterans, founded in 1927. Led from 1931 by Colonel de La Roque, under whom membership reached 150,000 in a couple of years, the movement developed into a kind of "political boy scouts' movement for grown-ups" (R. Rémond), though it was no less threatening for all that. This and similar groups received funding from maverick industrialists, notably the perfume manufacturer René Coty.

One of the biggest reasons for the growth of the extra-parliamentary Right was the development of a strong revolutionary Left, equally antagonistic towards "bourgeois

Poster warning peasants against the threats of communism. Xenophobic as well as anti-Bolshevik, such propaganda was not sufficient to prevent a good number of rural voters, notably in the Midi, from supporting the French Communists in the inter-war period.

*Le Communisme
C'est la mise en commun
tes troupeaux, tes biens
Ils sont à moi comme à toi*

democracy". In its party congress of 1920 – the so-called Congress of Tours – the Socialist Party had split. The majority broke away and under Bolshevik inspiration applied to form part of the international communist movement organized from Moscow. Once accepted, the French Communist Party came into being. The Socialist rump of the SFIO, led by the Jewish intellectual Léon Blum, retained some of its Marxist slant, but stayed an independent force committed to democratic reformism. Up until the mid 1930s both Socialists and Communists had a parliamentary presence. However, the Socialists remained true to a 1905 resolution not to participate in "bourgeois cabinets"; while the Communists, taking the Russian Bolsheviks as their model, saw parliamentary representation as only a small part of their activities. The split on the Left was mirrored on the industrial front by the formation of a Communist union to rival the Socialist CGT. Significantly the Communists rejected the tricolour and "The Marseillaise" in favour of the red flag of international labour and "The Internationale". Communist secretary Maurice Thorez compared the difference between the bourgeois democracy of the Third Republic and fascism to the difference between cholera and bubonic plague: both were deadly in the end.

The divisions within extra-parliamentary groupings to Left and Right were severe enough to allow the Centre considerable leeway in the 1920s. Yet three developments in the 1930s boosted the further growth of extremism: namely, mounting evidence of political corruption, economic depression and the rise in international tension.

"Electing a deputy these days," sneered a fascist newspaper, "is too often to give parliamentary immunity to a crook, a receiver of stolen goods or a dangerous imbecile." The close links which industrial and financial lobbies enjoyed with politicians were dramatically highlighted in 1934 by the so-called Stavisky Affair. Alexandre Stavisky, a Ukrainian Jew who had been naturalized as a French citizen, was up to his ears in municipal corruption when his death in suspicious circumstances aroused fears of a cover-up. The knee-jerk anti-Semitism of the right-wing press was amplified by the suspicion that Radical deputies were deeply compromised by corrupt dealings that they now sought to hide. On 2 February 1934 right-wing parties and the fascist leagues demonstrated in Paris, and led a march on the National Assembly which was only contained by violent police action. Some seventeen individuals died, and over a thousand were wounded in the mêlée. The government fell, and Communist counter-demonstrations led to further bloodshed.

The volatility of extremist politics was fuelled by economic difficulties. The Wall Street Crash on 24 October 1929 had produced a prolonged slump in the world capitalist system, though the shock-waves were slow to hit France. Indeed for two years after, politicians and industrialists were viewing France as an oasis in a crisis-ridden economic order. From 1931, however, it was becoming apparent that the great cycle of French prosperity, dating from around 1905, had drawn to a close. Exports were soon falling, industrial activity slowing down and unemployment rising. Slow to start, the slump was, moreover, particularly slow to end in France – it was only from 1938 that recovery was detectable. Production levels in that year stood at nearly a fifth lower than they had been in the previous decade. Agriculture was especially hard hit by a collapse in food prices (which paradoxically favoured those in work, whose purchasing power rose accordingly). Economic recovery in the 1920s had given some boost to the birth-rate, but the new circumstances caused a reversion to the more sombre long-term pattern. Deaths were outnumbering births from 1935 onwards. France's population in 1939 was to stand at 41.3 million – an increase of only two million since 1918. Over the same period, Germany's population had grown by ten million.

The German threat simply would not go away. Even the Maginot Line had failed to bring the sense of security which France had been seeking since 1918. It did not cover the Belgian frontier through to the Channel coast, as had originally been the plan. Third Republic politicians took this decision in 1932, partly on financial grounds and partly because of alliance with Belgium itself, which ended in 1936. Hitler's rise to power in 1933 on an anti-Versailles ticket set French governments a difficult problem – especially as they were formally allied with a British government wedded to policies of appeasement. In 1933 Germany withdrew from the League of Nations and introduced compulsory military service in 1935. In 1936 Hitler denounced the Locarno agreements of 1925, and occupied and began to remilitarize the Rhineland. The French stood agonizingly yet idly by. Nemesis seemed to beckon.

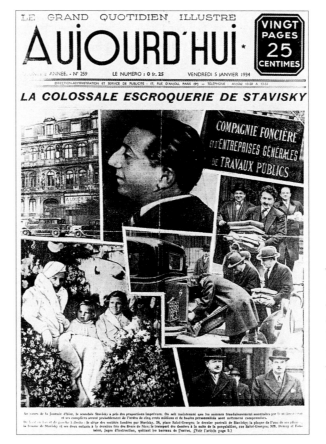

The disclosure on 5 January 1934 of the fraudulent activities of Stavisky was followed by the discovery of his body three days later. Although suicide is the most likely explanation, it was widely believed that his death had been engineered in order to protect accomplices in high places, notably in the Radical Party.

FROM THE POPULAR FRONT TO THE FALL OF FRANCE (1936–40)

International tension joined with the threat of internal fascism to push the Left to the fore. The riots caused by the Stavisky Affair – falsely, if fruitfully, perceived to be part of a fascist conspiracy – encouraged the Communist Party to reconsider its position. A switch in Stalin's international policy confirmed a change of heart. From late 1934 the Communists began to call for a united platform with the Socialists – a Popular Front – to resist fascism and introduce social and political change. The following year many of the Radicals subscribed to the movement as well, and the newly united Left won important gains in municipal elections. In the same year the Communist trade union returned to the fold of the CGT – indeed it effectively took it over. By 1937 the revitalized union would boast four million members. With extraordinary sleight of hand the Communists, who had formerly renounced the very idea of *la patrie*, now clothed themselves in the tricolour rather than the red flag, and intoned "The Marseillaise" as well as "The Internationale". Even Joan of Arc – "daughter of the People, sold out by her king and burnt by his priests" – enjoyed a period of left-wing approval. "Our party," announced the Communist daily *L'Humanité*, "is a moment in the history of eternal France."

That the movement for a Popular Front had struck a chord within the French nation was revealed in two ways. In the 1936 elections, campaigning under the slogan "Bread, Peace, Freedom", the united movement carried all before it, counting 358 deputies against 222 with the Socialists under Léon Blum as the largest party. Ominously, however, progress for the Communist Party was matched by growing support for the far Right. In the second place, the Left had still not taken power when a spontaneous working-class movement seized the country. Something like two million workers occupied their factories and workplaces, calling for the immediate implementation of Popular Front reforms.

The Left was taken aback by this movement; the first the secretary of the CGT knew about it was when he was contacted by telephone. Blum had formed a government composed of Socialists and Radicals – the Communists supported the government in the Chamber, but did not enter the cabinet – and he brought workers' leaders and employers round the table to thrash out a social policy with their help. The so-called "Matignon Agreements" of 7 June 1936 granted wage rises averaging 10 per cent, introduced the forty-hour week, established machinery for arbitration and conciliation, and laid down the principle of two weeks' paid holidays for all employees. Other important reforms followed. Measures were taken to stabilize grain prices, as an aid to farmers; to make the Bank of France more accountable (reducing the influence of the legendary "200 Families"); to increase the school-leaving age from thirteen to fourteen; and to undertake rearmament. The fascist leagues were also dissolved and driven underground.

The Popular Front showed a good deal of deftness in its approach to reform. The holiday provisions struck a responsive chord among the leisure-orientated working

The Spirit of 1936 **by Henri Cartier-Bresson. The provision of two weeks' paid holiday per year was, along with the reduction of the working week to forty hours, an integral part of the Popular Front's economic strategy of soaking up unemployment. It was perceived as making a significant improvement to the working classes' quality of life.**

classes – Blum claimed he had "injected a little beauty and sunshine into lives of hardship". Yet his government found it impossible to keep together both its parliamentary following and its mass support in what were clearly difficult times. The Spanish Civil War (1936–9) posed a real dilemma: to support the Republicans, as he wished, would lose Blum his Radical allies. In the end he opted for a studied neutrality which, however, disenchanted the Communists and many Socialists too. The poor state of the economy, moreover, negated the effects of his social reforms. The strategy of limiting the working week as a means of reducing unemployment was a spectacular failure: unemployment stubbornly refused to come down. Wage increases were offset by price rises. Industry was disrupted – production was lower when Blum left power in mid 1937 than at the time of the 1936 elections. A flight of capital put pressure on the currency, yet, by delaying a devaluation, Blum denied his government the chance of benefiting from a lower franc in export markets.

Beset from all sides Blum abandoned his post as prime minister in June 1937. There were several governments based on the Popular Front – including another led by Blum in early 1938 – that attempted to keep the political strategy intact. But social reform had been put on hold, and the popular enthusiasm which had greeted the elections of

Opposite **Miners in their work-clothes, following a political rally at a sports stadium in Montrouge outside Paris on 14 June 1936 to celebrate the end of their strike. The Popular Front was enormously effective in mobilizing militancy in the workplace, but less successful in rewarding it.**

1936 gradually dwindled away. It proved difficult to keep the Communists in line: their call for a general strike in 1938 proved a flop, and lost the Left credit. The fascist leagues had metamorphosed into right-wing political parties – de La Roque's *Croix de Feu* was now the *Parti social français* (French Social Party), boasting nearly a million members, while the former Communist Jacques Doriot formed the dangerous and rabble-rousing *Parti populaire français* (French Popular Party). On the international scene the picture was gloomy, too. In March 1938 Hitler had invaded Austria, and openly defied the international community to stop his continuing annexations.

The post-Popular Front government of Edouard Daladier bowed to what seemed the inevitable. In the Munich agreements of September 1938 the French and British ratified the Austrian Anschluss and also endorsed Hitler's claim to the Germanic Sudetenland in northern Czechoslovakia. Daladier attempted to regroup and reorganize the economy after the Popular Front era. The forty-hour week was extended to a forty-eight-hour week in 1939 as an incentive to employers. Firm financial policies were followed. A push on rearmament had the effect of boosting an economy slowly emerging from recession, and of bringing the armed forces up to scratch for conflict with Germany, which began to look increasingly inevitable. Only the Communists had voted against the Munich agreements of 1938. But they – like Stalin – were becoming disenchanted with the Western democracies' inability to cope with Hitler. News of the Nazi–Soviet pact of August 1939 shattered like a bombshell on the French political scene, and made for a depressing outlook when Hitler invaded Poland in September.

France and Britain went to war with Germany in September 1939 with little of the rhapsodic jingoism of 1914, but rather with a measured resignation, and with signs of political division very much in evidence. The loyalty of Communists – the party was outlawed almost at once – was very much in question. On the Right fear of Communist subversion damaged confidence in the war effort. "Rather Hitler than Blum", ran the anti-Semitic whispers. In early 1940 an envoy of Churchill, the British prime minister, reported to London that the French bourgeoisie was "gibbering with fright". The edge was taken off the suspense by a lengthy period of waiting while the two sides made military preparations. "Here, nothing," wrote a young lieutenant on the Maginot Line to his parents in February 1940. "Absolutely nothing. The only distractions are eating and sleeping. The situation is desperately reassuring."

Desperate reassurance was swiftly to give way to the blackest despair as, in May 1940, after eight months of "phoney war", the Germans launched an offensive. Since 1918 French generals had been planning to fight – and to fight in the way they knew best, namely, a war of trenches. The Maginot Line had been built on this assumption. They had failed to keep abreast of strategic thinking, which now aimed to bring mobility back on to the battlefield. Strategists like Liddell Hart and J.F.C. Fuller in Britain, Guderian in Germany and, at a less sophisticated level in France, the young cavalry officer Charles de Gaulle argued for the key role to be given to tanks, operating with air cover, to break like lightning through enemy defences and create havoc. Indeed the 1940 campaign was to prove an object lesson in the new strategy of lightning warfare

First had come the smart sedans, remaining quite elegant beneath their coverings of packages and mattresses; then came the sputtering old cars and the vans naively camouflaged with branches in the hope of escaping the black-crossed killers [Nazi aircraft]; and then comes the rearguard, the end of the misery, the flight of the country-folk and the have-nothings who walk along slowly ... the footsloggers, the bicycles laden with bundles, the tenacious mothers heroically pushing the baby's pram.

Writer Roland Dorgelès' account of the tragic procession in the summer of 1940 captures well the confusion and desperation of the so-called "Exodus", when between eight and ten million French people took to the road south. Enemy aircraft brought warfare to the civilian population far more directly than in World War I. Bombing of stations and rail networks produced havoc in northern cities. The urge to flee sprang partly from fear, partly from a misplaced belief that the government did not wish the population of a large sector of the northern departments in enemy hands,

The "Exodus"

as had proved to be the case in 1914–18. The rationale became bogged down in the mire of official indecision. The government tried to rally, and to organize urban defences in Paris in late May, but by 10 June the decision had been made

to move the government southwards, too, which added enormously to the confusion and panic.

A snowball effect operated, as villages and cities were abandoned by enough of their population to make collective life impossible. Cities were left deserted and empty, with abandoned cats and dogs roaming the streets, and, in the villages, the endless mooing of unmilked cows. Only 800 out of a population of 23,000 stayed on in the city of Chartres, in Troyes only 30 individuals out of 58,000. The receiving cities, in contrast, were full to the brim, with charitable agencies wringing their hands about the difficulty of feeding the bedraggled and limping refugees. In Limoges there were reckoned to be 200,000 individuals sleeping in the streets and gardens of the city. Bordeaux's population mushroomed from a quarter of a million to over 600,000, possibly more. This pell-mell crowd action was only calmed by the end of hostilities. Some, notably many Jews, had managed to cross the frontier into neutral Spain. But for others, a sombre trek back home soon began.

– blitzkrieg. The Germans attacked unexpectedly on 10 May through the Ardennes forest – which the complacent French high command had regarded as impassable by modern armies, and which was consequently neither within reach of the Maginot Line nor heavily defended. Some 1,500 armoured vehicles, commanded by Guderian, rushed headlong for the coast. When on 20 May they reached it, they had completed the encirclement of Allied forces, which fell back in disarray on Dunkirk. The French high command, old men for the most part, found it impossible to react swiftly enough. It took up to forty-eight hours for them just to get messages through to the front. Some 200,000 men of the British Expeditionary Force, plus 140,000 French troops, had to be evacuated by a flotilla including small boats sent from Britain in rescue. Cynically scenting the outcome, the Italian leader Mussolini declared war so as to pick up some spoils from a France which was palpably facing annihilation.

The German breakthrough sowed panic throughout northern France. Up to ten million people – two million of them from Paris – took to the roads, fleeing for their lives. The government joined the so-called "Exodus". Prime Minister Reynaud had attempted to bolster his authority by bringing the World War I icon, 84-year-old Marshal Pétain, into his government as vice-premier. He also introduced as junior war minister the 49-year-old de Gaulle – "he is a mere child!" commented one of the aged general staff. By early June, however, the government was on the road, stopping first at Tours, then in Bordeaux, before finishing up in the spa town of Vichy. With defeat staring him in the face, Reynaud proposed moving the government into the colonies so as to continue the struggle, while de Gaulle dreamt of falling back into the furthest reaches of the Breton peninsula. Pétain would, however, have nothing of it and, stepping forward, arranged an armistice to take effect on 25 June. The German army – whose great-grand-fathers had in 1871 acted as midwives at the birth of the Third Republic – was turning out to be the regime's undertaker. In the somewhat bizarre setting of the Vichy casino on 10 July 1940 the Chamber of Deputies voted overwhelmingly – by 568 to 80 – to entrust power to Pétain for the creation of a new state. The virtues of the Third Republic – its capacity for soaking up bitter social and political tensions within a liberal demo-cratic framework – were forgotten in the shocked recognition of utter defeat. The old regime's supporters were not allowed to put their case – leaving it to the Radical deputy Vincent Badie to shout above the mêlée, as the assembly broke up, "Vive la République, quand même!" – "Long live the Republic, all the same!" There would be worse epitaphs.

VICHY, OCCUPATION AND RESISTANCE

For France it was, as historian Marc Bloch put it, a "strange defeat" – unexpected, swift, devastating. The peace imposed by the Germans was Merovingian in its stark brutal-ity. France was permitted to retain her colonies and her navy (some of which the British Royal Navy bombarded into oblivion in the Algerian port of Mers-el-Kebir a few weeks later); but her army was reduced to 100,000 men, and 1.5 million troops were taken, effectively as hostages, to Germany. Alsace-Lorraine was incorporated into Germany. A kind of limited partition was imposed on France, the most important aspects of which were the designation of the north and the Atlantic coasts as a German-occupied zone, with the south forming a separate, non-occupied area. This Pétain called the *Etat français* (the "French state"), or "Vichy", as it was known after the southern spa town in which its government was based.

Pétain announced that the basis of the new regime would be "work, family, father-land" – and he meant it. The "liberty, equality, fraternity" of 1789 was to be replaced by the more homely triad of Vichy's would-be "National Revolution". The objective was to set straight, in the name of good old traditional values, all that had gone wrong with France. Though priding itself, like its leader, on being above factions, Vichy proved the most partisan and vicious of regimes, and spent much time and energy set-tling scores. Informing on enemies of the state was positively encouraged; each year its bureaucrats received nearly a million communications denouncing individuals. It cast its net wide for scapegoats. The politicians of the Third Republic were a special target: Blum, Daladier, Reynaud and others appeared before a political tribunal at Riom which ended, however, as a fiasco without sentences passed. Other groups that the Right and

Vichy poster for the Chantiers de la Jeunesse, the form of national service which all twenty-year-olds in the south were expected to perform for eight months – usually in forestry or environmental work. Behind the member of the Vichyite youth organization, the regenerative figure of a Gaulish warrior . . .

extreme Right had denounced in the 1930s also received attacks. Communists were beyond the pale, but so were freemasons – masonic orders were dissolved in 1940, and masons were drummed out of the teaching profession and the bureaucracy. So too were Jews – who received a special status in October 1940, and for whom Vichy reserved its most brutal attentions.

By such purges Vichy hoped to ground France in more traditionalist, patriarchal, authoritarian values. Strikes and trade unions were abolished. Corporatist committees, containing representatives of both workers and employers, had been introduced into industry to balance labour and capital. However, they invariably favoured employer over employee. The Catholic Church was incorporated into the regime's strategy, and prelates fell over themselves in saluting "the Pétain miracle", the "providential" marshal and so on. Religious teaching communities were given greater prominence within education – for a time religious instruction was enforced even within state schools. Freedom of speech and press freedom were quashed. Although the regime endeavoured to keep in touch with opinion through a veterans' league, there were never elections, nor even a referendum to endorse the political system. Nomination from above took the place of election at all levels of the state. If there was a Vichyite politics, it was one between variants of the Right – the ex-Communist Doriot, for example, based in the northern zone, was more actively collaborationist than Pétain, and even organized a French force to fight on the eastern front as part of the German army. Or else it was a kind of court politics similar to Bourbon Versailles: who had the marshal's ear and

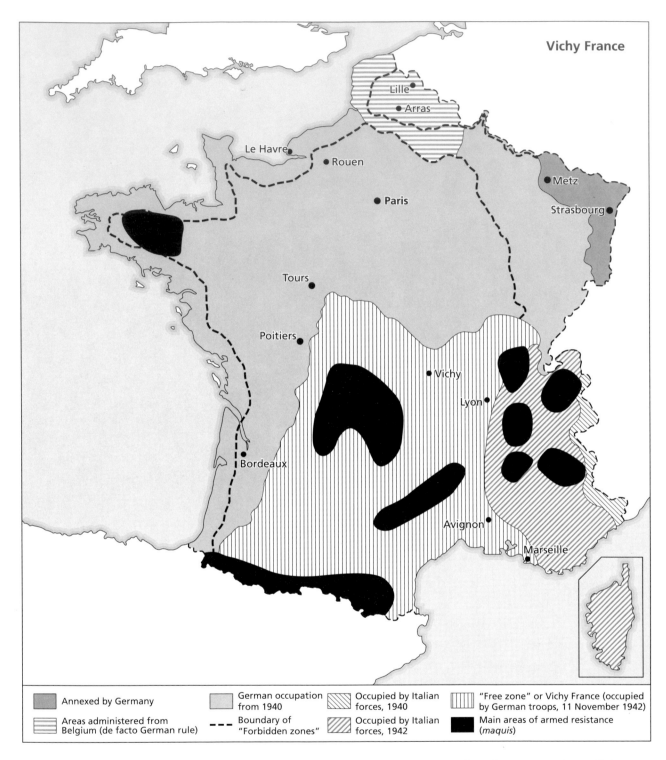

Vichy France

■	Annexed by Germany	☐	German occupation from 1940	▨	Occupied by Italian forces, 1940	▥	"Free zone" or Vichy France (occupied by German troops, 11 November 1942)
▤	Areas administered from Belgium (de facto German rule)	- - -	Boundary of "Forbidden zones"	▨	Occupied by Italian forces, 1942	■	Main areas of armed resistance (*maquis*)

France's defeat in 1940 resulted in fringe losses – Alsace-Lorraine to Germany in the east, Alpine territory to Italy – combined with a brutal redistribution of power. Much of the country was placed under "forbidden" status, occupied and/or ruled direct by German administrators. The Vichy government's so-called "independence" was cruelly exposed by German military occupation in 1942. Armed resistance was developed in upland areas by the so-called *maquis*.

whom he smiled at were key considerations. As with Louis XIV – with whom his prime minister, Laval, freely compared him – Pétain was the object of a mystique of leadership. He used the royal "we" in his edicts, and propaganda made of him a ubiquitous influence for Vichyite values, especially among the young. The regime fostered a cult of youth. "Be pure," adolescent boys in the youth movements were instructed, "be a man, be French …" The marshal's regime also introduced severe laws against pederasty – which were indeed to last down to the Fifth Republic.

Pétain's paternalism implied, moreover, a traditional stance on motherhood. In the National Revolution women belonged in the home, and should dedicate themselves to the sacred tasks of childbirth and bringing up the young. "The mother makes the family," the propaganda went, "and the family makes France." More favourable treatment for large families, complementing the family allowances introduced in 1939, was accompanied by legislation making divorce more difficult. The abortion laws were toughened up, too, and a female abortionist was executed in 1943. Education for girls was given a firm push in the direction of domesticity. Paradoxically, however, because a large part of the adult male population was imprisoned in Germany, many women were driven into gainful employment just to keep their families together. Work conditions, however, were now systematically biased against them.

In retrospect Pétain claimed that his task had been not simply to instil forgotten values into the French nation, but also to protect it from the horrors of direct Nazi rule. It is doubtful, however, whether Hitler ever had rule by Gauleiters on the agenda for France. Moreover the "shield" which Pétain later prided himself on holding up against Germany was singularly ineffective. This was true throughout, but particularly after November 1942, when Germany occupied the southern zone, and when Pétain's prime minister, the wily Laval, sought to inveigle himself into German favour by

In 1943 busts of Marshal Pétain came off the production line of the National Museum workshops, Paris, doubtless bound for every town hall in France. Vichy was marked by a highly developed personality cult centred on Pétain.

actively promoting France as part of the "New Order" in a Nazi-dominated Europe. Nowhere was this more evident than in the regime's enthusiastic anti-Semitism. Though it drew strongly from a vigorous native tradition, it was no less shocking for that, especially in a state which, since 1789, had been a world pioneer of Jewish emancipation. The special status given Jews by Vichy in 1940 was freely volunteered by the regime, without German pressure. Foreign Jews – many of whom had come to France specifically to flee Hitlerian persecution – were targeted first for rounding up. In June 1942 over 12,000 Parisian Jews, including young children, were rounded up in one swoop and held in a sports stadium, converted into a temporary concentration camp, prior to deportation. The wearing of a yellow star was made compulsory. In all, besides homosexuals and gypsies, who also felt the anti-Semite's wrath, over 75,000 Jews (about a third of them native French Jews) were deported. Only about 3 per cent ever returned – and none of the children.

The repressive arm of Vichy was increasingly turned against non-Jewish citizens from 1942 onwards, under Nazi prompting. The *Milice*, organized under Joseph Darnand in 1943 as a kind of home-grown political police, worked hard to root out opposition. It used torture systematically for the first time in France since before the Revolution of 1789. It had no shortage of victims, for hostility towards the regime was by 1942 and 1943 growing fast. Life had had to go on after the catastrophe of 1940, and this involved for most people, certainly in the north, some degree of compromise with the occupying forces – though whether one calls this collaboration is a moot point. There were enthusiastic collaborators: Breton, Flemish and Occitanian "nationalists", who saw a role for themselves in a more regionalist "New Order", were cases in

Procession of the Black Virgin at Moulins, 15 August 1941. The upper clergy was generally highly in favour of the Vichyite regime, which accorded the Church better treatment than it had received under the Third Republic. Here the bishop of Moulins leads a procession which combines two other Vichyite specialities: youth organizations and local folkloric groups.

point. Yet the total number of active collaborators was probably quite small – perhaps only about 150,000 individuals.

The stakes of association with the Nazi regime grew higher, moreover, as time passed, and as the French economy was subjected to a kind of rape at German hands. Pétain's "shield" was quite powerless to prevent this happening. By 1943 Germany was creaming off 40 per cent of France's industrial production and 15 per cent of its agricultural product. A quarter of all French meat was shipped out to the Third Reich and over half of the country's new aircraft, automobiles and machinery. France had become Germany's biggest supplier of war materials and it also became the third largest (after Russia and Poland) supplier of manpower. The system of forced labour service (*Service du travail obligatoire*, or STO) from early 1943 intensified a demand for labour which had been perceptible from the earliest days. Over a million French workers migrated to Germany during the war, to add to the 1.6 million soldiers also kept there.

These demands, on an already weakened economy, were highly damaging. Industrial and agricultural output dropped. As imports were few and costly, systems of rationing and wage-control had to be introduced. Even so, inflation was rife, with prices doubling between 1940 and 1944. A flourishing black market was unable to prevent serious damage to the population's health. Nutritional levels were lower in France than anywhere else in occupied Europe, with the exception of Italy. Rationing allowed for only 1,200 calories per day by 1943 – a recipe for malnutrition. It was little wonder that life expectancy dropped by some eight years in the Vichy period.

By associating itself so closely with an occupying force which imposed this level of privation on a developed nation, Vichy was effectively writing its own death-warrant. The handshake which Pétain gave to Hitler at Montoire in October 1940 had a high symbolic price. Vichy went beyond passive, defensive collaboration, placing France's military, police, communications and judicial apparatus very much at the disposal of the German occupiers. Its repressive policies, however, ensured it a broad and growing opposition. It created its own undertakers. To victimized Jewish, masonic and Communist opponents were added a good handful of republican refugees from the Spanish Civil War and, after 1943, huge numbers of young men wishing to evade compulsory labour service in Germany – not to mention all those increasingly disgusted by the damage being wreaked on French society by Vichyite policies.

Draft evaders from the STO swelled the ranks of a Resistance movement which had been slow to develop. In the early years of the regime opposition to Vichy had been sporadic, small-scale and highly personalized. Its amorphousness owed much to the originality of the situation in which resisters found themselves. Those in the Cévennes were following in the now faint footsteps of their Camisard ancestors under Louis XIV; but this was the exception. Broadly speaking, there was no script for resistance such as the Parisian *sans-culottes* and their descendants from 1789 to 1871 had had for revolutionary opposition. Resisters were obliged to improvise, then, to learn by trial and error. It was also new to have a movement of resistance involving the full range of the

Jewish yellow star, as worn in Paris from 1942. The regime's knee-jerk acceptance of anti-Semitism was to have a long-term effect in alienating some Jews from their adopted homeland.

The "scientific" Institute for Jewish Studies was established in Paris to research the nefarious impact of Jews on French society. In this poster the Jew is viewed as a cancer, rotting the fabric of every aspect of national life.

political spectrum. Though in the southern, Vichyite zone the traditional elites rallied to the regime, so that resisters were normally left-wing, resistance in the north had a much more politically ecumenical feel to it. Unity had, as ever, a strong symbolic element. "The evening the first arms arrived," a Burgundian peasant-farmer later reminisced, "we came to this cellar. I remember we sang the Internationale. We weren't Communists though. It was just that Pétain sang the Marseillaise, so we had to sing the Internationale."

The return of Communist militants to the fold after Hitler's attack on Russia in 1941 had brought into the Resistance some of the most zealous and committed of working-class militants. After the war Communists would claim to be the party of the *"75,000 fusillés"* ("75,000 firing-squad victims"). Though most Resistance networks tended to be localist in outlook, and confined to one or other of the two zones, the Communist-based "National Front" network straddled the border and came closest to being a national network. The forces of Resistance grew stronger by 1942 and 1943, as Germany tightened its political and economic grip on France. Sabotage, sheltering of and organizing escape lines for Allied airmen and agents and intelligence-gathering intensified. Armed action also began to be more common and the *maquis* – Resistance militants, refugees and draft-dodgers who established camps in the upland heaths of the Massif Central and the Alps – were increasingly important in this respect. Perhaps 20,000 strong in 1943 they had grown to 40,000 by early 1944, and had soared into six figures by the late summer.

The Resistance was never a mass movement in Vichy France: at the most, 1 per cent of the population was probably actively involved. The circulation of the Resistance press – prominent among which were the newspapers *Combat* and *Libération* – was about two million, though readership was probably far larger. Listening to BBC radio broadcasts was also an increasingly common clandestine act, which involved even greater numbers of "armchair resisters" (R. Kedward). Yet to be effective a movement like this required active, reflex support from the population as a whole; the Resistance agents had to move unrestricted, like fish in water. Just seeing and keeping your mouth shut was in this sense an act of supportive resistance. Continuing high levels of denunciations for underground activity showed that France was still split, and that the struggle continued to have some of the features of a civil war. Yet as the war progressed, it became increasingly apparent that the balance of tacit support was swinging in the Resistance's favour.

What these numerous and increasingly well-supported Resistance networks lacked, however, was overall organization. In the event this came from outside, through the agency of ex-junior war minister Charles de Gaulle. He had escaped to Britain in the rout of May–June 1940, and on 18 June launched his famous message on BBC radio, calling for the continuation of the struggle. He may have occupied the high moral ground, but at this stage he had precious little else in his favour. Though Churchill recognized him as the leader of French forces carrying on the armed struggle against

Opposite In a secluded farmhouse in the Haute-Loire department a budding group of the *maquis* receive firearms training, using rifles parachuted in by the Allies.

Vichy, he was largely ignored within France, and very few expatriate Frenchmen rallied to his cause. Early attempts by his "Free French" to win over French troops in the colonies failed. The United States, which came into the war in 1941, seemed to prefer to support internal critics of Vichy rather than this imperious and notoriously difficult outsider, in whom they claimed to detect dictatorial ambitions. Winston Churchill famously remarked that the "cross of Lorraine" – the insignia which de Gaulle had adopted for the Free French – was the heaviest of all the crosses he had to bear during the war. When in 1942 the Allies invaded North Africa – French colonial territory – they neglected even to inform de Gaulle.

De Gaulle was able to make himself useful to the Allies. He had, first of all, military advantages to exploit. Despite the failure of attempts to win over Vichyite Senegal to the Gaullist camp, by 1942 just about all the rest of France's colonial empire (with the notable exception of Algeria) had come over to him. When the Vichyite governor of Algeria turned coat and came over to the Allies' side, de Gaulle was able to work the situation to his advantage: the French armed forces and the Gaullist Free French were combined into the French Committee of National Liberation. De Gaulle took care to co-opt to it a smattering of Third Republic politicians like Pierre Mendès-France and Vincent Auriol. Three days before D-Day, when the Allies launched their cross-Channel offensive against Germany, the Committee declared itself the provisional government of France.

If de Gaulle and the Free French finally proved useful military allies for the British and Americans, they also had the considerable advantage of close contact with the internal Resistance forces. In January 1942 an agent of de Gaulle, the former Prefect Jean Moulin, had been parachuted into France with the specific task of co-ordinating Resistance networks. He was able to overcome geographical and political divisions within the movements, creating by May 1943 an umbrella organization. Moulin presided over this National Council of the Resistance, which incorporated all the major networks. He was soon afterwards captured and died under torture at the hands of Klaus Barbie, the so-called "Butcher of Lyon". His successor, Georges Bidault, continued Moulin's work, making the Resistance Council not just a military committee, but the basis for organizing a transition of power; trade unions and political parties were all represented within it. Political co-ordination was a delicate task. De Gaulle himself was something of an old-style patrician, far distant from the political views of much of the Resistance network, and many in his entourage were drawn from the pre-war Right. The Resistance Council's call for "real economic democracy" after the overthrow of Vichy, however, set down a marker which de Gaulle came to accept.

De Gaulle had by 1944 made himself a force which could not easily be ignored. He was bitterly resentful that the Free French did not figure in the Allied landings of D-Day, 6 June 1944 – though there were French troops involved in the campaign. He and the internal Resistance forced themselves into the scheme of things. In Paris the Resistance opened an insurrection on 19/20 August to put the German defensive forces on the back foot. Allied commanders eventually gave way to pressure and agreed

to include French military forces under General Leclerc in the liberation of Paris on 25 August. By that time a Franco-American force, with a large French component under de Lattre de Tassigny, had landed in Provence and was already advancing up the Rhône valley, liberating cities as it went. Meanwhile Resistance forces were co-ordinating with the Allies in mopping-up operations behind the advancing front.

On 26 August 1944 de Gaulle could make a triumphant procession up the Champs-Elysées in Paris. This traditional gesture was immensely important for a nation which seemed to have lost sight of the repertoire of political symbols inscribed in its republican past. De Gaulle went on to evoke a city "liberated by its population, with the help of the armies of France's allies". It would be churlish to suggest that others might have given the two factors a rather different weighting – irrelevant, too, for by lodging the French people and French armies at the heart of the overthrow of the Vichy regime and establishing a new myth of foundation for the new, Fourth, Republic, he allowed French society to approach the *après-guerre* in a mood of renewal – a mood soon, however, to be sorely tested.

American photographer Robert Capa captures the jubilation on the faces of Parisians as their city is liberated by de Gaulle and the Allies on 25 August 1944.

CHAPTER 10

Post-war France: Expansion and Beyond

"There was nothing else to do but work seriously and devotedly, struggle for food, see friends quietly, and look forward to freedom." The comments of the painter Pablo Picasso, who spent the war years in Paris, are probably more representative of the bulk of the French population than those militant minorities involved in either open collaboration or paramilitary Resistance activity.

The hopeful edge to the future which the involvement of the French in their own liberation had brought was, however, soon lost. Freedom carried a heavier price than had been anticipated. The process of establishing a new, Fourth, Republic was bitter and divisive, and formed part of the broader backdrop of the Cold War between the main victors, the Soviet Union and the United States. The prize of ultimate victory was scarcely glittering: the Fourth Republic soon settled into a round of parliamentary wranglings which recalled the stalemates and compromises of the Third. Politics was also increasingly poisoned by bitter colonial conflicts, at first in Indo-China (to 1954), and then in Algeria (to 1962). Deadlock over Algeria in 1958 led to a constitutional crisis, with the Fourth Republic giving way to the Fifth, supervised by a reinvigorated de Gaulle, its first president.

Some argued that the Fifth Republic had been tailored so exactly for the requirements of de Gaulle that it would not survive his removal. This has proved not to be the case. Despite the alarms set off by the politically unclassifiable May Events of 1968, which seemed to come close to overthrowing it, the regime survived his retirement from politics (in 1969). However, the presidency (from 1974) of the Centre-Right Valéry Giscard d'Estaing owed little to the Gaullist inheritance. This stabilization of the regime owed much to the unparalleled period of economic growth which France enjoyed from the late 1940s down to the mid 1970s – growth which brought major changes in styles of life and outlook among the French population.

RECRIMINATION AND STABILIZATION

"No serenity was possible," wrote Simone de Beauvoir, long-time friend of existentialist writer Jean-Paul Sartre, of the post-war period. "The war was over: it remained on our hands like a great unwanted corpse, and there was no place on earth to bury it." The events of autumn 1944 and spring 1945 had been uplifting indeed: the liberation of Paris and successive provincial cities; the incorporation of the internal Resistance forces into the regular army; the penetration of the German heartlands by the forces of de Lattre de Tassigny; and celebrations for victory in Europe. But the buoyant spirit of the times was undercut by more sombre events. News of the concentration camps was confirmed by the Russian arrival in Auschwitz in January 1945 and the return of French deportees in May. Accounts of Nazi atrocities brought home the enormity of the

The existentialist cafés of Saint-Germain-des-Prés

"The Saint-Germain-des-Près quarter has become a campus for the American collegiate set," noted American resident Janet Flanner sniffily in the summer of 1948.

The Café de Flore serves as a drugstore for pretty upstate girls in unbecoming blue denim pants and their Middle Western dates, most of whom are growing Beaux-Arts beards. Members of the tourist intelligentsia patronize the Rue de Bac's Pont-Royal bar, which used to be full of French existentialists and is now full only of themselves, often arguing about existentialism.

The arrival of American hordes in the aftermath of the Liberation and the Marshall Plan converted into a tourist attraction a number of Left Bank cafés which had a long history of supporting networks of artistic and intellectual social life. The Deux Magots had been an important centre for surrealist groups in the 1930s, while the Brasserie Lipp was a hang-out for the more politically oriented. Communist groups had other locales, painters and sculptors others, and so on. To this café society was linked a warm hotchpotch of night-clubs, jazz spots, restaurants, art galleries and small theatres, which formed at once the means of expression and relaxation of this diverse intelligentsia. Before 1944 these public locations offered warmth as well as companionship. "Towards the end

The Deux Magots, in the heart of Saint-Germain.

of the Occupation, in the winter of 1943/4, everyone came there to keep warm," one writer later remembered of the Café de Flore. "One had the impression that the first-floor room was a classroom. Sartre was installed at a little table, writing *Paths of Freedom*, Simone de Beauvoir, at another table, was writing *All Men Are Mortal* ... close by, Arthur Adamov was writing, too, doubtless one of his plays ..."

Jean-Paul Sartre came to be the star of the show, and American students would ask waiters if they could sit in his usual chair. The existentialist philosophy which he developed, in association with founding feminist Simone de Beauvoir, his life-long companion, derived from the German philosophers Husserl and Heidegger. The existentialists sought to base principles of human responsibility and action on the raw materials of human existence rather than on abstract, metaphysical ideas. Tinged with a strong pessimism, and a resistance to easy answers, the movement of ideas responded to the mood of the period.

The café scene helped to make the existentialists famous: Sartre was more widely known than any philosopher since Voltaire. Popular success also compromised their sociability. Early on, Sartre and de Beauvoir had moved to the basement bar of the Hôtel du Pont-Royal, where they had to write on barrels. "Sartre?" the owner of the Flore later commented, "He was my worst client. Hours scribbling on a piece of paper, sitting in front of a single drink, which he didn't renew from morning to night"

Cartoon by Jacques Sennep. While Simone de Beauvoir writes at a table, Jean-Paul Sartre approaches the bar at the Pont-Royal for an existential cocktail, and is offered a choice between Plato-flip, Nietzsche-fizz and Spinoza-gin.

Woman collaborator paraded shaven-headed through the streets of Chartres in late summer 1944. The happy crowds who had cheered the passage of General de Gaulle soon turned to resentment and spite, now under the tricolour flag. Fortunately, such attacks on women who had consorted with German troops did not last long.

Holocaust, and provided a kind of anti-fascist vaccination which would last decades. The explosion of the atom bombs at Hiroshima and Nagasaki to end the war with Japan in August 1945 also put a question-mark against the humane values for which most had thought they were fighting in the war years. Many would have their disillusionment completed by reports, from 1949, that the Soviet Union too had had its labour and concentration camps, and had indulged in its fair share of atrocities.

No one seemed to have clean hands. Waves of vicious recrimination against alleged Vichy collaborators and black-marketeers were able to gather momentum in the power vacuum caused by the overthrow of the Vichy regime and the retreat of the Germans. Even a moderate like Edouard Herriot had few qualms in envisaging "a blood-bath" to purge the country of its noxious elements. In the event, things were not as bad as at one stage looked likely. Talk of 100,000 summary executions now seems exaggerated; there appear to have been fewer than 10,000. Trials of leading figures such as Laval (sentenced to death) and Pétain (imprisoned for life) were the tip of only a moderately large iceberg. Some 30,000 to 40,000 individuals were tried and imprisoned for collaboration – and most had been released within a few years. In some barbaric vigilante action, prostitutes and other women alleged to have engaged in "horizontal collaboration" were stripped and their heads shaved.

Though such actions soured the fresh smell of freedom, the scale of violence involved was moderate compared to that experienced in France's past – from the Wars of Religion to the Paris Commune. Given the initial power vacuum – especially in the Midi – a good deal of preventive action was taken: civilians were disarmed from October 1944; and 100,000 individuals were taken into protective custody. De Gaulle's commissaries, who helped to set up the new local administrations, acted to heal rather than heighten animosities – not least because they feared a Communist takeover if passions got out of hand. There was thus a good deal of continuity between Vichy and Liberation administrative structures. The 11,000 dismissals for collaboration left most of the bureaucracy intact.

As "dictator by consent" for over a year, de Gaulle operated through a government of national unity that included all shades of opinion, plus some notable figures from the Third Republic. The call for reconstruction and radical economic and social action reflected the popular demand for a break with Vichy values, but was also a good excuse to end recrimination and encourage a fresh start. After four years' subjection to Nazi priorities under Vichy, the French economy was in dire straits. In fact it would take a long time for standards of living to improve – another cause of disillusionment among those who had expected better once the war was over. Only half the rail network was still in place, half a million buildings had been destroyed and raw materials were in desperately short supply. As a result there were numerous shortages – bread rationing continued until 1949 – and inflation was rampant. The government took advantage of the chastened mood of employers, many of whom had collaborated, to bring much of the economy (gas and electricity, many banks and insurance companies, Air France, Renault and so on) under state control. This was accompanied by radical measures of state welfare – notably the creation of an impressive social security system and, at the workplace, works councils. The vote was also extended to women for the first time.

The establishment of a new constitution proved, however, a painful process. A referendum in October 1945 revealed that 96 per cent of voters were against the continuation of the Third Republic, but it proved difficult to find something recognizably different to put in its place. Elections had revealed a quite new political landscape. The old Radical party and the Right had been decimated, and the largest party was now the Communists, who played to the hilt their wartime role as the *75,000 fusillés*. They shared the limelight with the Socialists and a new progressive Catholic grouping, the MRP (*Mouvement républicain populaire*), headed by ex-*Résistant* Georges Bidault. Above them all floated de Gaulle, whose call for a more presidential style of constitution incited the major political formations to take up contrary positions. De Gaulle resigned in January 1946 – a tactical move which was, however, to consign him to the political wilderness for more than a decade. The failure of the first constitutional project to attain a majority in the referendum of May 1946 led to the eventual passing of a revised constitutional statute, which commanded little public enthusiasm.

The constitution of the Fourth Republic ended up by strongly resembling that of the Third. In the twelve years to 1958, there would be more than a score of prime ministers. Control shuffled between different power blocs drawn from the three major parties, the Communists (the PCF – *Parti communiste français*), the Socialists and the MRP. The decision of socialist prime minister Paul Ramadier in May 1947 to eject Communists from the governmental majority ended the phase of "tripartism" and marked the political marginalization of the main working-class party – it was another thirty-four years before they would re-enter government. Under the influence of cold war attitudes, the PCF would be one of the most irreconcilable critics of the new political arrangements, which placed France solidly in the American camp. The spirit of post-Liberation solidarity and revolutionary optimism had broken irremediably.

DECOLONIZATION AND THE ADVENT OF THE FIFTH REPUBLIC

The political scene was dominated by a sense of stalemate, with party groupings clustering around the Centre because of what were perceived as threats from both Left and Right. To the Right de Gaulle seemed to be posturing in Bonapartist fashion as a critic of the parliamentary system. He campaigned against the second referendum on the constitution, then in March 1947 set up his own party, the RPF (*Rassemblement du peuple français*). He made a good deal of headway – the RPF won 40 per cent of the national vote in the 1947 municipal elections. But his mass rallies and man-of-destiny appearances were frightening to many, and he eventually backed off, retiring from politics once again in September 1952. "De Gaulle marched us at full speed to the Rubicon," the writer and faithful Gaullist André Malraux later recalled, "and then told us to get out our fishing rods."

The Communists had been critical of governmental power even when they had been in the government themselves. Eventually they had been ejected from office in 1947

Maurice Thorez at the microphone during the elections of 1947. Leader of the Communists from 1930 till his death in 1964, Thorez had spent the war in Moscow, but returned to become a government minister during the period of tripartism in 1945–7. His influence helped make the PCF one of the most hard-line of all Western Communist parties.

VOTER COMMUNISTE
C'EST VOTER POUR L'OCCUPATION RUSSE

CENTRE DE DÉFENSE DE LA CIVILISATION ET DE LA LIBERTÉ – PARIS

Poster issued by the Centre for the Defence of Freedom and Civilization during the election campaign of 1950. The end of "tripartism" and the advent of the Cold War brought a strong current of anti-communism into French politics.

for supporting Renault strikers protesting against government pay cuts. The cold war made the Communists feared as ruthless Party infiltrators, and the pro-Stalinist line followed by Maurice Thorez, the PFC leader, who had spent the war years living in Moscow, as well as by the Communist CGT trade union, seemed to give some credence to this belief. In fact, by contrast with Stalin, the Communists were far more interested in maintaining their support among the working class than in seizing power, and stayed well within the bounds of legality. However, when American President Harry S. Truman began in 1947 to preach containment of Communism throughout the world, the French political establishment was forced to make a choice between the two cold war combatants. The decision to throw in France's lot with the United States ensured unremitting PCF hostility, but had the considerable advantage of attracting Marshall Aid from America, which was crucial to France's economic recovery. France also played a part in forming the military defence league NATO (the North Atlantic Treaty Organization) in April 1949.

Although extremism was seen as threatening political stability, the voting system of proportional representation favoured the Centre parties. For electoral reasons and to emphasize their autonomy, the latter tended to accentuate differences between themselves. Thus the Socialists retained an anti-clerical aspect which set them at odds with the Christian Democrats of the MRP. The Radicals also made a comeback, and played a crucial role as tactical prop in a number of ministerial pacts. The relative stagnation at the heart of the political system was underlined by the rabble-rousing political campaign led by Pierre Poujade in the early 1950s. Based on a small shopkeeper mentality, which attacked the government for high taxes, and which was spiced with a fashionable anti-Communism and a vestigial anti-Semitism, the Poujadist party managed fifty-three seats in the 1956 elections.

Perhaps the only time in the Fourth Republic when a new mood permeated political life was the brief premiership of Pierre Mendès-France in 1954/5. A determined effort to extricate France from its serious colonial entanglements was accompanied by a programme of economic modernization that won a good deal of support. The cult of personality which appeared to be developing around his name made him a soft target. Moreover, though aimed mainly against unlicensed moonshine producers, his campaign to reduce alcoholism and increase milk-drinking had a comic element in such a wine-producing and wine-consuming society as France, which served him ill.

This political quagmire was a poor context for the resolution of problematic colonial issues. Insurrection in Madagascar in 1947, which resulted in the deaths of nearly 100,000 rebels, highlighted the seriousness of the issues. Indo-China was also by that time proving difficult to deal with. The nationalists in Vietnam were headed by Ho Chi Minh, who, following the withdrawal of the Japanese, set up a provisional government in August 1945. The possibility of France working with the Viet-Minh, however, was frustrated as a result of colonial administrators on the spot playing fast-and-loose with the Viet-Minh and with the Japanese occupying forces. In the hostilities which followed, the French use of former Nazi German soldiers who had been smuggled out of Europe along various "rat-lines" caused something of a stir in France, as did the troops' use of torture. It was as if the French were inflicting on the Vietnamese the kind of treatment which the Nazis had visited upon the French from 1940 to 1944. It took a major military defeat at Dien-Bien-Phu in 1954 at the hands of the Vietnamese general Giap – subsequent strategist of the Vietnamese war against the United States – to make the Indo-Chinese issue more than an academic question.

Negotiations skilfully conducted by Prime Minister Mendès-France helped France disengage from Indo-China less painfully than might have been the case. Mendès also proved accommodating towards Tunisian independence, and set in motion talks with Morocco which were to lead to its independence in 1956. Algeria was, however, altogether a bigger and more difficult problem. French since 1830, it counted one million Europeans out of a total population of nine million. Since 1954 the minority had been resisting a wave of co-ordinated violence conducted by the FLN (*Front de libération nationale*). All the major political formations in Paris were internally split over the Algerian crisis, while the frequently changing ministerial line-up made it impossible to develop a consistent political strategy. Military activity and bipartisan violence came to fill the vacuum. A savagely dirty war evolved, with atrocities on both sides. Bombs were detonated in mainland France, while in Algeria the French army began to use torture as a standard weapon of counter-intelligence. Intellectuals blew the whistle on these clear violations of human rights, but many French men and women and European colonists accepted such steps because they were expedient. The army was also determined to win at all costs. Many professional soldiers had felt humiliated by Dien-Bien-Phu, and wished to set the record straight.

Attempts by government to force the colonists into conciliatory reforms were only partly successful, while negotiations with the FLN ran aground on colonist intransigence. The strike against Colonel Nasser in Egypt by a Franco-British-Israeli force had other origins, but was further justified in French eyes by the fact that Nasser was supposed to be providing material aid to FLN rebels. The strike failed dismally, but the

"Suez Crisis" only strengthened French resolve that something had to be done. The war was not only politically divisive, its expense was threatening France's financial and economic stability. Secret negotiations were halted, however, by a sudden and unanticipated colonist *coup d'état* on 13 May 1958. Right-wing colonists seized the levers of power, and the French military establishment in Algiers felt itself unable to do any more than endorse their action. General Massu presided over the colonists' Committee of Public Safety – a reference to 1793/4 that made the call to keep the republic "one and indivisible" all the more patriotic. General Salan was heard to shout "Vive de Gaulle!" in Algiers, and de Gaulle announced himself willing to re-enter politics. The

Photograph of a routine episode in the war against Indo-China. Colonial wars in Indo-China, then Algeria – dirty, badly conducted, ill-conceived, and swimming against the tide of history – were to be the death of the Fourth Republic.

In the Algerian cities a war of bomb blasts and barricades developed. A ferocious policy of repression, including widespread and systematic torture, was unable to contain the rebellion.

rebel generals sent in parachute regiments to take over Corsica, while in mainland France nervous Parisians scanned the sky fearfully for parachute drops.

In this atmosphere of imminent civil war, with the major political formations in apparent deadlock, free agents within the political establishment began to fish in troubled waters. The idea of de Gaulle as political saviour was warmly endorsed by the Algerian colonists. De Gaulle's pose as man of destiny seemed to be reaching its justification. He distanced himself from the generals, evidently not wishing to lead a *coup d'état* which would leave him beholden to the military. His Resistance past also ensured him a following on the Left as well as on the Right. So he collaborated closely with President Coty to maintain every appearance of legality. On 1 June 1958 a chastened National Assembly agreed that de Gaulle should be recalled and given emergency powers for six months. The decision to draw up a new constitution was now a formality. This effective constitutional suicide by the Fourth Republic must have gone some way to vindicate de Gaulle's twelve years in the wilderness. When he returned to his Parisian hotel on the evening of 1 June he told the hotel porter, "Albert, I have won."

Winning, however, had its responsibilities. The new constitution de Gaulle drew up was very much made to his own measure. Many on the Left doubted that under its provisions they could ever climb to power. The focus of power was shifted firmly away from the National Assembly towards the president – along lines which de Gaulle had himself advocated in 1946. The practice of referendums was widened. The underlying conceptual framework was that the president should be above the mêlée and should resist and counterbalance various interest groups – political parties, unions, and so on. The new system also gave the president a good deal of leeway for a foreign policy independent from parliament.

The solution to the Algerian crisis was, moreover, very much a personal *tour de force* by the new president. At first he seemed to go along with the European minority; on a visit to Algiers, in which he received an ecstatic welcome by the Europeans, he commented, "Je vous ai compris" – "I have understood you" – an oracular phrase whose ambiguity would only become apparent in time. He soon realized that no military solution to the insurrection was possible, while most political solutions on offer bore too high a price. To assimilate Algeria into France ultimately risked – because of the high Algerian birth-rate – the chance of a Muslim majority in the French National Assembly. On the other hand, a solution based on a wholly French Algeria, with the power of the

The *pieds-noirs*

French decolonization in North Africa produced population displacements which are comparable with the more famous migrations in central and eastern Europe in World War II. From the early 1950s to early 1960s some 1.3 million Europeans were "repatriated" from Morocco, Tunisia and Algeria. Algeria provided the bulk of these, reflecting the greater duration of French occupation, and perhaps two-thirds of the "refugees" left between 1961 and 1963, as the Algerian War drew to a close.

The origin of the term *pieds-noirs* ("black-feet"), used to describe the returning colonists, is uncertain. At first they were called Algerians – Algerian Arabs were called first "natives", then "Muslims" – but this term became too loaded with ambiguity over the course of the 1950s. After 1955 they accepted the term *pieds-noirs* to describe themselves.

Though there was a *pied-noir* diaspora throughout the world, the bulk of the European population of Algeria settled in France, where they received compensation from the French government. Though they felt that this was well below what they were entitled to, the *pieds-noirs* appeared to bring little enduring bitterness into the metropolitan country with them, and set about making a new life with some gusto. The vast majority of *rapatriés* concentrated in cities south of a line between Bordeaux and Lyon. A young, fairly active population, they rejuvenated these areas, increased their birth-rates and boosted local economies. The influx of *pieds-noirs* caused little lasting hostility from the host population either, highlighting the importance of the economic environment – which was booming – in helping to integrate immigrant groups. Their Arab compatriots would prove less fortunate in the 1970s and 1980s.

European minority maintained, meant that the war might continue at unacceptably high costs. Having decided that no alternative was open to him, de Gaulle moved fast. In September 1959 he announced his readiness to accept Algerian self-determination, and entered into negotiations with the FLN. The result was the Evian agreements of 1962, which gave Algeria full independence.

The decision to grant Algerian independence led to a backlash by the European colonists. From 1961 they founded the OAS (*Organisation Armée secrète*), along with disaffected army officers (such as Salan), Rightists and disgruntled politicians in France (such as Bidault). The OAS conducted terrorist attacks in Algeria and mainland France, including a number of plots on the life of de Gaulle himself, and a further attempted *coup d'état* by senior army officers in Algeria in 1961. De Gaulle, however, prevailed. The problem of the European minority was "solved" by providing for their return to metropolitan France. Some 800,000 Europeans – *pieds-noirs* ("black-feet") as they were called – left Algeria, mainly settling in southern France. The war had caused some 20,000 French deaths, as against several hundreds of thousands of Muslim deaths.

The colonial catastrophe in Algeria pushed France further down the decolonizing road. In 1958 de Gaulle had offered the colonies of central and West Africa the option of independence without subsequent aid, or partial autonomy with continuing association with metropolitan France. Sekou Touré's Guinea took the former option, but the other states chose the latter. In 1960, however, the terms of the arrangements were altered in order to encompass full independence. France retained a number of overseas territories: the "DOMs" (*Départments d'Outre-Mer*) (notably Martinique and Guadeloupe in the Caribbean, and Réunion in the Indian Ocean), which enjoy full French nationality, including the right to elect deputies to the National Assembly; and a handful of "TOMs" (*Territoires d'Outre-Mer*), which have a lesser status and fewer political rights. Yet these are merely the appendix to what had been one of the greatest colonial empires in world history. De Gaulle closed this chapter in French history – and closed it definitively. Aid from metropolitan France fell fast, while trade with the colonies dwindled away, as France found its major trading partners inside Europe rather than outside it. Where the Third World had accounted for a fifth of French trade in the late 1950s, by the late 1970s it was down to a twentieth.

Whereas Fourth Republic foreign ministers had been endlessly harassed by colonial problems and their scope for action limited by the darkest days of the cold war (and by dependence on American aid), de Gaulle in the 1960s was able to pursue policies of calculated *grandeur*. He put something of a brake on the move towards European integration, famously vetoing the entry of Britain into the European Community, for example. He also withdrew France from NATO, developed an independent nuclear deterrent and sought out ways of establishing diplomatic links without slavishly seeking clearance at Washington. He took some pleasure in thumbing his nose at the "Anglo-Saxons" – as with his famous cry for a "Free Quebec" during a state visit to North America in 1967. This independent line highlighted the growing self-confidence of a France whose economy was pushing up the league of great powers.

THE "THIRTY GLORIOUS YEARS"

France had a more impressive economic performance than at any other time in its history stretching back to 1945 and lasting through to 1974. Its record stood up well against any of her international competitors. It was fashionable, especially amongst Gaullists, to contrast the Fourth and Fifth Republics. The former was allegedly scarred by frequent political deadlock and lack of political will; whereas the latter, with its more presidential constitution, allowed for a greater degree of continuity – and therefore effectiveness – in policy. Certainly the political calm and ministerial continuity that developed in the 1960s – in stark contrast to the more troubled days of the previous decade – provided a more helpful framework for social and economic policies to take effect. Yet the contrast was more apparent than real. The economic achievements of the Fifth Republic owed a great deal more to the groundwork performed under the

Soldiers and civilians, Arabs and Europeans mob General de Gaulle with enthusiasm in his visit to Algiers in June 1958. The photograph is a reminder of the large numbers of allies the French had among the Arab inhabitants of Algeria.

Fourth than Gaullists liked to admit – and more to some of the state-oriented social thinking mapped out in the early days of Vichy than most French people cared to acknowledge.

Perhaps the most evident symptom of the transformed economic environment of these *trente glorieuses* – the "thirty glorious years" from the mid 1940s to the mid 1970s – was a complete turn-around in the country's demographic performance. France's population started to grow fast – for the first time since the eighteenth century. Population rose from 40.3 million in 1946 to nearly 50 million by late 1958, and to 56 million by the 1990s. Improved medicine was starting to have a more long-term impact on the death-rate: life expectancy in 1946 was 60 years for men and 65 years for women; by 1965 the figures were 67 and 75 respectively, rising further to 72 and 80 by the early 1990s. Yet the major cause of demographic vitality was a post-war baby-boom, which continued well into the 1960s. The birth-rate was 50 per cent above pre-war levels for most of this time and, moreover, above average European levels. State encouragement, in the form of welfare arrangements and generous family allowances, played a part in this boom but was not a determining cause – the boom started under Vichy, before the welfare state was in place. The major determinant of the rising birth-rate appears to have been a healthy economic environment.

Much the same was true of the other main contributor to population growth. The baby-boom slightly depressed the percentage of women in the labour force in the 1960s, and it was immigration which took up the slack in the expanding economy. The number of foreigners resident in France had fallen in the repressive Vichy years to around 1.5 million. A massive influx in the 1950s and 1960s – encouraged by employers, who needed the labour supply, especially at the lower wage-rates immigrants would accept – boosted these levels significantly. By 1975 there were roughly four million foreigners, around half of whom were from the Iberian peninsula (especially Portugal), together with half a million North Africans. Immigrants composed some 8 per cent of the labour force – and formed 17 per cent of industrial workers.

A bigger, younger population gave a powerful injection of demand which in turn helped to trigger economic growth. The state was also a major player in the post-war economic revival. Bold nationalization policies were supplemented by the decision to institute a National Plan, the brainchild of former Cognac merchant Jean Monnet, whom de Gaulle appointed in 1946 to serve as the Plan's first commissioner. Government, business and trade unions were encouraged to work together to reach approved economic targets. The technocratic edge to economic decision-making was underlined by the creation in 1946 of a national administrators' college, the *Ecole Nationale d'Administration* (ENA), and "*énarques*" came to be the missionaries of the state-led economic revival, forming a back-room technical lobby of immense importance through to the present day.

The First Plan was established to last from 1947 to 1952, and made the reconstruction of the war-damaged infrastructure and the supervision of industrial recovery the main priorities. The focus was put on production – coal, steel, cement, tractors,

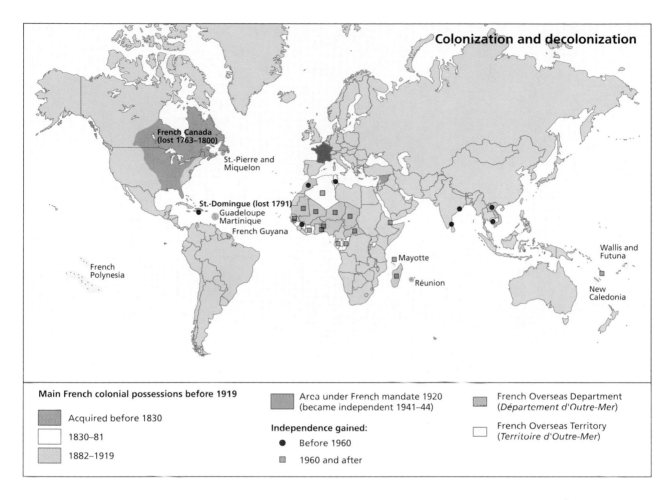

Colonization and decolonization

French Canada (lost 1763–1800)

St.-Pierre and Miquelon

St.-Domingue (lost 1791)
Guadeloupe
Martinique
French Guyana

French Polynesia

Mayotte

Réunion

Wallis and Futuna

New Caledonia

Main French colonial possessions before 1919

Acquired before 1830

1830–81

1882–1919

Area under French mandate 1920
(became independent 1941–44)

Independence gained:

● Before 1960

■ 1960 and after

French Overseas Department
(*Département d'Outre-Mer*)

French Overseas Territory
(*Territoire d'Outre-Mer*)

transport. The consumer was as yet the last in the line. France's performance was immensely assisted by Marshall Aid from the United States, which was particularly generous to France, and which helped maintain the pace of change right through to the early 1950s. By then new structures were emerging. Of key importance here was the Coal and Steel Treaty, brainchild of Monnet and MRP deputy Robert Schumann, which was arranged in 1951 with West Germany, and which formed the first step in the creation of the European Community.

Industrial performance was impressive: the years from 1950 to 1958 witnessed an 80 per cent increase in output, as the economy as a whole continued to grow at over 5 per cent a year. Agriculture was also part of the picture of dynamism: the "tractor revolution" helped to boost productivity on farms of all shapes and sizes. The number of tractors increased tenfold from 1946 to 1958. A sign of new levels of performance was the fact that, rather than hide behind tariff barriers, France was prepared to participate in the burgeoning economic community by submitting the agrarian sector to greater foreign competition. The Treaty of Rome of 1957, which established the "Common Market" of France, Germany, the Benelux countries and Italy, extended to agriculture as well as industry. Even though their position was bolstered by the price guarantees

France had built up an impressive colonial empire in the seventeenth and eighteenth centuries, notably in Canada, the West Indies and West Africa. Losing the so-called "Second Hundred Years War" (1689–1815) against Britain necessitated starting again almost from scratch. Algeria was colonized in 1830, but most French colonization took place from the 1880s until the First World War. Decolonization following World War II proved especially painful for France, including humiliating military defeat in Indo-China and devastating wars in Algeria.

and income-support mechanisms of the Common Agricultural Policy (1962), French farmers were still under a challenge to produce more efficiently. The challenge had a tonic rather than a depressive effect, with farmers seeking to reorganize and modernize in order to remain internationally competitive. The price of modernization, however, was that a large number of the workforce shifted away from agriculture. Farmers had composed over a third of the active population in 1946; by the mid 1950s the figure was drifting below 30 per cent, and by the late 1960s had hit a mere 16 per cent – drifting downwards to 6 or 7 per cent over the next decades.

The shake-out of agricultural labour was less painful than it might have been, because the rest of the economy was doing well enough to absorb the additional manpower. The regeneration of productive capacity began to work its way through into other areas of the economy. Besides industry the service sector of the economy was also booming. Up to the mid 1950s the Plan had seen heavy industry as its main priority; now a more balanced pattern prevailed, with housing and food production included. Economic recovery was by then beginning to have a major impact upon living standards. The trade unions had had to work hard in the aftermath of war to keep wages even within shouting distance of prices. The problem of inflation was temporarily resolved by the significant devaluation of the currency which de Gaulle imposed in 1962. Among other measures of monetary restraint he introduced a "New Franc" for every 100 old ones.

In the 1960s the trappings of consumerism hit a society long resistant to commercialism. Half of all households possessed a refrigerator in 1965 (only 7.5 per cent had done so in 1959); a car in 1966 (only 30 per cent had done so as recently as 1960); a television also in 1966 (as against 26 per cent in 1962); and a washing machine in 1968 (in 1954 a third of homes did not even have running water). The number of televisions rose from 1 million to 11 million between 1958 and 1973, cars from 5 million to 15 million over much the same time-span. Other indicators of consumerism attested to the depth of the transformation. Less than a fifth of homes possessed central heating in 1962; by 1982 it was over two-thirds. The number of supermarkets rose from forty in 1960 to 1,000 by 1970. New forms of leisure were encouraged by statutory provision for three weeks of paid holidays per year in 1956 – which was raised to four weeks in 1963 (and ultimately to five weeks in 1982). New forms of holiday such as the eco-friendly Club Méditerranée began to grow, and the increasing habit of taking off for *le weekend* spurred a craze for second homes. Indeed the number of *résidences secondaires* rose from 330,000 in 1954 to 1.7 million in 1975.

The new materialism made waves within the intelligentsia. There was a strong backlash critical of this "commodification" of French culture. Much blame was pinned on American cultural influence – *franglais* (Americanized French) in particular became the subject of hot debate. Yet cultural imports made a significant impact on French high culture. The revival of theatre from the early 1950s, for example, owed an enormous amount to foreigners based in France, notably Ionesco (Romanian), Beckett (Irish), Adamov (Russian), Obaldia (Panamanian) – and, later, Peter Brook (British). The

"theatre of the absurd" questioned the conventionalities of everyday life, as did, in another medium, the practitioners of the *nouveau roman* ("new novel"), such as Alain Robbe-Grillet, Michel Butor and Nathalie Sarraute. The *nouvelle vague* ("New Wave") in French cinema which emerged in the late 1950s – Truffaut, Godard, Chabrol and Rohmer all made their first serious features in 1959 – also celebrated rather than condemned overseas culture. Hollywood directors such as Alfred Hitchcock received adulation and homage from the New Wave directors.

Not everyone won prizes in the consumerist race; there were losers as well as winners. Geographically, "have-not" regions in the south and west contrasted with "have" regions to the north and east of a line running roughly from Le Havre to Grenoble. Many small businesses went to the wall when confronted with competition – textiles, leather and clothing industries were especially badly affected. Small-shopkeepers were hard hit, too, and formed the backbone of the politics of resentment preached by Pierre Poujade. Anyone on a fixed income suffered from the inflationary pressures of the 1950s and 1960s. Material life could be grim on the bottom of the pile. Much housing, badly affected in the war years and made a lower priority in the early phases of the Plan, was of poor quality. In the 1960s, for example, half of all dwellings lacked a bath or a shower, and nearly half had no inside toilet. Living conditions for immigrant workers, grouped together in veritable shanty-towns (*bidonvilles*) on the edge of cities, were worst of all. New housing for workers, notably the "HLM" (*habitations à loyer modéré*), was moreover often soulless, overcrowded and miserably maintained. The pleasures of

Two realities of working-class housing in the 1950s and 1960s: on one hand, the shanty towns ("*bidonvilles*"), lacking the most basic amenities. On the other, towering in the distance, the shabby anonymity of tower-block housing.

Two Citroëns

It was the sight of the new Citroën DS ("Déesse") in the 1950s that inspired writer Roland Barthes, semiotician of everyday life, to compare the modern automobile to a medieval cathedral. "Supreme creation of an era, conceived with passion by unknown artists and consumed in image if not in usage by a whole population that appropriates

A souped-up "Déesse" (*left*) and a "Deux-Chevaux" (*above*) in all their glory.

them as a purely magical object," he noted, before going on to describe the faithful caressing the door-handles and fondling the internal cushioning like so many holy relics.

The car was the ultimate status symbol in a society won over to the proclamation of status through consumer goods. Sitting by the kerb, "like a huge breathing oyster, about to snap off the leg of any passing pedestrian" (M. Larkin), the DS was for three decades an esteemed asset to any front drive.

It contrasted with the other main money-making car which Citroën produced in the post-war years, the 2CV

("Deux chevaux"). The 2CV, launched in 1948, had its roots in France's agrarian past. It had been modelled in 1935 as the TPV ("Toute Petite Voiture"), capable of transporting two peasants in clogs along with a 110-pound sack of potatoes, and was made saleable at considerably lower cost than most other models. The 2CV was in some senses the polar opposite of the DS in that it made a total aesthetic sacrifice for the sake of utility. Answering perfectly to the consumer demand for cheap, practical, personal travel, some seven million 2CVs had been sold when the model went out of production in the late 1980s.

the consumer society disproportionately benefited the rich: only 40 per cent of workers took a holiday away from home whereas 90 per cent of the bourgeoisie did so. The latter also dominated the elite positions within the higher education sector. When university expansion came in the 1960s, it was done on the cheap, creating resentments which would soon boil over.

THE EVENTS OF MAY 1968

With the benefit of hindsight, it is not impossible to grasp some of the origins of the Events of May 1968, which seemed to come close to overthrowing the government and indeed the whole political system. But we should not let retrospective analysis obscure the fact that what occurred in 1968 was essentially unpredicted and unpredictable.

Founded in 1945, *Elle* caught the wind of post-war interest in home consumerism and fashion. In the mid 1960s it was selling three-quarters of a million copies – a figure that had halved by the mid 1990s. The film star Brigitte Bardot, here gracing the November 1963 edition, could be counted on to raise circulation.

De Gaulle spoke for much of the political establishment when he declared the Events "incomprehensible". What started as a campus protest in Nanterre, on the outskirts of Paris, burgeoned into a round of barricades on the streets of the capital and a massive, nationwide workers' movement of revolt, which was dismantled only with difficulty. The Events were moreover suffused with new cultural forms, which highlighted the inadequacies of the existing party-political scene. Those in power had failed to respond to and absorb new social energies unleashed by economic modernization.

This was all the more surprising in that politics after 1958 had seemed to take a step towards the conventional and classifiable rather than the experimental. One of the effects of de Gaulle's coming to power in 1958 was that the Right and Left became clearly polarized into two sides, unlike the ragbag of often tiny formations which had characterized the Fourth Republic. In the constitutional referendum and in national and local elections in 1958, the Gaullists – grouped together into the UNR (*Union pour la Nouvelle République*) – gained three-quarters or more of the vote. In electoral terms there was de Gaulle – and then there was the rest. Important centrist formations under the Fourth Republic, like the MRP and the Radicals, were now sucked into the government majority. In addition, the use of referendums also worked to clarify and simplify the key issues.

The *bête-noire* issues of the Third and Fourth Republics were, moreover, becoming outmoded: the constitution was now fixed, clericalism and anti-clericalism were in

A classroom in the Sorbonne, May 1968, sees the sons and daughters of the bourgeoisie call on the proletariat to unite. The Events were an engaging mix of the ludic and the ludicrous.

their death throes as religious attitudes became more relaxed and less intransigent, and the colonial question had become a thing of the past. Economic questions now seemed to be of more substance in determining political choices. It was noticeable that the electoral geography of France – which had its roots, as we have seen, in the country's response to the Civil Constitution of 1791 – began to shift into new patterns from around this time.

There were some on the Left, including Mendès-France, who held that the cards had been stacked up too high for them ever to achieve power. Certainly, if it was to make any headway at all, the Left had to become better organized, and better able to articulate the grievances of working people. The two-tier electoral system established in the 1958 constitution made a run-off between a Left and Right candidate likely, so electoral pacts became part of the currency of political life. The politics of personality also contributed after 1958 to this simplification of the political landscape. Supporters began to treat de Gaulle as a kind of deity, which had the unlooked-for effect of boosting the prestige of his chief opponents. François Mitterrand gained enormous prestige in the presidential elections of 1965 (since 1962 by universal suffrage) simply by taking de Gaulle to a second ballot. In 1967 he gathered the old SFIO and a number of other socialist groupings into the FDGS (*Fédération de la Gauche démocratique et socialiste*), which transmuted in 1969 into the PS, or *Parti socialiste* (Socialist Party).

Mitterrand was the veteran of countless Fourth Republic governments, and from 1971 became undisputed leader of the PS. More than anyone on the Left he benefited from this personalization and repatterning of party politics. With the support of the Communists and other Left formations, the Socialists had done particularly well in the 1967 elections, putting the government coalition under some strain. In particular Valéry Giscard d'Estaing, leader of the *Républicains Indépendants*, who formed part of the government coalition, openly expressed reservations about government policy. The government was also attracting criticism for its inept involvement in dirty politics. It seemed clear, for example, that the French secret services had been in cahoots with the Moroccan secret police in the assassination of their opposition leader Ben Barka in Paris in late 1965. This scandal was whipped up because of the general context of economic malaise in France in 1967.

It was from the universities, rather than the industrial sector, that the first signs of discontent manifested themselves in May 1968. Student baby-boomers entering university in the late 1960s found the system incapable of coping with the tenfold increase in the student population since World War I levels. Poor conditions in the Nanterre campus of the Paris University stimulated student radicalism – in the event, over American conduct in Vietnam. This led to protests whose impact was amplified by police brutality. The trade unions reacted by calling for a one-day general strike, coinciding with a big student and worker march in Paris. Then critically – and quite spontaneously – student protest fanned out into a nationwide revolt, and between nine and ten million workers came out on strike, many occupying their factories.

There was undeniably a copy-cat element in this worker revolt, but it was fuelled by its own grievances – low wages, poor working conditions, unemployment, poor management practices and unimaginative trade-union leadership. There was, too, an awareness that the benefits of the consumer society had been slower to come to workers than to their social betters. The union leadership was as much taken by surprise as anyone. The PCF-backed CGT followed the party lead in condemning the movement and calling for the restoration of order; but the call by young workers, in particular, for greater participation in management was heeded by the other unions. Participation was also the watchword among many professional groups who joined in the protest: doctors, for example, journalists and workers in radio and television. Many schoolchildren took over their schools, too, attacking the hierarchical rote-learning aspect of *lycée* education, and calling for a less authoritarian form of teaching, which developed all aspects of the personality. The Odéon theatre in Paris was opened to the movement by its director, Jean-Louis Barrault. Night after night this venue, as well as the nearby Sorbonne amphitheatre, witnessed a kind of perpetual teach-in and complaints forum for anyone who chose to attend.

There was a variety of elements within the movement of May 1968. Its carnival character was combined with the call, from a minority of left-wing students and workers (Trotskyist, Maoist and anarchist), for political and social revolution. Underpinning it all was the more materialistic demand of workers for more pay and more control over their lives. All these elements were magnified, moreover, by the crass over-reaction and brutality of the police forces. They beat and tear-gassed indiscriminately, harming by-standers as well as protesters.

In hindsight one can see that the major movements of cultural politics in the last twenty-five years were spawned in the May 1968 Events. The 1917 Bolshevik script, preached by the Marxist Left, was arguably less significant in the longer term than other, less traditional forms of *gauchisme* ("Leftism"). The imaginative use of slogans and publicity images, which had close affinities to the advertising world, made conventional party publicity seem old hat. Amid a veritable firework display of political extremism of every kind, a number of important developments in cultural politics fell into place. The feminist movement, the "green" movement and gay politics, for example, all drew new strength and direction from 1968. The Events were a signal that French society was changing faster, and social expectations were being transformed more radically, than the political establishment had been able to accommodate. Extinguished almost as soon as it had begun, May 1968 embodied an important long-term message.

Yet 1968 was not settled in the long term but in the short. The forces of opposition were too deeply split to have much chance of success. Of crucial importance in the stability of the regime was, ironically enough, its sternest critic, the Communist Party, which ascribed the whole movement to left-wing deviation and petty bourgeois adventurism. Communist support was more than helpful to de Gaulle, who had come close to cracking under the strain. His loyal supporter from Algerian days, General Massu, stationed on the Rhine, had bolstered his resolve. For a figure who bore the hallmarks of an early twentieth-century elite education and training, de Gaulle had always dis-

The battle-lines on the streets of Paris, as dawn breaks. Police repression of the rioting provoked a wave of indignation against the regime.

played a surprising knack at communications. His famous speech on BBC radio on 18 June 1940 had made his name. His performances during the 1958 crisis and the Algerian troubles had been of sterling worth. Now, just as his government's fortunes looked at their lowest, he used the media to proclaim a determination not to quit. There would be, he announced, no change of government, no resignation from himself and no change of policies. His prime minister, the tough and resilient Georges Pompidou, dismantled the oppositional movement by offering wage rises of between 7 and 10 per cent to workers and increasing the national minimum wage. De Gaulle also called for fresh elections – a move which turned out to be a master-stroke, allowing a right-wing backlash to get organized in the face of the indeterminate and divided left-wing threat. In late June, elections gave the unified Right, now renamed the UDR (*Union des démocrates pour la République*), a massive majority of 358 out of 485 deputies – the largest right-wing vote in the history of the Fifth Republic hitherto, and

Operations room for the May Events, containing many of the posters which were spread around the walls of the city.

more than enough to take the wind out of the electoral sails of the far Left. Edgar Faure steered through some reform of higher education, establishing a good degree of decentralization for universities and allowing students increased participation in university governance. Campuses were the site of political chaos for some time to come; but there were no more insurrections.

Despite the glowing success of the 1968 elections, much of the old de Gaulle magic had disappeared in the crisis. The government's survival owed as much to Pompidou as to de Gaulle, yet the latter almost at once dismissed his prime minister – a move many interpreted as jealousy. Yet the old warhorse went on his terms rather than at the behest of the voters. In 1969 he put plans for Senate and regional reforms to a referendum, threatening to quit if he was not given proper popular support. The loss of the referendum – by 53.2 per cent to 46.7 – did not necessarily entail his removal, yet he chose to fall on his own sword. On 28 April 1969 he went on to the radio to announce tersely: "I am ceasing to exercise my functions as president of the republic. This decision will take effect from today at midday." He walked away from politics as he had done in 1946, but this time never looked back. He died in 1970.

Could there be Gaullism after de Gaulle? Indeed could there be a Fifth Republic after his departure? Georges Pompidou was the man who answered both questions in the affirmative. Though he lacked de Gaulle's penchant for self-aggrandizement, he

"The walls speak": Paris in 1968

A particular target of the rioters and *gauchistes* during the Events of May 1968 was the close control that the government kept over the media. Government domination of television was legendary – "the government in your dining-room," as the critics of television news put it – while freedom of the press was also felt to be compromised by unseemly ministerial pressures on editors. Official news was criticized not only in the content of the political activities, but also, implicitly, in their form. Tons of paper were used to make news-sheets, handouts, broadsheets and posters of every imaginable sort. More than that, walls in public spaces became a primitive canvas for critical expression, and anonymous graffiti became a political art form. Rather than defining a pragmatic programme of action, the multi-media communications of May 1968 offered a different kind of political language, one which hoped to transcend the banal and the routine, and to place, as the graffiti stated, "imagination in power".

The May Events had been sparked off in crowded and ill-equipped Nanterre campus – here staging a 1968 sit-in – which remained a hot-spot of student activism for many years afterwards.

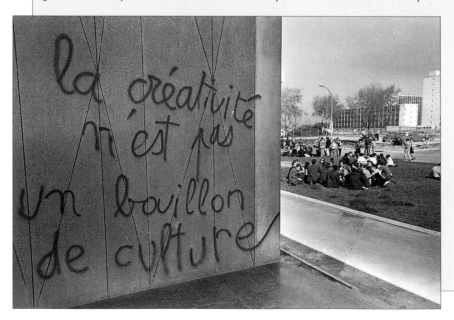

was a tough operator and shrewd enough to draw political sustenance from the Gaullist inheritance. Thus he maintained, for example, the independent foreign policy line which de Gaulle had developed. His commitment to Europe was strong too; he permitted an enlargement of the "Six" who had pioneered the Common Market into the "Nine" of the European Community (with Britain coming in along with Ireland and Denmark in 1972).

At home the weakening of the Left in the aftermath of the May Events and the subsequent right-wing backlash made his job initially easier. So did the continuation of the

De Gaulle's departure in 1958 found the Parisian daily *France-Soir* at the top of its influence, selling 1.4 million copies (only 300,000 twenty years later). This picture was taken by the great photographer Henri Cartier-Bresson.

long-term wave of prosperity which France had managed since the late 1940s. Average income increased by 4.5 per cent per person per year between 1959 and 1973. Pompidou tinkered minimally but sagely with the system which had served France well. The grip of central government was slightly relaxed in certain areas (notably control over the nationalized industries).

Pompidou became aware of, and then reacted to, a sea change that was occurring in the political meaning of regionalism. The spirit of decolonization had spread to mainland France. In 1965 the young socialist Michel Rocard had called on government to "decolonize the provinces", a demand that proved a landmark in regional thinking. Before, it was almost unthinkable for the Left, with its strongly centralizing, Jacobin tradition, to support regional power, which was usually the watchword of the backward-looking and traditionalist Right. By his measured programme for regional development Pompidou took some of the wind from the sails of this pro-regionalist Left. For the first time since their creation in 1790 departments had certain economic tasks taken out of their hands and placed in the control of assemblies at the supra-departmental, regional level. Certain major economic programmes also had the effect of stimulating the regions. Much of the aerospace industry behind the Concorde project was based in Toulouse, for example, while the building of the massive oil refinery at Fos, near Marseille, from 1970 onwards helped the Mediterranean economy. There was also gigantic tourist development – the flagship of which was the pyramidical apartment blocks of La Grande Motte on the formerly malarial Languedoc coastline. Ridding its beautiful beaches of mosquitoes made them fully inhabitable for the first time. Massive motorway building in association with private enterprise also helped to stimulate the regional economy. Major efforts were made in another branch of communications, the telephone system. The number of lines quadrupled in a matter of years rather than decades; where only one home in seven had possessed one in 1968, three-quarters did so in 1982.

Though he lost some of the left-wing voters whom de Gaulle had personally attracted, Pompidou maintained the right-wing umbrella formation which de Gaulle had developed. Under his guidance it became a formidable political machine. His choice of the mildly liberal Chaban-Delmas (who had served under de Gaulle in London during the war) as his first prime minister was a sensible measure which made post-1968 reforms possible. Chaban's growing popularity led Pompidou to replace him in 1972 by the more rigidly uncompromising Pierre Messmer. Continuing nervousness in government ranks at a possible repetition of 1968 meant that he stayed firmly authoritarian on public-order issues. Anyone who visited Paris in the late 1960s and late 1970s will remember the extraordinary police saturation there, which was maintained at all times. Protest demonstrations and marches would as likely be interrupted by police stooges and *agents provocateurs*. Police powers were still wide – and much used.

Paris was also, however, the centrepiece of Pompidou's calculated investment in the politics of cultural grandeur. To some degree this was a continuation of the de Gaulle era. De Gaulle's minister of culture, André Malraux, had in 1962 introduced heritage legislation which led to a major clean-up of all public buildings. The grime of centuries was peeled away from such cultural monuments as Notre-Dame to reveal a novel cleanliness that only the niggardly could bemoan. Malraux also aimed to spread high culture to what were seen as the culturally under-developed regions. In 1966 he opened at Le Havre the first of a dozen or more *maisons de la culture*, or cultural centres. These Malraux identified as the cathedrals of the cultural future. He viewed them as missionary outposts, dispersing the classical cultural heritage of the educated, particularly Parisian, elite. "In ten years," he announced in 1966, "this hideous word 'provincial' will have ceased to exist."

The *maisons de la culture* were not destined for a happy future. Although they did something to bolster the regional devolution which Pompidou was urging, the cultural suppositions behind Malraux's "civilizing mission" in the regions were old-fashioned and elitist. The consumer society had pulled to pieces many of the assumptions behind high culture. Television, records, pop music radio stations and the other media of the consumerist age all highlighted culture as pluralistic rather than unitary, popular

Opened in 1977, the Pompidou Centre proved to be the most popular museum and public building in France. The hordes of visitors placed a strain on the fabric, and in 1994 the building was closed temporarily to allow essential works and redecoration to be undertaken.

rather than elitist and diverse rather than canonical. More emphasis was placed on creativity than the passive reception of an agreed cultural heritage. Here again, the playful explorations of the 1968 Events had had a subtle but serious impact on the very terms of the cultural debate.

Though he maintained state support for the dozen or so *maisons de la culture*, Pompidou was more personally associated with policies of modernism and urban renewal within Paris itself. Purists have never forgiven him for utterly transforming the Parisian skyline – be it the futuristic business centre at La Défense, on the outskirts, or the Montparnasse and Halle des Vins skyscrapers and similar developments. The Beaubourg – soon to be Pompidou – Centre, which opened in 1977, was also devised and authorized under his presidency, as was the modernization of Les Halles after the main market of Paris was transferred to the suburbs. This showcase development of the city was accompanied by major efforts to improve the Parisian transport system and communications network – themes which would be carried further by Pompidou's successors.

COPING WITH RECESSION: THE PRESIDENCY OF GISCARD D'ESTAING

The sudden death of Pompidou from cancer in 1974 opened up the political arena once again. With the aid of up-and-coming Gaullist Jacques Chirac, ex-finance minister Valéry Giscard d'Estaing resisted the claim of Chaban-Delmas to represent the authentic Gaullist heritage, and secured the support of the Right. Giscard (president 1974–81) underlined the durability of the Fifth Republic, for he was not even a member of the Gaullist UDR party, but headed his own formation, the UDF (*Union pour la démocratie française*). Giscard had his work cut out, however, to impose himself on an electorate increasingly attracted by a Left, now resurgent after the dark days of the late 1960s. François Mitterrand had since 1969 welded together socialist groupings into a new, revitalized Socialist Party, and after careful negotiation with the Communists, the PS and PCF had agreed a Common Programme, to which other left-wing groupings added their support.

The Common Programme had led the Right to make much capital out of a "red scare" in the 1973 legislative elections. There was much dark talk of the communists in power, a constitutional crisis, the wholesale redistribution of wealth and so on. The united Left had come close to victory in 1973. In 1974 they just failed once again. The closeness of the result – 50.8 per cent to Giscard, as against Mitterrand's 49.2 – made some claim that their respective television performances in the campaign had been the deciding factor: Mitterrand had looked less snappy and in control than Giscard. Fear of the "Socialist risk" factor also probably counted, and wages were still rising and unemployment was still low. Yet if Giscard successfully surfed into power on the wave of the *trentes glorieuses*, that unparalleled period of economic prosperity was in fact just about to come to an end, creating a new set of political and economic headaches. Subtle changes were taking place in the foundations on which prosperity had been built: the birth-rate started to fall from the mid 1960s; industrial production stagnated from 1973 to 1981; unemployment levels rose from 200,000 in the 1960s to over two million by the early 1980s.

It was not just France which was running into economic trouble: the whole Western world was on the slide. The oil crisis of 1973/4 caused a fourfold increase in prices of oil from the Middle East. This was bad for every advanced economy, but particularly so for France. Unlike neighbouring Great Britain, it had no oil deposits and imported three-quarters of its energy requirements (Britain and Germany in contrast imported only half of theirs). The West would no longer be able to count on cheap energy, raw materials and transport, and a lack of competition from developing countries. Yet it was too easy in 1974 to see the crisis as a blip rather than a structural transformation. Government attempts to treat the crisis as a short-term one only had the effect of producing a devastating mixture of inflation, growing unemployment and economic torpor. Prime Minister Chirac's attempt to move out of economic crisis by going for growth produced a massive government deficit. Inflation, at 3.3 per cent in the late 1960s, jumped to 15.2 per cent in 1974. The appointment of economist Raymond Barre as Chirac's successor in 1976 stabilized the situation. Adopting a policy of austerity and monetary rigour, Barre proved an adept practitioner of crisis-management. Though inflation and unemployment remained high, the economy did moderately well, with dependence on oil being reduced by the development of nuclear energy within France. It was in these years, moreover, that France overtook Great Britain in the league-table of national wealth.

Economic difficulties cast a dark cloud over President Giscard's claim to be promoting the cause of an "advanced liberal society". A remote, cerebral figure with a technocratic background, his accordion-playing seemed a somewhat desperate bid to be seen as human. When his media image was cultivated, the results seemed trivial and condescending: he invited dustmen to the Elysée palace, for example, and adopted the practice of inviting himself to dinner with "ordinary" citizens. He did, however, preside over some quite significant liberal reforms. He lowered the voting age to eighteen. His educational reforms – notably the spread of comprehensive schooling at secondary level – aimed to provide greater social equality of opportunity. Government control over television and the media was also reduced.

Women's rights were a particular concern. France had been one of the last Western nations to enfranchise women, and even after they were accorded the vote in 1945, their position within society remained backward compared with other nations. Simone de Beauvoir's epochal work *The Second Sex*, published in 1949, had had surprisingly little long-term effect; it was only in the wake of 1968 that it was rediscovered, going on to become the bible of contemporary French feminism. On becoming president, Giscard appointed two women cabinet ministers: Simone Veil in charge of health, and journalist Françoise Giroud as secretary of state for the condition of women. Both proved effective in helping to further changes which had already begun to occur in women's status. In 1965 the surviving restrictions that stemmed from the Napoleonic Code were lifted – the right to open a bank account, for example, or to own property

President Giscard d'Estaing examining a pressure-cooker at an ideal home exhibition. Giscard's attempts to show the common touch rarely convinced.

without the husband's consent. In 1972 equal-pay provision was introduced for women (though it would be a long battle to enforce it effectively). The "right to choose" was a key women's issue: in 1971 some 343 women, many of them from public life, signed a manifesto in the *Nouvel Observateur* weekly, calling for the legalization of abortion, themselves admitting to having had an abortion. A law of 1975, directed through parliament by Simone Veil, responded to this demand by making the operation more easily and legally available, and thereby ending the dominion of the back-street abortionist. A law in 1974 built on a measure of 1967 to make contraception more freely available, too. Divorce was also liberalized in 1975.

Giscardian liberalism, underpinned by his quest for a relaxed, loose media image, was given some chance to establish its credibility when squabbling broke out on the Left between Communists and Socialists in the late 1970s. Indeed, for a time, Giscard had far more trouble within government ranks than with the opposition. His dismissal of Chirac in 1976 boomeranged badly. Chirac banged the door shut after him, and transformed the Gaullist UDR into the RPR (*Rassemblement pour la République*). The new party's Gaullist-sounding initials obscured the fact that it was a vehicle for his own ambitions, in which the old Resistance barons had little place. The RPR far outsized Giscard's own UDF. In 1977 Chirac stood for, and won, the post of mayor of Paris, which Giscard had created as a private fief for his friend Michel d'Ornano. Chirac's influence was sufficient to frustrate a number of the liberal reforms which Giscard had in mind, and which might have won him some support from left-wing voters. Giscard was obliged to move towards the Right, as a means of ensuring that his government coalition remained intact. The revival of the Left at the end of the 1970s also made his liberal claims seem thin.

Giscard's once relaxed presidential style had by then developed into something altogether stiffer and more imperial. His habit of being served first at official banquets and his decision to slow down and make less martial "The Marseillaise" were the kind of preoccupation with petty issues which irked many. His diplomacy also became a cause of concern. His call for the "globalization" of French foreign policy seemed a liberal enough gesture. Yet in Africa, in particular, he sponsored neo-colonial moves which looked frankly dynastic: French troops crushed rebels against Mobutu in Zaire in 1978, and supported then helped to overthrow the dictatorial Bokassa in the Central African Republic. His love of hobnobbing with the great also rebounded on him. Bokassa had offered him diamonds as a personal gift, and Giscard's evasiveness over this was an unexpected but significant vote-loser for him in the presidential elections of 1981.

By then he was facing a Left reunited around the candidacy of François Mitterrand – "the eternal loser", as Giscardian supporters sneered. Yet he was obliged to go to the polls when the Western economies were still in very poor shape. Barre had done a fairly effective job at stabilizing the economy in the mid 1970s, but when further oil price rises occurred in 1979, the government opted out of the difficult and probably unpopular policies required. Instead they sat back and waited for the 1981 elections, even as the recession seemed to be getting deeper and deeper. Because of the nature of the coalition which he headed, moreover, Giscard found it difficult to present himself as the liberal he claimed to be. It had been his misfortune to come to the presidency at a time when the world economy was leaving little scope for genuine liberal policies. In the 1981 elections he paid the price, and had to give way as gracefully as he could to "the eternal loser", François Mitterrand.

CHAPTER 11

The Mitterrand Years

François Mitterrand's election as president in 1981 and 1988 for two terms of seven years ensured him an enduring place in French political history. Only de Gaulle, who was in power for thirteen years (1944–6, 1958–69), approaches this span of time at the top of the political tree in the twentieth century. As France moved towards a new *fin de siècle* – which would also be a *fin de millénium* – this personal dominance under the constitution of the Fifth Republic contrasted strikingly with the feverish volatility of governments a century earlier, in the Third Republic's *fin de siècle* as well as under the Fourth Republic, which formed the workshop where Mitterrand's political apprenticeship took place.

Mitterrand maintained his grip on power through a mastery of political compromise learnt early in his career. Though he worked under Vichy as a civil servant, he was an active member of the Resistance, for which he was subsequently decorated. When he was a minister in his twenties under the Fourth Republic, his political party had a key role in propping up governmental coalitions, and he served endlessly on the ministerial merry-go-round. Though his career surely marked him out as a man of leftish principles, it was not always apparent what those principles were – despite his enthusiam in 1981, for example, he was a late convert to socialism. Though his integrity was confirmed in his odyssey through the oppositional wilderness from 1958 onwards, his ability to accommodate and to survive seismic shifts in the political terrain served him well as president after 1981, when he had to preside over governments drawn from right across the political spectrum.

On this point, personal destiny merged with constitutional stability. Despite the "custom-built" character of the Fifth Republic at its outset the regime had proved able to accommodate a president who was neither de Gaulle (Pompidou, from 1969), nor even a Gaullist (Giscard d'Estaing, from 1974). Mitterrand threw down further challenges to the Fifth Republic's constitutional arrangements. Not only did he begin as a president from the Left, he then from 1986 to 1988 (and again after 1993) continued as a left-wing president working with a right-wing government. The new doctrines of "cohabitation" of Left and Right within the same regime, and of *alternance* ("alternation") between the two wings, proved sufficient to meet those challenges.

THE APOTHEOSIS OF THE FIFTH REPUBLIC

From the very start of his presidential term, Mitterrand showed a sensitivity to history and social memory. He affirmed the great Socialist victory celebrations on the Place de la Bastille – traditional site of left-wing demonstrations – and made an early visit to the Panthéon, where national heroes are interred. There he honoured the memorials of Victor Schoelscher, the Second Republic politician responsible for the final abolition of slavery in French domains in 1848; of Jean Jaurès, the great Socialist leader assassinated in 1914; and of Jean Moulin, the Resistance hero. He also held a special reception

Opposite The Socialist electoral victories of 1981 produced a tremendous mood of elation: most of the young had never known a left-wing government. Hopes were soon to be dashed.

The departments of France

The framework and the nomenclature of the departments established in 1790 have proved surprisingly enduring. Named after local natural features – rivers like the Hérault, for example, or mountains such as the Hautes-Pyrénées – they have been increased through some additions (such as Savoie) and some sub-division (notably in the Paris conurbation). Moves towards greater devolution have tended to group departments together into larger regional units. Ironically, these have often drawn on the ancient provincial names (Brittany, Languedoc, Aquitaine, etc.) replaced in 1790 by a Revolutionary National Assembly (see p. 12).

for the ageing Pierre Mendès-France, who had been one of his own mentors under the Fourth Republic, at the Elysée palace. Significantly, "The Marseillaise" was changed back to its properly martial cadence from the regal/funereal dirge that Giscard had endeavoured to make it.

These important gestures aimed to bring into the mainstream of republican memory, and to offer constitutional endorsement to, a tradition of radical and social action which differed from the rather more triumphalist, right-wing political traditions with which the Fifth Republic had until now been associated. The respect for the past was confirmed in Mitterrand's appointment of Pierre Mauroy, a former history teacher, as his prime minister. Indeed a third of Mitterrand's ministerial team, and over a third of PS deputies, were teachers – earning the new administration the nickname of the *république des professeurs*.

The electorate, moreover, seemed eager to learn from "the teachers' republic". Mitterrand dissolved the National Assembly and scheduled new elections to bolster his position. The elections proved a triumph for the Left: the Socialists and Communists between them took 55 per cent of the national vote, winning an absolute majority. The Communists were very much the junior partner, with 9 per cent of the vote – leaving some to mutter that the "Common Programme" had been nothing more than a means of levering their traditional rivals for working-class votes into power. Four ministries were, however, awarded to the Communists – a machiavellian gift that bound the PCF to support the government if troubled times came round.

Mauroy's government honoured its socialist credentials by introducing an ambitious programme of social reforms, whose international impact was all the more pronounced coming as it did at a time when most Western governments were battening down the hatches under the pressure of economic recession. Civil and human rights were extended by abolishing the death penalty (which Giscard had last used in 1977), by reducing the policing powers of the courts and by freeing radio communication. Local radio stations were permitted in 1981, and in 1982 an independent broadcasting authority was established, weakening the tradition of state control in this domain.

A further important break with tradition was decentralization measures in local government. Gaston Defferre, the Socialist veteran and long-time mayor of Marseille, introduced legislation in 1982 aimed at reducing the power of the prefects. The right hand of government in the departments since their creation by Napoleon, prefects were renamed "commissaries of the Republic" and many of their former powers were transferred to the elected presidents of departmental councils. The powers of mayors and municipalities were also increased, and the twenty-two regional councils created in 1972 were given a broader remit, notably as regards economic development and planning. Corsica, the scene for some years of separatist violence, was also accorded a separate status.

The Socialist programme aimed to spread economic as well as political power. The 1981 Auroux laws promoted workers' rights to collective bargaining, shifting the balance of business power in favour of employees. In addition far-reaching and generous

Overleaf The Géode, constructed during the 1980s in the redeveloped La Villette park in Paris, is an entertainment centre containing a huge 360-foot cinema screen that shows nature films.

A distinctive characteristic of the presidents of the Fifth Republic has been a strong commitment to prestige projects. The Concorde, which by the 1990s was an ageing veteran of the sky, remained a questionable heirloom from the days of de Gaulle. In the 1980s the high-speed train, the TGV (*Train à grande vitesse*), after opening on the Paris–Lyon route, was expanded by government to run on other networks, involving massive investment in rail infrastructure.

The politics of cultural grandeur

projects, often planned by the international high-fliers of the architectural world, who showed lofty disdain for any criticism, were accompanied by massive publicity hype.

To the 1977 Pompidou Centre, designed by Englishman Richard Rogers and Italian Renzo Piano, were added

Pei's glass pyramid in the courtyard of the Louvre (the latter also earmarked for major redevelopment), the Opéra Bastille and the massive Arche de la Défense, opened to coincide with the 1789 bicentenary celebrations in 1989 in the La Défense development on the outskirts of Paris. Before the end of his presidential term Mitterrand also planned to open a new national library, the TGB (*Très Grande Bibliothèque*).

Presidents from de Gaulle onwards,

It was Georges Pompidou, however, who set the tone for prestige building projects, particularly ones located in the capital. Giscard continued this work. While freezing some of his predecessor's more over-ambitious plans, he backed the transformation of the dilapidated Orsay railway station into a museum, and approved the development of La Villette park and science museum. The tendency reached it peak under the presidency of François Mitterrand. Such

La Défense, the business and residential centre on the western fringes of Paris, developed in the 1960s and 1970s, is crowned by the Grande Arche. This commemoration of the 1989 bicentenary of the French Revolution is placed in a direct line down the Champs Elysées towards the Étoile.

to be fair, have also been associated with plans for urban renovation and heritage development that place France among the most progressive of European governments. The crumbling Marais district in Paris, for example, has been transformed into a superb showcase of the architecture and design of the seventeenth and eighteenth centuries. Mitterrand also considerably increased the share of the national budget allocated to the arts and culture.

increases were made to the state welfare programme. The minimum wage was
increased by 10 per cent, but this was dwarfed in importance by 25 to 50 per cent
increases in family allowances, housing subsidies and old-age pensions, along with
significant changes in medical benefits. The working week was reduced from forty to
thirty-nine hours, and a fifth week of paid holidays was introduced – a striking homage
to both the programme of the Popular Front and Fifth Republic leisure consumerism.

Who was to pay for this unparalleled largesse? The government introduced a wealth
tax on the largest fortunes and increased the tax liability of employers, but these steps
had only symbolic value, given the extent of additional state welfare commitments.
Mitterrand and Mauroy wagered on Keynesian-style policies triggering an expansion in
the economy which would absorb the new social costs. The government tried to turn
over a new leaf after Barre's austerity, and go for growth. To that end liberalism and
decentralization were accompanied by an extension of state economic power
unmatched since the Liberation. The state increased its control of the economy in
order to channel investment rationally. In the process they hoped to control
exchanges, boost exports and trigger rises in production. Legislation in 1982 saw five
industrial giants nationalized, plus the main private banks. State holdings in other
major businesses were increased to give a majority holding position. By the end of
1982 thirteen out of France's largest twenty companies were effectively in government
control. The proportion of the labour-force directly beholden to the state doubled, rising
to over 20 per cent, when supplemented by the 140,000 new jobs in the public sector
which the government went on to create, many of them in prestige cultural projects.

"I was carried away with our victory; we were intoxicated. Everyone … predicted
the return of growth by 1983. Honestly, I lack the necessary knowledge to say they
were wrong." Mitterrand's frank confession dates from as early as July 1983. By then
the high hopes of 1981 had largely evaporated, and the government was engaged in
damage-limitation exercises in enforced austerity. The Socialists had wagered on state-
led growth curtailing rising imports and stimulating exports. The "republic of teachers" had failed to do their maths homework. As they were later ruefully to accept, the
economic environment was almost wholly inauspicious for this scenario. Extra purchasing power within the French economy tended to be spent on imports rather than
home-produced goods, unsettling the balance of trade and weakening the currency.
There were enforced devaluations of the franc in 1981, 1982 and 1983. The rocketing
price of oil imports only made matters worse, and helped to send inflation spiralling
upwards. Despite the devaluations, moreover, the franc was probably still overvalued
on world markets, which made French exports uncompetitive. Ominously unemployment continued to edge upwards, passing the two million mark.

In these stormy economic waters Mitterrand, the political arch-survivor and past-
master in the skills of compromise, chose not to go down strapped to the mast of
unbending socialism. In classic austerity packages – notably in June 1982 and March
1983 – he and Mauroy took the deflationary path: wage and price freezes, cuts in
public expenditure, increases in health service charges, imposed ceilings on pay rises,

exchange controls and so on. The Right, of course, rubbed its hands in gleeful *schaden-freude*. It was given the chance to flex its muscles by the Savary law of 1984, which envisaged closer state control over private – which meant in effect Roman Catholic – schools. The opposition to this law owed little to the confessional struggles of the past. Indeed many Church leaders, long thankful for the dowsing down of the fires of anti-clericalism, were faintly embarrassed by the political capital which the Right made of the issue. It was privacy rather than Catholicism which parents valued most in Catholic private schooling. Four-fifths of them were not even practising Catholics, but such schools were favoured for their middle-class cachet, generous teacher–student ratios and reputation for academic success. A demonstration in Paris that rallied over a million persons – making it, by some counts, the largest public protest in French history – forced the government to back down and withdraw the legislation.

The growing unpopularity of the government was signalled even more clearly in the elections to the European parliament, which also took place in 1984. The Socialists slumped to a mere 21 per cent of the vote. Ominously many disgruntled voters chose to divert their votes not to the alternative left-wing party, the PCF, which did poorly, nor even to the conventional Right. A newly-emergent far Right, Jean-Marie Le Pen's frankly anti-immigrant but also clearly anti-Semitic National Front (*Front national*), became the crucible for grumbling discontent. It attracted 11 per cent of the vote – roughly the same as the Communists. In 1981 Le Pen had been unable to command the necessary support to put himself up in the presidential elections, and his party attracted less than 1 per cent of the votes in the 1981 legislative elections. A former Poujadist, Le Pen developed his organization cannily, building up strong support in regions with a large immigrant population, notably in the Mediterranean south and in some larger industrial cities. His racist opinions brought a new tone of resentment and viciousness into the political arena.

The Socialist magic lamp, it seemed, had succeeded in uniting the conventional Right and bringing forth the Le Pen genie. By 1984 it was clear that a change of direction was essential if the PS was to perform even passingly well in the 1986 legislative elections. Mitterrand consequently dropped Mauroy, bringing in as prime minister the young *énarque* (that is, graduate of the technocratic *Ecole Nationale d'Administration*), Laurent Fabius. Fabius aimed to shore up the economy by moving further and more systematically away from the social and economic programme of 1981. The Communists withdrew from the government – and many left-wing Socialists became disenchanted, too, as Fabius attempted to rehabilitate the government by stealing the clothes of the opposition. Priority was given to reducing inflation and increasing productivity. There were further public spending cuts, pay restraint and tax incentives to private industry. By the 1986 elections Fabius had performed moderately well according to his own lights. Economic growth was slow but steady, inflation was down to 5 per cent (it had topped 15 per cent in 1982) and exports were rising. Unemployment, at over 10 per cent, was still high, but early retirement and job-creation schemes had kept it within bounds.

Poster culture brings National Front leader Jean-Marie Le Pen and singer Michael Jackson, then touring France, into an uneasy juxtaposition. Le Pen's sloganizing called for "Frenchmen first", which meant defining second-generation immigrants as "ethnic", and therefore non-French.

Not only had Fabius helped to bring the economy round, he had also helped to make the idea of the social market economy acceptable within his own party and within public opinion generally. It remained to be seen, however, whether this was the basis for a successful electoral campaign. With fascistic extremism suddenly à la mode, and with the conventional Right making a strong showing in the opinion polls, the Socialists did not have left much of the optimism of 1981 to show for their five years in power. The success they enjoyed came from operating the economy in the spirit of Barre, Giscard and Chirac. This was hardly a strong endorsement in the eyes of an electorate which had been led to expect better in the heady days of 1981.

ADJUSTING TO POLITICAL ALTERNATION

Long before the 1986 elections the runes had been read. Could a Socialist president remain at the helm with a right-wing majority in the National Assembly? There were some who claimed that this was unthinkable – former premier Raymond Barre was among them. However, those rather better placed than he to benefit from a right-wing victory in 1986 – notably the RPR leader Jacques Chirac and former president Giscard d'Estaing – accepted the possibility of "cohabitation".

Cohabitation matured into a fundamental doctrine of republican constitutionalism under Mitterrand's term of office. After presiding over Socialist reform from 1981 to 1986, from 1986 to 1988 he was willing to take a back seat and allow premier Jacques Chirac, who led the right-wing majority in the Assembly, to call the shots. Mitterrand used his constitutional prerogative, however, following his victory in the presidential elections of 1988, to dissolve the Assembly and call for fresh legislative elections. These proved favourable to the PS and led to his appointment of Socialist premiers down to 1993. Victory for the Right in the 1993 legislative elections saw Mitterrand maintaining his hold on power, even as the government passed back into the hands of the Right.

In the stately progress of political alternation there were numerous confident predictions of Mitterrand's demise – prophecies that were given new impetus when he was diagnosed in 1992 as having a minor cancer problem. These proved ill-founded. Three factors helped his durability. First, the 1958 constitution placed so much power in the hands of the president that it proved difficult for parliamentary manoeuvrings to end a president's tenure, which had been grounded since 1962 in election by universal suffrage. Second, wherever possible Mitterrand treated foreign policy as his personal domain, using his growing stature as an international statesman to enhance his political reputation at home. At first, in 1981, he displayed a concern for human rights abroad that chimed with his principled domestic plans. The shift to "realism" in domestic economic policy was, however, matched by a move towards *Realpolitik* in international relations. His agreeing to the use of French troops in internal dissension in Chad in 1983 recalled the neo-colonial rashness of Giscard, while by 1985, he was even welcoming General Jaruzelski, the scourge of the Polish Solidarity movement, to the Elysée palace. The *Rainbow Warrior* affair of 1985 – in which French secret service agents destroyed a ship in a New Zealand harbour belonging to the Greenpeace movement, prior to its being used to protest against French nuclear testing in the South Pacific – also suggested a degree of presidential cynicism in the protection of state interests.

Such incidents failed to detract from the international stature which Mitterrand enjoyed. His apparent reversion to foreign policy positions viewed as authentically Gaullist won him support within France from traditional supporters of the Right. Though his commitment to a European future for France was well in advance of de Gaulle's conception of national sovereignty within a loosely affiliated Europe, in many other respects he proved as Gaullist as de Gaulle (and often more Gaullist than the Gaullists in the National Assembly). His role – and the participation of French troops – in the Gulf War of 1990/1 won plaudits. The timing of the crisis helped to ensure that, when in 1991 the French media drew up the balance sheet of his ten years in power, the prognoses were pretty favourable.

A further reason for Mitterrand's popularity, and the third factor explaining his political longevity, was his ability to distance himself from the hurly-burly of party infighting and to pose as being somehow above politics. While basking in any credit and popularity coming his way, Mitterrand proved particularly adept at using successive prime ministers as lightning rods for any unpopularity attracted by his governments.

This was particularly evident in the years of Chirac's premiership, between 1986 and 1988.

In a move, some said, of diabolic cunning Mitterrand had in 1985 introduced a degree of proportional representation into the election process for the legislature. The new system aimed to cushion the fall of the Left – a contingency which proved necessary. A low turn-out in 1986 highlighted the lack of fervour among the electorate. Though the Socialists performed moderately well in the event, the PCF experienced its worst election since 1932, and the Right far outdistanced the Left. On the Right Raymond Barre had represented the policies associated with his name since the late

Cartoon by Plantu from *Le Monde*, November 1982. Mitterrand and Margaret Thatcher, Britain's prime minister, shared a hearty dislike of each other, though the protocol of European partnership obliged a certain, sometimes vacuous, cordiality.

1970s; Chirac's Gaullist RPR had a strongly Bonapartist feel to it; and a revived Giscard made a play for the centre ground. Personal animosities, as well as policy differences, between the three men hampered the Right's effectiveness. The way in which proportional representation favoured the advance of the National Front also scaled down the victory of the mainstream Right. Le Pen's party registered the biggest gains for the far Right since Poujadist successes in 1956.

Though the swing to the Right was confirmed by local elections, the new prime minister found himself squeezed on the Right as well as the Left. Though he continued to have a guiding role (notably in foreign policy), Mitterrand gave Chirac a good deal of rope, hoping no doubt that he would hang himself by the time of the presidential elections in 1988. The time factor did indeed cramp the style of Chirac, who fancied his chances in 1988. With precious little time to prove himself by then, Chirac acted with the haste to which he was temperamentally disposed. While tending to remain at one with Mitterrand over foreign policy, he endeavoured to reverse the Socialist programme of 1981, cutting taxes on wealth, making further spending cuts and engaging in whole-sale denationalization and privatization schemes. The headway he made was, however, limited by the stock-exchange crash of 1987. He sporadically flirted with the far Right, whose votes he needed to count on in 1988. Le Pen's ripening racism, epitomized by his comment in 1987 that the Nazis' gas chambers had been only a "point of detail", put his party beyond the pale of the conventional Right. This was especially true in the context of the then current trial of Klaus Barbie, the "Butcher of Lyon" and torturer of Resistance hero Jean Moulin. Chirac endeavoured to speak to the concerns which lay behind the National Front's popularity by taking a tough line on law-and-order issues and on immigration. He inspired a crackdown on terrorism, while a 1986 law curbed immigration by insisting upon more stringent residence conditions.

By the time of the 1988 presidential elections Chirac was coming across as more than a little impulsive and rash. This allowed Mitterrand, who till very late had been coy about his candidacy, to portray himself as a reassuring embodiment of la France unie – "France united". Chirac's concern for law-and-order issues was represented as divisive and undemocratic, while Mitterrand championed a vague social welfarism, much diluted since 1981. In the event Le Pen polled 14 per cent of the votes on the first round and a third of these voters did not transfer their support to Chirac in the second round. Because of this squeeze on the Right Chirac was utterly outmanoeuvred, recording 46 per cent of the vote to Mitterrand's 54 in the second round.

The end to cohabitation was nigh. As in 1981 Mitterrand called legislative elections to give him a Socialist majority, with which he could work effectively in the National Assembly. The PS won the most seats. Their position was strengthened by a decent PCF showing, though the Communists chose not to enter the government this time. Chirac's RPR did best of the right-wing parties. Despite polling nearly 10 per cent of the vote across the country, the National Front was able to secure only one deputy.

The Left was back in power. But it was now a more cautious and pragmatic Left, which made fewer promises. If it roused less enthusiasm among many of its own sup-porters, conversely it alarmed fewer of its opponents. Mitterrand appointed Michel Rocard as his prime minister. An imaginative Socialist with a past in a left-wing faction of the PS, Rocard was now a staid individual who prized competence in running the economy over the transformation of society. If he had any wider ambitions, notably in the fields of decentralization and self-management, he anticipated achieving them by stealth rather than in head-on political tussles. Perhaps with an eye to inheriting Mitterrand's mantle in the 1995 elections – Rocard's presidential ambitions were leg-endary – he acted as a faithful agent for Mitterrand's policies. He kept to austerity poli-cies, even when this meant facing down major strikes in the public sector, and managed to keep the rate of inflation down. However, a slowing-down in the economy after the Gulf War led Mitterrand to replace him as prime minister in May 1991. His choice fell on Edith Cresson, who thus became France's first female prime minister.

Mitterrand campaign poster in 1988. Master of the subtle political manoeuvre, Mitterrand played the Jacobin card as his right-wing opponents were being tempted towards partisan spoiling against immigrant groups.

It was not to prove a distinguished choice. A competent administrator, with a decade of ministerial experience behind her, Cresson was one of the only very small percentage of female deputies. Though female voters in the Fifth Republic actually outnumber men, the proportion of women in the National Assembly has usually hovered at around 5 per cent. The Ministry for Women's Rights, instituted by Mitterrand in 1981 (and abolished by Chirac between 1986 to 1988), did not include in its remit the better representation of women among the political class. That cause, moreover, was not much advanced by Edith Cresson. She made gaffes almost from her first day in office. Her widely reported comments comparing the Japanese to ants and suggesting high levels of homosexuality among English males contributed much to the gaiety of nations but little to the cause of international harmony. Mitterrand's personal backing was turned against her by his political opponents, and her reputation never recovered.

The Antigone project in Montpellier

Rising in the 1980s between the run-down banks of the river Lez and the outskirts of the old city of Montpellier was a massive and ambitious project in contemporary urban construction masterminded by the flamboyant Catalan architect Ricardo Bofill. Brought in by Socialist mayor Georges Frêche in 1979, Bofill's Antigone project aimed to extend the city's heart in a way which did justice to one of the fastest-growing and most buoyant cities in France.

As recently as the 1950s Montpellier was a quiet provincial backwater town, whose wealth derived from a decaying woollen industry and the extensive vineyards of the department. But the economic boost to the regions, engineered by central government since the 1970s, has benefited Montpellier. So too has the more general shift in the French economy from agriculture and industry to the tertiary sector. Administrative capital of the Languedoc-Roussillon region, home to sunrise industries, Montpellier has also taken advantage of the adjacent tourist development of the Languedoc coastline. The 250,000 strong population in the early 1990s was three times the level of that of World War II and twice that of the early 1960s.

Though public office space and shopping complexes were provided, the Antigone project was essentially a residential scheme, targeted mainly for housing schemes. The design, which combines the geometry of the classical with the curvaceous sweep of the baroque, is a stunning example of urban postmodernism.

Building in Bofill's Antigone project, Montpellier.

The decision to replace her in April 1992 with finance minister Pierre Bérégovoy was a merciful release.

Bérégovoy's inability to hold the line against growing criticism of government policies, as unemployment climbed towards the three million mark, led to a major triumph for the Right in the legislative elections of 1993. Indeed this was the greatest victory in the history of the French Right with the opposition capturing four-fifths of the national vote and with the Socialists down to a low of 17.5 per cent. This led on to a further bout of cohabitation, as Jacques Chirac's nominee and ally Edouard Balladur, a former aide to Georges Pompidou, was called on to head the government. The vertiginous collapse in the PS vote underlined the distance the party had travelled away from its popular base. While Michel Rocard endeavoured to pull the party into shape after this terrible drubbing, Mitterrand's personal prestige suffered a tremendous blow and sank to an all-time low.

Just as right-wing voters in 1993 chose between the conventional and the far Right, so also the left-wing vote was increasingly fragmenting. The decline in Socialist support was accompanied by the rise of the Green movement – the two ecological parties began to make an electoral impact. This more fragmented political spectrum resulted, in part at least, from the 1985 legislation that had introduced proportional representation. Yet it also bore the marks of a changing social and cultural landscape.

THE SOCIAL AND POLITICAL LANDSCAPE

France under Mitterrand underwent no great transformation of the sort which had radically restructured its economy and its society in the 1950s and 1960s. The world economic recession continued, with all the social fall-out which that implied. Unemployment proved stubbornly difficult to reduce; passing the 2 million mark in 1981, by 1985 it had reached 2.5 million, and it failed to come down. At 4.1 per cent in 1975, it hovered around 10 per cent in the late 1980s and early 1990s. Inflation was reduced, but increases in average real wages were virtually nil through the 1980s.

Against this depressing backdrop the processes set in motion during the *trente glorieuses* continued to operate. It was from the very late 1970s that information technology began to make an impact on the business world, and this was relayed into domestic life. The *minitel*, for example – a videotext terminal plugged into telecommunications networks – was offered to telephone subscribers in lieu of a directory. Offering public information and a private means of exchange, the new gadget became commonplace. There were 10,000 terminals in use in 1982; by 1991 they numbered six million, and collectively registered nearly a billion calls. Televisions, between fifteen and sixteen million in 1980, had probably doubled in number a decade later; over 90 per cent of homes had one. The proportion of households with a car rose from 61 to 70 per cent between 1971 and 1981 and carried on rising. The market for top-of-the-range cars was particularly buoyant at the height of the recession, while gastronomic restaurants seemed always full. The economic downturn certainly did not signal the death of consumerism in French society.

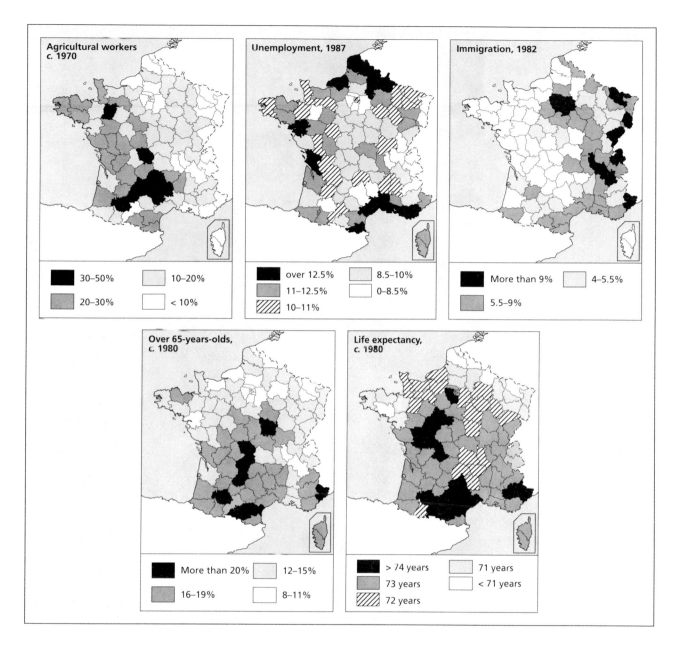

Agricultural workers *c.* 1970

■	30–50%	░	10–20%
▨	20–30%	□	< 10%

Unemployment, 1987

■	over 12.5%	░	8.5–10%
▨	11–12.5%	□	0–8.5%
▧	10–11%		

Immigration, 1982

■	More than 9%	░	4–5.5%
▨	5.5–9%		

Over 65-years-olds, *c.* 1980

■	More than 20%	░	12–15%
▨	16–19%	□	8–11%

Life expectancy, *c.* 1980

■	> 74 years	░	71 years
▨	73 years	□	< 71 years
▧	72 years		

The consumer culture was fundamentally urban. The proportion of workers in agriculture continued to fall – roughly 6 per cent of the total workforce in the early 1990s (and falling), compared with about a third at the time of the Liberation. Peasants counted for less in contemporary France in everything except emotion and nostalgia. However, their devotion to such forms of direct action as filling town squares with superfluous artichokes or cabbages, and pillaging and burning British lamb carcasses, highlighted their continued importance as a pressure group. If there was a slight increase in the share of the population living in the countryside, this stemmed from the increased popularity of commuting – a choice of lifestyle made easier by improvements

France towards 2000. The vestiges of the "two Frances" – a more industrial north and east versus a more agrarian south and west – remain in the Fifth Republic. Other more subtle geographies are also emerging, however, in regard to major social developments: unemployment, immigration, and the ageing of the population.

The popularity of the Minitel spawned a host of services and networks making use of the system. Minitel dating has proved particularly popular and has deprived the newspapers of a traditional source of revenue.

in road and rail communications. These "neo-villagers", along with tourists, at least brought added wealth back into many rural areas. The distance which such workers were able to put between their homes and their place of employment illuminated the continuing increase in the proportion of the workforce who were salaried – managers rather than small businessmen or property-holders. Where two-thirds of the labour force had been employed in agriculture or industry in 1945, two-thirds by the early 1990s were employed in the service sector of the economy.

Population patterns changed somewhat after the 1960s. The high birth-rates detectable from the 1940s slowed down, a development which seems to have been linked to more permissive sexual attitudes arising from easier divorce and new, more accessible contraception (notably the "pill"). From the late 1970s onwards the birth-rate was below its pre-war levels. The number of children adults regarded as ideal slipped from 2–3 to 1–2. Partly this was a consequence of increased social and geographical mobility, which had removed small children from the supportive network of grandparents and other kin. This tendency was partly offset by the excellent provision for infant education (half of two- to five-year-olds attended *écoles maternelles* in the 1960s, while by the 1980s, the figure was 80 per cent and rising). On the other hand, the high participation of women in the labour force also acted to reduce aspirations for large families.

Family patterns seemed to be in flux. A dip in the marriage rate from the 1960s reflected a sharp rise in couples living together outside marriage. As a result illegitimacy rates rose, from one-twentieth in the post-war years to between a quarter and a third in the early 1990s. Divorces too became more frequent, more than doubling between

A Paris street filled with Muslims at prayer. Islam became France's second religion during the Fifth Republic, with three million adherents. Arab workers were usually, however, far worse paid and less well-treated than their native French comrades.

the 1960s and the 1980s – nearly a third of marriages ended this way. The rise in the number of abortions pointed in a similar direction – from roughly 130,000 in the mid 1970s, when terminations became legal, to over 160,000 in the late 1980s.

However, the most significant demographic fact in the 1990s was also the one with the most ominous economic consequences for state and society – namely, the ageing of the population. The baby-boomers of the 1940s and 1950s started losing their teeth. In 1946 one French person in six was over 60 years old; by 1991 the figure was one in five. The situation will be even more pronounced in following decades. Increased life expectancy, and the spread of early retirement packages aimed at soaking up unemployment, means that there will be more individuals approaching retirement age around the millennium than ever before in French history. It will be between 2006 and 2010 that the peak birth-rate group of 1946–50 reaches its sixtieth birthday.

The ageing population means that there will be increasingly large numbers of economically inactive people in the future. One likely consequence of this is the continuing, and possibly growing, role of women in the workforce. The period after the 1960s saw the resurgence of female employment. Nearly 40 per cent at the turn of this century, it fell markedly in the post-1945 period, climbing again during the recession to reach 43 per cent in the early 1990s. Women were popular with employers, because they accepted lower wages than men, thereby keeping down production costs. Although a larger proportion of girls than boys left school with their *baccalauréat*, women were consistently to be found in the least well-rewarded sectors of the economy. Their marked under-representation among the political class was mirrored in the most prestigious professions and the higher echelons of business and bureaucracy.

Opinion polls and under-registration of the female unemployed suggest that high unemployment since the 1970s had a disproportionately heavy impact on women wanting to work. Indeed unemployment seemed to punish the most defenceless: as well as women, immigrants, the unskilled and young workers (especially in areas stripped of heavy industry by the recession) were particularly badly affected. Casualization of the workforce in many industries also produced more underemployment than can easily be quantified. Want and need, in the context of an increasingly materialistic consumer society, produced a backlash of delinquence. The crime-rate rose by 250 per cent between the mid 1970s and mid 1980s. Even allowing for increased police registration, these were woefully impressive figures. Unattached single males were the biggest offenders. Half of prison entrants were less than twenty-five years old, while three-quarters were unmarried. These developments triggered a sense of insecurity among the public at large, to which politicians of all parties became increasingly alert.

This state of public insecurity was an essential component in the rise of far-Right politics, and when wilfully mixed with the issue of immigration, it composed a vicious cocktail of hate. Paradoxically immigration became a political issue when it was in a phase of slowing down (from the mid 1970s) rather than increasing. France's economy had long depended on attracting unskilled or semi-skilled cheap labour; three-quarters of population expansion in the 1920s, for example, was through immigration. Indeed it has been calculated that around one-third of the French population in the early 1990s was a first-, second- or third-generation immigrant. Yet immigrants were no more numerous proportionately in the 1990s than they had been in the 1930s. Unchecked until the 1970s numbers stabilized at around four million – roughly 8 per cent of the total population.

Immigration was therefore as French as croissants. What made it a contentious political issue was the greater cultural visibility of the immigrant population in the middle of an economic recession. Past waves of immigrants had integrated themselves relatively painlessly through their jobs. Mass unemployment from the 1970s onwards knocked away the ladder by which they could climb within French society. In addition the immigrants tended to be concentrated to the north and east of a line between Marseille and Le Havre, and were particularly strongly represented in big cities. The fact that much of the most recent immigrant wave was also not white – Arabs from North Africa, Asians and Turks – made them easy targets, too. The religious issue may have counted for some: almost unobserved, Islam became the second religion of France. Town councils began to receive applications for mosque-building. The Muslim community endeavoured to knit together a full community on their own terms, sometimes overtly rejecting integration and the secular culture which French society offered. The 1980s also saw the emergence of a "Beur" culture followed by second-generation Arab adolescents, and largely on the margins of mainstream youth culture.

The rise of extremist intolerance towards immigrant groups should perhaps be seen as part of a wider picture of political fragmentation that was becoming clear by the 1980s. The transformation of society since 1945 had produced a sea change in political allegiances. The evaporation of the peasantry lost the Socialists and Communists some of the traditional heartlands of their support. In the same way the disintegration of the big proletarian cities, notably of the north and east, meant the break-up of former Communist strongholds. The proportion of the labour-force who were members of trade unions fell from 20 to 15 per cent by the late 1980s. The startling decline in the PCF – from the largest party in 1945 down to level pegging with the far Right in the late 1980s and 1990s – had less to do with politics than sociology. Though the PCF leadership proved singularly inept at adapting its policies to the times, the fact was that social change was destroying the old working class.

The political landscape was, then, increasingly fluid as the end of the century approached. The strengthening of the presidential system under Mitterrand was accompanied by the emergence of new political groupings and new political styles. These could be quite diverse in character. The National Front traced its lineage back to the 1930s. Immigrant support groups, in contrast, had to improvise: there were no strong indigenous traditions to follow. A good many of the groups on the Left conveyed something of the values arising out of the 1960s – and of 1968 in particular. The feminist movement is a case in point. Feminists were galvanized into forming a political pressure-group by the events of 1968. The experience of the May Events was negative, in the sense that many women discovered just how sexist most male-dominated left-wing groups really were, but positive in that it encouraged solidarity and mutual support, and provided models of cultural politics – lobbying, demonstration, artful publicity and outright provocation – which could be used to forge a specific political identity. The feminist movement was characterized by rifts and an obsession with theoretical issues in the 1970s and 1980s – another legacy of 1968! It was also relatively unsuccessful in linking up with the experiences and aspirations of working-class and immigrant women. The gay movement also drew strength and inspiration from the 1968 experience, though the foundation of the *Front Homosexuel d'Action Revolutionnaire* drew as much inspiration from the US Gay Liberation Front. Though the gay movement's impact on mainstream politics was not great, the heady early liberal phase of Mitterrand's presidency saw the revoking of anti-homosexual legislation that had been on the statute books since Vichy. The anti-racist movement – notably Harlem Désir's *SOS-Racisme* – had more effect, drawing its repertoire from the American civil rights movement of the 1960s as well as from French experience.

SOS-Racisme

"*SOS-Racisme*'s France is the France of 1789, the France of free contract, the France of rights respected." The comment of Harlem Désir, chair of the anti-racist organization *SOS-Racisme*, highlights one of the principal aims of immigrant groups: to get an equal chance in the home of the Rights of Man.

SOS-Racisme was founded in 1984 by Désir, himself of mixed racial descent, after young immigrant groups were spurred into action in the so-called "March of the Beurs" in 1983. This event was triggered off by the killing of a young immigrant in a Parisian suburb and took the form of an American-style civil rights march across the country. The aim was to publicize the conditions of discrimination under which young Arabs lived. The word *beur* derives, through a curious form of back-slang known as *verlan* (*à l'envers* = backwards), from *arabe*, and was assumed as a mark of identity by young, often second-generation adolescents, from

immigrant backgrounds. The movement, fuelled by clashes between immigrants and police forces in a number of major cities, endeavoured to give voice to a current of opinion on the margin of the political nation. This was in a climate, remember, when Arabs felt themselves under attack from the racist taunts of the National Front's leader, Jean-Marie Le Pen.

Marshalled with consummate skill by Désir, the movement took as its symbol a hand raised in warning, accompanied by the slogan: "Touche pas à mon pote" ("Hands off my pal"). It acted as an organization of solidarity, but also as a publicity machine, lobbying for legislation, fighting for legal assistance in discrimination cases and providing press releases to publicize the key issues and improve public relations. In the early 1990s the organization had 300 support committees spread throughout France and 25,000 members.

Occitanian graffiti: "We want to live in our country." The regionalist call from the Midi is given an extra twist by the mass tourism which the area experiences each summer, and by the increasingly frequent practice of "foreigners" – that is, French as well as non-French – buying up second houses in the choicest areas, thereby sending up property prices.

Another form of cultural politics to emerge strongly in the 1970s and 1980s was the regionalist movement, which was increasingly shaking off its reactionary and Pétainist aura. But the change from an agrarian way of life in many French regions had dealt a heavy blow to their indigenous cultures – in particular their languages. Many regional dialects and patois, for example, were dying out with the disappearance of older inhabitants: the Franche-Comté patois, the romance language of Lorraine and Occitanian in the Tarn and Cantal were all cases in point by the late 1980s. The historical drive towards one unified French language initiated their decline, but the process was hastened by the development of the spoken and visual media.

When government accepted the need for a regionalist economic programme, particularly from the 1980s, new life was breathed into these linguistic traditions. The state threw its support behind the learning of Alsatian, Flemish and Breton in schools in those areas, while Basque and Catalan also revived in association with the linked groups in the Iberian peninsula. Even prior to that, regionalism had been becoming a left- rather than a right-wing concern. A good illustration was the response to government plans in the late 1970s to extend a military camp on the Larzac plateau in the

Cévennes. When local peasants protested against the loss of their livelihoods the Left orchestrated massive, nationwide support. Big solidarity marches and demonstrations were held in Paris and throughout France. One of Mitterrand's first acts on becoming president was quietly to shelve the military camp project.

Within this movement inspired by Larzac was a strong current of ecologically minded post-1968 *gauchisme*. Indeed the Massif Central had become a favoured spot for ex-militants to "drop out" and pursue alternative lifestyles. This was one element within the development of a strong Green movement, which tapped into the guilty conscience of a consumerist, increasingly urban society. The first political impact of the Greens came in 1974 when the distinguished economist René Dumont stood for president of the republic on this ticket. The movement gathered strength in the late 1970s and early 1980s, and its support was buttressed by voters' loss of enthusiasm for government-style Socialism after 1984. Elections to the European parliament allowed the ecological movement to make links with and gather strength from the strong Green movements in other countries, notably Germany. Slow but steady progress at the polls was rewarded in 1988 when Mitterrand, less sure of the Communists as his political allies, and looking for other supporters on the Left, appointed Green leader Brice Lalonde (who had stood in the 1981 presidential elections) as minister for the environment. The Greens made strong progress in the legislative elections of 1993, drawing many normally Socialist voters into their camp.

PROBLEMS OF CULTURAL IDENTITY

Politics and culture have since 1789 at least been inextricably intertwined in France. Social and cultural solidarities, bound up with geographical region, family outlook and choice of profession, have long tended to dictate specific forms of political identity. The Vendée, for example, was indelibly marked by its treatment at the hands of the infant First Republic in 1793/4, and thereafter was pro-Church, anti-republican and Right-voting. The liberal professions, in contrast, were one of the social groups to lead and to do best out of the Revolutionary experience; they have tended to be anti-clerical and to vote for Radicals and Socialists. For much of the nineteenth and twentieth centuries the "party of reaction" faced the "party of movement", and a definable line between the two sides could be drawn on most major issues – whether these were lay schooling, colonial issues or constitutional arrangements.

This long-established fusing of political and social identity appeared to be breaking down in the last quarter of the twentieth century, under the pressure of social, economic and cultural change. Two countervailing developments seemed at work. First, there was the way in which all conventional party formations accepted and worked within the constitutional framework. Such stability was both a rare bird and a new arrival in recent French history. Second, and by contrast, a more diverse and colourful political scene was emerging outside or marginal to the parliamentary arena. Many of these unconventional groups offered new models of political engagement and new styles of cultural politics. "Left" and "Right" seemed suddenly to count for less than "green", "gay", *gauchiste* or whatever. So just as Left and Right had for the first time since 1789 managed to agree to work within the same constitutional framework, new cultural and political forms appeared, questioning the very terms in which debate was framed.

It is too soon to understand the reasons for these shifts of political and cultural identity in the Mitterrand years – or to gauge their likely impact. We can, however, explore generally how these forms developed. It seems clear, for example, that the new fluidity in political and cultural expression owed much to changes in access to information technology and telecommunications. Public access to information has always been a key issue for the French state. This has sometimes been restricted through censorship or, more typically with republican regimes, shaped through emphasis on lay schooling and freedom of speech. The early history of the Fifth Republic was marked by bitter debate about state control over information, notably radio and television. De Gaulle's famous scorn for the journalistic profession ("scribblers, wanglers and crawlers") was echoed in Pompidou's more guarded comment: "French television is thought of as the voice of France, at home and abroad." Many of the sharpest barbs in May 1968 were directed against government control of the media. News, it was held, was little more than the general addressing the nation.

State monitoring of the media, however, was greatly relaxed from the 1970s on, as the regime became more settled and as new information technologies came on stream. Giscard d'Estaing made moves in this direction, but it was Mitterrand's presidency which saw the biggest changes. From the early 1980s audio-visual freedom was proclaimed; private radio stations were permitted; an independent broadcasting authority was established to keep government at arm's length; private TV channels were authorized (the first, *Canal Plus*, opened in 1984); and cable and satellite broadcasting started to make advances.

The increased freedom of television was particularly significant in that the medium had become the means by which French people derived information, and it constituted a widespread form of popular leisure – to the nation's detriment, some felt. Opinion polls in the late 1980s found that while, on average, French people spent twenty minutes a day reading newspapers, they spent two hours listening to the radio and three hours watching television. The decline in newspaper reading was a particularly dramatic component in this story. A century earlier, at the time of the Dreyfus affair, France was the world's leading consumer of newsprint; as the end of the millennium approached, it found itself in eighth position within Europe and twenty-seventh in the world, on a par with Korea and Singapore. Competition from the electronic media was largely responsible for this decline. It is noticeable, too, how the *minitel* took over the role formerly played by the newspaper small-advertisement in addressing individuals' wants and needs.

The changes detectable in the news media reflected the growth of consumerism within French society. News had become a commodity to be consumed like cars, video-players or blue jeans. This commodification of culture began to have a noticeable impact on the way French history itself was viewed. As we have suggested, the French

"My French is rich," a headline from *Libération*, 24 February 1994. This incomprehensible phrase alludes to a stock construction of school English: "My tailor is rich." The headline announces a revival of the government attack on foreign terms (especially from Britain and the United States) being used where a French term was available. The laws against *franglais* were created in 1977, but have rarely been used.

past has long been a critical component of civic identity: the story of "the nation" constituted one of the ways in which individuals asserted their own political and cultural
identities. How history was written and how it was read thus proved a particularly
interesting yardstick by which late twentieth-century social and cultural change could
be registered.

When that last quarter of a century began, in 1975, the national bestseller list was
headed by two history books: Emmanuel Le Roy Ladurie's *Montaillou*, an account of
the Cathar heresy in a Pyrenean village of the same name in the fourteenth century; and
amateur historian Pierre Jakes Helias' *Le Cheval d'orgueil* ("Horse of Pride"), an account
of traditional Breton peasant culture. Their lead position was not as exceptional as it
might appear – history was a market leader among academic books throughout the
1970s and 1980s. Such commercial success reflected the quality and the orientation
of the French historical method in the wake of the so-called *Annales* "school" –
the historians associated with the famous journal of that name. The *Annalistes* had
endeavoured to revolutionize historical writing. Shifting the focus away from the
traditional chronicle of kings, queens and battles, they sought to recreate a "total
history", which examined broader time patterns – the *longue durée*, as master *Annaliste*
Fernand Braudel called it. Furthermore, they attempted to build bridges between history and the other social sciences – sociology, economics, demography, linguistics,

The weekly television show,
Apostrophes, was a cultural
trendsetter in the 1970s and
1980s. Its host Bernard Pivot
became a kind of literary
impresario and cultural ring-
master. Among his guests here
are Jacques Attali, sometime
personal aide to Mitterrand,
disgraced president of the
European Development Bank,
and writer and historian.

anthropology (as in *Montaillou*), oral history (as in *Le Cheval d'orgueil*) and so on. The result was innovatory forms of history writing which by the 1960s had conquered the academic establishment in France and turned the French historical method into a world leader.

Yet this can hardly explain its popular success, any more than the fact that both the 1975 bestsellers were brilliantly written. One must bear in mind that history was traditionally viewed in France as an intellectual crossroads where cultural identity was transacted. Both Le Roy Ladurie and Helias in their different ways evoked lost worlds – rural civilizations that were grounded, for all their manifest faults and problems, in enduring values. In this way history writing addressed a nostalgic itch, which other historians too numerous to mention capitalized upon. Agrarian life could be experienced by ever fewer French people; but it could be consumed vicariously by millions. Historians became chat-show guests, television presenters, newspaper columnists. History became a means by which the entrails of a changing society could be read. This "new history" caused political as well as social debate. There were those on the republican Right, in particular, who resented the disappearance of "event history", with its attendant dates and "facts", and school syllabuses were brought back hurriedly into line.

The phenomenon reached its high point with the bicentenary of the French Revolution of 1789. The event was bound to raise political disputes along well-worn lines: thus the pro-Church Right, marshalled by maverick Protestant historian Pierre Chaunu, attempted to conflate 1789 with the alleged "genocide" meted out by republican armies in the Vendée in 1793/4. Similarly there was ritual sniping between President Mitterrand and Mayor of Paris Jacques Chirac over the form the celebrations on 14 July 1989 in Paris should take. Beyond what might have been expected, however, three features of the celebrations shone out.

First, it was noticeable how virtually the whole political nation engaged in the events positively and constructively. This underlined the extent to which the republican values embodied in 1789 provided the established framework for political debate and civic affirmation. Second, the enthusiam which the commemoration evoked in towns and villages was also most remarkable. Huge numbers of local bicentenary committees were established, and many, encouraged and shepherded by professional historians, proved eager to find out about local history in the Revolutionary epoch. The bicentenary, then, prompted a search for origins and fuelled a quest for local identity that both chimed with the shift to a new cultural politics of the grassroots and highlighted a sense of uncertainty about cultural identity.

The third striking feature of the bicentenary was the extent to which Revolutionary culture was being commercialized. While historians held their Revolutionary conferences and wrote their Revolutionary books, radio and TV producers produced Revolutionary programmes and entrepreneurs fabricated their Bastille tee-shirts, guillotine earrings and tricolour underpants. This element was captured in its purest form in the massive procession organized on the evening of 14 July in Paris. Bastille

The official opening in May 1994 of the Channel Tunnel – here celebrated by French and British co-workers – marked a stage in the growing economic integration of the European Community. The new link has also triggered fresh debate on the thorny topic of Franco-British relations – and the construction of a European identity.

Day is usually celebrated here in the form of convivial neighbourhood street parties; these were pushed aside in favour of a glitzy parade, for whose co-ordination Mitterrand called in J.F. Goude, supremo of the advertising world. The procession was a stunning event and a huge success by its own, consumerist, lights: the streets were thronging with people, and foreign earnings exceeded $5 million.

"Take a good look at this; you'll never see anything like it again." Mitterrand's prophetic comment as he greeted the Socialist election triumph of May 1981 might as well have been applied to the bicentenary celebrations. The latter represented a forum in which very different conceptions of the past, the civic and the commercial, drawn largely from within the mainstream of French national life, were put together in what will probably be an unrepeatable way.

For all that was positive and fun about the event, it occurred at a time when some basic assumptions underpinning French nationality would soon be tested. France's integration into the European Community, which Mitterrand had doggedly pursued, seemed likely to have a major impact on the meaning of national identity. An enlarged role for the European Commission and Parliament, attachment to a single currency and a single market, support for the "social chapter" – all would be profoundly significant issues for the French as for every other constituent nation of the European Community. They appeared to be the prerequisites for mounting effective competition against the economic superpowers, Japan and the United States. "France is our homeland," Mitterrand had roundly declared, in his New Year's Eve speech of 1988, "but Europe is our future." The commemoration of 1789, then, was celebrating national unity at a moment when that very conception seemed in question. Events in Eastern Europe in the same year – notably the moves towards German unification – placed an enormous question-mark not only over the shape of the new Europe, but also the clout that the French would be able to command within it. Although it seemed quite possible that European integration might trigger a nationalist, or even regionalist, backlash, the sense – even the foreboding – of structural change and a transformation of cultural identity was clearly in the air in the 1990s.

If this was true in the international sphere, it was perhaps even more apt below the level of the nation state. A version of national unity was celebrated in 1989 at a moment when strong new shoots of cultural and political diversity were appearing within France. The national script would clearly need to be rewritten in major ways in the near future. For most within the political mainstream the Revolutionary device of "liberty, equality, fraternity" could still with justice be held aloft as the fount of civic values. But in the France of the late twentieth century they could also be severely interrogated. What "liberty" for those on the dole queues or in the desolate immigrant neighbourhoods of rotting industrial cities? What "equality" for all those minorities – farmers, Muslims, the young – and women, from whom the economic advantages of a consumer society have been largely withheld? What "fraternity" in a France where even the National Assembly became, with the emergence of the National Front, a site for the politics of intolerance and hate?

Not all the new political elements thrown up by France's swiftly changing political scene were challenges to it. Most of the Greens, for example, threw up bridges of accommodation to the political establishment. But there was nevertheless a growing danger of estrangement of these new political and cultural forces from the mainstream. This was made even more problematic by the utter collapse in the morale of the Left following its catastrophic showing in the 1993 legislative elections. In this context it is worth noting how the French intelligentsia, since Dreyfus the most vocal champions of civic and political rights, appeared to be detaching themselves from the political fray. Notable, too, was the extent to which the language of Le Pen came worryingly close – albeit usually in the form of unintentional pastiche – to the traditional republican language of civic integration. The slogan "France for the French" was not so very distant from the idea of a civilizing mission at the heart of nineteenth-century republicanism. The intense opposition shown by some towards so bland an event as the 1991 opening of Eurodisney suggested a similar anxiety over cultural identity. So too did a worrying resurgence of anti-gay opinion in the wake of the appearance of AIDS.

All developed nations towards the end of the twentieth century were grappling – some with greater success than others – with the problems and difficulties of multi-culturalism. France boasted a more distinguished record than most in integrating minorities: on numerous occasions the republic had risen to the challenge of bringing socially and culturally marginalized groups into the political fold. Yet integration had worked best when notions of French identity were relatively stable, and when economic circumstances were propitious. In the mid 1990s, with economic recession proving difficult to shake off, and with the uncertain venture of European integration looming, neither condition applied. With the grounds of political and cultural identity seemingly in flux, the French republic faced a considerable challenge, as the *fin de millénium* drew nigh.

Afro-American opera singer Jessye Norman, massively draped in the tricolour, performs "The Marseillaise". One of the high spots of the bicentenary celebrations held in Paris on 14 July 1989.

Chronology

c. 2,000,000 BC   Early hominid societies.

c. 30,000 BC   Old Stone Age.

c. 10,000 BC   End of Ice Age.

c. 6,000 BC   New Stone Age.

c. 1,800 BC   Age of Metal.

700 BC   Celts present throughout Gaul.

125–121 BC   Roman colonization of southern Gaul.

58–51 BC   Rome conquers Gaul.

177   First Christian martyrs at Lyon.

406   Major barbarian raids and settlement.

476   Roman Empire in west falls; Franks develop empire.

511   Paris established as Frankish capital by the Merovingian Clovis.

732   Arab forces defeated at Poitiers.

751   Carolingians assume power.

771   Charlemagne sole ruler.

800   Charlemagne crowned Emperor in the west.

843   Treaty of Verdun divides Carolingian empire.

987   Hugh Capet becomes king, establishing Capetian dynasty.

1095   First Crusade called by Pope Urban II.

1159   "First Hundred Years War" (to 1299).

1214   Battle of Bouvines.

1299   Treaty of Montreuil confirms end of "First Hundred Years War".

1302   Estates General convened.

1309   Papal residence established at Avignon.

1328   Philip VI succeeds to throne, establishing Valois dynasty.

1337   Hundred Years War between England and France (to 1453).

1346   English defeat French at Crécy.

1347   Loss of Calais to the English.

1348   Black Death breaks out leading to huge population losses.

1356   English defeat French at Poitiers.

1356   English capture King John II "the Good".

1358   Jacquerie rising in northern France.

1360   Peace of Brétigny signed between England and France.

1415   English defeat French at Agincourt.

1431   Joan of Arc burnt at the stake.

1438   Pragmatic Sanction of Bourges secures monarchy greater control over papacy.

1453   Battle of Castillon, the final battle of the Hundred Years War.

1470   First printing presses in France established in Paris.

1477   Death of Charles the Bold, duke of Burgundy.

1482   Treaty of Arras incorporates duchy of Burgundy into France.

1494   Italian Wars (to 1559).

1515   French victory at Marignano.

1516   Concordat of Bologna confirms king's rights over French Church.

1525   French defeated and Francis I captured at Pavia.

1534   Affair of the Placards pushes government into overt repression of Protestantism.

1534   Jacques Cartier leads expedition to Canada.

1539   Edict of Villers-Cotterets makes French the language of all legal and official documents.

1559   Treaty of Cateau-Cambrésis ends Italian Wars.

1561   French Wars of Religion (to 1598).

1572   Saint Bartholomew's Eve Massacre: prominent Protestants murdered in Paris.

1588   Day of the Barricades by Catholic League in Paris.

1589   Henry IV succeeds to throne, establishing Bourbon dynasty.

1594   Croquant peasants rise in the south-west (to 1595).

1598   Edict of Nantes ends Wars of Religion.

1598   Treaty of Vervins with Spain.

1618   Thirty Years War against Austria and Spain (to 1648).

1622   Peace of Montpellier reduces Protestant garrison towns to two.

1624   Richelieu enters royal council as principal minister (to 1642).

1630   Day of the Dupes consolidates Richelieu's hold on power.

1631   First national newspaper, the *Gazette*, established.

1639   Nu-Pieds revolt in Normandy.

1643   French victory over Spain at Rocroi.

1643   Louis XIV becomes king of France.

1648   Treaty of Westphalia ends Thirty Years War.

1648   Fronde (to 1652).

1659   Treaty of the Pyrenees concluded with Spain.

1661   Colbert, finance minister (to 1683).

1667   War of Devolution (to 1668).

1672   Dutch War (to 1678).

1685   Edict of Fontainebleau revokes the Edict of Nantes.

1689   War of the League of Augsburg (to 1697).

1701   War of Spanish Succession (to 1713).

1702   War of the Camisards in the Cévennes waged by Calvinist peasants (to 1704).

1713   Treaty of Utrecht ends War of Spanish Succession.

1715   Death of Louis XIV: parlement of Paris installs duke of Orléans as regent of Louis XV (to 1723).

1740   War of Austrian Succession (to 1748).

1756   Seven Years War: France suffers heavy losses at England's hands (to 1763).

1775   Flour War; rioting over grain shortages.

1778   War of American Independence: France joins rebel colonies against England (to 1783).

1783   Treaty of Versailles: France makes some colonial gains.

1788 Estates General convened to meet in May 1789.

1789 (20 June) Tennis Court Oath: the National Assembly swears not to disband until basis of a new constitution has been established.

1789 (14 July) Bastille stormed in Paris. French Revolution starts.

1789 (Autumn) Peasant revolution; the abolition of feudalism.

1792 Outbreak of war with Austria.

1792 Louis XVI overthrown and First Republic declared.

1792 September Massacres: vigilante gangs murder prisoners in Parisian gaols.

1793 The Terror (to 1794).

1795 Directory, a new constitutional regime, is established (to 1799).

1799 Napoleon overthrows Directory and creates Consulate.

1801 Pope and Napoleon sign Concordat, re-establishing Catholicism.

1804 Napoleon crowned Emperor: creation of First Empire.

1804 *Code Napoléon* (Civil Code) issued.

1808 Peninsular War in Spain begins.

1812 Napoleon defeated in Moscow campaign.

1814 Napoleon deposed and sent to Elba.

1815 Napoleon's "Hundred Days" end in defeat at Waterloo.

1815 Bourbon dynasty re-established on throne in person of Louis XVIII.

1830 French conquest of Algeria begins.

1830 *Trois glorieuses* (27–29 July) force Charles X to abdicate, ending Bourbon dynasty. Louis-Philippe, duke of Orléans, becomes king.

1848 July Monarchy falls.

1848 Second Republic is declared, Louis-Philippe abdicates and a Provisional Government is formed.

1848 "June Days"; repression of Paris radicals.

1851 *Coup d'état*: Louis Bonaparte seizes power.

1852 Second Empire, president Louis Bonaparte appoints himself emperor Napoleon III.

1870 Franco-Prussian War.

1871 Paris Commune; loss of Alsace and Lorraine to Germany. Third Republic declared.

1898 Emile Zola publishes "J'accuse": the Dreyfus Affair.

1905 *Entente Cordiale* between France and Britain.

1914 First World War (to 1918).

1914 Battle of the Marne.

1916 Battle of Verdun.

1919 Treaty of Versailles; Alsace and Lorraine reincorporated into France.

1924 Dawes Plan for German reparations.

1925 Locarno Treaties between France, Germany and other powers.

1929 Decision to build Maginot Line.

1934 The Stavisky Affair.

1936 Popular Front government unites Communists, Socialists and other Left groups.

1938 Munich agreements signed by Daladier.

1939 World War II (to 1945).

1940 *Etat français*. End of Third Republic; establishment of Pétain's Vichy France.

1944 D-Day Allied landings.

1944 Overthrow of Vichy regime.

1946 Fourth Republic established.

1954 Algerian War begins.

1954 Vietnamese defeat French at Dien-Bien-Phu.

1957 Treaty of Rome establishes the Common Market.

1958 Deadlock in Algeria leads to constitutional crisis: the Fourth Republic gives way to the Fifth.

1962 Evian agreements grant Algeria full independence.

1968 May Events; students and unions stage massive anti-government protests.

1981 François Mitterrand elected president (re-elected 1988).

1994 Official opening of the Channel Tunnel.

Picture Acknowledgements

Magnum. **287** Nicolas Tikhomiroff/Magnum. **291** Keystone/Sygma. **292** Photos: Citroën, Neuilly-sur-Seine. **293** Collection & photo: Vintage Magazine Co. Ltd., London. **294** Guy Le Querrec/Magnum. **296** Bruno Barbey/Magnum. **297** Bruno Barbey/Magnum. **298** Gérard-Aimé, Paris. **299** Henri Cartier-Bresson/Magnum. **301** J.C. Martel/Archipress, Paris. **304** Raymond Depardon/Magnum. **307** Bruno Barbey/Magnum. **310** Leonard Freed/Magnum. **311** Photo: Sygma. **314** Steve McCurry/Magnum. **316** © Plantu, Paris. **318** Dominique Aubert/Sygma. **319** S. Couturier/Archipress, Paris. **322** Dominique Aubert/Sygma. **323** Abbas/Magnum. **326** Bisson/Sygma. **327** Photo: RV. **330** S. Bassouls/Sygma. **332** Regio Bossu/ Sygma. **335** Yves Forestier/Sygma.

Bibliography

General Works

Atlas historique de la France contemporaine, 1800–1965. Paris: A. Colin, 1966.

B.S. Anderson and J.P. Zinsser, *A History of Their Own: Women in Europe from Prehistory to the Present*, 2 vols. New York: Harper & Row, 1988.

J. Ardagh and C. Jones, *Cultural Atlas of France*, Oxford: Facts on File, 1991.

P. Ariès *et al.* (eds), *History of Private Life*, 5 vols. Cambridge, Mass.: Belknap, 1987–90.

L. Bergeron, *Paris: Genèse d'un paysage.* Paris: Picard, 1989.

G. de Bertière de Sauvigny and D.H. Pinkney, *History of France.* Arlington Heights: Forum Press, 1977.

M. Bloch, *French Rural History: An Essay on Its Basic Characteristics.* London: Routledge Kegan Paul, 1966.

M.J. Boxer and J.H. Quataert (eds), *Connecting Spheres: Women in the Western World: 1500 to the Present.* New York: Oxford University Press, 1987.

F. Braudel, *The Identity of France*, 2 vols, New York: Harper & Row, 1986 and 1988.

F. Braudel, *Civilisation and Capitalism*, 3 vols. New York: Harper & Row, 1982–4.

F. Braudel and E. Labrousse (eds), *Histoire économique et sociale de la France*, 4 vols. Paris: PUF, 1970–82.

F. Brunot, *Histoire de la langue française des origines à 1900*, 12 vols. Paris: A. Colin, 1905–53.

A. Burguière and J. Revel (eds), *Histoire de la France*, 3 vols. Paris: Seuil, 1989 and 1990.

H. Clout, *Themes in the Historical Geography of France.* New York: Academic Press, 1977.

R. Collins, *The Basques.* Oxford: Blackwell, 1986.

R. Dion, *Les Frontières de la France.* Paris: Hachette, 1947.

————, *Le Paysage et la vigne.* Paris: Payot, 1990.

G. Duby (ed.), *Histoire de la France*, 3 vols. Paris: Larousse, 1982.

————, *Histoire de la France urbaine*, 5 vols. Paris: Seuil, 1980–5.

————, *A History of Private Life*, 5 vols. Cambridge, Mass.: Belknap, 1987–90.

G. Duby and M. Perrot (eds), *A History of Women in the West*, 5 vols. Cambridge, Mass.: Belknap, 1992–3.

G. Duby and A. Wallon (eds), *Histoire de la France rurale*, 4 vols. Paris: Seuil, 1975–6.

J. Dupâcquier (ed.), *Histoire de la population française*, 4 vols. Paris: PUF, 1988.

J.B. Duroselle, *Europe: A History of Its Peoples.* London: Viking 1990.

P. Goubert, *The Course of French History.* New York: Watts, 1991.

A. Guérard, *France: A Modern History*, 2nd edn. Ann Arbor: University of Michigan Press, 1969.

H. Le Bras, *Les Trois France.* Paris: O. Jacob, 1986.

H. Le Bras and E. Todd, *L'Invention de la France.* Paris: Seuil, 1981.

E. Le Roy Ladurie, *Times of Feast, Times of Famine: A History of the Climate Since the Year 1000.* New York: Doubleday, 1971.

R. Mettam and D. Johnson, *French History and Society: The Wars of Religion to the Fifth Republic.* London: Methuen, 1974.

L. Mirot, *Manuel de géographie historique de la France*, 2nd edn, 2 vols. Paris: Picard, 1947 and 1950.

J.R. Pitte, *Histoire du paysage français*, 2 vols. Paris: Tallandier, 1983.

X. de Planhol, *Géographie historique de la France.* Paris: Fayard, 1988.

R. Price, *A Concise History of France.* Cambridge University Press, 1993.

E. Todd, *The Making of Modern France.* Oxford: Blackwell, 1991.

————, *The Causes of Progress.* Oxford: Blackwell, 1987.

P. Wolff (ed.), *Univers de la France et des pays francophones* (multi-volumed series, covering histories of individual provinces and cities). Toulouse: Privat, 1967–.

Introduction

Annales: Economies, Sociétés, Civilisations (appears six times per annum)

J. Ardagh and C. Jones, *Cultural Atlas of France.* Oxford: Facts on File, 1991.

R. Barthes, *Mythologies.* Paris: Seuil, 1957.

M. Bloch, *The Royal Touch.* London: Routledge, 1973.

F. Braudel, *The Identity of France*, 2 vols. New York: Harper & Row, 1986 and 1988.

R. Cobb, *A Second Identity.* Oxford University Press, 1969.

E. James, *The Franks.* Oxford: Blackwell, 1988.

————, *The Origins of France: From Clovis to the Capetians 500–1000.* London: Macmillan, 1982.

J.R. Pitte, *Histoire du paysage français.* Paris: Tallandier, 1983.

X. de Planhol, *Géographie historique de la France.* Paris: Fayard, 1988.

E. Weber, *Peasants into Frenchmen: The Modernization of Rural France 1870–1914.* Stanford University Press, 1977.

Before the Middle Ages (Chapters 1–3)

a) Before the Romans

P.G. Bahn and J. Vertut, *Images of the Ice Age.* Oxford: Facts on File, 1988.

J.L. Brunaux, *The Celtic Gauls: Gods, Rites and Sanctuaries.* London: B.A. Seaby, 1987.

J.G.D. Clark and S. Piggott, *Prehistoric Societies.* New York: Knopf, 1965.

J. Guilaine, *La France d'avant la France: du néolithique à l'âge de fer.* Paris: Hachette, 1980.

————, *La Préhistoire française.* Paris: CNRS, 1976.

J.J. Hatt, *Celts and Gallo-Romans.* London: Barrie & Jenkins, 1970.

R. Joffroy, *Le Trésor de Vix: Histoire et portée d'une grande découverte.* Paris: Hachette, 1962.

A.P. Phillips, *The Prehistory of Europe.* Bloomington: Indiana University Press, 1980.

S. Piggott, *Ancient Europe*. Edinburgh University Press, 1965.

S. Piggott, G. Daniel and C. McBurney (eds), *France before the Romans*. London: Thames & Hudson, 1973.

T.G.E. Powell, *The Celts*. New York: Praeger, 1958.

M. Ruspoli, *The Caves of Lascaux*. London: Thames & Hudson, 1987.

N. Sandars, *Bronze Age Cultures in France*. Cambridge University Press, 1957.

C. Scarre (ed.), *Ancient France: Neolithic Societies and their Landscapes, 6000–200 BC*. Edinburgh University Press, 1983.

A. Sieveking, *The Cave Artists*. London: Thames & Hudson, 1979.

D. Trump, *The Prehistory of the Mediterranean*. New Haven: Yale University Press, 1980.

b) The Romans

T. Cornell and J. Matthews, *Atlas of the Roman World*. New York: Facts on File, 1982.

J.F. Drinkwater, *Roman Gaul: The Three Provinces, 58 BC–AD 260*. Ithaca, New York: Cornell University Press, 1983.

P. Garnsey and R. Saller, *The Roman Empire: Economy, Society and Culture*. London: Duckworth, 1987.

C. Goudineau, *César et la Gaule*. Paris: Errance, 1990.

P. Grimal, *Roman Cities*. Madison: Wisconsin University Press, 1983.

A.H.M. Jones, *The Decline of the Ancient World*. London: Longman, 1966.

A. King, *Roman Gaul and Germany*. Berkeley: California University Press, 1990.

F. Millar, *The Roman Empire and Its Neighbours*, 2nd edn. London: Duckworth, 1981.

M. Pobé, *The Art of Roman Gaul*. Toronto University Press, 1961.

A.L.F. Rivet, *Gallia Narbonensis: Southern France in Roman Times*. London: Batsford, 1988.

R. Van Dam, *Leadership and Community in Late Antique Gaul*. Berkeley: California University Press, 1985.

E.M. Wightman, *Gallia Belgica*. Berkeley: California University Press, 1985.

A. and P. Wiseman, *Julius Caesar: The Battle for Gaul*. Boston: Godine, 1980.

c) The Merovingians and Carolingians

B.S. Bachrach, *A History of the Alans in the West*. Minneapolis: Minnesota University Press, 1993.

D. Bullough, *The Age of Charlemagne*, 2nd edn. New York: Puttnam, 1973.

G. Duby, *The Early Growth of the European Economy: Warriors and Peasants from the 7th to the 12th centuries*. Ithaca, New York: Cornell University Press, 1974.

P. Galliou and M. Jones, *The Bretons*. Oxford: Blackwell, 1991.

P.J. Geary, *Before France and Germany: The Creation and Transformation of the Merovingian World*. New York: Oxford University Press, 1988.

W. Goffart, *Barbarians and Romans AD 418–584: The Techniques of Accommodation*. Princeton University Press, 1980.

R. Heer, *Charlemagne and His World*. New York: Macmillan, 1975.

R. Hodges and D. Whitehouse, *Mohammed, Charlemagne and the Origins of Europe*. London: Duckworth, 1983.

G. Holmes (ed.), *The Oxford Illustrated History of Medieval Europe*. Oxford University Press, 1988.

E. James, *The Franks*. Oxford: Blackwell, 1988.

————, *The Origins of France: From Clovis to the Capetians, 500–1000*. London: Macmillan, 1982.

R.M. McKitterick, *The Frankish Kingdoms under the Carolingians, 751–987*. London: Longman, 1983.

P. Périn and L.C. Feffer, *Les Francs: A la conquête de la Gaule*. Paris: A. Colin, 1987.

M. Todd, *The Early Germans*. Oxford: Blackwell, 1992.

J.M. Wallace-Hadrill, *The Barbarian West, 400–1000*, 3rd edn. London: Hutchinson, 1967.

————, *The Long-Haired Kings*. New York: Barnes & Noble, 1962.

S. Wemple, *Women in Frankish Society: Marriage and the Cloister, 500–900*. Philadelphia: Pennsylvania University Press, 1981.

The Middle Ages and the Early Modern Period (Chapters 4–6)

C. Allmand, *The Hundred Years War*. Cambridge University Press, 1989.

M. Barber, *The Two Cities: Medieval Europe, 1050–1320*. London: Routledge, 1992.

C. Beaune, *The Birth of an Ideology: Myths and Symbols of Nation in Late Medieval France*. Berkeley: California University Press, 1985.

J. Bergin, *The Rise of Richelieu*. New Haven: Yale University Press, 1991.

M. Bloch, *Feudal Society*. Chicago University Press, 1962.

————, *The Royal Touch*. London: Routledge, 1973.

F. Bluche, *Louis XIV*. Oxford: Blackwell, 1990.

R. Bonney, *Society and Government under Richelieu and Mazarin: 1626–61*. London: Macmillan, 1981.

R.M. Briggs, *Communities of Belief: Cultural and Social Tensions in Early Modern France*. Oxford: Clarendon Press, 1988.

————, *Early Modern France: 1560–1715*. Oxford University Press, 1977.

P. Burke, *The Fabrication of Louis XIV*. New Haven: Yale University Press, 1992.

J. Calmette, *The Golden Age of Burgundy*. New York: Norton, 1962.

R. Chartier, *Cultural Origins of the French Revolution*. Durham: Duke University Press, 1991.

N.Z. Davis, *Society and Culture in Early Modern France*. Stanford University Press, 1965.

G. Duby, *France in the Middle Ages, 987–1460: From Hugh Capet to Joan of Arc*. Oxford: Blackwell, 1991.

J. Dunbabin, *France in the Making: 843–1180*. Oxford University Press, 1985.

R. Fossier, *The Cambridge Illustrated History of the Middle Ages: 350–950*. Cambridge University Press, 1989.

J. Gillingham, *The Angevin Empire*. New York: Holmes & Meier, 1984.

P. Goubert, *The Ancien Régime*. New York: Harper & Row, 1971.

P. Goubert and D. Roche, *Les Français et l'Ancien Régime*, 2 vols. Paris: A. Colin, 1984.

M. Greengrass, *The French Reformation*. Oxford: Blackwell, 1987.

————, *France in the Age of Henry IV*. London: Longman, 1984.

E.H. Hallam, *Capetian France*. London: Longman, 1980.

O. Hufton, *The Poor in Eighteenth-century France*. Oxford University Press, 1974.

C. Jones, *The Charitable Imperative*. London: Routledge, 1989.

R. Knecht, *Francis I*. Cambridge University Press, 1982.

J. Le Goff, *Medieval Civilisation: 400–1500*. Oxford: Blackwell, 1981.

————, *The Medieval Imagination*. Chicago University Press, 1988.

————, *Time, Work and Culture in the Middle Ages*. Chicago University Press, 1980.

E. Le Roy Ladurie (ed.), *L'Etat baroque*. Paris: J. Vrin, 1985.

————, *L'Etat royal*. Paris: Hachette, 1987.

————, *The French Peasantry: 1450–1660*. Aldershot: Scholar, 1987.

————, *Montaillou*. New York: Vintage, 1979.

P.S. Lewis, *France at the End of the Middle Ages*. London: Macmillan, 1968.

J. Lindsay, *The Troubadours and Their World*. London: F. Mutter, 1976.

H.A. Lloyd, *The State, France and the Sixteenth Century*. London: Allen & Unwin, 1983.

R. Mandrou, *Introduction to Modern France: 1500–1640*. New York: Holmes & Meier, 1976.

R. Mettam, *Power and Faction in Early Modern France*. Oxford: Blackwell, 1988.

A.L. Moote, *Louis XIII, the Just*. Berkeley: California University Press, 1991.

R. Mousnier, *The Institutions of France under the Absolute Monarchy, 1598–1789*. Chicago University Press, 1979.

N.J.G. Pounds, *An Economic History of Medieval Europe*. London: Longman, 1974.

M. Prestwich (ed.), *International Calvinism: 1541–1715*. Oxford: Clarendon Press, 1985.

D.L. Rubin, *Sun King*. Berkeley: California University Press, 1992.

P. Sahlins, *Boundaries: The Making of France and Spain in the Pyrenees*. Berkeley: California University Press, 1989.

J.H.L. Salmon, *Society in Crisis*. London: Methuen, 1975.

S. Shahar, *The Fourth Estate: History of Women in the Middle Ages*. London: Methuen, 1983.

F. Simone, *The French Renaissance*. London: Macmillan, 1961.

N.M. Sutherland, *The Huguenot Struggle for Recognition*. New Haven: Yale University Press, 1980.

V.L. Tapié, *France in the Age of Louis XIII and Richelieu*. Cambridge University Press, 1974.

France Since 1789 (Chapters 7–11)

a) General Works

F. Caron, *An Economic History of Modern France*. New York: Columbia University Press, 1979.

R. Cobb, *A Second Identity*. Oxford University Press, 1969.

A. Corbin, *Women for Hire: Prostitution and Sexuality in France after 1850*. Cambridge, Mass.: Harvard University Press, 1990.

A. Copley, *Sexual Moralities in France: 1780–1980*. London: Routledge, 1989.

M. Crubellier, *Histoire culturelle de la France (XIXe–XXe siècles)*. Paris: A. Colin, 1974.

G. Dupeux, *French Society: 1789–1970*. London: Methuen, 1976.

S. Hoffman, *France: Change and Tradition*. Boston: Harvard University Press, 1963.

B. Jenkins, *Nationalism in France: Class and Nation since 1789*. London: Routledge, 1990.

C. Jones, *The Longman Companion to the French Revolution*. London: Longman,1989.

T. Judt, *Marxism and the French Left: Studies in Labour and Politics in France, 1830–1981*. Oxford: Clarendon Press, 1986.

Y. Lequin, *Histoire des Français: XIXe–XXe siècles*, 3 vols. Paris: A. Colin, 1983–4.

M. Lévy-Leboyer, *The French Economy in the Nineteenth Century*. Cambridge University Press, 1990.

J. McMillan, *Housewife or Harlot: The Place of Women in French Society, 1870–1940*. Brighton: Harvester Press, 1981.

A. Moulin, *Peasantry and Society in France since 1789*. Cambridge University Press, 1988.

R. Rémond, *The Right in France from 1815 to de Gaulle*. Philadelphia: Pennsylvania University Press, 1969.

J. Scott and L. Tilly, *Women, Work and Family*. London: Routledge, 1986.

J. Seigel, *Bohemian Paris: Culture, Politics and the Boundaries of Bourgeois Life, 1850–1930*. New York: Viking, 1986.

E. Shorter and C. Tilly, *Strikes in France: 1830–1968*. Cambridge University Press, 1974.

D. Thomson, *Democracy in France*, 5th edn. Oxford University Press, 1969.

C. Tilly, *The Contentious French*. Cambridge, Mass.: Belknap, 1986.

G. Wright, *France in Modern Times*, 4th edn. New York: Norton, 1987.

T. Zeldin, *France, 1848–1945*. Oxford University Press, 1973.

b) 1789–1914

M. Agulhon, *The Republican Experiment, 1848–52*. Cambridge University Press, 1983.

————, *Marianne into Battle*. Cambridge University Press, 1981.

K. Baker, F. Furet and C. Lucas (eds), *The French Revolution and the Making of Modern Political Culture*, 3 vols. Oxford: Pergamon, 1988–90.

E. Berenson, *The Trial of Madame Caillaux*. Berkeley: University of California, 1992.

J.D. Bredin, *The Affair: The Case of Alfred Dreyfus*. New York: Brazillier, 1986.

H. Brunschwig, *French Colonialism, 1871–1914*. New York: Praeger, 1966.

M. Burns, *Rural Society and French Politics: Boulangism and the Dreyfus Affair, 1886–1900*. Princeton University Press, 1984.

————, *Dreyfus: A Family Affair, 1789–1945*. New York: Harper Collins, 1991.

R. Cobb, *The Police and the People, 1780–1820*. Oxford University Press, 1970.

H.A.C. Collingham, *The July Monarchy, 1830–48*. London: Longman, 1988.

W. Doyle, *The Oxford History of the French Revolution*. Oxford University Press, 1989.

S. Edwards, *The Paris Commune*. London: Eyre and Spottiswood, 1971.

G. Ellis, *The Napoleonic Empire*. London: Macmillan, 1991.

F. Furet, *Interpreting the French Revolution*. Cambridge University Press, 1981.

R. Gibson, *A Social History of French Catholicism, 1789–1914*. London: Routledge, 1989.

R. Harris, *Murders and Madness: Medecine, Law and Society in the French Fin-de-Siècle*. Oxford University Press, 1989.

F.W.J. Hemmings, *Culture and Society in France, 1789–1848*. Leicester University Press, 1987.

C. Heywood, *The Development of the French Economy, 1750–1914*. London: Macmillan, 1992.

L. Hunt, *Politics, Culture and Class in the French Revolution*. Berkeley: University of California Press, 1984.

D. Johnson, *France and the Dreyfus Affair*. London: Blandford, 1967.

P.M. Jones, *The Peasantry in the French Revolution*. Cambridge University Press, 1988.

J. Landes, *Women and the Public Sphere in the Age of the French Revolution*. Ithaca, New York: Cornell University Press, 1988.

J. and M. Lough, *An Introduction to Nineteenth-century France*. London: Longman, 1978.

C. Lucas (ed.), *Rewriting the French Revolution*. Cambridge University Press, 1991.

J. McManners, *Church and State in France, 1870–1914*. London: SPCK, 1972.

R. Magraw, *France, 1815–1914: The Bourgeois Century*. London: Fontana, 1983.

J.M. Mayeur and M. Rébérioux, *The Third Republic from Its Origins to the Great War, 1871–1914*. Cambridge University Press, 1984.

J.M. Merriman (ed.), *French Cities in the Nineteenth Century*. London: Hutchinson, 1982.

————, *The Red City: Limoges and the French Nineteenth Century*. New York: Oxford University Press, 1985.

M. Miller, *The Bon Marché: Bourgeois Culture and the Department Store, 1869–1920*. Princeton University Press, 1981.

P. Nord, *Paris Shopkeepers and the Politics of Resentment*. Princeton University Press, 1986.

M. Perrot, *Workers on Strike, 1871–1890*. Leamington Spa: Berg, 1987.

P. Pilbeam, *The French Revolution of 1830*. New York: St Martin's Press, 1991.

D. Pinkney, *Napoleon III and the Rebuilding of Paris*. Princeton University Press, 1958.

A. Plessis, *The Rise and Fall of the Second Empire, 1852–71*. Cambridge University Press, 1983.

R. Price, *A Social History of Nineteenth-century France*. London: Hutchinson, 1987.

————, *The French Second Republic*. Ithaca, New York: Cornell University Press, 1972.

R. Shattuck, *The Banquet Years: The Arts in France, 1885–1918*. New York: Vintage, 1958.

B.G. Smith, *Ladies of the Leisure Class: The Bourgeoises of Northern France in the Nineteenth Century*. Princeton University Press, 1981.

D. Sutherland, *France 1789–1815: Revolution and Counter-Revolution*. London: Fontana, 1985.

J. Tulard, *Napoleon: The Myth of the Saviour*. London: Weidenfeld, 1985.

M. Vovelle, *The Fall of the French Monarchy, 1789–92*. Cambridge University Press, 1984.

E. Weber, *Peasants into Frenchmen: The Modernization of Rural France, 1870–1914*. Stanford University Press, 1977.

————, *France: Fin de Siècle*. Cambridge, Mass.: Belknap, 1986.

R.H. Williams, *Dream Worlds: Mass Consumption in Late Nineteenth-century France*. Berkeley: California University Press, 1982.

S. Wilson, *Ideology and Experience: Antisemitism in France at the Time of the Dreyfus Affair*. Rutherford, New Jersey: Farleigh Dickinson, 1982.

T. Zeldin, *France 1848–1914*, 2 vols. Oxford University Press, 1973.

c) Twentieth century

A. Adamthwaite, *Grandeur and Decline: France, 1914–40*. New York: Routledge, 1993.

M. Agulhon and A. Nouschi, *La France de 1940 à nos jours*. Paris: Nathan, 1984.

J. Ardagh, *France Today*. London: Penguin, 1990.

S. Audouin-Rouzeau, *Men at War, 1914–18: National Sentiment and Trench Journalism in France during the First World War*. Cambridge University Press, 1992.

R. Austin and H.R. Kedward (eds), *Vichy France and the Resistance*. London: Croom Helm, 1985.

J.P. Azéma, *From Munich to the Liberation, 1938–44*. Cambridge University Press, 1984.

J.J. Becker, *The Great War and the French People*. Leamington Spa: Berg, 1986.

P. Bernard and H. Dubief, *The Decline of the Third Republic, 1914–38*. Cambridge University Press, 1985.

S. Berstein, *The Republic of de Gaulle, 1958–69*. Cambridge University Press, 1990.

S. Berstein and P. Milza, *Histoire de la France au XXe siècle*, 4 vols. Brussels: Complexe, 1981.

M. Bloch, *Strange Defeat*. New York: Norton, 1949.

D. Borne, *Histoire de la société française depuis 1945*. Paris: A. Colin, 1988.

M. Cook (ed.), *French Culture Since 1945*. London: Longman, 1993.

M. Ferro, *The Great War, 1914–18*. London: Routledge, 1973.

J. Flower (ed.), *France Today*. London: Hodder, 1993.

H. Footit and J. Simmonds, *The Politics of Liberation: France, 1943–5*. Leicester University Press, 1988.

J.R. Frears, *France in the Giscard Presidency*. London: Boston, 1981.

P. Fridenson (ed.), *The French Home Front, 1914–18*. Providence, R.I.: Berg, 1992.

W.D. Halls, *The Youth of Vichy France*. Oxford: Clarendon Press, 1981.

C. Hirchfeld and P. Marsh (eds), *Collaboration in France: Politics and Culture During the Nazi Occupation, 1940–4*. Oxford: Berg, 1989.

A. Horne, *The Price of Glory: Verdun, 1916*. Harmondsworth: Penguin, 1962.

————, *To Lose a Battle: France 1940*. London: Macmillan, 1969.

J. Jackson, *The Politics of Depression in France, 1932–6*. Cambridge University Press, 1985.

————, *The Popular Front in France: Defending Democracy, 1934–38*. Cambridge University Press, 1988.

————, *Charles de Gaulle*. Cambridge University Press, 1990.

D. and M. Johnson, *The Age of Illusion: Art and Politics in France, 1918–40*. London: Thames & Hudson, 1987.

R.W. Johnson, *The Long March of the French Left*. London: Macmillan, 1981.

H.R. Kedward, *Resistance in Vichy France*. Oxford University Press, 1978.

————, *Occupied France: Collaboration and Resistance, 1940–4.* Oxford University Press, 1985.

T. Kemp, *The French Economy, 1913–39.* New York: St Martin's Press, 1972.

A. Kriegel, *The French Communists: Profile of a People.* Chicago University Press, 1972.

J. Lacouture, *De Gaulle,* 3 vols. London: Collins Harvill, 1984–6.

M. Larkin, *France Since the Popular Front, 1936–86.* Oxford: Clarendon Press, 1988.

J.F. Macmillan, *Twentieth-Century France: Politics and Society, 1898–1991.* New York: Macmillan, 1992.

M. Marrus and R.O. Paxton, *Vichy France and the Jews.* New York: Basic, 1981.

H. Mendras, *The Vanishing Peasant.* Cambridge, Mass.: MIT Press, 1970.

H. Mendras and A. Cole, *Social Change in Modern France: Towards a Cultural Anthropology of the Fifth Republic.* Cambridge University Press, 1991.

A. Milward, *The New Order and the French Economy.* Oxford: Clarendon Press, 1970.

E. Mortimer, *The Rise of the French Communist Party, 1920–47.* London: Faber & Faber, 1984.

M. Ophuls, *The Sorrow and the Pity: Chronicles of a French City under the German Occupation.* New York: Dutton, 1975.

R.O. Paxton, *The Vichy Régime: Old Guard and New Order.* New York: Knopf, 1972.

A. Prost, *In the Wake of War,* New York: Berg, 1992.

J.P. Rioux, *The Fourth Republic, 1944–58.* Cambridge University Press, 1987.

G. Ross *et al., The Mitterrand Experiment.* New York: Oxford University Press, 1987.

J.F. Sweets, *Choices in Vichy France: The French under Nazi Occupation.* New York: Oxford University Press, 1986.

J.M. Winter, *The Experience of World War I.* New York: Oxford University Press, 1988.

V. Wright, *The Government and Politics of France.* New York: St Martin's Press, 1989.

V. Wright (ed.), *Continuity and Change in France.* London: Allen & Unwin, 1985.

T. Zeldin, *The French.* New York: Pantheon, 1983.

Index